More Praise

"The Holy Grail of marketing has been found! *Ask, Listen & Repeat* has revealed the complete combination on how to unlock the door to master communication on a supreme level. This knowledge applied in your business, will allow you to operate with the skills of a master marketer. Just consider yourself getting a PhD in knowing what to say and how to say it to anyone anywhere!"
—*Sue Lynn Smith, doTerra*

"Not since Dale Carnegie's *How to Win Friends, and Influence People* has there been a more modern and updated book on how to build lasting relationships. If you diligently follow the steps of *Ask, Listen & Repeat*, you will find that your relationships will have more clarity, direction and fulfillment."
—*Viggo Madsen, Owner, Invest In You*

"The MISSING LINK for the 21st Century business. FINALLY!!! The key skills you MUST build in order to be truly successful in: business/network marketing, family and life. *Ask, Listen & Repeat* is exactly the kind of information I needed earlier in my networking career. This book should be required reading before anyone sets out on any entrepreneurial endeavor. The education obtained from this book is easily worth millions of dollars. Implementing it—priceless. I wish I had it decades ago when I started this journey. Be sure to have a highlighter, a pen, and a notebook as you read, digest, and enjoy this book."
—*Diane Walker, Senior Executive, SendOutCards*

"It's been said that we become the average of the five people we spend the most time with. Before finishing *Ask, Listen & Repeat*, you'll understand why Clay Stevens' life, relationship and business success principles are at the top of my list! Clay's teaching through masterful storytelling will have you on the edge of your seat. The wisdom and insight packed between these two covers will show anybody how to begin, foster and maintain amazing relationships, putting them on the path to personal and professional success!"
—*James Wood, Co-Founder & Senior Director, The Cash Coupon*

"A 'must read' for anyone interested in building in-depth, long-lasting relationships, at home and at work. At last an engaging book that reveals the secrets for success in corporate achievement and network marketing in a novel format with quantifiable tools—so that progress can be monitored and adjusted as necessary."
—*A. Maughan Lee, President, Synergy State University*

"If you are in the Network Marketing Industry—this is a MUST have book!"
—*Phoenix Sagen, World Ventures*

"The more you read, the more excited you will be to try out the formulas yourself! It is amazing the amount of information in a book on relationships. Just imagine—if every company took the challenge to use the formulas in this book what a difference they could make in the world!"
—*Judi Brooks, Branch Manager, Bank of America*

"Relationships create Real Results! *Ask, Listen & Repeat* is a textbook for building strong, productive, predictable and long-lasting relationships. *Ask, Listen & Repeat* is a critical element of success in everything we do. You too can become a Relationship Magnet by mastering the skills taught in this book and sharing them with others."
—*Pat Patterson, National Marketing Director, Juice Plus+*

"Experts in the field of communicating and connecting are often lost in rhetoric or statistics; Clay Stevens is an exception. In this book he shares his secrets in an engaging story filled with likable characters. It will generate a shift into a realm of communication not accessible before you picked up this amazing book."
—*JeanneLauree Olsen, Chaplain, highly regarded international speaker*

"I absolutely love the book, it is really a training manual!!!! I will be implementing so much of it in our trainings—starting RIGHT NOW!!"
—*Tim Braff, Founding Member, The Singles Matrix*

"This is an instant masterpiece. It shows us how to create life-long relationships through a very engaging story. We now have a deeper awareness of exactly why and what magnetizes people to us and what repels people away from us. This is imperative to a fulfilling life and it is the key to the shift that is needed across the globe to create the world we dream of, one of truth, understanding and love."
—*Che'lisa Corey, Triple Diamond Executive, It Works Global*

"Clay Stevens does a masterful job of teaching the critical skills for developing rapport and deep level trust so that people will want to come towards you and then will want to go with you. *Ask, Listen & Repeat* is a must-read for any entrepreneur looking to make massive improvements in the way they do business and in the way they live life."
—*Pamela Herrmann, small business social media marketing consultant, radio host and creator of Social Media 101*

"This is such an amazing book. I'm hanging onto every word!!! *Ask, Listen & Repeat* is an intriguing story chock-full of valuable lessons which are entwined through the experiences, thoughts, challenges, and successes of the interesting characters. This book skillfully unlocks the secrets to success!!! Have a highlighter and pen/paper handy while you enjoy this book!"
—*Mary Hill Lane, Independent Distributor, Xango*

"I have used the principles taught in *Ask, Listen & Repeat* to rapidly increase my massage therapy practice. I would highly recommend this book to anyone serious about learning how to gain the skills necessary to be successful in any business—one relationship at a time."
—*May F. Popham, Downtown Massage Therapy Clinic*

"This book is powerful. After reading it, I felt like I had just attended a life-changing week long seminar. I learned new ways to nurture and build strong, lasting relationships. This book gave me insight into how I was doing in my relationships and the tools to more positively influence people, whether in personal relationships or business relationships. It is a must-read for those who want to be successful, not only in business but also in their personal lives."
—*Laraine Chamberlain, Founder, Chamberlain Leadership*

"We went 'from bricks to clicks' implementing the lessons taught here in building our business. *Ask, Listen & Repeat* is a novel that should be read more than once and not taken lightly. This book gives us those things we need to understand in order to succeed in all walks of life."
—*Dave and Lori Smith, Senior Executives and Master Trainers, SendOutCards*

"*Ask, Listen & Repeat* is the 'beef' that everyone needs. It's got to be shared. 'Success is a result of valuable and lasting relationships.' In *Ask, Listen & Repeat* Clay Stevens brilliantly demonstrates how you can learn, practice and apply skills that enable you to have meaningful communication and quickly begin rewarding life-long relationships. This book can change your life!"
—*Kenneth Orgoglioso, National Marketing Director, IDTLP Trusted Advisors*

"WOW!! Clay has done it again! Building on the foundation from his last book, *Six Figures in Six Months, Ask, Listen & Repeat* leads to improving relationships, which are the gateway to success in EVERY ASPECT of life. *Ask, Listen & Repeat* has given us an effective way to evaluate and improve every vital relationship in our life. This book will be at the top of the reading list for our team."
—*Marty & Allyson Mickelson, Premier Distributors, Lifevantage*

"Clay has captured the essence of what makes the BEST relationships go 'round, both personally and professionally. With Clay Stevens as our mentor we can now confidently build our relationship skills and have the 'ride of our lives!' Clay masterfully reveals the 4 personal interaction keys that allow us to put our lives in 'overdrive' as we enjoy predictable income streams through meaningful interactions."
—*Merrie W. Hudson, Executive National Vice President, Arbonne*

"Being a leader requires having certain skills and capabilities. Creating relationships is the most important aspect in building a successful business. In his book *Ask, Listen & Repeat,* Clay Stevens teaches you to manage your relationships, not only in business, but in life. Read Mr. Stevens' book carefully, put its principles into practice and watch your business flourish."
—*Kim Evans, 4-star Golden Circle, Isagenix*

"If you want to take your relationship marketing business to the highest level possible, mastering the skills of asking and listening are like adding a sprinkle of pixie dust—the magic appears. This book shows you how to do just that!"
—*Stephanie Brua, Nerium International*

"I have read many books about building relationships, creating a business, and how to sell and understanding one's self. I could take about a dozen books off my shelf and replace it with this one book. It is a manual for living a great life and having a wonderful relationship with your spouse, family, friends, business partners, customers, employer, employees, and anyone you meet in your lifetime. Thank you Clay, it has changed my life."
—*Joseph Sousa, Realtor, Keller Williams Westfield*

"I have sold over a billion dollars in the Orange County real estate market as a top producer. I have told myself a million times; listen, listen, listen… Never have I thought to use the repeat concept in such a powerful way as fully as Clay explained it in the here and now. Not just a book or novel, but a firm road map for future success."
—*Mac Mackenzie, Realtor, Coldwell Banker, Orange County, CA*

"*Ask, Listen & Repeat* is a home run! The practical wisdom shared through the engaging characters is applicable for anyone, but especially for those in direct sales and network marketing. I am excited to get copies to all my leaders so they can enhance their skills from the lessons they learn!"
—*Rhonda Voss , Senior Executive Unit Leader, AVON*

"*Ask, Listen & Repeat* is a great follow-up to *Six Figures in Six Months*. Most people overlook the importance of building relationships in network marketing. Leaders can take advantage of teaching these simple steps that will create less dependence and give encouragement to their leaders."
—*Dan and Mylisa Graham, Vice Chairman Marketing Directors, Youngevity Founding Members*

ASK, LISTEN
&
REPEAT

Life-long Relationships from
Meaningful Interactions

May you take this & help thousands to have the life they want!

Clay St

Clay Stevens

Founder of Ri Training and Author of *Six Figures in Six Months*

TRAINING

ASK, LISTEN & REPEAT

Clay Stevens

Acknowledgements

Special thanks and grandest appreciation goes to all the people who believed in the dream of *Ask, Listen, and Repeat.*

I received help and encouragement from my wife, Carol, as well as from mentors, family, friends and business partners. Notably Frank and Ruth Harmon, Lillian Heil, Viggo and Joy Madsen, Royal Fletcher, and William Black have been invaluable in the creation of this book.

Furthermore Carol Stevens shared her expertise and commitment in designing and creating a publishable product. Lastly, I also want to acknowledge the team at Hedgehog Solutions for their dedication and expertise, especially for meeting impossible timelines.

The true stars of this book, however, are the characters. Without them there would be no story to tell. They are a composite of many people who have been willing to do something different, and to learn, practice, and apply the principles that create success in developing life-long relationships.

Introduction

"The biggest communication challenge people have is listening too little and talking too much. You never learn anything when you are talking. The key to effective communication is to be interested instead of interesting!" —Clay Stevens

For too long practical methods, understandable approaches, and fundamental practices that help people relate more effectively with one another have been largely unavailable to the general population. Most people have an innate feeling that relationships are the heartbeat of every aspect of life. This feeling is, in fact, true. The need to develop strong and positive relationships is so pervasive among the human family that it touches and influences all facets of life. In fact, relationships determine the quality of personal and professional experience. This book reveals the extent to which relationships do this, and provides expertise for creating, maintaining and improving relationships.

To get an idea of how important relationships are to human experience, to personal success and quality of life, consider this: Have you ever been talking with someone when you suddenly become aware that they do not appear to be interested in you or what you are talking about? When this happens does it build trust between you and the other person? Does it help you feel like they sincerely care about you? Does it build confidence that you can share your thoughts and feelings on a deep level? Compare this with the times when you are talking with someone and suddenly feel that you can tell them anything. While you are interacting in this way, did you feel like you were the only person in the world to that person at that time? Like there was nothing more important and no-one else on their radar but you? Every part of your life would be dramatically better if the people you talk to each day felt this way during and after your conversations.

People who are perceived to be the best conversationalists actually do very little of the talking; and yet they know so much about the person they are interacting with. Meaningful, purposeful communication of one's intention to give and share creates the deep connections necessary to develop a level of trust that builds lasting relationships.

This book and the fundamental three-step process of Asking, Listening, and Repeating are keys for really understanding what people want their life to be like. These keys are like the clues on a treasure map. Learn, practice and apply this simple pattern and people will openly share their goals, dreams, and passions because they trust, feel cared for, and believe that you truly understand them, their passions, needs, and wants; what makes their specific circumstances unique; and the depth of their commitment to take action to change a self-proclaimed undesirable situation.

Ineffective, meaningless, inconsequential relationships thwart productivity, rob you of joy and happiness, and cause significant life challenges. This is why having productive, healthy, positive relationships is so important: because personal success and happiness are built on trusting, caring, meaningful human interaction.

After many decades of classroom teaching, corporate training, a successful career in direct sales and conducting hundreds of workshops and speaking engagements I have witnessed that most people don't understand and are not being taught that people and relationships are essential to success in every endeavor. I wrote this book to teach about this most central and critical issue, and to provide practical methods to initiate, maintain, and improve powerful, positive relationships that last a lifetime.

My experience with teaching the Ask, Listen, and Repeat process is that people find it liberating and immediately applicable to their life. Learning how to communicate effectively builds great relationships, sharpens perspective, reduces feelings of conflict, improves the value of your service, enhances understanding, enlivens the desire for teamwork, shifts accountability to where it belongs, magnifies the capacity to achieve intentional results, and deepens personal and professional satisfaction.

I hope this introduction to relationship dysfunction and the simple Ask, Listen, and Repeat process as a way to discover the underlying causes of unsatisfactory relationships will help you achieve greatness in your personal endeavors, community ventures, and professional responsibilities and aspirations.

Author's Note:

This book is written in a novel format so that you can experience through the lives of the characters how the principles taught here can be implemented into real-world circumstances. However, the core principles of the book are taught in the center section. If you want to move straight to the activities and principles without reading the entire book you can get the bulk of the content by reading chapters four through twelve.

There are also activities included in many of the sections intended to help you to learn the importance of building relationships, of increasing the value of your service, and of being able to confidently invite others to take appropriate action that creates the results they want. Learning along with the characters is encouraged!

The appendix contains formulas, equations, and calculations for the Relationship Rating, Trust Quotient, Warning Label, Value of Service Score, and Conversion Ratios.

Mastering the skills and knowledge in this book will help you become the kind of person that others will both hear and feel. The process of Asking, Listening, and Repeating will become the keystone to help you and those whom you influence succeed personally, professionally, spiritually, and emotionally.

It is my grandest desire that you learn, practice, and apply the contents of this book and include it in your personal toolbox for success.

1

Let's Get On With It

The horses are strangely restless in the trailer tonight—maybe because there is a full moon out, or maybe because the weather is warmer in early spring. In some ways I am glad they are uneasy; they are keeping me awake and alert.

My name is Matt Ivey, and I have been driving Ivey Ranch horses to a race track, rodeo, or fair every week or so for the past couple of years. During the week I make sure the truck and horse trailer are washed and in good working order and that all the tack is in place and in full repair, including tools to mend anything that might break or malfunction during each weekend's event. I take great care to ensure that the horses are well taken care of. After all, their success is what keeps our ranch in business.

I feel proud when I hitch the trailer up with the "Ivey Ranch" name and logo on the side and back, especially when I see the sign that carries my name, "Driven by Matt Ivey" spelled out in script lettering on the truck doors. I am not really complaining, I think my father is preparing me to take over the family business one day. I have overheard him say many times to my sisters that every ranch owner must know every aspect of the business.

For me, that business is tending to the horses and making sure our ranch's animals show well. As soon as school is over on Friday afternoons, I load enough water and feed for whatever event the horses are participating in and hitch up the trailer with the prized animals. Then it's out on the road again. Most of the time, I enjoy being at the events. There's lots of activity and excitement through the whole weekend of races and events. But getting ready to go and getting the horses home again is definitely hard, thankless work, and it's far away from any limelight, which tends to shine on the rest of my family, rather than me or the horses.

There are a lot of horses on our ranch. I say "ours" but it's really my father's operation. He is a state champion rodeo star. My sisters are award winners in their individual events as well, and like my dad, they are as pampered as the horses. If I think about it, I'm probably jealous that they travel together in a palatial motor home. And sometimes I resent it anytime I think about my sisters' getting pretty much all of my father's attention and admiration. Still, I figure that they only get this treatment because they are in the spotlight with him.

The worst part, though, is that I can't really get away from the spotlight. Their pictures, newspaper articles, and magazine clippings are pasted all over our house and ranch office. Shoot, the trophy case in the entry way of the house has been expanded at least three times to hold their awards, trophies, and ribbons. It suddenly occurs to me that I might be somewhat responsible for helping my sisters win the attention I wish I was getting. Without my hard work, they couldn't perform. Oh well. I really don't want the spotlight; it's a relationship with my dad I really covet. But he doesn't seem to see me in the same way he sees my sisters.

Bang! One of the horses kicking the side of the trailer brings me back to reality. For a moment, a bit of pride swells up in my chest because my father has entrusted me with horses, truck, trailer, and all of the tack and other gear. All told, all of the things I am responsible for are worth about a quarter of a million dollars.

Thinking about what I am being trusted with relieves some of the pain I feel about having no real relationship with my dad. I am seventeen and he trusts me with this. Not many other kids my age have this kind of responsibility. In fact, there are about five other guys who work on the ranch and none of them have their name on the side of this truck. So it seems there are even a lot of adults who don't instill this kind of confidence either. I smile the rest of the hour-long trip to the race track.

I put the horses in their stalls and bed down for the night. Dad will be here tomorrow and will want to start his pre-race routine as soon as he gets here, so I had better be ready when he arrives. The noise of other trainers arriving with their horses makes it hard to sleep. I know most of them. Around midnight, Oscar Lambert announces his arrival with his very familiar, and highly customized horn blasting. Oscar is almost an institution among the trainers 'cause he's been around so long. I'm not sure what it is about him, but everyone knows and loves him. When we walk around together everyone smiles, waves, and says hi to him. Oscar is about as close a friend as I have on the racing circuit. When we are talking it feels like there's no one or nothing else in the world more important than that moment.

I think Oscar has taken a special interest in me because he also started doing this as a teenager. He and my dad have been friends for a long time, and my dad seems to trust Oscar's advice about people. From time to time they even play cards.

Since I am still somewhat awake, I get up to help him get his horses unloaded. I yell, "Hi" and wave to him as he is preparing to back up his trailer next to the barn. He motions me to help guide him so he doesn't have to get out of the truck to check. When he gets parked, he turns off his truck and gets out. He meets me about half way to the back of his trailer.

We shake hands and he says in his gravely scratchy voice, "It's good to see you kid. Thanks for helping me." As we walk to the back of the trailer to open the ramp to unload the horses, he grumbles, "I am getting too old and stiff to do this alone."

As I look at Oscar, I think, "I could make a lot of money on the fairgrounds midway challenging people to guess Oscar's real age." He looks and walks like he's about seventy, even though I know he's only about fifty.

"You should find something else to do besides this kid," Oscar says in a weary voice. "These 1,200 pound hyperactive beauties will beat you to death by the time your my age. I am tired of getting stepped on, kicked, bitten, leaned on, pushed, and pulled all over creation."

Working to open the tailgate I realize it's locked. "Where's the key to the lock," I yell as I fumble in the dark, unable to see what I am doing. Oscar mumbles something grumpy about having to have the right key to get into anything anymore. As we unlock the trailer ramp he is still talking. "It's not a normal world these four legged beasts live in, and it breaks young men down in the long term too. I sure love them, but they are a handful in the excitement and unfamiliar surroundings of races and rodeos," he rambles on. "And each one of them is different. You have to handle each one in its own way."

After we get the horses settled, Oscar reaches into his pocket and opens a fortune cookie left over from his dinner. He reads it out loud: "If you don't change your direction, you are likely to end up where you are headed." Bending over to sit in his favorite lawn chair next to a small stack of hay between the stalls, here he motions to himself as he hands me the fortune, saying, "Look at me kid, and you'll get a glimpse at where you'll end up if you don't change the direction you're headed. I think am pretty darn good at building life-long relationships, but I would encourage you to follow that example instead of my career. Unless this is all you want in life, I would tell you to do as I say, not as I do."

Like I do every week, I retrieve a beer from the cooler in the back of Oscar's truck, open it, and hand it to him as I sit down.

Taking a huge drink and letting out an equally huge belch, Oscar asks "What are you doing up so late? Your dad will be showing up in a few hours and he will be in a hurry to get everything done. You better get to sleep. You know it will be a long day tomorrow." I know he's right and figure we'll talk later. As I get up to leave, Oscar points to my trailer and teases, "Sleep fast kid in the Ivey Holiday Inn."

I chuckle, though I don't really find his comment that funny. Climbing into the bunk at the front of the trailer, I lay there, staring at the darkness, unable to sleep. Oscar's words haunt me all night. Like a movie, scenes from Oscar's life play in my mind over and over again: Drinking three or four beers each night so he can sleep, then drinking three or four cups of coffee each morning to wake up because drinking beer makes him sluggish. It pains me to watch his slow, painful movement that makes him take thirty minutes or more to do work I do in ten minutes. The foul language and colorful metaphors. Though his vulgar jokes make me laugh, I'm not always happy with the crude and crass things he says about women.

I don't really sleep. Finally the alarm goes off, and I have never been happier to be fully awake. Oscar is a nice enough guy, and he does actually get his work done each day, but I take comfort thinking that I won't be doing this kind of work much longer. My goal is to replace my dad as manager, and someday be sole owner of the ranch, living like my sisters instead of camping in a drafty horse trailer in the back lot of the fairgrounds or race tracks. Chuckling to myself, I remember Oscar's reference to the "Ivey Holiday Inn."

It's raining. Even though I am glad to be awake, I am very aware that rain makes everything more difficult and messy. Reluctantly, I feed and water the horses, and make all the necessary preparations for the day. Then I sit down under the overhang of the barn, watching some of the owners and ranch managers arrive. While I am waiting for my dad to show up, I become aware of a very interesting contrast: the hired hands are sitting on hay bales, some asleep sitting up, using their dirty wet coats as pillows, but the owners, riders, family, and friends are all clean, well-fed, and rested. None of them are dirty or mussed. Not a hair or shirttail out of place. And I begin to doubt. Seeing me, Oscar comes over and sits down.

"I used to do that too," he says. Quite a contrast in lifestyles isn't it? My advice? There's nothing wrong with working for a living, but make sure that what you work at can give you the life you want. When do you graduate from high school, kid?"

"In a few months," I say, a bit agitated that he always calls me "kid."

Oscar smiles shaking his head, and recalls out loud, "I remember when I was in high school. I had big dreams of conquering the world. But I never quite got past the gates of the ranch, or the fences of the fairgrounds. I have lived a pretty good life kid, but there is a whole world out there to explore, and you seem way too smart and ambitious to be stuck doing this every week. What are you going to do after you graduate? I mean, what would you do if you could wave your magic wand and do anything in the world?"

"No-one ever asked me that before," I replied, contemplating the idea of limitless possibilities. "I think I would like to visit foreign countries and see how others live."

"Yeah, but that's vacation stuff," Oscar interrupts. "I mean what do you want to do when you grow up; what are you passionate about?"

I sit up straight, look Oscar in the eye and exclaim, "I would love to play professional football. But my five foot, ten inch, 145-pound frame doesn't support that dream. What I really want is to learn how to run a successful business. I want to run and someday own Ivey Ranches. My dad is training me to take over the ranch. That's why he has me learning this part of the business, so that I will know exactly how to manage it as part of the whole operation!"

Chuckling, Oscar shakes his head again and declares, "That's what they all say. That's what I said to my dad. Walking away he asks sarcastically, "Do I look like I own or run one of these outfits?"

As Oscar leaves I look down at a small river running along the side of the barn and think to myself, "I don't ever remember having a conversation like this before with anyone." It feels good to consider the future. It didn't seem strange to have that conversation with Oscar; he has those kinds of conversations with everyone. Watching a rainbow begin to form across the field it occurs to me that Oscar knows more about me than my dad does. In fact, as I think about it, Oscar seems to know more about everyone than anyone. And not just the gossipy stuff, he knows important things about people: their hopes, dreams, and passions.

When Oscar comes back, he sits down, holding a cup of coffee. I ask him, "How do you know so much about people?" His eyes light up as if I have just put a quarter in the juke box. With a smile he says, "Success in anything is built on the strength of the relationships you have with people." Putting his hand on my shoulder he continues, "Remember last night, when we unloaded my horses and I told you each one is different? Well it's the same with people."

"What does understanding about horses have to do with knowing about people," I ask, not connecting the dots.

Oscar continues as if he is holding court, "Everyone thinks, talks, and responds differently to things. And just like last night, when you needed to have the right key to unlock my trailer to get the horses out, you need to have the right key in order to get people to really talk to you. When you unlock people, they will tell you almost anything. However, every person requires their own personal key to get inside. You couldn't have opened the lock to my trailer with the key to your truck because the locks are different. You needed the right key for that specific lock. People are the same way, and at the most basic level, the key to unlocking them begins with three principles."

I sit here for an uncomfortable amount of time, waiting for Oscar to hand over the blacksmith's secret to forging a key to relationship success. Unfortunately, Oscar doesn't just blurt it out; he wants to be asked for it.

"Okay what are the three things?" I plead, finally relenting in the uncomfortable silence.

Oscar smiles as if he is now free to reveal the most important secret he can share. "First, people need to know if they can trust you. Second, they need to know if you are good at what you do. And third, they need to know if you sincerely care about them."

"That's it?" I respond, disappointed, as if the deepest secret to success was as anti-climactic as counting to three.

Putting his cup of coffee down and looking me squarely in the eye, Oscars says, "I think you are missing the importance of the lesson. Let me dig a little deeper here." He pauses, maybe concerned about overloading me with information, but seems to want to make sure I understand what he believes are critical principles of building life-long relationships. He continues, "Matt, a few minutes ago you asked me how I know so much about so many people. Well, I have learned to start forging a personalized key for each person by being curious about them. I ask what they think about and what makes them tick. And because I am simply being interested in them and their life, they trust me; and because I use what they tell me to better serve them, they know I am good at what I do, and they know that I sincerely care about them. They know I just want them to have a better life, and so we get along great. Take your dad for instance. Even though we work as competitors, deep down he knows I care about him and the smooth operation of his ranch, and from time to time we talk about how to do things better. Growing from our mutual respect is trust." Oscar pauses, looking up, "Speaking of your dad, here he comes now."

It's about 10:30 AM, and before both feet are out of his truck my dad is already barking out orders like a drill sergeant. Un-summoned, Oscar's cautionary words, "That's what they all say," come back to my mind. "He didn't even thank me for all I have done to get ready for his arrival," I think, "When I am running things I will remember to show a little more gratitude to my ranch hands." It seems that my dad missed Oscar's "Key-making" class. It would be fantastic to have him take an interest in my dreams like Oscar does, or even just come over to me and ask about the trip, or how I slept. Momentarily I consider that Oscar might be right; there is a great big world out there to be explored and maybe this isn't the life for me.

The weekend event produces two firsts, a second, and a fourth place finish for the ranch. Not a bad payday for my dad. I sometimes wish I got paid a percentage of what we make at these events. But for me, win, place, show, or no-show, I get paid the same amount. Remembering Oscar's three keys I think, "Not exactly what I would call a real motivation to be good at what I do." Now that the races are over and the crowds are gone, the weekly excitement is over. The horses and tack are loaded, and I am ready to get on the road home again.

Shaking my hand, Oscar unexpectedly holds on for a brief moment as he reminds me, "Don't forget what the fortune cookie said, 'If you don't change your direction, you are likely to end up where you are headed.'" Looking deep into my eyes he says, "Find something you can love that will give you the life you want."

Oscar's eyes reach somewhere into my soul before he releases my hand. I get in my truck, reach out the window, rub my personalized sign on the door for luck, and head for home. But Oscar's parting words gnaw at me as I drive. It's an obvious statement, of course: 'If you don't change your direction, you are likely to end up where you are headed.' I am headed home right now and

I hope I get there following the road I'm on. But maybe there's more to this fortune cookie and Oscar's warning than just what the words mean. The picture of Oscar getting out of his truck the other day comes back vividly. If that's where I am headed, then this course is not the one I want to follow. But if it gets me to running and owning a ranch it's the path I'll follow. Oscars advice is a little confusing. How can "unlocking relationships with the right key" possibly be the most important thing to success?

The truth is, my dad is pretty successful, but I can't see that he has the best of relationships. I have never even had one conversation with him like the one I had with Oscar over the weekend. So who do I believe, dad or Oscar, I ask myself? I can see at least some evidence that Oscar may be right. I don't have much evidence at all about my dad, but I know how it makes me feel when he treats me like an employee.

The school year ends, and graduation day is finally here. I am so excited to get on with my life. My mind is wandering while the administrators gloat about how great the school is and what wonderful achievements the students have accomplished. But it doesn't mean much to me. No one is here to celebrate with me anyway. Who knows where my parents are. It's obvious what ever they are doing is more important to them than this.

Again, Oscar's words of warning pulse in my head: "That's what they all say. That's what I said to my dad. Do I look like I own or run one of these outfits?" If I'm not important enough for my dad to even come to my graduation, why in the world would he ever leave an entire business operation to me? I begin to wonder if I really am just a handy worker with the right last name. The thing is, if one of my sisters were going to read a poem in the park, he would declare it a family holiday.

It occurs to me that I need to pay closer attention to my own best interests since I don't appear to be important enough to the "executives" in my family to show up on such an important day in my life. It seems my home is run more as a business than as a family. It's obvious that my dad is the CEO and everyone, including my mom, is subordinate to him. As I think about it, I can't ever remember a time when my mother ever did anything against his wishes. So it's no wonder she's not here either.

By the end of the ceremony I have decided to change my life and maybe become more interested in others than I have been. Starting with Larry. He's my best friend, snoozing in the chair next to me. Maybe I won't have to do this on my own. I nudge him to wake up; graduation is over. Time for the next phase to begin.

With graduation and a few weeks of summer behind us, Larry and I are off to the river to water ski in the boat he got as a graduation present. Larry works at his dad's tavern, which he hopes to take over some day. For now he gets to work all the worst shifts. This has a very familiar ring to it, I think, as we launch the boat. It's a nice break from the daily grind of our usual, seemingly meaningless work. Laying there in the boat with the warm sun on us as we drift down the river, we begin to plan our escape from the "no way out" situation we both feel we are in here at home.

Larry says, "Any place we go seems to be better than where we are now."

I add, "It feels like we are both working at dead-end jobs, flunkies with no future. I have been working for years now at the worst jobs on the ranch. It doesn't seem as if I will ever own the ranch or even manage it for that matter."

Within a few months Larry and I have plotted our getaway, finding the perfect little town next to a river down south to live in. The weather is awesome most of the time and there seems to be plenty of work for a couple of hard working, ambitious high school graduates. We decide to make our move in the spring.

Time is going by quickly. Thanksgiving is already upon us, and I have been working fulltime for my dad at the ranch for six months now with no promotion in sight. Each week at the race tracks, Oscar and I have our little counseling sessions about life, relationships, and success. I wonder why my own father isn't having these conversations with me. He never seems to talk to me about anything except what he wants me to do next.

Oscar shares his own stories of life on a ranch where no one sees you but everyone depends on you. He tells me every week that he had planned to leave his father's ranch to see what else the world offered, and to show his dad how valuable he was to the operation, but he never did it. Even though he had opportunities to leave, he always told himself that the animals would suffer and that the job wasn't so bad. Each time he told me that story I could see the regret in his eyes and on his face.

The lack of recognition for my work and the similarity between my life and Oscar's stories open my eyes to the real possibility that my life will someday turn out just like Oscar's. Like the fortune reads, "If you don't change your direction, you are likely to end up where you are headed." But I just can't see myself hanging around fairs, rodeos, and horse shows as a slave for my dad and sisters twenty-five years from now, and it is almost spring.

Spring comes and one day, early in the season, I get up before dawn like I do every other day. But, instead of going to the barn, I pack everything I own in my car, pick up Larry and his small boat, and, like escaping prisoners, we start our journey without a word, note, or phone call informing anyone where we are going. Two days later we are in our little river-front utopia. We both find jobs and a place to live not fifty feet from the river's edge, where we dock Larry's boat. During the week we work for a canal company digging footings and forms for cement irrigation ditches. It's hard work, long hours, and great pay for eighteen-year-old kids. We spend all or most of our money water skiing, boating, partying, and having a fabulous fun time in the sun. We think our little bachelor pad is the perfect place to have parties, so we become pretty popular with the locals, at least among the guys we work with.

For weeks we plan to have a semi-formal gathering with our church group. I look forward to sitting together inside with our friends instead of being scattered all over the yard on the ground, picnic style. But when our guests arrive it is painfully obvious that the only furniture we have are a couple of lawn chairs and a plastic folding table. The pizza comes, and to my embarrassment we hadn't even thought about plates, paper towels, and silverware. Realizing that we don't really have any of those things, one of the girls seizes control of the situation, moving our festivities outside. She tears the pizza boxes into little pieces and uses them for plates. Vivid reflections from the fairgrounds return to my mind. The memory of eating pizza on bales of hay using the box tops as a table and drinking soda pop straight from the bottle haunts me. Everyone is laughing and having a good time, but this is a miserable disaster for Larry and me.

The next day Larry and I ski up the river for a few miles and then decide to float down stream like we did before we "ran away". Relaxing in the boat as it meanders down the river, Larry and I discuss the disaster and embarrassment we both feel about yesterday's party.

As we survey the scenery surrounding us Larry mentions quietly, "I love the reeds growing at the river's edge. They are always tall and green. They don't ever seem to get sick or die."

I look at the alfalfa fields bordering the river bank, and add, "It's interesting that the green of the reeds and the fields only stretches a short distance from the river."

Larry looking even further away remarks, "The further I look into the distance the bleaker it becomes. Look at the small dirt hills and scanty brush."

"Yeah but we are in the middle of the river," I joke. "I relish the sun, water and just enjoying the fruits of our work."

We're silent for a little while. I watch a hawk flying overhead, effortlessly soaring on the wind, but purposefully looking for his lunch, and it occurs to me that although I have escaped the physical fences of the fairgrounds like Oscar challenged me to do, I am at the mercy of the winds and luck for my survival. Living here is a lot of fun, but my life working in the canals is no closer to escape than working for my dad was: different work, same story. I am living day-to-day, meal by meal, without any direction. The word direction gives me a chill even though it's a hot, sunny day.

The cold feeling turns into a haunting memory of Oscar's fortune cookie, "If you don't change your direction, you are likely to end up where you are headed." I sit up and realize that my life is a lot like this boat on the river, or the hawk overhead, aimlessly drifting on the wind or water currents without any deliberate movement in a specific direction. In that moment I recognize why my father hasn't given me any recognition. What had I ever done to prove I could do more than play and transport horses? What success had I accomplished to prove to him the value that is within me?

Looking at Larry I confess, "I think it's time to start growing up and getting on with a real life."

"That same feeling came over me yesterday when we moved the party outside," Larry admits.

Without any hesitation I agree and urge, "Maybe it's time to go home and start over in more familiar circumstances. Let's get on with it."

Larry starts the boat, and with renewed determination we speed to our riverside Xanadu. We put the boat on the trailer and spend the next few weeks saving every penny we can to go home and get our lives on track to become something. During those weeks, I often anxiously ponder about what I am going to say to my dad when I get home. We have never talked about anything that really matters, and I need his help. How can I find the key that unlocks my dad so we can start important conversations, especially after having left without notice and without communicating with him since?

It's warm and sunny as we pull up to Larry's house. His mom and dad come out to greet us and welcome him home. My anxiety is somewhat relieved seeing Larry's reception. But his parents are not mine, I think, while we unpack his stuff and unhitch the boat. As I start the two mile trek home, my mind shifts from visions of a new life working on and then taking over the family ranching operation to the absence of my parents at my graduation, Oscar's warnings, fortune cookies, and his lifestyle example. I find myself sweating and breathing more heavily as I turn the corner for home. I can see my dad at the end of the driveway. Larry's father must have called him to let him know that we had arrived. As I get closer, I see a very different picture from the scene I left at Larry's.

Dad looks like he has a head full of steam worked up, ready to explode. I have seen that look once before at the races when a groomsman made a mistake that cost us a race. Dad immediately fired him, and left the guy to get back to the ranch for his belongings by himself. Surprisingly he blocks me from going into the driveway. To avoid running him over, I swerve and park at the curb in front of the house.

Before I can get all the way out of the car, dad is yelling at me: "You can't park there either," he roars waving his finger in my face, "This place is reserved for employees, friends, and family."

Stunned, I ask, "What do you mean?"

"When you left six months ago, you turned your back on the family and our business," he bellows, "I have known since you were born that you wouldn't be worth much. You have always been a source of contention for your mom and me. You have always been the runt of the litter. Too small and weak to play sports, and now too dumb and irresponsible to ever be the boss here.

You'll never be anything more than a gopher or menial laborer. You were a mistake then and now it would be a bigger mistake to let you come back. Go find somewhere, anywhere else to live," he snarls. As he turns back towards the house; he finishes his tirade, warning, "It's obvious that fun and your friends mean more to you than we do. So move your car or I'll have it towed away."

The door to the house slams shut. All of a sudden it begins to rain on what has been a bright sunny day. It wasn't really raining; the truth is that I am crying so hard it looks like rain. Any hopes I had of living or working at my dad's ranch are dashed, crushed in this single moment. Never in my wildest dreams did I imagine this kind of scene upon my return. It's several minutes before I recover from the shock of what I just experienced. I get back in my car and drive away, knowing that my dad's towing threat is not an idle warning.

As I drive around town, my heart is beating almost out of my chest and my mind races to find meaning for and a solution to this situation, but I find none. I understand his anger at my leaving, but I never expected this. I guess Oscar had been right all along; dad did just see me as another employee or ranch asset to be used, monetized, and thrown away. The more I think about it, the more my emotions turn from sadness and shock to anger. With nowhere to go, I just keep driving.

As I drive, I pass houses, farms, and ranches that I have seen hundreds of times before. They have been there for decades, handed down from one generation to the next. Many of the people living there are long-standing family friends. Passing Bill Rena's ranch I unconsciously slow down, almost to a stop. Bill is a good family friend, but I don't know why I am slowing down here. I continue down the road for a few miles, and then the feeling to turn around returns. Reluctantly I decide to stop and talk to Bill. Approaching his driveway, I start convincing myself that the way things are going today he won't even be home. After all, he travels as much as I used to when I was working with my dad. But, turning into the driveway, I see his pickup. I knock on the door and amazingly he answers. He reaches out welcomingly, shakes my hand, and invites me to come in.

"What brings you out this way Matt?" he asks.

I sheepishly respond, "I just had a very interesting experience with my dad. He told me that I wasn't welcome there anymore, and that he felt that when I left I had betrayed him, the family, and the business. I came home because I am ready to put my life together and move forward. But now I am not sure what to do."

Empathetically Bills says as he leans back on the couch, "You probably don't know it but your dad was pretty upset when you left. It's interesting that you would use the word 'betrayed' just now. I actually talked to your dad after you left and he used the same word when he told me about it. Maybe you should give him some time to heal now that he knows you're back. Why did you leave in the first place, if you don't mind my asking?"

I offer what feels like a feeble excuse as I fidget with a book on the coffee table in front of me, "I felt a little like a slave I guess; living at home, working on the ranch that I pictured as one day being mine, but then never getting any encouragement, appreciation, or even a decent paycheck. My dad seemed to have more respect and a better relationship with all of his employees than he did with me. I guess all that, combined with some advice Oscar from the King's ranch gave me, encouraged me to escape, to be free for a while."

Bill leans forward and asks curiously, "What did Oscar tell you that made such an impact on you?"

Looking up more confidently now I share, "If you don't change your direction, you are likely to end up where you are headed, and that parents make promises they don't intend to keep."

"Let me give you some unsolicited advice Matt," Bill offers forcefully. "Only take counsel from people who are where you want to be. From people who are successful doing what you want to be successful in, or those who live like you want to live. Guidance from people who pretend to be successful is guidance coming from those uncommitted, unproven, and unwilling to live according to the principles they teach. What they know may be right on target. But they are unsuccessful because they are uncommitted and unwilling to apply what they think they know, and so their experience with success is unproven. "So," he pauses, "Now that you are home again, what do you want to do?"

Wondering why I never had a conversation like this with my dad before, I respond, "Bill, now that working for my dad is not an option, I need to take some time to consider other possibilities. I hadn't ever expected what has happened over the past hour or so."

Bill then asks a very interesting question that forces me to commit without 'telling' me to commit. He says, "On a scale from 1 to 10, how serious are you about really making some decisions about your future?"

Pausing for a moment because I recognize the importance of the question, I answer, "I am a nine or a ten."

Without any hesitation at all, Bill proposes, "I would like you to stay here and work with me on my ranch. I have always been impressed with your work ethic, ability to handle animals, and your willingness to take them to events all over the countryside week after week, and month after month. Anyone who your dad trusts like that is certainly capable and worthy of working here."

Temporarily relieved I ask, "When can I start?"

"I have a one bed, one bath, hired-man's bungalow out by the horse barn. It's not very big, but it has everything you need: bed, small stove, sink, refrigerator, and shower. You can stay there. If you care to eat with us tonight you are welcome. Dinner is at 6:30. I'll make sure your dad knows you are okay, and that you will be here if he needs you."

It was nice to feel wanted, or at least welcome somewhere after the ordeal with my dad. That night, while lying in my bed it begins to rain again right there in that bungalow. I visualize fairground fences popping up around me, but console myself with "This isn't so bad." As I fall asleep on a wet pillow, I am afraid that Oscar and I are going to be life-long soul mates and weekly pals. My last conscious thought is, "maybe I should be grateful I am sleeping indoors and in a bed. At least I am not sleeping in a drafty horse trailer, or in my car on the side of the road somewhere." I doze off hoping that tomorrow is a new day with a new direction.

The sunlight peeking through the window on the west wall wakes me up. I lay here for a few more minutes thinking about the advice Bill gave me last night, "Only take counsel from people who are where you want to be. From those who are successful doing what you want to be successful in, or those who live like you want to live." Clearly I don't want to live like Oscar lives. I have been running away from that for over a year now. Oscar might not be completely ignorant of everything about success, but he's not making it work for him.

As I pour milk on my cereal, it comes to me; what Oscar is really good at is relationship building. Professionally he isn't where I want to be, but in regards to what he claims is the "most important thing," relationships, he is extremely competent. He just doesn't get paid for those skills. Maybe Oscar missed his calling. Maybe he should have been a relationship teacher or someone who deals with people instead of a ranch hand. Oscar knows the underlying principles, and is able to forge special keys to unlock people. When it comes to relating to people, Oscar can and does.

All of a sudden I feel better about following Oscar's counsel and advice about unlocking relationships, but figure it's okay to leave the other things he taught me alone. After all, didn't Bill explore my circumstances, goals, and aspirations before giving me any advice or proposing that I work here? And Bill does live like I want to live. Nice house, new pickup truck, and a beautiful ranch. With both Bill and Oscar as examples, I am pretty sure I believe that following Oscar's advice about relationships is worth mastering.

My job with Bill includes exercising horses, cleaning stalls, tending to all the livestock, mending fences, watering, cutting and baling hay, maintaining equipment, and doing all kinds of odd jobs found on a horse ranch. For the most part I am free to come and go as I please, as long as the work gets done. After a few months my dad still hasn't called or visited. It doesn't surprise me, though I still feel a little shell-shocked from his angry outburst. I am settled now at the Rena Ranch and feel like I am getting along pretty well. I don't see many of my friends though. Larry has gone off to college, and I don't really even have many other friends in the area anymore. The loneliness is starting to get to me a bit. Animals are fine, but they don't make the best conversation.

One day, I decide to take a chance and call Suzie, one of my old high school girlfriends and invite her to go to dinner with me. She agrees, and when I pull up to her dad's place to pick her up I recall the dream I have about owning a place like this: A ranch style home with five bedrooms and four baths; an office on the main floor with a mountain view on twenty acres of land with a river flowing through one side, and a county maintained road on the other; a white fence surrounding the whole property and a barn with horses in the back. It has been a long time since I allowed myself to dream this vividly. It feels pretty good to reminisce about old times and to be reminded of the vision I have of a place like Suzie's dad's property.

Driving back to the Rena's I am completely engrossed by the vision of my dream property. Suddenly I find myself skidding off the road, around a corner, and sideways into a telephone pole. It takes a minute or two to regain my wits. Realizing I am not hurt, I sit in the car for a full five minutes, thinking that this is great because I need some practice in panicking. I am about ten miles from town and about five miles from the Rena's. Finally, I get out of the car, and on a very dark two-lane country road I start walking home; home, that's an interesting thought. I am calling my one-room apartment at Bill Rena's ranch, home.

Walking in the dark makes it easier to see that my current life is all too familiar. My tiny bedroom growing up, my cot in the front of the horse trailer, the tiny unfurnished house Larry and I shared on the river side, and now a one-room bungalow at the Rena's. The vision of the ranch house and property I had just a few minutes ago is certainly gone now. As I walk I ask myself, what am I missing? Is Oscar right? Are relationships the key to everything? How can relationships fix any of this? I start thinking that I couldn't have messed things up more if I had tried. I don't remember there being any clouds in the sky, but there on that cool black night it starts to rain again.

"Get a grip on yourself, Matt," I scold myself, oddly remembering that my dad used to call these kinds of moments and feelings, "pity parties." I am not going to give in to them anymore, I think with a new-found determination. It's kind of funny actually that I should remember something my dad said in this moment, when my broken relationship with him is the very reason I am in this situation. No more pity parties, I decide as I begin to walk a little faster towards the Rena's.

About thirty minutes into my journey, Bill's wife, Alicia, stops and picks me up.

"I saw your car a few miles back and was worried sick about you," she pronounces in her warm, motherly voice. "I am relieved to see you're safe and sound walking down the road. I pictured you out in a field or in the ditch."

Alicia is like all of those mothers you see on TV shows from the 1950s, I think as she chides and empathizes with me both at the same time.

After a few minutes she asks, "What are you going to do now?"

Taken a bit by surprise I interpret her question to mean, what do I want to be when I grow up or what do I want to do as a long term career. She listens intently as I tell her, "I think it's probably time for me to get on with my life and make some decisions about what I really want to be someday that I could be passionate about. I think I will enroll in college."

Alicia, though nodding her head in agreement with my plan, clarifies her question, "What I meant was, what are you going to do about your wrecked car?"

"Oh, that. Sorry," I answer, ignoring the embarrassment that surely shows on my face. "I'll have it hauled to the junk yard and then begin working on my plan." She reaches out and gives me a pat on the shoulder and with a comforting smile she says, "It always looks darkest before the dawn breaks. Everything is going to turn out fine. Just keep working to get better, and you'll see."

The next morning Bill comes out to the barn and asks about the car and the plan Alicia told him about. He has an unusually excited tone in his voice as he comments, "I was beginning to wonder when you were going to see that you are much more than a ranch hand. Maybe your little car accident is the thing you needed to help you consider the future more seriously. What is it that you think you might want to study? What are your interests and passions?"

My mind returns to a very similar conversation I had with Oscar. I say in an unsure voice, "I think that I want to learn more about business. I am pretty good with numbers and understanding what they mean and how to use them."

"Anything else?" Bill continues.

I recognize the curiosity approach that Oscar uses, and reply more confidently, "I am not really sure what all the choices might be. The good news is that I will have some time to figure it out. I will have to take a bunch of general classes before I choose my major."

Bill seems sincerely interested in what I want, and this kind of conversation seems to create a bond of trust between us. Why don't they teach this in school, I wonder? It seems that if Oscar and Bill understand this and they work with animals all day, then everyone working with people should be able to learn this lesson. "My dad could use a lesson or two on this topic," I think, chuckling grimly to myself.

Bill interrupts my mental vacation saying, "When you are ready to apply to school let me know. I will be happy to help you in any way I can with letters of recommendation or anything else I can do."

My gratitude overcomes me while thanking him; I reach out and give him a big hug! The truth is that I have been faking sincerity for a long time now. But I am truly sincere in my appreciation for all Bill and Alicia have done for me: taking me in, offering me a job, talking to me, and worrying about me. This is the relationship I wish I had with my own parents.

That evening as I am feeding the horses, I realize that this might be a pivotal moment in my life. I have a strange feeling that, though in some ways I have taken some steps backwards, somehow Bill's encouragement and support have given me strength to move forward and take a bold step in the pursuit of my future.

Over the next few weeks I submit my application to State College as the next step in my life plan. Then one day, a few weeks later I had the feeling that it might be a banner day. As I work on the barn door I notice that Alicia is running towards me with a letter in her hand.

She shouts, "It's here, it's here! Your letter from State College. Open it, open it. I can't wait to find out what they say about your application."

Furiously tearing into the letter like it's a Christmas present; I begin to read it aloud, "You have been accepted for the winter semester." I'm a little stunned: by some small miracle I have been accepted. Alicia and I joyously dance for a few moments right there in the barn. I am sure the horses and cows are chuckling at this sight. I am so excited that it doesn't even dawn on me that I have no idea how a person with a high school GPA of 2.2 could get into any college. Right now I don't care how I got in. I don't know if Mr. Rena pulled strings to get me in, or whether he had my dad do something to help me. I hope the fortune cookie quote will prove true as I move in this new direction.

January comes with still no word from or sight of my dad. I am off to State College, and I really wish that I had his blessing. But I am accepting that this wish will probably just stay a wish. I am moving on with my life and I don't want to risk a repeat of our last encounter. I figure he will find out that I am going to college however he finds out, if he even cares to find out. In that moment I take charge of my own life and I am looking forward to going back to school.

I really end up enjoying school. Time flies by; it's already the end of my third semester and I need to declare a major. I'm leaning towards financial planning. I only have one more semester of general education classes and then I will be working exclusively in my major. At this point my experiences with the fairgrounds, the riverside, and the Rena Ranch are helping me see the greater opportunity offered here at the university. I feel like I am really responsible for my life; no one is checking up on me. I succeed or fail based on how I decide to work. Those who are here to learn do learn and become something, and those who don't want to learn don't seem to stay long. After a few semesters I am really starting to learn what I am good at and what I don't care for.

As I work on an assignment I think about what Oscar might be doing right now? Then I think about Larry, and then my dad as I ponder about what they might be doing. My dad seems very intelligent and successful, but he also seems very lonely and void of meaningful relationships that transcend the superficial. Wow, I am even starting to sound like a college student – "transcend the superficial." When I think of my parents they don't seem particularly close. They are married, but seem to be living separate lives within the same house.

Then I realize that I don't really have any close friends or relationships that I consider life-long either. Funny how the sun is actually covered by a dark cloud in the exact moment I discover that I lack real, deep relationships in my life. It's really eerie, like a sign from God or something.

Over the next few months a longing to have better, deeper relationships develops within me. I turn to God and my personal experience and observations for some answers, help, and encouragement, and begin to develop a list of things I most want in my romantic and platonic relationships. I think about the people whom I admire and respect most and include these attributes in my list With attributes based on these people, my list grows longer: inspirational, emotional strength, hard-working, action taker, innovative, aggressive, logical, decisive, great planner, dreamer, resourceful, motivated, enthusiastic, loyal, independent, responsible, versatile, persistent, visionary, problem solver and leader. My list continues to grow while I finish the semester.

On the first day of my fourth semester I find myself in Biology. The students are being assigned lab partners and we are supposed to find our partner and sit next to them for the entire semester, beginning right now. I have a piece of paper in my hand with my partner's name on it; Ann Wentz. Wandering aimlessly around the classroom, I bump into someone from behind. Turning around to apologize for my clumsiness, I discover that I have run into Ann, my new lab partner! I think to myself, "If God answers prayers like this, I should be praying every day. If I waved a magic wand I couldn't have created a more perfect match to the list I had been creating for a girlfriend or wife. Looks aren't everything I know, but they are something, and Ann is beyond belief.

Over the next few classes and lab assignments, I become more deeply enamored with her. She is spectacular: good looking, smart, articulate, outgoing, and in every other way a perfect match to the characteristics on my list. After a few weeks of psyching myself up, I ask her on a date. Happily she agrees. I don't know why it is, but first dates are always a little awkward. Asking the superficial, data-centric, preliminary questions so we can have something to talk about is painful to me. I have a difficult time with this initial "get to know you" phase of dating. Ann, however, is wonderful at this game.

She tells me about her family and some brief details about her background, "My father and mother are both college graduates. My dad is a professor here on campus. I came to State College on a swimming scholarship and am studying fine art. I have already sold several art works, and have published illustrations in globally distributed magazines. I love to ride horses and I still have one of my own. I am not on the swim team now because I just returned from a foreign exchange program in South America. I plan to work as a freelance artist until I finish my degree. I am a bit embarrassed to admit this, but the reason I am taking Biology as a senior is because I don't like it, so I put it off for as long as I could. So what about you? Tell me about what you are up to here at State College."

After hearing her stories of family activities and her closeness to her brothers and sister, it seems prudent to keep my dysfunctional family a secret for as long as possible. I don't want to alert her to the fact that my situation isn't as idyllic as hers, so I give her as few details as possible. "I am from a small town in the country. My parents own a horse ranch. I have two sisters, and am majoring in financial planning," I hope she won't press for more detail. Of course if this date works out and our relationship becomes more serious, the details will come out, but I really want her to get to know me before I trouble her with the details of my background.

Over the semester our relationship develops into something really great. I have never had so much motivation to study in my life. I want her to think I am the best student ever, and that I would or could fit into her family. Almost every day I make up some kind of reason to visit or talk to her. My streak of days seeing Ann is only broken by the Thanksgiving holiday. I drive home to the Rena Ranch for the break. A feeling of loneliness and despair comes over me. I am not sure exactly what love feels like, but I can tell you that I never want to be away from Ann for this long again.

Ann is suffering from the same agonizing empty feeling at her home. As she walks to the barn to take a ride she thinks about past Thanksgivings and the usual happy time she has with her family and friends. But this one is different. Galloping across an open field she suddenly becomes aware that the weather is turning cold. She turns back to the barn and confides to her horse that the semester is winding down, and that the Biology class she dreaded in the beginning of the semester is turning out to be a great blessing. She tells him that her "forced" time with Matt as a lab partner is coming to an end soon, and even though it's only been a few days, she misses the late night talks and contrived study sessions at the ice cream store.

Throwing her arms around the horse's neck, and resting her head on him, she softly says, "I think I might be falling in love with him. This time away from him has made me recognize how much I enjoy being with him," she admits candidly while rubbing his neck. "The little bit I know about his family life makes me think it has been challenging, and so I think he could use some family support during the holidays. That's it," she exclaims loudly as she throws her arms up in the air startling the horse. "I will invite him to stay in town and visit us each day during the Christmas break. But how?" she asks aloud as if the horse could offer the answer. "How can I ask him to stay and be with my family without appearing too forward?"

The plan takes shape as she puts her horse away. During the week before finals, she plans to study alone with Matt in the library. It shouldn't be too hard to get him to agree, he is always making some excuse to see me. When we are alone I will ask what his plans are for the Christmas break, and then I will know for sure what he is thinking. Maybe.

Matt returns from Thanksgiving break on Saturday, a full day early from vacation, and immediately calls Ann. She answers and sounds surprised that I would call at the first opportunity when I got back, Matt thinks. Maybe she is just happy to see me. After all, during the call she did invite me to Church tomorrow.

Ann, thinking about her carefully laid plan remarks to herself, "Step one is complete. He gladly accepted my invitation." As she waits for an opportunity to begin step two, her mother unwittingly assists the plan by asking Matt to dinner. Even though Ann is sure he is beginning to sense that something is going on, he isn't letting on at all.

As Matt rings Ann's doorbell, an unsettled feeling comes over him. But that goes away when Phil, Ann's father answers the door, reaches out and pulls him into the house with a huge smile on his face and welcomes him warmly.

Ann remembers nervously, having boys meet my parents always seems to be awkward, But this time seems different somehow. Usually dad talks for a minute or two and then leaves us alone. I am surprised when, after about five minutes of the usual small talk, mom and dad are opening up and accepting Matt as if he has been a part of the family for a long time. Dad interrupts the conversation by inviting Matt to help him get his snow blower started. Mom and I go to the kitchen to finish getting dinner ready. We are going about their different jobs in silence when all of a sudden the sound of the roaring snow blower motor fills the air. Success is achieved in the shop, Ann grins.

Her mom catches her smiling, and deviously says, "That's the same look I used to get when your father did things like that for my dad. I was so proud of him that I couldn't help but smile just like you are right now. Seems he is pretty special to you Ann." Just then dad and Matt come in from the shop.

"Sounds like you got the snow blower going," Ann says quickly, with a bit of relief in her voice, momentarily avoiding responding to her mom's obvious insinuation about Matt.

Dinner time at the Wentz's is like the kind you see on TV, but only imagine in real life Matt muse's. It's like having Sunday dinner with the perfect imaginary family; great food, interesting discussion of the topics of the day, curious questions about events and plans for the coming week, and a feeling of togetherness. I don't ever remember eating together very often growing up; let alone having civil conversation at mealtime.

Ann moves quickly to clear the table and together we wash the dishes. Now that dinner is over, Ann escorts me to see her horse and we talk about her adventures dashing through fields, riding along dangerous mountain trails and through orchards as a teenager. But I can see something is on her mind. Just as we are at the front door she asks me, "What are your plans for Christmas?"

Matt calmly and naturally responds, "I don't really have a family per se to go to." This might be the perfect time to let Ann know the details about my situation with my dad. The story makes her cry, and after a few emotional moments she invites me to spend the holidays with her and her family during the break. Either she is feeling sorry for me like she would a lost puppy dog, or she is really beginning to feel something for me. At the moment, I don't care what the reasons are, I am glad to accept the invitation.

Over the Christmas break I spend a lot of time with Ann's family and watch them interact with one another. This is the kind of family I am going to have some day, I promise myself. One where everyone supports and encourages instead of competing for family resources like vultures waiting for their prey to die so they can enjoy the feast. Ann and I have a great time without the pressure of school hanging over us.

On one hand I am glad the semester is over; we both got an A in Biology, which is of course, no surprise to Ann, but it's a great achievement for me. On the other hand, I am a bit panicked that our contrived time together is over. During the break, we go on walks, ride horses, play games with her family, and talk about everything from politics and religion to hobbies and our deepest fears and desires. Our relationship is becoming very serious, and I love every minute I spend with Ann.

Winter turns to spring. Time is flying by and Ann is scheduled to graduate in a few weeks. Our future beyond that is uncertain, and when I think of a future without her, a lonely, empty feeling like the one I had last Thanksgiving returns. I decide that the time has come to make our relationship a permanent one.

My plan is set; everything is in place. Ann agrees to hike to the waterfalls with me. I make up some excuse about wanting to learn about framing a scene for a fictitious art project for one of my classes. When we get there, she takes great care to help me understand about positioning items in a picture and how the eye follows certain shapes and colors. "It's as if you are creating a relationship between the scene and the person looking at the picture," she says.

Step two is being put into place while we are on our hike. I have arranged to have two horses ready when we return and right on schedule, with the help of Ann's brother, they are brushed, saddled, and rearing to go. Ann may suspect that something is going on, because her brother, who doesn't care at all about horses, is waiting at the barn to greet us with groomed and prepared horses to ride. But if she suspects something is going on, she isn't letting on.

I lead her on the route to the old apple orchard she used to ride on as a child, and right in the middle of that orchard I stop and get off my horse. I take her hand and pull a ring out of my pocket. She looks at me with a tear in her eye and as I ask her to marry me I can feel my heart pounding. My whole life hangs on what that tear in her eye means.

2

And So It Begins

Everything is a blur. The minister is telling Ann to take me by the right hand and to recite her wedding vows. My mind is racing as I flash back to when we first met, our first date, and our first kiss. I am aware that I am not fully paying attention to her as she is saying "to have and to hold." I'm lost in the thought of our new life together as a family. A family that I hope would be more like Ann's than mine. Once again my parents were a no show. My dad seems to be absent in my life at every important point I can remember. In that second I make a promise to myself that I will always work to build strong family relationships. In some ways I promise myself that I will be a chain breaker, to build relationships instead of testing them. My family's history of dysfunction doesn't have to be part of my future. This is my opportunity to change my direction.

I return to the proceedings just in time to hear Ann say, "For better or for worse, for richer, for poorer," which vaults me into the future. How will I ever provide for her like she deserves and what about raising children and having a comfortable home and retiring some day? Again the vows interrupt my diversion. She is all the way to, "I promise to love you unconditionally, to support you in your goals, in good times and bad, regardless of the obstacles we may face together." I am thinking about what trials we will face and wondering how we will face them? I return fully to the ceremony when Ann takes my hand and puts the ring on my finger. Looking into her eyes, a feeling of gratitude swells within me, helping me believe that whatever life throws at us we will be able to handle it, as long as we are together. The minister pronounces us man and wife, and tells me that I can kiss Ann now for the first time as my wife.

After our honeymoon we come back to our familiar college surroundings, only now we are inseparably linked together. Somehow each decision takes on a more serious and monumental weight. Ann is doing art jobs while I complete my last year and a half of studies. I imagine what it will be like to have a rewarding career doing something I love. To be able to afford a car that I can depend on to get me to work and that Ann can use to run errands without having to worry. Our small apartment with used furniture and non-matching pots, pans, dishes, and silverware seems appropriate for college students but I must admit it is a sore reminder of the fact that I promised Ann a bigger more fashionable home with a yard, new furniture, kitchen utensils and appliances made after I was born. However it is great to be home. Our first child is born during my last semester. A healthy boy and despite these humble beginnings it's great to have a family that is happy to see each other at the end of each day.

There is only a month or so left in school. This is the time when most students either get jobs or begin worrying because they don't have one yet. As I work on an assignment the phone rings. I beat Ann to answer it and I talk for a minute or two. I hang up the phone and grab Ann. She is very surprised at my outburst until I tell her that I got a job working for Collation Money Systems, a small finance and budgeting company for low income families who have challenges meeting their obligations. Collation is certainly not my dream job, but it's a start. What a relief it is to have a job locked down before graduation. This job will almost certainly get us out of these student living conditions. I tell Ann, "I am thinking of not attending my graduation ceremony. There is just too much historical pain involved with my family's lack of support to seriously consider going through all that again."

Ann responds compassionately, but asks me to consider her family's situation and their support. I really hadn't fully appreciated the fact that I do have at least one side of the family that supports and encourages. This is what it must feel like to be one of my sisters.

After graduation, Ann and I spend a few days looking at houses we could afford in neighborhoods that were within commuting distance to my job. We learn that the reality of not having much of a credit history and working at a job with meager wages make it impossible for us to buy a house. Our current situation may be a stepping stone professionally, but the living conditions we can afford are limited to basement apartments. This is a long way from the lifestyle I want and promised myself to provide for Ann and our family. I figure the only way out of this basement is to learn all I can about record keeping, tracking results, and efficient budgeting. If I can become a professional at offering these services, my boss, Mr. Jaynes will certainly notice and be forced to give me raises.

The weeks turn into months with little or no change in my situation. Ann has to do art projects in our living room. She works around our son's sleeping schedule. As I open the door after a long day's work, I find Ann working on the final part of a project that is due tomorrow morning. My heart sinks as I survey the situation in amazement. Our son is crying, the dishes haven't been done and the house looks as if a tornado has passed by. Ann is still in her pajamas and it looks as if she hasn't taken the time to even brush her hair. She looks at me with tears in her eyes and asks if I can help her by giving her the peace she needs to complete her work.

I take our boy and get him ready for bed. He asks me to tell him a story that will help him dream good dreams. I think for a moment and tell him a story of a man who has been down and out on his luck. He lives in the front of a horse trailer and must work to overcome problem after problem. Happily, he marries the girl he loves, and with the help of a few great people along the way, the man learns to become better each day. And in the end he becomes honored. His family lives in a big house and they love each other very much. By the time I finish the story he has fallen asleep. I sit there for a moment staring at him sleeping so peacefully.

As I sit there Oscar's words "This isn't so bad" ring in my ears. I look around me and think to myself, I am turning into Oscar! Everything about this existence feels like I'm settling for something I don't really want. Oscar, me, and the people I work with each day live paycheck to paycheck with little or no hope of ever escaping the captivity of lack and want. As fast as Oscar's words of surrender had come a minute ago, his fortune cookie came to mind now, "If you don't change your direction, you are likely to end up where you are headed."

While I clean up the house, wash and dry the dishes, make Ann a sandwich and take a shower, I replay Oscar's hay bale training on the importance of relationships. He used to tell me that success in anything is built on the strength of my relationships and that there is some kind of key to unlock people, based on trust, professionalism, and sincere caring. I drift off to sleep waiting for Ann to come to bed, still not knowing how to make Oscar's blacksmith's secret create power in my own life. How is any of that going to get me out of this apartment or help me increase my earning power at work? My last conscious thought is a saying of my favorite university professor: "When the student is ready, the teacher will appear." I am so ready for things to change.

A couple of days pass and Mr. Jaynes calls me into his office. He has a deep voice and a menacing look about him. Today he seems more gloomy than usual.

He asks me, "Have you noticed that many of our clients ask specifically for other agents instead of you?

Taken back by his accusational tone and demeaning question I respond saying, "I haven't noticed them asking for others, specifically; but now that you mention it, everyone seems to have a larger work load than I do. Why do you ask?"

He stands up and responds saying, "Because people don't seem to like you. You are the best we have at putting together creative solutions for our clients. However, the technical part of what we do is only part of the value of our service. You are concentrating on the superficial part of our clients. You get their basic documents and information and then excuse them, telling them you will call in a few days with a plan or budget that will meet their needs.

You may have also noticed that you haven't received a raise since you have been here."

As Mr. Jaynes pauses, I brace myself for the worst. But he continues intently, "In this business, young man, we get paid to create results for our clients, and the best way to do that is to gain people's trust. To invite them to tell you more about their life, their circumstances, what they think might be the cause of their challenges, and what relief might look and feel like. This is a relationship business, not a budgeting, planning and financial strategy business. Learn to ask questions, and then take some time to listen, really listen, to what your clients are saying. Then ask more questions to get clear on what they want their life to be like. I'm not talking about what they need to get by. I mean so that they can create something fantastic of their life. When you learn that, more people will come in here asking specifically for you, and I will be happy to pay you more because you will be worth more to the company. I hope you take this little talk to heart. I have my eye on you."

On my way home after work, it occurs to me that every important lesson I have ever learned comes to me like being hit with a two-by-four on the head. Maybe I am deaf or insensitive to learning when someone whispers or talks normally. It seems I need to be severely shaken to have my senses stirred. Maybe my dad has been right all along. Maybe I am not cut out to be a huge success in life. Maybe basement apartments, lack, and want are all I will ever have. Maybe Oscar is more right than I knew when he said, "This really isn't so bad, is it?"

I open the door to our apartment and find Ann and our son asleep on the couch. I help her tuck him into bed, and then I share what Mr. Jaynes said. I begin complaining about how I am working really hard, but I'm not really getting anything out of this job, and that I feel like I am letting her down because we don't have anything. Then I cap the night off by telling her I am going to begin looking for another job.

It is clear that I have depressed both of us by the time we retire for the night. It's a good thing it is Thanksgiving weekend; although right now I don't feel like I have much to be thankful for. Maybe something as simple as having a few days to get myself together is a place to start.

Ann is up bright and early preparing a Thanksgiving feast. This is the first year we will be celebrating the holidays away from Ann's family. I offer to help in the kitchen and discover that our utensils and pans are woefully short in supply and utility. I wonder if anything in my situation is working out. Lacking a roasting pan, we cook a turkey in the biggest sauce pan we have; fortunately it's a pretty small turkey. We have a good laugh over the cooking situation.

What else can we do but laugh? Ann tells me that Thanksgiving is her favorite holiday. She loves it when the family comes together to watch football, and of course she loves the smell of turkey, gravy, mash potatoes, homemade cranberry sauce, and her dad's homemade pumpkin pie. And even though this is certainly not a feast of that magnitude, it is what we can do in our current circumstances. Certainly we have enough for the three of us.

I appreciate her willingness to overlook this year's deficiencies, but I have to hide my own disappointment from her. I think, "She is completely missing the point. She is working as a mother and artist, I am working my guts out and still we don't have a proper pan to cook a turkey in! Somehow this has got to change or we are definitely going to end up where we are headed."

Putting my own feelings aside for the moment, I say instead, "This is the first year I will get to actually carve the turkey. And here is my first attempt at making your fathers pumpkin pie. It was a bit challenging because not only was it my first attempt making pumpkin pie at all, but I had to make it in a salad bowl. It doesn't look very pretty, but it tastes pretty good, if I do say so myself."

Ann tastes it and agreeingly says, "With the right utensils this may become an Ivey family tradition."

Just then the phone rings. I answer and talk for a few minutes before giving the phone to Ann; it's her mother. She is calling to make sure Ann has everything under control on such an important occasion. Ann retreats into the other room but not out of earshot. Matt can hear Ann's side of the conversation.

Ann admits to her mother, "I burned the gravy." Her voice becomes a bit teary when she says, "I feel a little like a hick cooking in pots and pans that were never meant for this type of celebration. I wanted everything to be fantastic on our first Thanksgiving on our own and the one day that Matt has off. I miss the smells of your kitchen, mom. And today has been nothing like my memories growing up. In fact nothing seems to be like I remember."

Crying now, she adds, "I love Matt and our son, but nothing is working out like I thought it would when we first got married. Matt works so hard for the meager money he gets. I can contribute some, but I want Matt to feel like he is doing enough to make me happy. He seems pretty upset about our lack of basic cooking utensils. I know he is not angry at me, I think he is comparing himself to his dad and the lifestyle he provided as Matt grew up. He has an expectation that he is only doing his part if my life is comfortable and I have everything I need and want. But his job is just not generating enough income to make that happen right now. He is working twelve to fourteen hours everyday to provide for us. We do have enough money to live each month, but I can't see when this will end. He is hardly ever around and I feel like we are living parallel lives. I think of how you had to scrimp and save for everything you ever had. In fact I don't remember ever having new carpet or new furniture."

Her mother patiently waits for Ann to finish and begins to respond in a loving, soft tone saying, "Love and family are what matter most; the relationships you create along the way are the most important thing. Material things are nice, but I wouldn't trade anything in this world for your dad and the relationship we have."

Talking to my mom always gives me comfort, Ann thinks, and that's when it comes out, "I am also pregnant."

"Have you told Matt yet?" her mother asks.

"Not yet," replies Ann nervously. "I don't know how to tell him without putting more pressure on him. Things aren't going well at his work and he feels like he can barely provide for the three of us. How will he feel when he finds out there is going to be another addition to our family?"

While Ann is in the other room, Matt is lost in his own heart break and disappointment; not really paying attention to Ann's conversation with her mother now he thinks, I'm sitting in the living room with my head buried in my hands. I completely miss Ann's grand announcement to her mother about the baby. I just remember the life I promised Ann, and the reality is that this life is a far cry from anything I imagined when we were dating.

By the time Ann hangs up the phone we are both wiping tears from our eyes and have to fake putting on a happy face, pretending that everything is fine or that it would someday be fine if we just keep on working. The good news is that we do have each other, although right now that seems like little consolation.

"I feel like a failure," I humbly share. You deserve so much more than this and I'm not making it happen.

Lying in bed that night my lamentation turns into determination. I am determined to succeed no matter what. The trouble is I don't know what or how to do anything about it. As I drift off to sleep, my heart is heavy with a feeling of sorrow for our lifestyle. Just before I nod off I remember what Alicia Rena told me when she picked me up on the side of the road after my car accident: "It always looks darkest before the light of dawn breaking. Everything is going to turn out fine. Just keep working to get better, you'll see."

I get to work early on Monday morning. I am serious about taking Mr. Jaynes' advice to heart, changing my approach from efficiency to effectiveness. I schedule thirty minutes for every appointment instead of fifteen so that I will have plenty of time to talk to my clients. And even though they all say they want to change their circumstances, I know they all need the same things: discipline and control to handle their funds wisely. Over the next few weeks I listen to different stories with the same ending. I create financial strategies and plans that include information I never had discovered before experimenting with this new-found interest in people and their motivation for a different future based on a new direction. I feel like I really am interested in each client and the results are beginning to show. What a great trick! Mr. Jaynes has given me a great secret, and as far as I can tell it's working. He seems happy, my work load is increasing slightly, and I'm not getting called into his office like a schoolboy being punished.

The reality of this job, however, is becoming obvious. It is a dead end job, and in order for things to change, I have to change things. I spend my lunch hour each day searching for a new job; a job where I can start fresh and really use my university degree and new-found skills and experience.

Christmas time comes, and as we sit in front of the tree all decorated and lit up, Ann gives me the best present ever: she announces that she is pregnant. Our family is growing and she looks so excited as we watch the snow outside our tiny living room window. I am excited for the baby to come. At least this part of our marriage is working well. Then all at once the realization that I am going to be a father again hits me like a ton of bricks. The pressure to make more money and care for a family of four mounts in my mind.

I think about my job and being there to help families get what they want in life, while mine is in worse condition than many of theirs. The fact that I have Ann and now two children somehow consoles me. I can't explain it; I just felt like they are the anchors in my life, the only things that are truly stable. As darkness falls outside our basement home, the phone rings and like an alarm clock it seems to startle both Ann and I. As I hang up the phone I jump for joy, almost hitting my head on the low basement ceiling.

Ann is surprised by my sudden out burst and demands to know, "Who was it!"

Strutting around the living room like a rooster, I tell her, "I got the job working for Perpetual Wealth Financial. It's a national financial planning company. The good news is that I will be starting in two weeks and I will be getting a raise. The bad news is that we are going to have to move closer to the big city." Ann responds excitedly, and as fast as a pregnant woman can, she gets up and dances with me around the living room.

We spend the next few weeks looking at houses we think we can afford with my new salary. The one we like best is a small, new, red-brick ranch style home in a classy neighborhood; the only house on the block with less than 5,000 square feet. It is certainly the odd house in this neighborhood, but that's one of the things we like most about it. While we are taking a second look, a woman from across the street comes to greet us. She has a big smile and warmly announces herself as Sara Thoms.

Sara is genuinely happy that someone is seriously considering this house. "Although it's new," she says, "It's been vacant for a long time now. It's a great house but not what most people want when they look at this neighborhood." She seems really interested in us. She's asking a million questions about us and is talking so fast that there is no time to answer. "This is a great neighborhood with fantastic schools and a nice grocery store around the corner. There are commuter trains and a bus stop three blocks away," she informs us without taking a breath.

Sara and Ann become friends immediately. They talk for a full half hour while I walk around the house and quite frankly begin feeling a little like the Clampetts from "The Beverly Hillbillies." We are about to be the poorest family in the smallest house in the neighborhood. But Sara Thoms' welcome and our love of this little house induce us to buy it. A calm feeling comes over me as I realize that I have climbed out of the basement. No more sleeping in the front of drafty horse trailers or underground. Finally we are on our way up.

After an hour bus ride and a two block walk, I arrive at the corporate headquarters of Perpetual Wealth Financial. My company mentor Josh greets me and another new hire named Jane Passmore with a warm smile and a firm handshake. As we walk to the Human Resources Department Josh begins explaining our initial job responsibilities, which include developing financial strategies and plans for families.

While we are filling out our paperwork and getting situated in our little cubicles, it dawns on me that it seems kind of strange to trust a recent college graduate with only a year or so of experience who is living in a 2,500 square foot house and has only one car in disrepair with planning people's path to prosperity, financial security and generational wealth succession. I love the challenge though, and I'm going to learn all I can from my peers and supervisors.

In the months to come I am usually the first to work and the last to leave, which of course separates Ann and I for much of each day. Ann is an awesome support partner. She spends a lot of time with Sara from across the street, and in fact joined her in a home-based business called XL-8. She seems content to go to a few meetings from time to time and buy products that make our life better. Ann's freelance art work helps her make a financial contribution to our family. And she is awesome at stretching our money go as far as possible. She sews clothes, drapes, tablecloths, and everything else we need. She cans fruits and other goods, and uses leftover's as many times as possible. I swear this is the fourth day in a row we are eating casserole for both lunch and dinner. I console myself by acknowledging that she is working as hard as or harder than I am to make our house a home. She decorates the house and calls me at work almost everyday. Today I realize that she has invented a game called, "Guess what I did today?"

When she calls this afternoon the first thing she says is, "Guess what I did today?"

I respond with my usual, "I have no idea," and then asks "What did you do?"

Excitedly she boasts, "I refinished the kitchen table and chairs so that they look brand new!"

Her passion for this kind of work is great because we certainly need to fill in the gaps of what we don't have financially. In a short time and with hard work she is creating a castle for the Ivey family to grow, be happy, and create memories in.

It is the income from her art work that makes it possible for us to go on family outings and vacations; usually to her parent's house. It feels good to go there once in a while, but I long for a real vacation. One where you don't have to do the dishes, make the bed, vacuum, trim trees, and mow the yard.

Every day I catch the early bus to work. Jack, the driver, welcomes me aboard. Sitting in my unofficial reserved seat my heart sinks a little, realizing that, except for the house we live in, very few of the things I dreamed of growing up, worked for in college, and promised Ann on our wedding day to provide, are ours yet. For the rest of the hour ride, I wish for what I want, knowing all the time that wishing will never produce what work will. For the first time since I started riding the bus I am grateful for the time to just think without paying attention to anything else. I am so caught up in my thoughts that I almost miss my stop. Jack honks the horn to get me to notice that I am supposed to get off.

I meet with Josh for my first quarterly job review. He asks, "How are you doing; how are you feeling now that you have had some time to get used to being here?"

I respond saying, "I feel great. I am starting to really learn the business and I think my work speaks for itself."

He takes a deep breath, sighs, and then tells me, "I agree that your financial plans and strategies are clever, creative, and unique. We knew you could do that when we hired you. But there is something missing in your approach. Something that will keep you from the success you are capable of. I don't know exactly what it is, but I think it has to do with really understanding your clients on a deep level before you begin putting a plan in place."

I had heard this message before. My heart sinks a little as I sit back in the chair, folding my arms and legs as I realize that I haven't changed my approach enough. First Oscar, then Bill, then Mr. Jaynes, and now Josh! I am obviously not getting the message!

"This is not the minor leagues anymore," Josh continues. "Our clients count on us to create results that transcend this life. They count on us to help them make retirement and generational wealth possible. You are lagging behind the other Floor Level Planners we hired at the same time you came. In fact Jane Passmore has been awarded with the Distinguished Service Certificate due to her exemplary customer satisfaction survey scores. Please know that I think you are a valuable contributor to the company and department. And I challenge you to improve on the human side of our business in the next quarter."

Shocked and a bit dismayed, I slowly walk back to my desk, and for the first time I really examine what I might be missing. A quote I heard in my first tax planning class comes to mind, "Faking it creates failure a thousand times faster than taking the time and effort to learn it and make it." In that moment I realize I have been faking sincerity for a long time now, and everyone seems to be able to see it but me. Maybe it's time to implement some of what I am learning and teaching others in my own life. I ask myself what I want in life, and then begin to plan a path out of my own dilemma.

I begin by thinking that Ann deserves more than I am providing, and as I sit here in my cubicle, the advice my dad, Oscar, and Bill have given me in the past comes front and center in my mind. What I see is illustrated by a saying I've heard hundreds of times before, "If it is to be, it's up to me". I write this at the top of the white board, and underneath that I add Oscar's emotional plea telling me to, "Find something you can love that will give you the life you want." Then in a completely different color I write Bill's admonition to "Only accept advice and counsel from those who are succeeding in the area you want to succeed at."

I love the work that I am doing, but it's not giving me the life I want. So I begin to ask myself what I can do to create more income, and who can teach me? Almost immediately the inspiration starts coming. In fact it's coming faster than I can write. In a few minutes I have a lot of options written on my white board. I probably should write them in a less public place, but I always think better when I can see what I am thinking in big print, and this is the only place that accommodates my thinking process. About thirty minutes into this exercise Jane Passmore stops by unannounced to ask a question about a strategy for one of her clients.

I think, but don't say, "You are the belle of the ball. What can I possibly say that will help you, and why should I help you look even better than you already do? Of course this way of thinking overlooks the fact that helping her means helping our clients." I continue to myself, "You are on the fast track up the corporate ladder, ahead of me," jealously and self-pitying. "You are my rival and nemesis." Before I can answer she notices my list on the white board.

She changes the subject by asking, "What are you doing?"

Confessing that I am considering possible options to make more money, I tell her, "I'm not in any kind of financial trouble or anything, I just want to provide a better lifestyle for my wife and kids, and I am exploring options." Inexplicably confiding in her I continue, "I am tired of old furniture, mismatched appliances, undependable transportation, and a myriad of other little things that by themselves don't amount to much, but all together wear on me. And I have a second child due in the next month or so."

She grabs the eraser and wipes the board clean, except for the quotes from my dad, Oscar, and Bill. Then she sits down and candidly shares, "I have had similar feelings and so I will give you some advice. First of all, you don't want anyone else here to know that you are considering other options. Management is watching us very closely as candidates for promotion because we are the next generation of leaders here. Everyone admires your work, dedication, and innovative solutions to challenges our clients have. That's why I have come to see you; to get your insight on a problem I am having with one of my clients. You might consider additional options within the company as a way to make more money and demonstrate that you're dedicated to the organization. The company offers night classes right here on campus for employees and clients in almost every area of financial planning. I would advise you to go to Craig in Human Resources, or to Mrs. Jensen directly, and ask if there are any evening class instructor opportunities that you can take advantage of. Taking the initiative to offer to teach some night classes will make you look good, and the income should relieve some of your financial pain."

I lean back while contemplating the possibilities Jane had just explained and how they might affect Ann and me. It's not clear how much time went by but when I come back to reality, Jane is still there staring at me.

I break the silence by asking her, "Sorry, for getting lost. What question did you come in to ask me?"

She says as she stands up, "It really doesn't matter; you have much bigger challenges to consider."

For the first time in my life, I see what is missing. Just now Jane seemed to really care about me, which created trust between us. And that's when I saw her as a professional who might be able to help me get what I want, instead of my competition. She did what Oscar had been talking about those years ago: she unlocked me and let the horses out. That's why she earned the award and that's why she is succeeding. She focuses on relationships. She's not my enemy, adversary, competition, or nemesis; she's my friend and professional colleague and I should take her advice and make an appointment with Mrs. Jensen. But first I should probably find out as much as I can about the night class program we offer.

Up to this point I have been completely oblivious to the company's class offerings, the times and days classes are offered, the teachers, or anything else concerning it for that matter. I am on my way to the Human Resources office to get acquainted with the training programs we offer before going to the company president, Mrs. Jensen. I ask Craig, the Director of Human Resources, if there are classes he has trouble finding instructors for. He is eager to tell me that there are two: Budgeting and Record Keeping. He explains how much I would make as an instructor, and the process for becoming an instructor. I start selling myself as the one who can alleviate his pain by telling him much of what I think he wants to hear about my qualifications in these two subjects. I venture a weak offer to teach both courses if Mrs. Jensen will approve.

While I am telling Craig that I am on my way to talk to her right now to inquire about teaching in addition to my regular responsibilities, he stands up, shakes my hand and says, "I would love to make the introduction and see if she will approve you right now." Craig waves as we pass Mrs. Jensen's assistant and we walk right in to her office.

Greeting him cheerfully she asks what we are up to. Craig quickly explains, "Matt here has shown remarkable initiative by coming to see if he can teach some night classes."

Turning to me, she asks, "Why do you want to teach at night after a long day in the office?"

Before I can answer Craig jumps in giving a bottom line reason, "It's part of his long term succession plan at the company."

Nice answer Matt thinks, much better than I would have given. Mrs. Jensen agrees under the condition that it won't affect my normal duties or responsibilities. Craig assures her, "Don't worry. This evening assignment will enhance Matt's daily work. I'm confident that anyone who would ask about this extra opportunity is just the kind of person we want doing both jobs."

Craig and I leave as fast as we came. We whisk past the administrative assistant, and as we pass through the floor's cubical farm I ask him, "Why didn't you want me to respond to her question about why I want to teach?"

He replies as if to teach me an important lesson, "I didn't want her to think you might be dissatisfied doing what you are doing now, or that you would be distracted by this additional assignment. I know her very well and her personality type won't allow for long explanations or long pauses for thought before giving a response. So I thought I would step in and get to the bottom line for her. I hope you don't mind." Approaching his office he continues, "You just seem like you really want to begin immediately, so I made that happen for you. Here is the schedule of courses we need instructors for. The budgeting course starts next week on Tuesday's and Thursdays at 7:00 PM and record keeping begins in a couple of weeks on Mondays and Wednesdays at the same time."

He hands me the pay form and asks me to send him a short bio that he can put on the website for promotional purposes, and tells me that I need to attend a brief orientation at lunch on Friday to make sure that I know the logistics of grading, class materials, lights, locking doors after class, and et cetera. I sign the form, agree to attend the orientation meeting, and return to my cubicle. I sit down at my desk, and staring at me like a neon sign are the words at the top of my white board, "If it is to be, it's up to me." "Find something you can love and that will give you the life you want." "Accept advice and counsel from those who are succeeding in the area you want to succeed at."

I realize that I initiated the sequence of events that made all this possible and I also recognize that without Josh's honesty, Jane's advice, and Craig's encouragement, none of this would be happening. So the quotes from my dad, Oscar, and Bill seemed tailor-made to help me get what I want. It is at this moment that I think of Ann and what I am going to tell her when I get home about my new income opportunity. On the bus ride home I start thinking of important points that I want to make to soften the blow of taking on this extra assignment at work since I now wouldn't be getting home until after 10:00 PM four nights per week. I think of mentioning how she might use the extra money, and that teaching includes the additional benefit of putting me in contact with other managers and executives who, according to Jane, are looking for leaders; and leadership means raises. I also think that this additional responsibility will be temporary until we get our finances under control and I begin earning promotions.

When I get home Ann welcomes me and asks, "Guess what I did today? I got flowers at a 75% off sale and planted them all around the house. They make everything so much brighter. She looks at me and can tell right away that something is going on. I begin to explain, trying to make a compelling case for my professional ambition.

She listens intently and asks curiously, "Why do you want to work the extra hours."

Feeling the pain, both of working more and of not having provided well, I say, "I am feeling some pretty significant emotional pain about the scarcity of resources I am providing."

Empathetically Ann says, "I will agree to support you if this is really a temporary situation. But there is one condition to my agreement: you need to schedule going with me to the next business development conference for the home-based business I joined with Sara."

Relieved, I smile and answer, "No problem. I would love to spend the time with you anyway."

The first few weeks of double duty are a bit hectic. I am getting in the flow of a new schedule, leaving at 6:00 AM, working until 6:00 PM and then teaching classes until 8:30 PM or so, and riding the bus home. I eat reheated dinners by myself at 9:30 or so and then go to bed so that I can do it all over again the next day. The classes are going well and over the next few months it seems more than a coincidence that at least once per week Josh, Craig, and sometimes even Mrs. Jensen pop into my classes for a few minutes. I interpret this as a sign that they are hearing great things about me and want to see and hear first hand, the brilliance of my teaching.

I support my belief with the fact that each week they stay longer and longer to listen and even sometimes corroborate what I am teaching. At last I may be on my way up the corporate ladder, I think as I walk home later than usual because the bus broke down and we had to wait for another to come and rescue us. The bus challenge doesn't spoil my mood because this quarterly review with Josh was much better than the last one was. I have begun to really pay attention to the clients I am working with, and the results are showing up in my customer satisfaction survey scores. In fact, Josh told me that he recommended me to receive the Distinguished Service Certificate. Maybe I have finally broken out of the fences of the fairgrounds and escaped the reeds of the riverbanks to take control of my future.

Ann is really starting to learn the business she is in. As I am heating up what Ann made for dinner, I find a folder lying on the kitchen counter. I open the folder and begin looking at her notes and a couple of interesting looking graph reports entitled P.E. Profile. There are red, yellow and green bars across the page. The first report has a lot of red and not much green. But in the most recent report most of the red has disappeared. The report divides the different areas into three main categories. Ann's greatest amount of progress is in the first part of the report entitled "Improve Yourself". I think I will write a little note at the top of the second report congratulating her on the obvious improvement, hoping she'll see this note as some kind of secret encouragement when she looks through these files. Although I have no idea what any of it means, I feel like I should support her in this since it seems to make her happy, and fills a void in our lives caused by my long hours at work.

As I put the reports back I discover an income report showing that she has gone from buying some basic products and services at wholesale prices to getting those products and services for free. And this month she is actually making a small profit. A feeling of pride swells up in me as I say under my breath, "Way to go Ann!" There is also a picture of Sara Thoms giving Ann some kind of award and putting a bronze colored pin on her blouse. My wife is becoming some kind of home-business celebrity. No-one at work is giving me lapel pins or taking pictures of me.

As I walk into the bedroom to change my clothes to avoid spilling dinner on my suit, I see a brass colored lapel pin on Ann's blouse draped on the chair. It says, "Brass Achievers Level" on it. Going back to the kitchen, I remember the picture in the folder on the table, and thumbing through the rest of the papers is a sheet that describes five promotional levels in her business: Copper, Bronze, Silver, Gold and Platinum. By the looks of things, Ann has been promoted twice! I should probably look into what she is doing and see if any of my clients can use XL-8 as a bridge for the income gap that many experience, and to see whether what she is learning can help me get promoted; twice!

The XL-8 business development conference comes and we get up sooner than I want to on a Saturday morning. Ann insists that we get to the event a bit early to get good seats. Good seats, I think. How many people will be at a Saturday morning business seminar? I have a hard enough time getting people to my classes on weeknights, and I am a professional financial consultant.

Our neighbors Sara and her husband Steve welcome us as we arrive. They usher us to some kind of special reserved seating in the front of the auditorium.

I am amazed; there are hundreds of people here. I am not real clear on the purpose of this meeting, but it doesn't take long for me to get the hang of it. Steve Thoms is the established leader of this group. They love him, and in some ways seem in awe of him and what he has accomplished. I had no idea that I am living across the street from a celebrity. A woman introduces Steve and the crowd goes crazy with applause as if he were a rock star. Wow, I think. No one does that when I come into the office. The list of his accomplishments as the way shower in XL-8 is long and the magnitude is great. I am quickly gaining an appreciation for how great a man Steve is. Humbly Steve accepts the praise and invites us all to sit down so that we can get started.

As he starts to speak it becomes really obvious that he has everyone's full attention. In fact you can hear a pin drop in a room of over 300.

He begins by asking, "I want all of you to close your eyes and ponder for sixty seconds what you feel like you have to offer others."

I reflect on the request and think about how strange and quiet a big room with hundreds of people can be.

After about thirty seconds, Steve interrupts the silence saying, "Keep your eyes closed and continue to consider what you offer others. Some of you might be thinking about our products and services, and others might be thinking about the income offering side of the business. Still others might be considering your own time and talents and how using them to serve others might be what you bring to the table. You might also feel like your words of encouragement, advice, counsel, financial resources, friendship, experience, compassion, skill, knowledge, or perspective are what you offer to others. What ever you are thinking, I want you to consider for just a second, the method that you use to approach others as you invite them to take advantage of what you offer. Do you jump on them, smother them, attack, cajole, manipulate, coerce, trick, or bowl them over with your enthusiasm–letting them know that you have something that could change their life if they would just listen to you? Now, open your eyes because I want you to come back to a new world of becoming aware of the people in your life–the ones you already know, and those you don't–becoming aware in such a way that they will ask you to share what you offer because it applies to them, and will learn from you how they can best take advantage of it.

"I want to remind you that it's your personal effectiveness in critical areas of the business and relationship-building that makes it possible for you to share what you offer with others." Matt writes a note to Ann saying, "Oscar told me about the importance of relationships years ago, sitting on a bale of hay. This helps me connect what he told me to other parts of my life."

Steve continues, "And of course we measure our competence in areas like contacting, presenting, following-up, asking for the business, answering questions, overcoming objections, promoting products and events, using systems people can duplicate, transferring skill and knowledge, and a myriad of other skills with what we call Personal Effectiveness Points or PEPs. So when you hear the term PEPs you will know that it's a way to quantify a person's level of skill and knowledge that he or she has in any specific area of the business or their personal life. For example: if a person has high PEPs in asking people to take action, then they would probably have a high conversion rate for people they asked to take action compared with the number of people who actually take action. The catch phrase we hear all the time in regard to this is 'higher PEPs equal higher checks.'"

Matt whispers to Ann, "This is so cool, a way to measure your ability to build relationships."

"Shh, I can't hear. We can talk about this later," Ann whispers back, annoyed by the interruption.

"So with that said," Steve goes on, "Let me share with you that people experience the results they are committed to! Those who are committed to mediocrity, lack, and want will continue to experience this as long as they think, act, and remain committed to those results. Those who adopt success philosophies and commit to abundance, wealth, and freedom experience that result by increasing the value of their service and becoming the kind of person others will listen to and follow.

"Success comes by enrolling people in their own life; by helping them learn how to take a proactive role in their life and the circumstances that create success as they define it. It is a result of having high Personal Effectiveness Points or PEPs, which helps build relationships based on trust, constructed on the foundation of effective communication of your intention to give and share. Effective communication is established when you invite and encourage your prospects and team members to talk about and share their hopes, dreams, passions, problems, and challenges. The relationship this kind of interaction creates enables you to better serve them by proposing appropriate solutions that will alleviate their pain, and by motivating them to take your recommendations when you ask them to take action.

"That is all success is: getting people moving towards you, then with you. Being interested instead of interesting is the relationship magnet that draws people towards you. People want to be around people whom they believe are truly interested in them, and who are interested in helping them achieve their life's purpose and overcoming their challenges."

As Steve pauses to take a drink of water Matt thinks, "Holy cow, this guy is tough when he talks about mediocrity, and he has no fear of speaking his mind. This is the first time I have ever heard anyone speak so frankly. His tone and matter-of-fact mannerisms remind me of my dad talking to some of his ranch workers. It also reminds me of one of dad's sayings, 'The truth may be hard, but it's always the truth. And knowing the truth is always better than not knowing it.' I have thought of at least ten different ways I can use this information when I teach my night classes and when I interact with my prospects, clients, and colleagues at work. And then there's Josh my mentor, and Bruce, my manager, and of course Ann and the kids. This is awesome. I circle the question: 'What do you offer others?" along with the principle: Value of Service."

Steve picks up where he left off, "In order to be of value to others you have to become the kind of person others will listen to and follow. The purpose of these monthly conferences is to help you learn and practice relationship-building principles and concepts, including personal interaction skills. Let's continue with another question: Ask yourself, who am I, and why should anyone care? I don't mean to demean anyone, that's not the point of the questions. Think of it this way: at the end of the day people are looking for leaders. People want to associate themselves with someone who is willing to learn, practice, and apply principles that create results, not hype and hopium. So the questions, who am I? and why would anyone care? are intended to help you see that living small doesn't serve you or anyone else. Your success in any area of your life is determined by your willingness to learn, grow, and become the kind of person others will follow."

Matt's mind wanders for a moment as he thinks about this question and his relationship with his dad, "He never saw me as adding greater value to anything, or really doing anything at all other than the responsibilities he gave me. And since I wasn't increasing my PEPs, he wasn't increasing my responsibilities or pay. This is incredible. I wish I had known this years ago."

I rejoin Steve's dialogue as he says, "At the fifty-thousand-foot level, relationship-building principles and concepts include things like service, trust, the ability to relate, curiosity, dot connecting skills, commitment requests, and a desire to learn and be teachable, often while teaching others to do the same. At the ground level, success is rooted in your ability to think and act like a mentor and not like a protective parent, coupled with your guiding philosophy of living on purpose, with purpose. Learning, growing, living, and sharing in this way will help you make better decisions and develop personal effectiveness that create success in business, and in all aspects of your life.

"At the core, success demands that you acquire effective skill and knowledge in talking, listening, relationship development, trust building, skill transfer, and a few other competencies. We must achieve the ability to influence others to see who they really are and who they could become if they begin their own journey of profound change, focused on developing their own potential. We qualify for success in life through a process of learning, practicing, and applying correct principles in their proper sequence.

"Did you get that?" pausing briefly for us to consider. "We qualify for success. Not by punching a time clock, or working a long time. But by using our time and efforts to learn, grow, develop, and become something. No matter how long it takes; no matter how challenging the work is; no matter how bitter the disappointments may be. The reward we gain will be in direct proportion to the type of person we have become along the journey we walk. The easy way may provide temporary trinkets; conversely, the path of building basic strengths, skills, and knowledge delivers treasures untold, treasures that transcend the monetary, and last an eternity.

"History proves that current circumstances and situations don't really matter to those who decide to succeed. Those who blame or make excuses use circumstances as reasons why they can't prosper. However, you have the power to learn, practice, improve, and the ability to take appropriate action, all of which will give correct direction to your life; helping you form new habits and ways of thinking and being.

"The success you enjoy depends on many things, and underneath it all, success depends on you and your willingness to build personal effectiveness in the skills and knowledge that create the results you desire. The single most important determinate of success is you! You are the difference; not who your friends are, what you own, your childhood experience, or position in the company. Of course, they are all important, but on the phone, at the meeting, and in the presentation, it's you, people are buying into, more than anything. The shortest route from wherever you are to wherever you want to be is the one paved by your willingness to improve."

I sit almost paralyzed and in awe, thinking, "Talk about hitting me right between the eyes with enabling power. I am pretty sure Steve is talking directly to me! I had some challenging circumstances growing up, and the bottom line is that I can use them as learning experiences and move on, or I can use them as excuses for 'living small' as he put it. No wonder Steve doesn't have any difficulty filling an auditorium and I can barely attract twenty-five to my classroom. No wonder Ann has been promoted twice and I have not been promoted at all. She is actually implementing these relationship lessons, while I have been focusing on creating a single transactional book of business. There is no way I am missing this meeting again."

Steve begins to write on a chalkboard behind him, "The first and most important concept to master is," Steve writes in big letters: "YOU ARE A SERVANT. One of the guiding characteristics of those who create lifetime relationships, job-dropping residual income, and generational wealth is service. They acquire the desire to serve others. They focus on serving prospects, customers, and associates. They place the needs and desires of others before their own. This speaks to the concept that people don't care how much you know until they know how much you care!"

Listening intently, Matt pauses to consider for a moment, "This is why I relate well with Oscar, Bill, Phil, and now Jane and Josh. Matt scribbles in his notebook, "It seems to me that they care deeply about my success and happiness. When I am talking to them it feels like they are more concerned with my well being than their own. I wonder how or even if I can increase my PEPs in this seemingly critical skill."

Steve extends his point saying, "Because no-one is born with this characteristic, it can and must be learned and duplicated if you are serious about creating a strong and profitable business. Duplicating the power of service will accelerate your business by leaps and bounds. Those whom you serve will learn that success is based on their becoming the kind of person others are attracted to. Service is like honey to the bee, it creates a culture of people focused on helping meet the needs of others, and by natural consequence on having their own needs met. This creates a healthier, wiser, freer, more ambitious team, whose collective service flows over everyone who engages with them.

"It is my belief that everyone has the capacity and power to learn, grow, and develop into effective people who take appropriate action to influence their circumstances and architect the life they want, rather than being an inanimate object to be acted upon, tossed to and fro by every wind of change. It is this capacity and power that enables you to focus on others and serve them. This service in a leadership role begins by providing information, help, and encouragement to everyone on your team. In turn, everyone in the group will follow your lead. Even those who have spent a lifetime working in a competitive environment can learn the better way. They will experience that cooperation through service creates better results at an accelerated pace. A team of people who serve one another will accomplish more than all of them could accomplish separately.

"People need to know three things about you before they will open up and begin creating a fantastic relationship with you: 1) Can they trust you? 2) Are you a professional? and 3) Do you care about them?"

Matt's mind wanders momentarily again, "I can't believe what I am hearing. If I closed my eyes I would swear that Oscar is standing on that stage talking right now. He told me years ago that success in everything in life is based on relationships, and that the key to unlocking all relationships is forged from these same three things Steve presented just now. My conviction that no matter how broke and lame Oscar is, he seems to be a master relationship builder, is apparently correct."

Steve further explains, "The factor that causes a prospect or team member to engage with you in any kind of relationship is the way they feel about you. And the thing that will keep them with you is how they feel they are treated by you. This is particularly evident in the demand today for stellar service and its impact on building customer loyalty. The reasons customers choose you, the products, and XL-8 is likely to be based on the value of your service, which encompasses trust, value for, and concern for them. The reason associates choose to partner with you is because they feel like they can trust you, and that you are really going to succeed with or without them. It's usually not how much you know, but how much you care and the value of your service that attracts them. Maya Angelou said it best: 'People will forget what you said, people will forget what you did, but people will never forget how you made them feel.'

"Service comes in many forms," Steve adds. "Teaching prospects what our products do and don't do. Helping prospects and customers understand exactly what results our products create. Following up with customers to ensure they are satisfied with their purchase. Making sure customers understand how to use all of the features and realize the benefits of the products they buy. It can also come in the form of making trial offers, gifting some products for them to sample, granting discounts for their initial purchase, and full disclosure about returns, refunds, and money-back guarantees if they don't like or want to keep the products, along with communicating your appreciation for their business. People love to know you appreciate them and their business. Thank you cards or emails go a long way to creating great relationships. Recommend new and improved products that will meet their needs, even if XL-8 doesn't offer them. Make recommendations to complimentary products and provide notices of updates or improvements to products they are already buying from you, as this is usually welcomed.

"These are only a few of the ways to connect and build relationships that let your customers know you are thinking of them not only as a paycheck, but as a person. And at the end of the day, people will not only buy more from you if your value of service exceeds their expectations, but they will be happy to refer their family and friends to you because you have treated them so well.

"Think of any really good server at a restaurant. They make a science of unobtrusively evaluating the needs of customers, and catering to those needs. There might be executives in a high-level business meeting with a rigid time schedule at one table, while a couple celebrating their twenty-fifth wedding anniversary sitting at another, and a family enjoying a birthday celebration sits at yet another. A skillful server can fill the role expected of them at each table, simply by observing the behavior of their customers and adapting accordingly. By asking a few high-yielding questions and observing behaviors and responses to the normal business of seating customers, getting water, and order-taking, a server can adapt to meet more than the food and beverage needs of customers; they can make this experience one that will create repeat business for the restaurant because of the way their customers feel they were taken care of. For example: I participate in a monthly leadership conference at a location near our corporate offices. And each month after the event is over, we go to dinner. And you know what? Out of the twenty-five or so dining choices we have in the surrounding area, we always end up at the same place. In fact, we always end up with the same server. His name is Goose, and he makes sure that we get taken care of. He knows that no matter what, he wants us to have a relaxing, fun evening. He gets tipped well, and he gets tipped frequently because we always come to that restaurant and specifically to him for service.

"I use a particular bank in the town I live in: not necessarily because it's the best bank in town, but because the manager; Judy, delivers the highest value of service I have experienced anywhere in the financial services industry. In fact, I don't even refer to the bank by its proper corporate name; I call it the Bank of Judy. And I am sure that if Judy ever left that bank and went to another one, I would follow her there. Let me explain briefly what I mean. When the bank charges us for something that we didn't expect, Judy makes it right. When we need to expedite something, she gets it done. And when we need to waive wait times for checks or some other service, Judy takes care of us. In fact, Judy called me once when I was out of town on a business trip and notified me of an impending problematic situation. She told me how to avoid the problem, and worked with me right then and there to prevent the problem from ever becoming a problem. That's why I call it the Bank of Judy. I know that the bank's corporate policies and procedures don't really promote this kind of service, because I have visited other branches of the same bank in neighboring cities and states, and they don't do these same things. But she works for me; and I will always be her customer.

"I go to a chiropractor named Dr. Chris Chapman, who has an unbelievable memory. He sees somewhere on the order of a hundred people every couple of weeks, and he always remembers names without fail. He also remembers the little things about people that make them unique, and he remembers stories about them. He greets everyone by name and chats with them knowledgeably about their personal lives, their family, and their circumstances. And boy, do people eat this up! This kind of attention does a number of things: It establishes his credibility. Patients are much more comfortable knowing they are in the care of someone who knows them well, which translates to an assumption that he remembers the details of their treatment with this same conscientiousness. It builds relationships, which means that his patients are more likely to follow his post office visit instructions more carefully, which in turn increases the likelihood that their treatment will be successful. It also makes his patients willing to recommend him to friends, and his business becomes even more stable and profitable."

Matt takes a break from writing in his notes and thinks, "Wow all this from simple little things that make such a huge difference to the long term success of your business. This must be what Mr. Jaynes, Josh and Jane have been talking about."

Steve continues with his explanation saying, "I suspect that Dr. Chapman takes a few seconds to jot down the gist of conversations in each patient's file after each visit and then reviews the file before patients arrive.

"In your business and in life outside the business, you may want to take advantage of the many ways you can stay in-touch with your customers, associates, family, friends, and colleagues. Besides the "vital statistics", record hobbies, spouses' names, birthdates, or topics of conversation. Keep track of their goals and dissatisfactions. How many kids they have? When their anniversary is? What they do professionally? What kind of car they drive? What kind of car do they wish they were driving? The little things can mean so much to those with whom you interact. Make the effort to do something extra for your customers every time you do business.

"For instance, I know a woman who has a customer that is homebound. She includes a blank greeting card with her order each month so that the customer can write to her daughter in a distant state. She doesn't charge for this, but there is no chance that this customer will ever abandon her. She does similar things for her other customers and her retention rate is over ninety percent. So think of things you can do that don't cost much, or anything at all, that will keep your customers coming back month after month. Doing these things is more about knowing your customers and understanding what makes them tick.

"I would recommend that you put your customer's names and phone numbers in your cell phone. And when they call, answer the phone! Even if it's inconvenient, answer the phone and tell them you will call back in a few minutes. People I have taught this to have doubled and tripled their incomes.

"Use positive language to express your appreciation and expectation for the next order. A positive reminder, such as 'see you again next month,' or whenever their next order time is.

"Always make sure to smile. It's hard to beat a sincere smile in this day of anger and rage. Keep in touch with your customers between orders. This can be in the form of an e-mail or a 'special report' that you think would interest them."

"And last but not least, refer your customers to each other. If you have customers who would benefit from working with a colleague, refer them. One of the best ways to keep your name in front of your clients is to send them referrals who say 'Steve Thoms suggested I call.'

"Life-long relationships begin when you focus on helping others get what they want regardless of what you want. Find out what they are passionate about; why their feet hit the floor in the morning; what keeps them awake at night. You can easily find this out by asking them, 'If you could change anything in your life what would it be?' Listen to their response, and then follow up by asking 'How would your life be different if you had or got that?' Most people will begin to really tell you what they want their life to be like at this point. Again, listen carefully to what they are saying and then ask 'On a scale from 1 to 10, how serious are you about having or getting that?'

"Are you seeing a pattern here? I won't steal the thunder for the next seminar's topic, but there is a very powerful, very specific recipe for success in this business and in life. You can increase the value of your service very quickly and simply if you follow the pattern I just demonstrated to you, and if you can be immensely curious about people.

"Some say that 'this is a relationship business' and that 'you must learn to love people in order to have a strong and profitable business.' Loving people is important if you are talking about relationships. The 'Love everyone in order to build a strong and profitable business' part is not completely true, at least in the beginning. There has only been one person who has ever lived that has loved everyone and he was crucified thousands of years ago. The truth is that you don't have to love everyone. In fact, you don't even have to like everyone. However it is essential that you learn to be curious about them. Curiosity is the absolute best way to create, nurture, and maintain life-long relationships. An interesting thing happens when you learn to be curious about people. You will learn to like them and then in time the liking will turn into love and respect.

"Let me tell you a story about a man with five children. His oldest was a little rebellious and did things that the father didn't agree with. For example the father was the football and baseball coach at the local high school. He loved sports, but had a very narrow view of which sports were meaningful and which ones the 'rebellious' kids engaged in. The child in question loved skateboarding, a sport the father loathed as a waste of time. In fact he chided the child about doing something of value with his time. The more the child skateboarded, the greater the strain on their relationship. As he looked for ways to connect with this son, the father had an idea. He decided to watch the world championships of skateboarding. It was then that he gained a great appreciation for the difficulty, elegance, and athleticism of skateboarding.

"So what does that mean to you? Well before the father was curious enough to find out what skateboarding was all about, he couldn't love or even like it. And to have his son engaged in what the father considered a valueless sport, somehow cheapened his son's value as a human being. So I submit to you that you don't have to love others to begin the relationship. In fact, it might not even be possible for you to love or like others until you have begun to be curious enough about them to discover what they love, who they are, and why they are the way they are. Until curiosity enters the equation, the best you can feel is nonchalance or indifference about others. And that is not a great place to begin any relationship.

"Before I end this morning I want to make sure that I give you some skill mastery practice. This month I challenge each of you to talk to at least one person each day and find out three things you could be curious about them. Keep a little journal and include the name of the person you talk to and what you found out about them that made you curious. If you want to, you can also include how the conversation went when you deepened it by asking more questions."

Steve thanks us all for coming and encourages us to be in our seats for the evening recognition meeting that starts at 7:00 PM. The lights in the auditorium come up and what was a silent room of hundreds becomes a beehive of indiscernible noise. Several people come up to Ann to comment on what they learned and tell her how great Steve was. Many ask her what she learned. I am surprised by her popularity, and when Ann introduces me to her 'entourage' almost everyone comments on how great she is as their leader. Of course, no one could agree with that more than I do. I tell everyone how proud of her I am.

When the crowd thins down Ann asks me, "How did you like the meeting? What did you like best? Did it help you understand what I am doing, and do you think this could be useful to you in your work?"

Eagerly Matt shares, "This was one of the most insightful seminars I have ever been to. Steve is quite a presenter and his questions were profound. It seems that he is focused on helping you all to become better people so that others will naturally be drawn to you, listen to you, and take the action you recommend." Glancing over my notes I remember several pertinent points that Steve made: "I love the way he invited all of us to look inward to determine the value of our service to others. When he asked 'What do you offer others,' and 'Who are you and why would anyone care,' I was taken back, just a little. But when he brought it back to the three foundational principles of successful relationships: 'Do they trust you, are you good at what you do, and do you care about them,' I understood his logic. I am going to use a lot of what I heard here today with my clients and night school students. I am going to take his challenge to increase the value of my service to a level that exceeds expectations into everything I do at work and at home. I do have a couple of questions for you, though: what are high-yielding questions? And what is the process Steve talked about for building strong relationships? He talked today about the 'value of service,' which seems to be like an ingredient to a larger recipe of sorts."

Excited that Matt had a great experience Ann explains, "Steve is always helping us to become better people, and his emphasis is on becoming the kind of person others will listen to and follow, and then becoming the kind of person other leaders will follow. To answer your questions on an elementary level, high-yielding questions are questions that require more than a one word or simple phrase answer. Think of when you come home and I ask you how your day was. This is not a high-yielding question because you can answer it by saying it was good, or bad, or you might even shrug your shoulders and say nothing at all. But if I ask you to tell me about the most amazing thing that happened in your day today, you are compelled to open up and describe events or people, what they did, and how it affected you. This requires more than just a one word or simple phrase answer. So the second would be a high-yielding question. Your second question or observation is correct. High-yielding questions are a part or 'ingredient' as you put it, in the value of our service recipe. This all fits into a sequence for relationship development that Steve calls; Ask, Listen and Repeat."

Thinking back to Steve's presentation Matt says, "I am very intrigued by the notion that curiosity is the key to building lasting, meaningful relationships; that we can learn to like and then love others when we begin with simple, non-judgmental curiosity about people's lives and circumstances. This is incredibly empowering. If Steve knows this much about all the other ingredients of the successful relationship recipe, I can't wait to learn more in the next meeting."

Not wanting to lower Matt's enthusiasm Ann reluctantly informs Matt saying, "Steve only presents at our events once per quarter."

Disappointed that the most amazing training and trainer won't be available for three months Matt responds, "How irritating, I am eager to learn the entire recipe as fast as possible."

Ann interjects saying, "Steve does do a weekly training conference call that I am part of. They are on Thursdays at 10 AM, but I can teach you what I learn from the calls, if you are interested in more training."

"When are the calls?" Matt asks.

Ann answers hesitantly knowing Matt will be at work when the calls are conducted, "They are on Thursday's at 10:00 AM."

"Well then I will depend on you to teach me what you learn in those calls," I say, surrendering my grand scheme to learn the skills and knowledge Steve so eloquently presents as fast as I can.

That night at the recognition meeting, Ann earns an award for personally enrolling new people. I am a little embarrassed when Ann is called up on stage to receive her recognition because she has me come up on the stage with her. But when she receives a second award, one for personal production points, I learn to appreciate the limelight and the view from the stage looking out on the audience. This is my first taste of this kind of recognition, and even though it isn't meant for me. I see the power in it. Seeing the potential of on-stage recognition, I quickly become enthralled with the spotlight being on the stage provides. Ann has built a small team of Associates with a few committed to the leadership track, and that small profit she was making, has now grown enough to create a clothes budget for her and the kids.

What Ann is learning and doing is very inspiring, and I am more determined and focused than ever on getting promoted myself, and working my way up the company ladder. The following month, I earn the Distinguished Service Certificate and get to be recognized as employee of the month on the company wide phone conference. Summer is coming to an end and Matt's son is beginning pre-school in a few weeks.

Matt begins to implement what he's learned from Steve. Every morning he reads a note card that says: "What do you offer others," on one line, and "Who am I and why would anyone care," on another line. The three foundational principles of successful relationships are written below the first two lines and read: "Can they trust you, Are you good at what you do, and Do you care about them." On the back of the card are the incomplete concepts of using high-yielding questions to get clients and students to talk to him, and the idea of some greater interaction process of Asking, Listening, and then repeating the sequence. This morning, right after I complete my morning ritual of reading aloud the note card, Bruce, the Department Coordinator calls me into his office.

"Matt," Bruce begins, "I want to commend you for making great changes in your approach to your prospects and clients in the past little while. I don't know what kind of personal improvement you are doing, but it's working. Josh reports that you are becoming the kind of leader we want. I also want to remind you that Rome wasn't built in a day, and that personal improvement takes some time before it manifests itself in your everyday life. I want to personally tell you we had a leadership slot open up a few weeks ago and we chose Jane to fill that position. I also want you to know that the decision was a hard one, and that you were a very close second to her. It all came down to performance and results and Jane simply has better numbers over a longer period of time. I also want you to know that we are keeping a close eye on you, and I hope to be able to have a different conversation with you soon. Keep up the improvement and good work. We need more people like you around here."

I am understandably disappointed, but as I return to my office I am able to feel glad for and supportive of Jane, too. She is becoming a trusted colleague and will be a great manager. She has become a great example to follow and she has been willing to share with me things I need to learn to be better.

As I sit contemplating my future here, my cell phone rings. It's Ann's mother. They are on the way to the hospital. The time has arrived for the baby to make its appearance. Without hesitation I run for the door and call Bruce on the way out to tell him that I need the rest of the day off and probably tomorrow too. He knows that Ann is about to give birth and jokingly says, "This is a very strange way to show your devotion to management." Laughing, he congratulates me and tells me to get going. This would not be a good time to be late.

Author's Note:

There is the mathematical equation in the appendix at the end of the book for this chapter.

3

Onward and Upward

Now that the second child has come to our family, I talk to Bruce about extra assignments that I can do on weekends to help me earn extra money. Because I am receiving excellent reviews from clients and my staff members, he feels like he can give me more responsibility. That increases my income a bit but it does take me away from Ann and my family more and more. I know it bothers her that I am away a lot. When it gets to be too much, she tells me that it seems like I am married to my job instead of her. I do work a lot: four nights a week and now regularly on weekends, too. But I do this so Ann can live in a house with modern appliances, furnishings, cooking utensils, and gadgets that make her life easier and more comfortable.

Actually, we have what has become our "signature" conversation to thank for seeing what my work is doing for our family. Ann has continued that game she began early in our marriage. Every so often she calls me at the office toward the end of the day and asks, "Guess what I did today?" I play along, of course and guess, "You got a manicure, or finished one of the three books you are reading." According to the game, she always stops me in mid-guess and today she says, "I bought a new sofa." As I listen to Ann describe the sofa, I think to myself, "The extra hours and effective work are beginning to provide some relief to our financial stress." Last week, I remember that Ann called and said, "Guess what I did today? I bought a new lawn mower." It is such a great feeling that a new sofa or lawn mower isn't a financial crisis in our home anymore. Even though these are very small things I love being able to begin to provide the things Ann deserves.

Time is going by so fast. The snow is piling up in our front yard as we prepare Thanksgiving dinner. This is the first Thanksgiving holiday in our new house. I pull out the salad bowl while looking for our serving plate. Ann begins to laugh remembering last year's disastrous cooking situation. This year our laughter isn't a mask for pain; things really are getting better. We are a long way from being rich but at least we can cook a pumpkin pie in a normal pie plate.

We sit down for dinner and each of us takes a turn talking about the things we are grateful for. Retreating into my own little world I reflect on all that I have learned in the past year. Ann turns to me and invites me to share my feelings. I proclaim, "This year has been the best ever. We have a new baby girl, a new house, a new job, pots and pans that work, and the thing I am most grateful for is the relationship lessons I have learned this year." Looking at our children who are obviously too young to understand, but not too young to feel my passion I share, "Your mother comes from a family where everyone likes, loves, and supports each other. So the importance of service and relationships are second nature to her. But I have spent the past years learning how to implement skills that she grew up with." Our little boy looks at me as if I had been speaking Martian and then asks Ann if he can start eating. Ann on the other hand looks deeply in my eyes, grabs, and then squeezes my hand in recognition that I have been through a lot. And even though we don't have much to show for the work, things are improving.

Going over my numbers for the week as I do every Friday afternoon to check my progress and plan for next week, I notice some amazing things. This quarter my new accounts grew by over 16% and my retention increased by 11%. The investment of time to learn how to serve is making a marked difference in the results I am creating for others and myself. My old boss, Mr. Jaynes was right. My up-sells increased by 12% and 41% of my sales now come from existing customers. As I lean back in my chair taking a moment to bask in the good news, I'm reflecting on the reasons for the improvement and can clearly attribute them to my understanding of the three principles: 1) people do trust me, 2) for the first time in my life I can say that I am good at what I do, and 3) I do sincerely care about my prospects and clients. Just as I am really relaxing and thinking this is what Jane knows that gave her a leg up in the promotion conversation a few months back, the phone rings and startles me back to reality.

Bruce is calling to ask me to come to his office right away. When I arrive at his door I find him sitting back in his big black chair. He tells me to sit down and relax. He announces without fanfare or build up, "Matt, you are going to replace me as the Department Coordinator. I have been promoted to Division Manager and I can't think of anyone I enjoy more to work with than you." Leaning forward and putting his elbows on his desk as if to say that the pleasantries are over, he explains; "You will have more administrative responsibilities now, and so you need to prepare for some late nights and some weekends in the office. I am leaving you a great situation with a great department that runs well, and so I am expecting great things from you. The raise you are going to get should offset the fact that you will need to quit teaching night classes."

Matt is elated, relieved, and terrified all at the same time. This is the moment he has been working for since he joined the company. Because of the last promotion conversation he had with Bruce, he feels the need to ask, "Why did you choose me for the promotion?" Bruce responds reassuringly, "Because you don't just show up each day and meet the minimum expectations. You are innovative and creative. Our clients love you and the service you provide them. You get more positive customer feedback comments than anyone else in the department. Let me read you one, 'Matt seems to know everything about us and what we would like our life to be like now and in our retirement. He is a credit to the company and we tell all of our friends about him and his personal service to us.'"

Bruce takes the report in one hand and slams it down on the table for loud and transitional effect. "So Mr. Service, now we want you to teach others in this department to do what you are doing. I will move out of this office this afternoon so you can move in tonight or before work on Monday. I will begin to train you on your responsibilities, reporting, and success criteria next week. Your staff meeting begins at 8:00 AM on Wednesday's so make sure to dig in before then and get acquainted with your team and the procedure manual for this position."

Back at my cubicle I stare out the windows behind my row of colleagues, thinking, I can't believe it. I have been promoted. And it happened in large part because of the things Steve and Ann are teaching me about how to do what Oscar so adamantly talked about in regards to success all those years ago; "The key to success in everything," he told me, "was building relationships." Speaking of relationships, I need to share this fantastic news with Ann and plan some kind of celebration with her; nothing too spectacular though since I didn't celebrate her promotions. Although in my own defense I didn't even know she had been promoted.

Ann and I attend her quarterly XL-8 business development conference. Steve is presenting again and I felt like I will get a whole college course in one day by listening to him. Ann smiles as we get out of bed because she knows that today that we will be together and for at least today, she feels more important than my job. Her feeling is mostly right. However, I do want to learn all I can from Steve so that I can be better at work so I can provide a better life for Ann.

After the normal introduction about who Steve is and why we should care, Steve calls the meeting to order. Everyone quiets down and he begins by asking a couple of questions from the skill mastery practice he assigned to us the last time he spoke. It's silent for a full thirty seconds, before he reminds us of what the homework project was. "You might remember," he says in a irritated tone. "You were supposed to talk to at least one person each day and find out at least three things you could be curious about them. You were to keep track of the name of the person you talked to and what you found out about them that made you curious. The assignment for the over-achievers included how the conversation went when you deepened it by asking more questions.

A man in the middle of the room offers an initial response, "I talked to a couple this morning who met in the business. They merged their businesses and are now married." A woman sitting in front of us said, "I talked to a man last night who told me he lived in Honduras for two years. He met his wife's family there and when she came to the US as a student they reunited and now are married. He was the first XL-8 associate in Honduras." Steve comments on her report saying, "You may not know this, but the first foreign country XL-8 expanded into was Honduras, and now there are ten Double Platinum's and twenty Platinum's who have come from that expansion. If the man you were talking to was the first XL-8 associate there you were talking to a multimillionaire, and our guest speaker for tonight's recognition meeting; the new President of XL-8, Orson Flint. Now that you know more about your conversation subject how much more could you have learned about him?

"Each day every one of us has the opportunity to take a few minutes to create a relationship close enough to learn specific things about the people we meet. Those of you who took the challenge seriously are in a much better position to make the new year the best one ever. Those of you who didn't, well, you can start moving onward and upward from this moment. Now, let's take this to a deeper level. What did you learn more generally about people, and how might you be able to help them by offering the value of your service?"

Ann speaks right up and explains, "It seems that everyone has a story. Each person has unique twists, turns, and passions." A woman from across the room declares, "Everyone seems to be similar in that we have a deep desire to have a different life and most seem willing to learn, change, and work to make that life a reality." A man from the front row confidently comments, "Most everyone I talked to during the month was focused on how bad things were for them, what they lacked or wanted, and the circumstances that caused their dissatisfaction with life. It seems that we need to be looking for people willing to share their passions, who are also willing to learn, practice, and apply success principles in their proper sequence." Steve interrupts the man in mid speech and excitedly shares, "This is exactly what we are going to be working on in this training."

He thanks everyone for sharing and continues saying, "The only way success on a large scale can happen is for each of us to increase the value of our service, so that more people will be drawn to us and to the success doctrine of building lasting relationships, which result in a strong and profitable business.

"Today I want to focus specifically on the concept of relationships. Let me ask each of you a simple question: 'Do you purposefully develop relationships or do you just let them come and go like the wind on a spring day?' Take a minute and reflect on the quality of relationships you have. Ask yourself why you are in these relationships? More specifically, examine each of your relationships and ask, 'Why is this relationship important?'

"Success in life, and specifically in this industry is based on the value of your service and the long-term relationships you create that are built on trust. So now you should know what I am going to talk about next quarter. But today I want you to take some time to seriously consider investing in relationships that promote, encourage, and inspire success. This also means that you might divest, eliminate or minimize relationships that degrade, discourage or impede progress to your greater causes and higher purposes.

"Make friends and become likeable. The number one reason anyone engages with you in any positive relationship is because they like you. Tonight Mr. Flint will talk about how to foster lifelong, meaningful relationships through effective communication; not just talk or idle prattle, but effective communication and interactions, and how they are the keystone of a relationship revolution that I am eager to be part of. But I don't want to steal any of his thunder for tonight so let me get back to the idea of relationships in general.

"Relationships mainly fall into two categories: relationships that reward and relationships that rob. Understanding the difference and arranging your relationship portfolio towards success will propel you towards the progressive realization of your worthwhile dreams."

Using the projector Steve advances to a slide entitled, Nine Critical Mistakes. He tells us, "When people make one or more of these mistakes they put their relationships in a position to rob them of success in some aspect of their life."

The first bullet on the slide says, "Listening to the wrong people and taking advice from people who are not where you want to be or who are not experiencing the result you want." Immediately, Matt thinks, "Holy Cow, this is exactly what Bill Rena was talking about when he warned me about listening too much to Oscar about success strategies in life. But it also corroborates the idea that I should adhere to Oscar's advice about building relationships."

Steve's second bullet point is, "Letting indecisive people continue to be hesitant to take action. Sometimes we let people rob us and themselves by allowing them to postpone taking action. Some people use excuses to avoid taking action or making decisions. This robs them and you of a meaningful relationship because neither of you is progressing toward any kind of success. Indecisive people will avoid taking action for as long as you let them."

Third, "Spending time with people who aren't or won't take action. This is where the eighty/twenty rule applies. You should invest eighty percent of your time working with twenty percent of the people. That might sound like your being cold or callous. But, here is the advice my mentor gave me when I was faced with this problem. She told me to only work with the willing, because the others won't take any action that will improve their life or yours."

Putting a star by both of these notes Matt considers, "My own clients do both of these things all the time. I can't believe these two problems exist outside of my profession. It makes me crazy when people won't or don't take action that they know will improve their life."

Steve's fourth point is, "Often we are quick to take orders from customers and then we fail to follow through to make them converts of our products, services, and the income offering. You invest a lot of time, money, and effort to convert a prospect to a customer or associate. You contact them, do a presentation, find out what their pain is, and recommend a solution to their challenges. Congratulations! However, it is several times easier to turn existing customers or associates into converts who order or interact on a scheduled, consistent basis than it is to continually recruit new customers and associates."

Ann looks at Matt writing feverishly in his notebook. He whispers, "This is a huge problem with the entry level planners and the other department coordinators I work with. They are all focused on creating a single transactional book of business. It seems that creating lifetime customers is the only business model that will ever create huge success." Ann thinks gratefully that Matt is taking this seriously. Steve seems to be teaching him a lot about how to achieve success in his job. I wonder how I might be able to help him see that these principles also apply to our personal relationship as well."

Refocusing on Steve's presentation, I read the fifth point: "Being indifferent to customers and team mates." Matt writes as fast as he can while Steve talks about this point saying, "People often make the costly mistake of recruiting customers and associates, and then assuming they'll remain customers and associates without maintaining and growing those relationships. Before you invest your time and money going after new customers and associates you do not currently have a relationship with, consider the following statistics:
1. Repeat customers spend thirty-three percent more than new customers,
2. Referrals among repeat customers are one hundred-seven percent greater than non-customers,
3. It costs six times more to sell something to a prospect than to sell that same thing to a customer,
4. It costs five times more to attract new customers than it does to retain current customers,
5. A five percent improvement in customer retention can cause an increase in profitability of between twenty-five percent and eighty-five percent."

Relating these ideas to his work, Matt ponders these points contemplatively, "I wonder how many managers in my company know what Steve knows. It seems like they must not. They certainly don't consciously train anyone at our company to increase the value of their service and to build relationships on purpose, with purpose. I wonder why? If what Steve is talking about is true, we could increase our profitability by at least twenty-five percent this year. That would be huge. Maybe I should use this as my secret advantage to move up the management chain. If I increase the profitability of my department twenty-five percent by teaching just this one concept, I will certainly stand out as the best candidate for a Division Manager position."

"The sixth mistake is," Steve continues, "Disregarding the needs, wants, and desires of others. There are many who either forget or don't even think about what their prospects, customers, or associates need or want. As incredible as it sounds, many people start conversations with 'This is what we do, and this is how we do it.' The real problem with this philosophy is that it does not give prospects, customers, or associates any reason to ever personally care about you or what you offer. When you lead with what you do, and how you do it, you ignore their needs, not allowing them to consider why they would engage with you or enroll in the program, and you leave your prospects to connect the dots about whether what you offer might matter to them.

"Your doctor doesn't do this. He or she begins your visit by gathering information. You usually fill out a simple survey, the nurse takes some vital sign information, and then when the doctor comes in, he or she looks at the charts and then begins a conversation with you to find out what your pain is. You see, the doctor may prescribe some medication or treatment for you, but they are not in the pharmaceutical or pill distribution business. They are in the 'resolving human pain and discomfort' business.

"What would you think if they walked in with the newest, latest, greatest bottle of pills, and started talking about the features and benefits of a specific kind of medication? And without even asking you how you feel or where it hurts, they prescribed the bottle of pills they had and then sent you a bill. Those pills might help relieve some of your pain, or they might make it worse! Who knows? Not even the doctor could predict the outcome of this kind of treatment. One thing is for sure, you would never return to that doctor again. And certainly you wouldn't take your children there, nor would you refer your family and or friends to that doctor.

"Well that's what you look like when you walk into conversations with guns blazin', explaining the features and benefits of what you offer before you know anything about what your prospect's life is about: what they want more of; what they want less of; what they need that they can't get doing what their doing now; what they dream of; what they might be avoiding.

"I would encourage you to change your approach from 'Here's what I do' to, 'What do you need or want that you don't have now?' The cornerstone of successful relationships is to discover precisely what others need and want. Until you know that, what you think, have, or offer is of little value to those you talk to. They will simply have no reason to care; no reason to listen; no reason to take any action you might recommend. Why would they? We will talk about connecting the dots in a few months."

Stunned, Matt whispers to himself, "This is amazing. No wonder some or even many of my clients are hesitant to take action or don't take any action, ever. They know they are being sold something they don't want or need by someone who is highly motivated to sell the flavor of the month. They might be motivated to move if we solved specific individual challenges with products and services intended to create those unique and explicit results."

Steve's seventh point is, "Not asking high-yielding questions. This mistake creates tremendous misunderstandings. When we have conversations with people, we interpret what they say through our own mental, emotional, and spiritual filters. When we base our understanding on what we think we hear them say, we start mentally processing responses to challenges and situations they may not have. We will be teaching an entire section on listening later in this training series. You will become a professional in this critical area."

Nudging Ann, Matt says, "This is twice he has talked about high-yielding questions. He keeps saying that mastering it is paramount to successful relationship building. When and how can I learn more about this?" Ann whispers back briefly, "Let's talk about this later. I don't want to miss anything."

"Eighth," Steve continues is, "Not listening to what people are actually saying. This problem is HUGE. When we have conversations with people, we interpret what they say through our own mental, emotional, and spiritual filters. When we base our understanding on what we think we hear them say, we start mentally processing responses to challenges and situations they may not have. You present a solution that contradicts or doesn't create the result they want. This is not a great strategy for long term success in any part of your life, certainly not in our business. We will be teaching an entire section on listening later in this training series. You will become a professional in this critical area."

"This seems to go back to being curious," Matt thinks. Flipping back through my notes from Steve's last conference presentation I remember him saying, "You don't even have to like everyone. However, it is essential that you learn to be curious about them. Curiosity is the absolute best way to create, nurture, and maintain life-long relationships." And his homework assignment was centered on being curious. Oscar taught me that being successful even in the horse business was based on building relationships through curiosity.

"Ninth but certainly not least" Steve moves on, "Being out of integrity. Many have learned how to talk the talk. They have the jargon down, and are so excited and anxious to begin enrolling customers and associates that they promote hype and hopium. What they should do is offer real solutions to problems they truly understand and can articulate. When you talk to people, find out what their challenges are and then under-promise and over-deliver the remedy to their pain. Do what you say you're going to do when you say you're going to do it."

Almost without taking a breath Steve plunges ahead, changing his focus from mistakes to the types of relationships XL-8 associates should consider investing in, saying, "In our business there are five types of relationships that fuel your business engine. Without productive relationships with these five types of people you will have a beautiful, bright shiny business, but it won't produce any meaningful result." Matt sits back in his seat wondering if Steve is going to talk about relationships outside XL-8. Matt whispers softly, "I bet he doesn't know that there are people here to learn about improving associations other than his network marketing business relationships." Just then Steve announces, "Of course we all have many relationships outside of the business: family, friends, church, community groups, neighbors, colleagues at work, and others. I will talk briefly about those in a few minutes, but we are in a business seminar and so I want to start with the proper focus for this meeting. Then we will do an exercise that can expand your skill and knowledge for all the relationships in your life.

"The next few presentation slides show the five types of relationships that are necessary to a thriving business, and I will talk briefly about each: First are Prospects. Before anyone ever buys from you or enrolls on your team they need to know that they can trust you, that you are a professional, and that you care about them. If you fail the test in any of these things you will not convert prospects to customers, or customers to associates. Prospects will follow your recommendations only when you develop a trusting relationship based on listening to their concerns and questions, and interacting with them as human beings; not by how fast you can talk, or by how much you know."

Advancing the slide to the second relationship type, Steve continues, "Savvy business people focus on making sure that they exceed their customer's expectations and they provide them with rewarding experiences. They know it's much more cost-effective to continue to sell to an existing customer than it is to recruit a new one. A customer list is one of the most valuable assets any business has when it represents deep relationships, relationships where you know about your customers' and team members' lives, dreams, and goals. This allows you to provide valuable service and opens the way to up-sells, cross-sells, and enhanced sales.

"Third is Associates. The main thing your team members need to know is that you are betting on them, not against them. Very few people have a support team that encourages them; that is glad to see them; that cheers when they achieve results. You can develop and maintain a great relationship with your team members by first getting to know them. Find out what their life circumstances are: What kind of work do they do? What their family situation is? Are they married? Do they have children? What are their dreams and aspirations? You can also develop strong, life-long relationships with your associates by helping them build their business. This might be in the form of counseling or coaching sessions, or it might also be personal help showing presentations, three-way calls, follow-ups, and bigger meetings that your associates put together.

"Developing great relationships with your associates will help them stay in the business even in challenging times because they are part of a team or community of people pursuing their dreams, goals, and passions. You can make them feel like they are part of the team by inviting them to go with you when you build the business. Or by volunteering to work with them to get them started, or to get them re-engaged. You can also send cards, letters, or emails, and make special efforts to ensure that they know about new products, promotions, events, special opportunities to be with up line, tele-calls, and other situations that promote the business.

"Your relationships will also be enhanced if you make sure that your associates receive experiential training in the critical skills of the business, whether you provide it or someone else does. You will be the hero if you provide each person on your team with opportunities to practice the skills related to the appropriate phase of the success pattern they are working on. Helping them to put a personal improvement plan in place will further enhance your relationship, and should instill confidence in them that they can achieve success when they envision it on purpose, with purpose.

"Fourth is; Mentors. A mentor or coach can be the difference between your ultimate success and massive failure. The relationship you have with your up-line is critical because they can help you accelerate your progress if you let them, call on them and use them. They are highly motivated to help you and will be as committed to your business as you are. That is to say that they won't invest more time in your business than you are devoted to invest. If you only invest four hours working in your business, then don't expect your up-line to invest ten hours. The best way I have found to create a powerful relationship with my up-line is to treat that relationship with the utmost respect and consideration. In fact, I would teach you that your relationship with your successful up-line is more valuable than your relationship to your customers or associates. You can replace your customers and team members, but your up-line mentor is your teacher in all circumstances, so this relationship is critical to your success. Don't misunderstand what I said. I said your relationship with your *successful* up-line. Learn from, listen to, and follow your successful mentor's advice, counsel, and example.

"Never, never, never complain about those who are teaching you to be successful to anyone who is not in a position to help you create success faster and with less frustration. Generally speaking this includes complaining about your spouse to your children, your up-line or mentor to your down line, or your manager to subordinates at work. The catastrophe this causes can't be fixed. Success in everything is built on trust and belief in others. If that is betrayed, then those affected will be infected with a virus so strong it will spread to others like wild fire. You will lose the confidence and relationships with those around you faster by doing this than anything else that can happen. So if you are in the mood to destroy your family, team, or organization say negative things about your teachers and partners and watch the cancer consume your world in a matter of weeks or months.

"Lastly is the relationship you have with the company. This can be very valuable. When I call customer service, or the training manager, or Mr. Flint, they know who I am. Because I invest in these corporate relationships I can get things done faster and with a lot less challenge. They frequently tell me things others don't know, and I always have advanced notice of promotions, special events, and announcements ahead of everyone else. You can foster a great relationship with the company by going on a tour of the facilities, scheduling a minute to talk to key people like the founders, the president, vice presidents, and important supply chain managers, customer and associate support managers. This includes the sales manager, product development manager, distribution manager, and the training manager. Building relationships is not a function of business, it's the only way to do business.

"Of course we all have many relationships outside of the business: family, friends, church, community groups, neighbors, and work colleagues, so we will move on from the critical business relationships to a more general discussion. Here are a couple of things to consider about all the relationships you have. Let me begin this segment by asking you a couple of questions: What kind of relationships do you have now? Do you have relationships that reward or rob you? Who are you listening to? Who gets a vote or voice in your life? Who are you listening to, and do they have a vested interest in your success? Do they have what you want or live like you want to live? Have they succeeded in the area you want success in? Who are you taking advice from? It's commonly thought that your life will become like an aggregate of the lives of the five people you spend the most time with. This applies in a broader context: if you want a long lasting marriage and you spend most of your time with people who are consistently moving in and out of romantic relationships, then that could become a problem for you," Steve points out.

Matt replays several conversations he has had with Oscar and Bill in his mind. This is what they have been teaching me all along, Matt thinks. Oscar told me, "Success in anything is built on the strength of the relationships you have with people." And Bill's advice was, "Only take counsel from people who are where you want to be. From those who are successful doing what you want to be successful in, or from those who live like you want to live. Guidance from people who pretend to be successful is advice from those uncommitted, unproven, or unwilling to live according to the principles they teach."

I submit to live according to this counsel, thinking, maybe it's time to learn from the experience of others instead of clumsily going along making the same mistakes they made; reliving the pain they already paid the price for.

Steve pauses for a moment and the silence of him taking a moment to confirm within himself that he wants to follow his teaching outline brings me mentally back to the meeting. Steve resumes saying, "We are going to do something now that I have never done or seen done in one of these meetings. Each of you is going to invest the next hour with one person in this room that you hadn't met before you came today. When we begin please don't talk to anyone else except the person you are partnering with. Sixty minutes should give you plenty of time to do the assignment I am about to give you. During the hour, open your note books to a fresh page and write down the different kinds of relationships you have. For example you might have a relationship with your parents, a spouse, customers, or neighbors. You might write your relationships in terms of categories like romantic, familial, professional, friendship, collegial, and or something else that works for your unique situation. Once you have written the kinds of relationships you have, take a moment and write some specific names of people you have relationships with. Then rate each relationship from 1 to 10. 1 is a relationship that robs you, and might be one you are considering ending or learning how to strengthen. A 10 is a relationship that is so powerful that nothing could ever pull you apart.

"Before you begin I want to give you some final instructions. It is often said that showing up is fifty percent of success. Let me remind you that another forty percent is showing up with a high value of service, and the other ten percent is showing up ON TIME! You are all adults so I am going to just tell you to be back in the room ready to move forward sixty minutes from right now. Get with your partner, the hour begins NOW!"

Matt not knowing anyone in the room looks at Ann for some advice. Ann has already chosen the woman sitting next to her and suggests that her new partners husband and Matt work together on the first part of the assignment. Ann and her partner Sally Whitman move to the back of the auditorium to work together. Matt invites Mark Whitman, Sally's husband to move to the stage where Steve had been a few minutes earlier. The stage gives them room to work where they can face each other. Sitting down they open their notebooks and Matt notices that Mark's notes are very orderly and his penmanship is perfect. Thinking to himself, mine are not nearly as organized, and my penmanship looks as if I graduated from the physician's school of handwriting. It seems silly right now, I think, to notice how distinctive our notes are, but the difference is unmistakable.

Mark and I talk for at least ten minutes about family circumstances, hobbies, recreation experiences, goals, passions, ideas about the conference, the story of how Mark enrolled in XL-8, and his favorite memories of the business. It seems that we hit it off right away. I really like Mark, and I think the foundation of a new friendship has been laid. We each take out our paper and start to write names on the list. After a few minutes, Mark has the idea,

"It might be more efficient if we categorize the kind of relationships that we each have and then put specific names within the categories. This is how we teach people to make a names list when they begin in the business," he adds. We brainstorm categories for a few minutes and then take about thirty minutes to fill in the blanks and rate our relationships. Not wanting to be late given Steve's warning, we return to our seats again. In a minute or two, Steve gives a five-minute warning, and tells everyone to wrap up our conversations.

Ann and Sally come and sit down and we talk for a few minutes about the activity. There is a lot of chatter and noise in the room where just a few minutes before it had been very quiet. Ann and Sally keep right on talking as if they have never moved. It seems like they have begun a great friendship. While they are talking, I notice Ann's notebook, which is opened up on her lap. Looking at it I see a few interesting things. Ann has rated almost all her relationships higher than I had. She also listed our children ahead of my name on her list. What does any of that mean? Does she really have better relationships than I do? Are our kids more important than me? It might mean nothing at all, but it does bother me that she put the kids ahead of me. Maybe it's a mom thing I think, in an attempt to soothe my feelings."

Personal	Professional
Family	Mentors
Ann (9)	Steve Thoms (6)
Kids (8)	Oscar & Bill Rena (8)
Parents – Frank, Ruth, Molly (3)	Company Associates & Colleagues
Grand parents – Bob & Mary (6)	Leadership team members –Tracy, Ben, Larry (7)
Siblings – Brent, Lori, Richard (6)	New Colleagues –Mark & Sally Whitman (7)
Parents in law – (7)	Craig in Human Resources (7)
Friends	Mrs. Jensen (5)
Larry Sielliger (8)	Bruce Jenkins – Division Manager (7)
Kurt Board (5)	Susan Lee – Customer Service Manager (7)
John Banks (5)	Josh (7)
Brad Williams (7)	Prospects
Members of the conference (5-7)	People on my hot, warm & chicken list (3-7)
Jack the bus driver (8)	Friends I haven't met yet (Don't know them yet)
Community & Organizations	Customers & Students
Lee Gardner – Junior Achievement (6)	Everyone who has purchased from me 1 or 2x (6)
Terry Lloyd – Future Business Leaders of America (8)	Those who occasionally purchase from me (7)
Tina Johal – Boy Scouts (7)	Those who are on autopay (8)
School Board Members (1-7)	Night Class students (6)
City Council (1-6)	Church Members
	Art & Michelle Pratt (6)
	Maughn & Carol Wagner (7)
	Todd & Christine Anderson (7)
	Brent & Darla Warner (6)

Steve calls the meeting back to order and invites everyone to settle down. While his assistants close the doors to the auditorium so that we can begin discussing the activity, I show Ann my quick list of relationships. I'm a little ashamed of already sneaking a peek at Ann's list. But there is really no time to worry about this now.

Steve starts right on time. As always, Steve starts out by asking us some questions. He begins with, "Why do you think I had you all invest this precious time doing this activity?" In the middle of his question, a couple and two other men walk in. As soon as they enter the room the tension becomes obvious. Unsurprised by this incident, Steve invites them to come up to the front of the room and asks, "Did you fully understand the directions for the assignment?" Each nods their head that they did and one tries to make an excuse about why he and his partner are late. Steve smiles and reminds them, "This is a business conference for a multinational billion dollar company leading a revolution of success."

Changing his focus from them to the audience for a moment, he asks, "Can anyone tell the whole group what fifty percent of success is?" A woman towards the back shouts, "Showing up is fifty percent of success." Steve nods in agreement and then asks, "What is forty percent of success?" A man in the front row shares, "Showing up with a high value of service." Again Steve responds in agreement saying, "That is exactly right." And then he asks, "What is the other ten percent?" To my surprise Ann yells out, "SHOWING UP ON TIME!"

Without further explanation or demonstration Steve invites the people who were late to take their seats and then talks about the damage we do to relationships when we don't do the things we say we are going to do, when we say we are going to do them. "Being out of integrity is a sign that we talk the talk but we don't walk the walk. Showing up late is a relationship buster and immediately encourages others to rate your relationship at a 1, defining it as a relationship that robs; one that they might consider ending! It demonstrates that the value of your service is substandard. So thank you for showing up, and I hope you have learned that a fifty percent relationship is one that robs instead of rewards."

Matt is taken back by the power Steve takes on this issue thinking, wow, that was really harsh. Doesn't he care that they might be offended? Surprisingly, the one who made an excuse at the front of the room, thanks Steve, for keeping him and the others accountable for their actions and showing great leadership. It was evident to him that Steve cares enough about them to build this relationship through accountability. He further said that Steve showed that he doesn't want to make critical relationship mistake numbers two and nine: "Letting people avoid taking action for as long as you let them." and "Being out of integrity."

Steve acknowledges his apology and returns to the question he asked a few minutes ago: "Why do you think I had you invest a precious hour doing this activity?" A voice comes from the back saying "It helped me to realize that I have a lot of relationships in my life." A woman at the end of my row adds, "It made me aware of the quality of my relationships." Another woman offers, "I calculated the average of my relationships and it scared me. More than anything else, I want to learn how to increase the quality of these relationships."

Steve thanks everyone for their responses and then tells us, "Increasing the quality of all of our relationships is the key to determining how valuable our service is. A year or so ago I developed a three-step process that will help you calculate the quality of your relationships. There is a little bit of math involved here so bear with me and we'll be fine. If you have questions, please ask as I move through each step. Those of you who have calculators on your cell phones are welcome to use them, but please be sure to disable the ringer. In a few minutes you will calculate what I call your Relationship Rating. Your Relationship Rating is a critical ingredient in your value of service recipe.

"Step One," he shares, "Add all the scores you put beside each relationship. And if you put some kind of range beside a relationship like a volunteer group you work with, then you need to take the lowest number of that group and use it. If you failed to put a number beside a relationship, then you don't get any points for that. Divide the total score of all the relationships you wrote down by the number of relationships you wrote down and that's your Basic Relationship Rating.

"For example suppose you add together all the numbers of the relationships you have and they equal one hundred. Then you count the number of all the different relationships you have and they equal twenty. Then you take one hundred and divide it by twenty. The result of this simple division gives you the first important number in your Relationship Rating. In this case it is twenty out of one hundred or five; $(100 \div 20 = 5)$.

"This number doesn't make you good or bad, right or wrong, smart or dumb. It is simply your estimation of the quality of all the relationships you have. So don't get too excited or worked up about what this initial number might be. Remember this is Step One of the process, and knowing is always better than not knowing. If you categorized your list, then you could do this same activity for each category of relationships you have and analyze your relationships that way. You can also take individual relationships and work through this exact same process. You determine the level of granularity you want to work with."

As Matt does his own calculation he tells himself, "I have a total number of 257 from 48 different relationships, for a relationship rating of 5.4." Glancing over at Ann's notes and seeing that she has 6.9 circled, my mind is racing now to find some meaning in the differences in our results. Ann doesn't seem too wound up about her score. But if these numbers are somewhat precise, then Ann's relationship rating is almost 20% higher than mine! Holy cow, I have a lot of room to learn and improve.

Moving on to Step Two, Steve begins with the question we are all asking ourselves, "So what does this really mean?" Steve asks rhetorically. "First, take your relationship rating number and multiply it by 10. For example if you have an initial number of 6.2, then multiplying that by 10 would give you a 62." Well at least I am over 50%, Matt thinks consolingly. My 54 could be considered at least a D in some classes. Whew, at least I'm not failing."

Steve continues his explanation of this second number, "Now let me explain what this number means both generally, and specifically to your individual relationships. Generally speaking if the number from step two is below 50 then you are doing things either consciously or unconsciously to push people away from you more than half the time. Now before I gave you a way to measure this, somehow you innately knew that the quality of your relationships is low. The good news is that now you can calculate your suspicions."

Matt leans back in his chair and puts his hands over his eyes and deeply considers the ramifications of this. There is such power and potential in this simple exercise, he thinks. There is still one step left in this Relationship Rating exercise and already I can think of a dozen ways I am going to use this at work to help myself and my colleagues improve client and work relationships. Why don't they teach this anywhere else? It is simply blind luck that I am even here learning this right now for myself. If we hadn't moved into the neighborhood with the Thoms', Ann wouldn't have enrolled in XL-8, none of what I am learning would be part of my skill set or knowledge set to help me become the kind of person others can trust and follow. Thank heaven for the little miracles."

Steve's allusion to the last time he talked to us brings me back to the room. He says, "I was talking about the idea of getting people to move toward you and then with you. Consider for a moment this scenario: An associate or colleague comes to you because he is not getting the results he wants. You work through step one with him and determine his Step One score is a 5 and hence his Step Two score as a 50. That would mean that he spends an estimated 50% of his time and effort drawing people toward him. And it also means that 50% of the time he is pushing people away. Would it be any surprise to you that he is not getting the results he wants? What is more, he is probably unaware that he is doing things that are repelling people and damaging his relationships.

"Now for Step Three; let me bring this down to a more precise level. If you assessed a singular relationship at a 7 in Step One, then your Step Two number would be a 70. And as I said a few minutes ago, that means 70% of the time you are doing things that are attracting that person to you, and that's good right? It also means that you are repelling that person away from you 30% of the time, and that's not so good right? Step Three, however, tells us the real story of what's truly going on in your relationship with this person. The bottom line of the calculation of Step Three is that your relationship with this person is really only at 40 percent."

Turning to the white board at the side of the stage Steve responds saying, "Thank you for the question. I really want you to get the breadth and depth of this concept, especially that you understand it drives success in relationship building." Writing now, Steve puts a really big '70' at the top of the board and then underneath that he wrote an equally big '30'. He explains, "If you have a 70% relationship with someone, that might seem fine at first glance. On the surface, you could even feel like this is a relationship that is rewarding; but what about the remaining 30% of your association? How does that part really affect your interactions and resulting relationship? Let me show you: If you take the 70 and subtract the 30 you end up with 40 or 40%, which is a more accurate analysis of where that relationship is. Here's another example: If you have a 90% relationship with someone then your Relationship Rating with them in all reality is discounted to 80%."

Steve pauses for a few minutes to make sure that there are no more questions and to let people digest the magnitude of what he just taught. Matt is kind of reeling at this point. He was disheartened when he thought he had a 54, but now that he does the deeper math he can't believe it! Fretfully he thinks, my real relationship rating is only an 8! That's right, 54 minus 46 is a whopping 8! That wouldn't even be cataclysmic if it were an earthquake. This would certainly explain why I struggle so much with people. It looks like 92% of the time I am consciously and subconsciously doing things that push them away from me. The precision of this exercise hit me between the eyes like a two-by-four. Happily, I keep coming back to Steve's quote, "Knowing is always better than not knowing," but I always seem to find out the things that I am really bad at. Wouldn't it be nice for a change to learn that I am really good at something? Well, maybe that's the purpose of training. If I sat in a room learning how good I was, it probably wouldn't help me much. I decide that I am grateful for the lesson and more committed than ever to take some specific action to improve my Relationship Rating in the coming months.

Steve interrupts my mental side trip by inviting all of us to "Take three minutes to write down what we considered was easy and hard about this activity. Look closely at what people or person you estimated yourself having the most powerful relationship with, and what people or person do you have the least powerful relationship with. Finally, do a quick evaluation of a few things that you are aware of that might push people away from you, and a few things that you are consciously doing to draw them toward you.

The three minutes begins right now!"

Steve interrupts the three minutes of deafening silence created by people thinking, reflecting, and writing by asking, "By the raise of hands how many of you were able to put a number beside every person's name on your list?" He shares a deeper concept, "If you didn't, then you are unsure of the value of your service to those people and your doubt shows up as a low number in your interaction ratio."

Looking at his list, Matt realizes that he didn't put a number by all the relationships he wrote down. Maybe that's why Ann has a higher relationship rating than I do, he thinks. Maybe I am unsure how to serve because I worry more about me than the person I am interacting with at any given moment in time.

Steve continues by asking, "How did your partner help with this assignment?" A man from the front left side of the room shares, "None, we didn't talk at all. We stayed together and talked about what time it was and checked with each other to see how far along we were." Matt's partner, Mark Whitman emphatically says, "We discussed ideas about different kinds of relationships we could list. I realized that this is exactly what we teach new associates to do when they enroll; like making a names list."

Steve deepens this line of questions by asking, "By the raise of hands how many of you put the person you just spent time with on your relationship list?" Only about twenty hands go up, including mine, I think gladly. I notice that Ann's, and Mark and Sally Whitman's hands are also up. Steve's countenance changes as he sees that only a relative few included the person that they just invested an hour of their life with. He follows up by asking, "How many invested time getting to know the person you chose to be with for the past hour?" Again only a small number of hands go up. He seems pretty upset now, seeing that associates and some leaders in the company that he loves so much were oblivious to the fact that they just initiated a relationship right here in the conference, and for the most part they missed seeing that relationship as being important enough to include.

"So here's what I think I just witnessed," Steve declares in an irritated tone. "There are 150 pairs of human beings who were together for an hour with no one else to talk to, and immediately after I talked about the importance of relationships and the value of service, only about five to ten percent of you all could immediately apply the lesson!" Ann grabs Matt's hand in re-assurance that they had applied the lesson. It's painful to hear Steve say, "I am amazed that it appears that most of you really believe that success is just a matter of showing up! Fifty percenter's," he rebukes, "Fail in school, business, and in life. You must understand that showing up is not enough! In order to create massive success in any part of life, you might consider the idea that providing a high value of service is just as important if not more important as showing up for the sake of showing up. So back to the original question, why did I have you do this activity? I had you do the exercise for some specific reasons. One of them was to see if you could apply what you had just been taught. I would strongly encourage you all to choose to be more aware of the relationships in your life. If you are serious about making a real difference in the world you need to learn to make a significant difference in the lives of the people you wrote down and the people you meet the rest of your life.

"Before I give you your skill mastery practice assignment today, I want to make sure that you know it is my grandest desire to help you all become professional relationship builders. The only way that you can truly serve the world is by sharing all that you offer. Now for your skill mastery practice: this month you have two assignments: First, today I want you to talk with at least one of the people on your relationship list. Your conditions of victory for that conversation are to improve your Relationship Rating with them through a highly curious conversation. You have the entire month to complete the second assignment. I want you to teach the lesson I taught you today to at least one person. Someone who is not here today. You can get together with others who are here today and compare notes and ideas if you wish, or you can just use your own notes if you choose. You have the entire month to share the importance of building relationships with anyone else in your world that isn't here today."

Steve thanks us all for coming and encourages us to be in our seats for the evening recognition meeting which starts at 7:00 PM. The lights in the auditorium become bright and it seems like everyone is beginning to talk about what they learned and how they were going to share with someone else this month. Still stunned by what he learned about himself today Matt sits and ponders while he watches several people come up to Ann to comment on what they had learned and how great Steve is. Many ask her what she learned and if she had a plan in place to discuss this meeting in more detail. Their attention to Ann makes me think of the first part of Steve's skill mastery assignment: "Improve one of the relationships you have on your list." Looking at my notes I recall that I rated my relationship with Ann at a 9 or 90%. But what that really boils down to is only an 80%, or in academic terms a B-! Wow the most important relationship in my whole life is only a B-. I also rated my relationship with the kids at a discounted 70%. It hurt to realize that my relationship with my kids was barely above a D! Consoling myself I said quietly to myself, "The good news is that I have at least one relationship that is at the B level. And the best news is that that relationship is the most important one in my world. So it's not all bad."

Still sitting there while Ann talks to her team members, it occurs to me that I haven't even thought once that my relationship with Ann is only at a B level or that my relationship with the kids is only at a C- level. I have been taught my whole life that it's my job as the husband to provide the family with what they need to live and have a good lifestyle, and if I did that, everything would be fine. At this point I realize that this is what dad did, and I don't think it really worked out that well for him. In that moment I decide to call Larry, my old high school friend. I rated my relationship with him at an 8 which I now know is really only a 6. I talk to Larry for a few minutes, asking him about what he's doing and how things are going. When he asks me where I am and why I am calling him now, I explain that I just want to make sure to keep our relationship going. We have had so many experiences together that I just didn't want time and distance to shrivel and die. We talk for a few more minutes and then hang up. For a minute I feel pretty good about this relationship stuff until I begin to consider what to do to improve my relationship with Ann.

As I am in deep thought about Ann and our relationship my cell phone buzzes. It's an emergency message from Bruce. I need to excuse myself and rush to work. I borrow the car from Ann, and as I am driving I think how counter-productive this is in light of Ann's comment about my being married to my job and my commitment to be with her at the conference. This is definitely not improving my relationship rating with Ann. But what am I supposed to do? I also need to keep my relationship with Bruce intact or everything will fall apart. When I pull in the parking lot at work I am stuck on the thought that we only have one car and that Ann has to rely on the Thoms' for a ride home tonight. That thought increases my commitment to outperform my colleagues and get promoted next.

I am gaining a definite advantage over my fellow department coordinators by learning, practicing and applying what Steve has been teaching me. Division Manager is in my sights now. I comfort myself by thinking that weekend dedication to the job shows my commitment to the company and in turn they will reward me when it comes bonus and promotion time.

After work, I pull into the driveway at home and see that the lights are off, Ann is still not home. I call her and she tells me that she is at a restaurant with Steve and Sara. She invites me to come join them. When I arrive, Steve is holding court in the back room with those who wanted to stay late and learn more about the business and how to make it work more effectively. Ann meets me at the door and we sit at the back of the room. I apologize for leaving, but Ann seems more disappointed than mad. Either way she views my leaving as me choosing my job over her.

On the way home it's silent in the car. I'm trying to think of ways I can increase my relationship rating, and the things that might be contributing to my abysmal score. Wow. An 8. I think the dog I had growing up had a higher score than an 8. But if that's true then what did my dog do that I am not doing? I come up with a few things. Maybe I'm on to something. When I came home from school he came to greet me. He wagged his tail and was excited to jump up on me as a welcome home. He didn't make judgments about me and how I dressed, how much money I had, or what my social status was. He was sincerely interested in being there for me.

How eager am I to be there for others, regardless of how it affects me? I am pretty sure that I am much more interested in how things affect me than how I affect others. Just as we pull into the driveway I make a mental note to write a question on a new line on the front of the little card I read each morning. It should say, "What can I do to serve others today?" Opening the door for Ann, I realize that now I have the second ingredient in Steve's recipe for success.

Attending the evening recognition meeting at the January conference, I get to see Ann being promoted to the third level in her compensation program. Sara puts the new Silver promotion level lapel pin on her blouse. I am so proud watching her get rewarded for learning and implementing new skills and knowledge about relationships in her business. She is really using the things that Steve and Sara have been teaching her, and it is paying off. Her PEPs are over fifty now. She has a team of over fifty Associates and about thirty customers. She has six team members who are consistently working and being promoted along with her. The best news is that she's making pretty good money now, and she can afford to start looking for a car of her own.

A few weeks later I pass Sara on the sidewalk as I leave for work. She smiles and wishes me well. I respond telling her, "Ann is expecting you. Just let yourself in."

"Hello," Sara says anxiously as she knocks and opens the front door. "Come in and make yourself at home," Ann answers, inviting Sara to join her at the kitchen table.

Sara asks, "What does Matt think about the business, your success and progression?"

"He loves what Steve is teaching him and is very supportive of my work," Ann shares. "He is using what he is learning from Steve at work and it's making a big difference in the results he and his team are getting. He loves the money I am making, but I think he feels a little out of sorts about the fact that we depend on that money. And he is concerned about how leadership responsibility for me in the business will affect my attention to family responsibilities. I feel like he uses the fact that I stay busy and have good team relationships to justify his not being here as much. But overall he has been great."

"You are very lucky Ann," replies Sara. "Not everyone has a supportive spouse or support team to help them. I want to talk today about how to help you grow your business even faster so that you will be able to pay more time and attention to your family. Now that you are at a leadership level in the business it is critical for you to focus on teaching your team to create A+ relationships with their prospects, customers, and team associates. I know

Steve has really been teaching a lot about this lately, and our results have been amazing. Since we have been concentrating on relationships our business has grown like never before. The good news is that developing great relationships is relatively simple to do. Not necessarily easy, but simple. Initially it does take time and effort, but in the end you actually invest less time working with people whom you have a relationship with than you do trying to work with people you don't have a positive relationship with. I have learned along the way however, that if something like creating relationships is easy to do, it's also easy not to do. That is to say, it's easy to invest a few minutes to learn about people so that you can better serve them and it's also easy to ignore the relationship part and just start blabbing about how great our products, services and company are. So the important lesson to learn from this is to concentrate on what result you are working to create. If your goal is to move through prospects quickly in an attempt to sort the 'good' ones from the 'bad' ones then you can ignore the relationship building part of the conversation. However if your goal is to get people moving toward you and then with you then you get to change your approach and quickly build rapport with your prospects. Building the relationship first may take a few more minutes but more of the people you talk to will engage with you. And after all isn't that what you want?

Speaking of goals, at this point in your business, your goals need to shift to be more focused on helping your team builders to qualify for leadership. You have a great responsibility now not only for yourself, but for a rapidly growing team."

"That's true in more ways than one," Ann interjects. "Thanks for being such a great friend and mentor to me Sara. I value our relationship more than you can imagine."

"Your turn is coming Ann," Sara reminds. "You will have plenty of opportunities to share your gifts and talents with many others as your business grows."

After Sara leaves, Ann calls Matt's office but gets to his voicemail. His assistant notices that it's Ann and picks up the phone. She tells Ann that Matt is in a meeting and that she will give him the message to call her back as soon as he returns. Meanwhile Matt is sitting outside of Bruce's office because it is time for his quarterly review again. He is less nervous than he has been in the past but these reviews are always a little stressful he thinks waiting for what seems an eternity. Bruce calls for him to come in and invites him to take a seat. Bruce rarely minces words and today is no different.

He begins saying, "Let me tell you Matt, this company has always been about creating and rewarding results not attendance."

Not sure if this is a good or bad commentary on his performance, Matt is unconsciously rubbing his hands together as Bruce uncharacteristically pauses; maybe for dramatic effect or maybe to collect his own thoughts. I don't know but it makes me very nervous.

Bruce continues, "You came here with a fresh set of eyes and a unique approach to helping our clients and now you have become very good at making them life-long customers. By the numbers: your department's customer acquisition costs are down 150%, while your new accounts grew by over 20%. Customer up-sells increased by 23%. 46% of your business comes from existing customers. Your retention rate increased by 11%. And in last quarter's customer satisfaction surveys, your department has the highest cumulative scores in the whole Division."

"It seems that you and your department provide stellar value that attracts new customers and helps keep the customers you do attract. Keep this up and I will be fighting you for a top floor promotion some day. Some day that is, but that day is not today," he said in a slightly sinister voice pausing again. Today I want to congratulate you for earning Perpetual Wealth Financial's Manager of the Quarter award. This is a prestigious award. You were competing against Jane and all the other Department Coordinators and all other managers at every level of the company. In the years I have been here, you are one of the only Department Coordinators to win this award. In fact I think only Terri Hesslip, now the Vice President of Sales, is the only other one to have won this award as a Department Coordinator. Earning this award puts a lot of executive eyeballs on you and gives you credibility upstairs in ways you can't imagine yet. I am not sure how you have made such dramatic improvement in such a short time, but I would encourage you to keep up the fantastic job you are doing. Pausing, he says, "I think that does it for this review." Closing my personnel folder, he asks, "On your way out could you invite my assistant to come in here?"

Back at my desk, I call Ann to play my own version of 'Guess What I Did Today'. Ann is elated at the news and offers to have a special dinner waiting when I get home. By the time I hang up the news had spread throughout the department and everyone comes over to congratulate me. Jane brings a picture of an Elephants ear mounted on a piece of cardboard as a memento of listening to leadership, teachers, prospects, and clients. It's so hard to compete against someone who is so supportive. But compete I will. This is just the encouragement I need to keep learning and working.

Over the next several weeks Ann and I sit at the kitchen table after the kids are in bed and discuss what she is learning on her daily visits with Sara and weekly training meetings with Steve. Today, just as Ann and I sit down the door bell rings. It's Steve and Sara, what an awesome treat. Ann had told Sara about my award and they have come over to congratulate me with some cookies and milk. We all sit down and talk for a little while. We don't get a chance to have a celebrity in the house very often and I think about taking advantage of the moment.

With Steve a willing conversation captive, I throw out a statement hoping that he will respond, "Many of the people who come into my office are a bit lost or confused about the future."

Steve takes the bait and asks, "What do you think people are looking for today, Matt?"

Taking time to finish off the last of my cookie I begin, "Ideally, leaders are looking for potential leaders to mentor; people are looking for someone who can and will actually lead them to achieve all that they are capable of. But in my experience at work, managers are just pretending to lead, when they are really only coaxing or cajoling their direct reports to do the heavy lifting so they, and I mean the 'leaders' here, can reap the reward. Not much value to that kind of service is there? These kind of 'leaders' aren't bad, necessarily; they just haven't experienced a true leader/mentor in their own lives who really cares and is willing to make a stand; a stand for something greater than their own self-interest." I pause, pleased with my answer.

"So let me ask you something Matt," Steve fires back with his own question. "If you could change anything about your organization what would it be?"

Immediately I respond, "I would like to teach others in my department what I am learning from you. I have been somewhat successful at increasing my personal Value of Service and Relationship Rating but I am not sure if I can teach others to do the same."

"How would your department be different if you could do that?" Steve seems truly interested in the possibilities here.

"I think it would help us to create better results for our clients and then, of course, for ourselves," I reply.

Suddenly Steve becomes more serious saying, "You think it will help you? You think?"

Sara, reaching over and grabbing Steve's hand, gives him that "Take a breath and relax look."

Steve sits back in his chair and calmly asks, "Matt would you be open to a little counsel?"

"I would love to hear your thoughts," I respond, not realizing what is about to happen.

Steve begins with a few questions, "A minute ago you mentioned results. So Matt, what result are you committed to create? How will you know if you are making measureable progress towards that result? The thing is, if you don't know what result you want, you can't know what to change. And if you don't know what to change, you are stuck depending on luck or chance to succeed. Is that what you teach your clients to do?"

"Of course not," I'm a little defensive. "I ask them what result they want to create and then ask them on a scale from 1 to 10, how committed they are to creating that result. If they respond with an 8, 9 or 10 we develop a plan that will predictably produce that result."

"Very good," says Steve. "What is your conversion ratio of prospects to clients?"

"I don't know. We don't track this number at all," I answer. "We track customer acquisition costs, total new accounts, customer up-sells, business that comes from existing customers, and retention rates."

"Okay," says Steve. "Let me approach this using your method of score keeping. How would your Department be impacted if you could double, triple or even quadruple just your total new accounts in the next six months?"

Chuckling I respond with, "I would be elected King. Although I don't think that scenario is possible."

Steve continues, "You are only missing one important step in your process. If you will find out why your prospects and current clients want their stated result, and get them to describe how their life will be different when they experience that result, they will take your recommendations and advice because they will know you sincerely care about them, that they can trust you because they will know that you are good at what you do. Does this sound familiar?"

I am reminded of Oscar. "I heard this from a trusted childhood friend, and again from you a few months ago."

"Now you know the deeper lesson Matt," Steve admonishes. Let's return to the question I asked a few minutes ago. "How will your business be different if your team learns what you have learned?"

"First off," I begin, "We will convert more prospects to clients. And if our programs, products, and services actually do what we advertise, all of our other numbers will increase as a natural result of having more people taking the actions we recommend during the enrollment process."

"I couldn't have said it better myself," Steve responds. "That's why Ann is progressing in her business so rapidly. She has mastered this process and is teaching others to follow her example. She is in a similar leadership situation as you. Her title is different, but her job isn't. She must teach other leaders to teach their team members to learn, practice, and apply success principles in their proper sequence, beginning with increasing the value of their service, and building relationships on purpose, with purpose. So now that you and I know what you want, and you have acknowledged why you want it, what are you going to do about it?"

4

Transactions and Transformations

The new quarter begins and I'm ready to makes some changes. I start by changing my weekly department meeting's agenda. I begin each meeting with a brief accountability reporting of conversion ratios, something we've never done before, followed by a short training session about relationships, value of service, and the selling process. I end with a skill mastery practice for my team to complete during the week. This new focus has a definite effect on my team numbers; so much so, that my prize pupil is promoted to be a department coordinator. As I'm sitting in my office, relishing the idea that I am successfully teaching others to succeed, it occurs to me that I might have lost that competitive edge because everyone I teach now knows the secret sauce of my success.

Although this worries me for a minute, the thought follows that teaching others to be successful is actually the key to my becoming an executive. I will succeed because I'm sharing this, not because I'm keeping it a secret. And that is really the best part of the whole concept. Success comes from sharing and expanding my circle of influence. Hoarding knowledge is counter- productive to success.

The snowy cold weather gives way to spring flowers and then to summer's heat. Ann's business is going well. Her relationship rating is climbing and so is her team's overall Relationship Rating. Leaders are emerging from her group at an accelerated pace, and she seems to be the poster child for learning, adopting, and teaching success principles in their proper sequence.

As I did my morning email check, I receive an urgent message from Bruce; "As soon as you get this message come and see me, no matter what you are doing." Worried, I hurry to Bruce's office with a thousand ideas going through my head. I'm not sure what is going on, but my first thought is, "I am being fired." Then I think, if that were true I wouldn't have had access to my email account, so it must be something else. Maybe someone on my team is being fired. Maybe the company is going bankrupt or is being merged with some other company. When I get to Bruce's office he can see that I am very tense.

Bruce reclines in his chair, puts his hands clasped on top of his head as he likes to do and invites me to, "Relax."

"Relax," I echo. "How can I relax with a message like yours greeting me first thing on a Monday morning?"

He smiles and then announces, "I have been promoted to Regional Manager and you are going to replace me again. Only now you are going to be the Division Manager."

Stunned for a moment, Matt just sits there.

"Well aren't you going to say anything?" Bruce asks.

"I don't know what to say," Matt acknowledges. "First, congratulations ᴜ᛫ your promotion. You will be great. Second, I want to thank you Bruce for mentoring me and believing in me, and third, I am very curious why you and the executives here would promote me ahead of Jane and others?"

"Let me tell you Matt," Bruce begins. "I told you before that we reward results above everything else here and simply stated, your results are better than anyone else's. And your record for teaching others to create excellent results has not gone unnoticed on the top floor either. I fought for you as the most qualified person for this position because your department's customer acquisition costs are down 500%, while your new accounts grew by over 20%. Customer up-sells increased by 34%. 65% of your business comes from existing customers. Your retention increased by 17%. And in last quarter's customer satisfaction surveys, your department has the highest cumulative scores. In short, Mr. new Division Manager, your department is the most profitable in the company. And now as your new Regional Manager my mandate to you is for you to teach your Department Coordinators to do what you have been doing. You are creating quite a stir Matt. Keep this up and you will be joining me on the Executive floor before long. Now get out of here before we both get all emotional."

On the way back to my office I think incredulously, the stuff Steve teaches really works! The three underlying principles and a few of the general topics Steve has taught me over the past months have helped me create these incredible results. Still walking to the elevator, I take the 3x5 card out of my pocket and read silently to myself: Do they trust you? Are you good at what you do? Do you care about them? The value of service really is rooted in my Relationship Rating. As I get off the elevator on the way to my office I remember my own monthly analysis of relationships, both personal and in my department. My own general Relationship Rating increased from an 8 to a 32 and each of my team members increased by an average of 25%!

My assistant Kayci meets me just outside of my office, and asks with the same concerned look on her face I had just a few minutes earlier, "What was the big meeting with Bruce about?"

"How did you know about the meeting?" I ask, surprised that she knew where I had been.

"There is very little that goes on in this department that I don't know about. That's why you always have what you need before you need it, she exclaims!"

Matt smiles in agreement and appreciation and informs her, "We are moving upstairs. We have been promoted to Division Manager and I am taking you with me." She screams, gives me a big hug and then gets her note pad and starts planning our move.

I go into my office to consider Bruce's mandate to teach my Department Coordinators what I have been doing. How am I going to do that? As I ponder this challenge, it only takes me about one minute to plan my first move: call Steve Thoms and invite him to do a workshop. Interrupting Kayci's planning frenzy, I ask her to "Get Mr. Thoms on the phone for me." She dials him and then transfers the ringing phone to me.

"Hello this is Steve," comes the voice on the phone.

"Hi Steve, this is Matt Ivey from across the street."

"What's going on Matt, how can I help you," Steve asks.

"I need to ask you a favor," I reply anxiously. "I was just promoted at work."

"Congratulations Matt," Steve interrupts.

"Thank you," I continue. "The main reason I have been promoted is because I and my department have been creating noticeable results here at work, and those results have come from applying the principles you have been teaching me."

"Well I appreciate your compliment," responds Steve. "I am glad that you have put them to good use. Ann seems to be having similar results as well. So what's the favor?"

"Well," clearing my throat nervously, "I am wondering if you might be willing to do a workshop with my new organization here at my office. I thought if I could have anyone stand in front of my team and teach them how to build better relationships faster and with less frustration, it would be you."

"Again, thanks for the compliment. You may be giving me too much credit," Steve acknowledges. "How many people do you have in your organization?"

"I have five Department Coordinators and my executive assistant," replies Matt proudly.

"I will have to carefully consider dedicating a whole day for such a small group," Steve contends.

My ego sags as I slump in my chair.

"Why do you want me to do the workshop, Matt?" Steve continues.

"With this promotion, I have been given a mandate," I reply, feeling kind of desperate. "I am supposed to duplicate my results within a larger organization. I am not sure if I can teach other leaders to teach their team members to do the same."

"So what I hear you saying Matt is that you feel comfortable teaching individuals to implement what you have learned but you're anxious about teaching other leaders to do the same. Is that right?"

"I think that might be true," I agree. "What if they start asking questions or challenging me on any particular point? You are pretty forceful when you teach and no one is in any position to question you or your knowledge."

"What you perceive as an advantage Matt, is really the biggest challenge for me in my business. Everyone on my team is a volunteer. They are motivated by many things but none of them are motivated by fear of being fired. They look to me as an authority on the success they want to create, and so some of them follow my advice and counsel. However, very few of them actually do what I encourage them to do with consistent precision and diligence. In all reality, you have a degree of control I don't. So in many ways it will be easier for you than it is for me. From what Ann tells Sara and me, you are on a fast track to executive leadership, so your team members should look to you as the 'all knowing, all powerful Oz' as well. Some might be jealous because you were promoted ahead of them, but they didn't get promoted because they weren't listening or applying what they were being taught. So what could you say if anyone decides to challenge you?"

After a few seconds of silence, Matt responds carefully, not wanting to say something stupid: "I might be able to use what you said as an advantage. I could just come right out and say, if you do what I have done, you will have a credible claim on the same success I have enjoyed. If you fail to learn, practice, and apply these principles, you will continue to have the results you have always had."

"Bravo," Steve says in a congratulatory tone. "Now you're thinking like the leader Ann has been talking about. Remember a few months ago, when the group of people came in late and tried to make an excuse for their ineffective behavior? What was their response to me holding them accountable for their actions?"

"They actually thanked you," Matt remembers. "They said you showed great leadership in making it clear you cared enough about them that you would build this relationship through accountability. You showed them that you didn't want to only talk about relationships, and then make critical relationship mistakes by letting them avoid taking action and being out of integrity."

"That's right Matt," responds Steve. "Remember, more than anything else, people are looking for a leader. Someone who can and will actually lead them to achieve all that they are capable of. Give me a minute to think of how I may be able to help you. I have one more lesson to teach in the series Ann is enrolled in. Are you going to attend that session?"

"I wouldn't miss it for the world," I quickly respond.

"Let me turn on my computer and check my schedule," Steve suggests. "When are you thinking of doing this workshop?"

"I will arrange my schedule to accommodate yours," Matt is excited Steve is considering it.

"My schedule gets crazy this time of year," Steve interjects searching for available dates and times. "Let's see, I will have to make a few phone calls to see if I can clear a day between the next conferences. I will have to get back to you Matt. Sorry for the delay in answering your question, I just want to make

Are you with me?

sure I can keep any commitment I might make to you."

"Thank you for even considering this," Matt responds.

"I will call you back on Friday with an answer and a date for you if I can fit it in," Steve says, "Keep up the good work in fostering great relationships. I will talk to you on Friday, goodbye."

Later that week after my Friday leadership meeting I sit down in my office chair just as the phone rings. "Good news," says Steve Thoms excitedly. "I also want to thank you. Your request has helped me get my training schedule organized. Arranging my training events months in advance is not my favorite thing, and your call helped me to get in gear. Unfortunately, I do not have an open date to do the training you requested until October. However, there is good news. Next month I will be doing the last training module in the sequence I set out for the group Ann is in.

"As you probably know the highest promotion level in XL-8 is the Platinum level. Yesterday, during our monthly conference call with my Platinum colleagues and with your proposal and Ann's progress in mind, I posed the idea of inviting one guest or couple to this year's Platinum retreat. This has never been done before, but I figured if the leaders could catch the vision of having one person or couple being with a group of Platinums for a few days it would help everyone to grow their groups with a little more purpose.

"The good news I spoke of a minute ago is actually three-fold. First, my proposal has been approved. Second, I want to extend the invitation for you and Ann to be my guests at the retreat. I recognize that Ann is building a huge team; her results have been astounding, and your invitation helped me create a win for me, Ann, and hopefully for you as well. And third, if you and Ann can be our guests, then you can learn everything you need to know to teach your team what the six, seven, and eight figure earners in XL-8 know about building a strong and profitable business through meaningful relationships.

"There are a couple of commitments you will need to make in order for us to be in agreement. First, you will need to make sure to attend the business development conference in a few weeks with Ann and her team as you have in the past. Second, in order to be in integrity you will need to commit to train your team on all the things you are learning at our conferences and the Platinum retreat. So the ball is now back in your court Matt. Can you and Ann commit to come along with Sara and me to this working retreat?"

"We would love to come with you," I respond ecstatically. "Ann will be so surprised and excited when I tell her tonight. Of course we will need the travel logistics, and what the next topic will be when present in a few weeks so that we can be prepared for it?"

"Excellent try Matt," counters Steve coyly. "I can't divulge that until the business development conference when you all arrive. I don't want people to get ahead of themselves planning for the next training while they need to focus on mastering the training they just received."

"I understand Mr. Thoms," I say, as the conversation turns more professional. "I also agree to teach my team here at work the things I learned from the first two trainings and what I will learn at the conference retreat in preparation for our April event."

"Excellent," Steve indicates agreeably. "I will have my assistant send you the information on the trip so that you and Ann can begin to prepare. Remember that this is a business trip, not a vacation. So come prepared to work, listen, and learn. Thanks again Matt for your invitation and the subsequent events that have occurred as a result. I look forward to having Ann and you accompany us, goodbye."

As I hang up the phone, I revel in my new position in the company, thinking, "I am on my way to a corner office on the executive floor. I am so excited about my promotion, the status, and yes, the raise associated with this new position. This kind of salary makes it possible to say yes to Steve's invitation without worrying about how much it will cost, what I would have to sacrifice for the next year to pay for it, or how I would explain the cost benefits to Ann to get her to agree to go. I must admit, I love the idea of being at the same level as my initial company mentor, Josh. I look forward to developing a healthy competitive relationship that drives both of us to record breaking results.

Just then the phone rings again. It's Ann. She asks, "How is your day going and then gives me the infamous 'Guess What I Did Today' question. I am so relieved that my new position doesn't put stress on our relationship when she informs me she just hired a housekeeper. I am thinking that my plan is working and I am quickly providing the kind of life that my dad gave us and the kind of lifestyle Ann deserves.

After we hang up I start planning my next training. There are a couple of things Steve showed me that seem so foreign to anything I have been taught: first, that life-long relationships are built and strengthened through accountability, and that I am out of integrity when I let people choose not to take the actions that will produce the result they said they want and have committed to create. Second, that finding out why they want what they want and getting them to talk about how their life would change if their desires were met is my responsibility.

I have no real idea how to do this, but it seems like it comes back to the ideas of being curious about people, and being interested instead of interesting. I begin to write on the whiteboard as a reminder of what I want to accomplish when I have interviews with my managers. As soon as I finish writing the last note, the phone rings again.

This time, it's Kayci informing me that Dayna, the Silverado Department Coordinator is here and would like to talk to me for a few minutes. When she asks whether she should send her in or make an appointment, I reply "Send her in, I would like to talk to her for a few minutes."

Dayna comes in, shakes my hand, and congratulates me on the new promotion. She begins saying, "I am eager to learn from you Matt. It seems you are becoming a bit of a legend here. I have been here three years, and I am glad that someone who has real floor experience is moving up the ranks. Your department was killing all of us each month in pretty much every category," she offers, fishing for some kind of response about management.

Resisting the temptation to agree with her, or further her point I respond with a simple thank you for your compliment. Wanting to understand her better, I continue, "I am glad to be working with such a talented group of leaders. Bruce has created a region that is the envy of all other Division Managers. Thanks for coming to see me like this Dayna. I would like your opinion on a few things. First, if you could change anything in your department what would it be?"

Without any hesitation she answers, "Getting more clients and selling more of what we offer to the clients we have."

"Really," I say inquisitively while I glance at my notes on the whiteboard. "What do you think is keeping that from happening?" This is good, I think, proud of myself for being interested in what she has to say, instead of jumping in and telling her about value of service, relationships, and conversion ratios.

It is silent for a full twenty seconds. She looks at me, caught by surprise that I didn't attempt to dazzle her with my brilliance and expertise. Finally, she offers, "I have no real idea. I know I shouldn't tell you that as my new boss, but I don't think anyone else does either. That's why I told you a few minutes ago that it's nice to have someone who has actually been massively successful at the floor-level moving up. This way you can teach all of us how you did it. So what is your plan for teaching all of us?" She asks expectantly.

"Let me answer you by asking how your department will be different when you have more clients and up-sell to existing clients?" I take another strategy from Steve's playbook.

Again without any hesitation she answers, "Morale will be better. People will do more work because it will have more purpose to it. We will all make a lot more money, and I think we will have more pride in what we do, and our recommendations will have more relevance to our prospects because more of them will be engaged and invested in the interaction."

I pause and then carefully respond, "My plan is to help you and every other department coordinator in this Division learn the simplicity of doubling and tripling your numbers in the weeks and months ahead. And that's what you want isn't it?"

She nods her head in the affirmative as I continue. "So on a scale from 1 to 10 how serious are you about getting more clients and up-selling more of what we offer to our existing…?"

Before I could say 'clients,' she responds, saying "Twelve. I am at a twelve!"

"Okay. Then I will share one of the keys briefly with you now. You are going to get to learn how to succeed personally, and how to teach others the key foundational skills required for success in this business."

"Sounds like you have a plan and I am excited about that," Dayna interrupts. "I am excited to work with you Matt and I look forward to hearing and learning from you." She stands up, shakes my hand again, and as fast as she came, she's gone.

After she left, I relived the conversation. Talking to Dayna was actually fun, even though I am sure she was just sent to find out what the new boss was going to be like, and she knows almost nothing about me or what my plans are. But from that short discussion I know so much about her; what she wants, what her pain is, and what her level of commitment to create a different result is. And I learned this all in a few minutes of casual, curious, interested conversation. Steve must be a genius for helping me see this. I wonder if the questions I am asking are what he refers to as high-yielding questions. But I guess I will get to wait to learn that later. For now I am grateful to have what I have. And even with the limited knowledge I have now, I am seeing game-changing results."

I can't wait to get home to have this kind of insightful conversation with Ann. It occurs to me on the way home that she probably already has this skill, and unbeknownst to me she has been having these conversations with me for months. Actually that makes me smile. I figure I should reconcile myself to the reality that I have been and probably will continue to be a participant in her skill training.

When I walk in the door Ann asks, "What are you doing home so early?"

I have obviously surprised her.

"I am so embarrassed about this mess," she confesses. "I am working on a craft project, and didn't expect you to be home before I had a chance to clean up." More calmly now she asks again, "What are you doing home so early?"

I can't even wait to say "Guess what I did today. "I have some great news to share about my day. I have been talking to Steve Thoms about him doing a workshop for my team at work and today we had a great discussion about my request. He asked me all kinds of questions about why I wanted him to do it and what my goals were as you can imagine."

"Sounds like Steve," Ann interjects.

"And at the end of the conversation he told me that he wouldn't be able to do the event, but that he would teach me how to do it myself."

"How is he going to teach you," Ann asks suspiciously?

"I committed to come to the next XL-8 training with you, and teach my team the things I am learning at the local events based on what I see and hear. Then he suggested that I could get a much deeper understanding by going to the upcoming Platinum Retreat with you as his guests!"

"What?" Ann replies doubtingly. "Only Platinum's are qualified to attend those meetings and you know that I am not at that level yet. So how is it that we can go to this event?"

Meeting the speed and pitch of Ann's speech, I respond, "He proposed that every Platinum leader be allowed to invite one guest or couple on their team to attend as a promotion of some kind and his idea was accepted. He has invited you and me to come with Sara and him to attend the event. I told him that we would go, and so I'm really not asking if it's okay with you, I'm really reporting on an agreement that I made with Steve. I hope you're okay about what I did."

"I'm more than okay with it," Ann says as she hugs me. "I am so excited to go and be part of that event. This is an honor and something no one ever gets to do. I am curious though, why did he invite us instead of almost anyone else?"

Smiling, I tell her, "Primarily, because you are creating amazing results and are a rising star in his organization because you are learning, practicing, and applying his system; but also because I attributed my professional success to the principles he teaches. I want to teach it too since I have seen it working. In all reality he has a passion for helping people, especially when it comes to creating success through lasting relationships. He is impressed that I am actually using what he is teaching and this is another way he can further his passion for helping others. And guess what else I did today?"

"At this point I don't think anything would surprise me," Ann says as she sits down at the dining room table still in disbelief.

"I had the greatest conversations with people today; especially with one of my Department Coordinators, Dayna. It was so empowering to feel like I had complete control of a conversation by being curious and interested, instead of feeling like I needed to manipulate or coerce to get her to do what I wanted. It was awesome to experience real human interaction at a deep and meaningful level. I was so excited about my conversations with Steve and Dayna that I just couldn't contain myself, which is why I had to come home to tell you face to face. By the way the house and yard look awesome. You are doing such a great job handling everything here and with your XL-8 business. You are amazing and I am so glad that we are together. Is there anything I can do to make your life easier?"

"My life is filled with ease," Ann responds candidly. "We have a new house, new furniture, a cleaning lady, a landscaper to take care of the lawn, money in the bank, and I have a new car. Ease is not what I lack. The one missing element in our home is a fulltime husband and father."

I pause for a moment, then tried to explain where I was coming from: "I think I can relate to your feelings of loneliness and solitude. However, my dad taught me that it is my responsibility to provide for my family and my wife's responsibility is to provide love and warmth in the home. And that having money is a husband's trade-off for not having much family time. My dad also taught me that ultimately a husband and father must choose between money and time because you can't have both. So from my perspective it's better to have money than time. When you tell me that your life is filled with ease, I breathe easier, believing that I am doing exactly what I am supposed to do. Obviously your experience is very different from mine. What are your expectations Ann?"

"I guess I want to eat my cake and have it too, "Ann replies sadly. "I watched my mother scrimp and save her whole life so that my brothers, sisters, and I could have the basics. That kind of stress has worn my mother down. Growing up I wanted us to have more, but at the same time my dad was able to be there for us. I need a husband, and our children need a father to teach them what I can't. I look ahead and I just can't see how our current situation is ever going to change. That's why I enrolled in XL-8; so that you wouldn't have to work so hard to make money. So that we could have both time together and money to enjoy life without the stress of jobs and bosses. I look across the street and see the Thoms' and wonder what it would be like to live like they do. Steve is home as often as he wants to be, and can go and do whatever he wants, whenever he wants."

Ann is almost in tears and I can't believe I hadn't ever seen this. "How come I didn't know this before?" I ask.

"I guess we just didn't have high enough relationship PEPs to have this kind of conversation," Ann responds.

Grateful to understand her better, I say "Thank you for sharing your feelings about this. I will be more sensitive to getting home earlier and being less distracted when I am home. You know, I have had a great day. Today I had three of the most compelling conversations I can remember." We sit for a few minutes longer as I take time to rub Ann's shoulders.

At work I recognize that word is out among the Department Coordinators. Mr. Ivey's intention is to teach them something revolutionary, something they had never heard before. Most Divisions have a weekly meeting with their Department Coordinators. Typically these meetings are very long and drawn out. Not many look forward to them, and for the most part they are not particularly productive. Combined with my desire to change that dynamic, and in light of my commitment to Steve I decide to begin training my leadership group as a part of our weekly meeting. This way the assignments I will give them will be weekly instead of monthly like Steve does it.

In our first meeting, I greet each of them with a welcoming handshake and call them by name as they come in. I want to learn about each of my Department Coordinators, and by demonstrating what Steve taught me using them as guinea pigs, I can show them what I want them to do with their own team members, prospects, and clients. I begin by telling them that this meeting will be different from the meetings other Divisions have. Of course we will discuss the traditional numbers, and I will add a few other ways we need to measure success as well; but this is not only about the numbers. The numbers are a result of how good we are at certain skills directly related to, but hidden underneath those numbers. So today we are going to start off in a different way. Each of us is going to take sixty seconds to tell the others who we are and then tell us something interesting about yourself that no one else in the room knows.

You all will need to take a note or two about the others in the group. This is going to be part of an exercise later on in the meeting.

Dayna speaks up first saying, "I am from San Francisco, California. I have worked here three years and I am the first one in my family to earn a college degree."

Jaylin goes next, "I am married with two children. I am a new Department Coordinator and my husband and I met at a rodeo."

Ray jumps in enthusiastically, "I was born in Toronto, Canada. I went to college at Arizona State University and I am training for the upcoming Olympics."

Shelly finishes writing and then says somewhat spitefully, "I have worked here four years and have been Employee of the Month three times. I am the first in my family to have been born in this country."

Mylisa tells us her name and then spells it out for us. She explains, "Mylisa was my mother's way of making sure that I always knew that I was her little girl; hence My Lisa. One interesting thing about me is that I love sports cars."

Kayci, my assistant takes her turn noting, "It's very interesting that all of us have a "y" in our name. I have worked here for five years with three different bosses. Mr. Ivey is the first one who thought to take me with him when he was promoted."

Pausing for a moment before taking his turn, Matt contemplates what Steve or Bruce might say right now. Dayna's words a few days earlier help me decide to ignore the fact that I have been here the least amount of time of anyone in the room. I choose to focus instead on results and what causes those results.

"Let me start by telling you something about me that none of you knows. I proposed to my wife while she was sitting on the back of a horse." Thankfully that broke some of the tension for everyone, including me. "I started working here at the bottom of the ladder, as a floor level financial planner, and have served as each of you do, as a Department Coordinator. From this moment on we are going to do things a bit differently than other Divisions. While other Divisions concentrate on single transactional sales methods, we are going to focus on gaining repeat buyers by building lasting relationships and increasing the value of our service to our prospects and clients."

"The good news is that it doesn't take any extra effort or time to create these kinds of relationships. It takes focused, disciplined, long-term-oriented work. You may be wondering what that means. Let's begin with an exercise. Jaylin, if you could ask Mylisa anything about what she said a minute ago, what would you ask her?"

A little shocked that the spotlight is on her, Jaylin smiles and says, "I would ask why she decided to become a financial planner?"

"Why would you ask that question?" Matt responds.

Feeling a little nervous now, Jaylin says, "Because we all work at a financial services company, and she is a manager here?"

"Very interesting," I say. "Thank you for being honest and for risking a little by participating. There is nothing at all wrong with Jaylin's question. It just seems a little out of place. When Mylisa introduced herself she didn't say anything about financial planning. She talked about her name and sports cars. We need to increase the value of our service by building relationships through curiosity. Is there anything Mylisa said in her introduction that any of you are curious about?"

Dayna interjects, "I would want to know more about the sports cars she mentioned. What kind she likes and what interests her about them."

Ray jumps in saying, "I would want to know if she has any sports cars of her own."

"Excellent," I say, wanting to refocus the conversation. "Both of you chose to pursue the sports car angle. There is a lot about what Mylisa told us that we could be curious about, including her name and its meaning in her family. My point in all this is that at the core, success in our business demands that we acquire effective skill in talking, listening, relationship development and trust building. In order for us to become the model division for the rest of the company we need to help our clients succeed according to their definition of success, not ours. People need to know three things about you before they will open up and begin creating a fantastic relationship: 1) Can they trust you, 2) Are you a professional and 3) Do you care about them.

"Being curious about what they share shows them that you are listening, that you are a professional and that you sincerely care about them, all of which tend to build trust between people. Close your eyes and ponder for sixty seconds what you feel you have to offer others." After about twenty seconds I interrupt the silence, saying, "Some of you might be thinking about different products and services, and others might be considering time and talents, and how using them to serve others might be what you bring to the table. Maybe you thought words of encouragement, advice, counsel, friendship, experience, compassion, skill, knowledge, or perspective are what you offer. Whatever you are thinking, I want you to consider for just a second, the method you use to approach others as you invite them to take advantage of the features and benefits of our products and services."

"Do you jump on them, smother them, attack, cajole, manipulate, coerce, trick, or bowl them over with your enthusiasm—letting them know that you have something that could change their life if they would just listen and take action? Now open your eyes. I want you to become aware of the prospects and customers you have. I mean the ones you already know and those you don't know yet. You need to be so completely aware of your prospects and clients that they will trust you to only offer them products and service that apply to them, and you will honestly tell them how to best take advantage of those services.

"Our own effectiveness in relationship building is what makes it possible for us to share what we offer to others. Let me introduce you to the way that we measure our competence in this and every critical area of our work. We use Personal Effectiveness Points or PEPs. People with high PEPs have consistent success in helping people learn how to take a proactive role in their own lives. They do this because they build trust-based relationships. Effective communication is established when you invite and encourage others to talk about and share their hopes, dreams, problems, and challenges. The relationship this kind of interaction creates enables you to better serve them by proposing solutions that will produce the results they want or that will alleviate their pain. When you do this it motivates them to take your recommendations when you ask them to take action.

"In Mylisa's case the solution might be finding a financial strategy that will enable her to open her own sports car museum or start a race team. The thing is that from a 30 second conversation, we may not really know what her passions are. But we need to start the conversation where she begins, with what she gives us, and then go from there. If we do that she will become more proactive in the conversation and will begin to move towards us, and then with us as we recommend solutions to the challenges and passions that she does have. That is all success is: getting people moving towards you, then with you. Being interested, instead of interesting, is the success magnet that draws people towards you.

"Find out what they are passionate about, why their feet hit the floor in the morning, what keeps them awake at night. You can easily find this out by asking them what are called high-yielding questions. These are questions that require a thoughtful answer, like, "If you could change anything in your life what would it be?" Ask this question, listen to their response, and then follow up by asking "How would your life be different if you had or got what you want?" Most people will begin to really tell you what they want their life to be like at this point. Again, listen carefully to what they are saying, and then ask, "On a scale from 1 to 10 how serious are you about having or getting that?" Knowing this will enable you to actually provide recommendations that others will take action on.

"You can increase the value of your service very quickly and simply if you can be immensely curious about people. Teach prospects what our products do and don't do. Help prospects and customers understand exactly what results our products create that relate specifically to them. Then follow up to ensure they are satisfied with their plan. These are only a few of the ways to connect and build relationships, and they are all ways that let your customers know you think of them not only as a paycheck, but as a person you care about. When the value of your service exceeds their expectations, people will not only buy more from you, they will also be happy to refer their family and friends to you because you have treated them so well."

"So why doesn't everyone here do it this way if this method doesn't take longer or take more effort and you can guarantee that it will produce great results for our clients and the company?" Shelly asks smugly.

I'm glad Steve and I had that conversation about being challenged. "I don't know why everyone doesn't do it this way," I respond purposefully. "Maybe the sales guru's of the past have focused so much on closing and sales techniques that the importance of stellar relationships has been lost over time. What I do know is that for the past few months everyone in my department has been and continues to be the most productive, most profitable department in the entire company because they implemented these principles I am discussing with you today. I am pretty sure that's why I am sitting in this chair; to help teach these skills to others, beginning with you."

I conclude the meeting by asking each of them to give me their weekly report. I assure them that if I have any questions about the numbers, I would ask them individually. I also inform them that each of our meetings will usually end with some skill mastery practice assignment. This week I challenge each of you to find out at least three things about your team members, prospects, and current clients that they could be curious about. I ask them to keep a little journal and include the name of the person they talk to and what they find out about them that makes them curious. Finally, I ask them to include how they can help to increase their value of service by deepening the conversations using high-yielding questions.

It only takes a few seconds for everyone to leave. Sitting there for a few minutes alone with my thoughts, I hope they know how important this is and that they need to take the assignment seriously.

Looking through the reports it seems interesting that Mylisa's customer acquisition cost is the highest of the group. Dayna's weekly average for new account enrollments has been static for over three months in a row. Ray's customer up-sell numbers are awful and drag the whole division down. The good news is that everyone's customer satisfaction scores are at least fair. Everyone except Jaylin's, that is. And Shelly's department is the most consistent. Nothing too flashy or negative, just consistently above average and below excellent. "What can I do that might help improve my relationship with Shelly so that I can really provide value to her?" I wonder leaning back in my chair looking out the window.

What Shelly seems to be upset about is that I got promoted instead of her. I am running things. I have the spot light. She said when she introduced herself that she had been Employee of the Month three times. Maybe I need to let her be the shining example of progress. How can I do that though? A few minutes pass while I am in deep thought, and then I remember how Steve chastised me for not tracking conversion ratios, and said they are a baseline number he used to keep his finger on the pulse of his organization.

What if I invite her to be a test case department that pays attention to a number we don't currently track? As soon as I thought of this I hurry to Shelly's office to talk to her. On the way there I remind myself to be interested instead of interesting. Me being interesting doesn't seem to make her feel warm and cozy. So I need to position this new project by telling her how it will make her look good.

"Hi Shelly," I say as I knock on her half-opened door. "Do you have a few minutes? I want to run an idea past you."

"I guess I do," she replies, somewhat bothered by the interruption.

Not put off by her reticence, I continue: "Shelly, I think we might be missing an important step in our process. Do you know why I have been talking about understanding why our prospects and current clients want the results they tell us they want, and getting them to describe how their life would be different when they experience that result by taking our recommendations and advice?"

Cautiously Shelly says, "I think because you feel like we will convert more prospects to clients and more clients to lifetime partners in our book of business?"

"Exactly," I respond. "You used the perfect word in your answer, convert. However, I can't see anywhere in the company where anyone tracks conversion ratios. Are you aware of anyone in your department, the division, or the company who tracks conversion ratios of prospects to clients? It seems we keep the raw numbers, but we don't pay any attention to the conversion rates in any of the steps in the enrollment or up-selling processes. Shelly, how would your department be impacted if you could double or triple just your total new accounts in the next six months?"

"I would be ecstatic," she replies cynically.

"I want to do an experiment using your department as the test group," Matt offers. "I want you to examine the enrollment numbers each week and keep track of the individual conversion rates at each step. My hypothesis is that you will see exactly where the challenges are in the enrollment process which will give you a huge edge in focusing your department training on those specific problem areas. I will be happy to give you full credit for the experiment if it goes well, and if it doesn't then you will know for sure that I am not as good as I think I am. Will you do it?"

"Let me think about it this week and get back to you," she says, not sure if she fully believes me about the credit part.

Walking back to my office, I am feeling pretty good. This "olive branch" meeting seems to have been very productive for a couple of reasons. My relationship with Shelly feels better already, and if the experiment works she will be a greater ally. On top of all that our division is going to be famous in the company. There doesn't seem to be a downside to this.

Our next Friday meeting begins much as it had the previous week. I state that, "Our division mantra is going to be 'Building relationships is not a function of business, it's the only way to do business.' I invite everyone to take a minute and reflect on the quality of the relationships you have. Ask yourself, 'do you purposefully develop relationships?' 'Why are you in these relationships?' And more specifically, examine each of your relationships and ask 'why is this relationship important?'

"I want each of you to take three minutes with each person in the room to ask them anything you want to know about what they told about themselves in last week's meeting. Find out at least three things you are curious about the members of this team."

When the time is up I ask them if they feel their relationship is better with their fellow managers than it was a few minutes ago. I also ask what did you learn?"

Mylisa responds, "I learned from Ray that his family has sacrificed along with him on his Olympic journey, so after the Olympics he wants to visit New Zealand with his family as a reward."

"Excellent discovery, Mylisa," I remark. "And do we have any programs that could help him with that goal? If so, are they different than what you would have recommended based on what you knew about Ray two weeks ago?"

"Yes we do offer programs that would benefit him, and they are very different from what I would have recommended two weeks ago without this new information," Mylisa admits.

"So, based on those three minutes, is there some product or service we offer that you could now specifically recommend to the person you talked to, that you wouldn't have considered before that conversation?" After a short pause, I continue, saying, "Relationships mainly fall into two categories: relationships that reward and relationships that rob. Understanding the difference will save you time, effort, and an incredible amount of frustration." I then talk briefly about the nine mistakes Steve shared with the XL-8 group a few months ago that give relationships the power to rob us. Then I ask everyone to write the ones they need to work on.

At this point I think it might be helpful if we could have a discussion about what people wrote down. I ask if anyone wants to share what they wrote.

To my surprise, Kayci speaks right up, "I have at least three: Listening to the wrong people, Spending time with people who aren't or won't take action, and Not listening to what people are actually saying."

"And how has that worked out for you generally speaking Kayci?," I hear the mix of frustration and relief in her voice.

Thinking for a moment Kayci responds, "Not very well. I have received a lot of bad advice from people who have not ever been successful in life, and I have suffered many, many, misunderstandings because I thought I knew what people were saying, when in fact they were saying something completely different."

Smiling at her, I remark, "Excellent observation Kayci. Now I want to invest some time in helping all of you see relationships in a different way. I want each of you to choose a partner. You and your partner are going to be together for the next half hour." I continue by explaining the remaining Relationship Rating instructions, the full activity, and the equations for calculating the measurements with the team, mimicking Steve's example.

After that half hour, each of them look a little more humble. Especially Shelly, who apparently decided to take this exercise very seriously. Maybe she is tired of the traditional politics, and can see that I am not her enemy. Or maybe my olive branch effort earlier relieved some of the resentment she felt about me. Whatever the reason, she seemed to get a lot out of this activity. I appreciate that, remembering how much it affected me when I went through it with Steve. Like me, they are all shocked and a bit ashamed of how low their Relationship Ratings are.

I tell them that their numbers are all very similar to what mine was when I did this for the first time. I assure them that none of them are in jeopardy of being fired or demoted as a result of this information, and that no-one would know their rating. There is a collective sigh of relief, especially after I tell them that with focused effort I have quadrupled my rating and increased my department's average score by twenty-five percent in the past quarter.

I finish the meeting by asking each of them to take one minute to tell the group one interesting item in their weekly report that might go unnoticed if they weren't there to give an explanation.

Mylisa shares, "I noticed a slight decrease in my departments' customer acquisition cost this week. I think that a greater percentage of prospects became clients this past week, but I don't know for sure. I will keep an eye in this."

Dayna offers, "The weekly average for both my personal and department new account enrollments went up a bit. I don't know for sure yet, but it seems that my team members took to heart my training on value of service that you challenged us to do."

Ray declares, "My customer up-sells were dropping each week for the past five weeks, and this week they were stable. I hope we have reversed the trend."

Jaylin adds, "I wasn't sure about the customer satisfaction scores. So I did a synopsis of our customer satisfaction surveys, and found that we have the highest cumulative scores we have had in months."

Shelly completes the report saying, "You should be able to easily see what happened in our department this past week. Pretty simple really, some things are up and some down. It's the normal ebb and flow of the numbers from week to week."

It seems Shelly and I still don't have a total easing of tensions just yet, Matt thinks. Shelly does, however, leave a note on the top of her report saying; "It will be interesting to collect this data in the weeks to come."

I ask for one last item before we end the meeting. Kayci hands each of them a small piece of paper with this week's skill mastery practice exercises on it. As she does I take the opportunity to thank each of them for their diligence in their work, their commitment to do the skill mastery practice from last week, and their attention to increasing the value of the service we offer.

"This is what I would like you to do this week to practice building strong, lasting relationships going forward. First, make a plan to improve on the areas needing improvement. Second, look closely at what people or person whom you estimated you have the most powerful relationship with, and what people or person whom you feel you have the least powerful relationship with, and do a quick evaluation of a few things you might be aware of that might push people away from you and a few things that you are consciously doing to draw them toward you. Third, talk with at least one of the people on your relationship list and have a purposeful, meaningful, highly curious conversation with them. Lastly, I want you to teach the lesson I taught to you here today to at least one person in your department. You can get together with your team the other managers here and compare notes and ideas if you wish or you can just use your own notes if you choose. Share the importance of building relationships with at least one other person in your department."

To my surprise I am the first one to leave the meeting. I smile as I walk out of the room because there is a lot of discussion, note sharing, and strategizing happening. My team is discussing how they are going to complete the skill mastery practice this week. They are beginning to come together as a team. This is what Ann and Steve must feel like when they leave their meetings with their groups. It's not surprising that they get a great sense of fulfillment from these kinds of moments.

A few days later Ann and I are sitting in the front row waiting for the quarterly training session with Steve to begin. Ann has some kind of assignment for the meeting, but she won't tell me what it is. She tells me that it's a surprise. I save her a seat next to me; which is no small task. We are surrounded by her rapidly growing team. They seem to have as much admiration for her as she and the other leaders have for Steve. The announcements and preliminaries are complete and Ann comes out to edify Steve. She does a great job highlighting his accomplishments and helping us know why we should listen, learn, and implement what he is about to teach us. When she finishes, the crowd stands up and applauds energetically. Those standing around me seem to be cheering as much for Ann as they are for Steve. Steve walks out on stage, graciously accepts the admiration, and invites us all to sit down and take out our note books.

He begins by saying, "Thank you all for being here today. I know it's earlier than usual and this special training session will last a bit longer than our normal training conferences. I want to make sure that you get all that you need about today's topic in one meeting so that you can put it into immediate action tomorrow instead of next month. So let's get started, shall we?

"Success is founded on trust that is a product of good relationships. In the last conference I talked about drawing people towards you and then with you, and the magnet that makes this possible is trust. Trust is also the glue magnet that pulls people toward you, that keeps them engaging with you over the long term, possibly for the rest of your life. A strong and profitable business or organization is a result of trust built on the foundation of the effective communication of your intentions to give and share.

"People must be willing to be vulnerable in order to trust. They must be willing to put their guard down, take a chance that you will like, love, and lift them, instead of hit them between the eyes, make fun of, or take advantage of them.

"Trust motivates people to give you permission to help them. Trust is what causes them to take action when you give them recommendations, advice, or counsel. That is all that success in this business is, building trust that gets people moving towards you, then with you. People want to be around people whom they can trust and have a great relationship with.

"When you contact, present, and follow-up, help them create a picture of their life as they dream of it. If you ask high-yielding questions, which we will talk about in a later conference, and listen carefully to their responses, you can immediately create trust with people. Even a basic level of trust will make people feel comfortable and safe with you and they will begin to hope for a better life with your help.

"Here are a few things to consider about trust: A person with low trust PEPs is primarily worried about themself, is scarcity-minded, resents others' success, and is insecure, controlling, manipulative, reactive, guarded, anxious, suspicious, fearful, rigid, self-centered, and defensive. Low trust PEPpers see others as rivals and are typically more concerned with quantity than quality. Here are some phrases that low trust PEPpers use: 'It's someone else's fault,' 'It's not fair,' 'I didn't understand what to do,' 'They let me down,' 'I always get cheated,' or 'The deck is stacked against me.'

"A person who has high PEPs in trust is primarily concerned with others and their success. High-trust PEPpers are abundance-minded, secure, peaceful, sharing, supportive, open, assured, flexible, and accommodating. They typically see others as friends, they are sincere, and concerned with quality instead of quantity.

"Trust is really comprised of two parts: a feeling component, and a confirmation element. The feeling part is based largely on either positively influencing people toward us as part of providing the solution to their pain; or, we can negatively impact trust by influencing others away from us as a further contribution to their pain. When you take the emotion out of your beliefs and values, you can easily discern that people, places, and things attract or repel you in certain situations. This part of trust is a feeling of peace and confidence.

"The confirmation part is based on a track record of performance. It is the time-tested calculation of experience that confirms our trust or mistrust of people. When you do what you say you are going to do, when you say you're going to do it, it builds a track record of trust that things and circumstances will be exactly as you have promised. This confirming track record attracts not only new people, but gives staying power to the ones who are already within your sphere of influence.

"For example, I have been to hundreds, maybe even thousands of business presentations. Often I hear someone who is in 'convincing' or 'manipulation' mode say those famous words 'Trust Me!' Or they ask, 'Would I ever do anything that wouldn't be right?' When a prospect hears these things, I would advise them to carefully evaluate what they are being asked to trust in.

"If you or someone on your team finds themselves saying, 'trust me,' something has gone woefully wrong somewhere in your relationship, long before the 'trust me' moment. Something is repelling your prospects, customers, or team members. You see, it is the feeling that people are moving away from you that compels you to ask them to trust you.

"Let's take a minute right now and answer in your mind the questions from the slide on the screen. Rate yourself on your paper from one to five. One is absolutely not or no and five is completely or absolutely yes."

1. Think for a moment about whether your team members, customers, neighbors, and co-workers really trust you? Do they absolutely know that you will do what you say you're going to do, when you say you're going to do it? Remember the question is; do they believe in you? Not, do you believe in you?

2. Do your customers and associates believe that you have their best interests at heart?

3. If one of your team members came across information that was potentially damaging, would they share it with you or hide it from you?

4. Do people tell you things they would never tell anyone else?

5. Do people perform at their highest level when they work with and for you?

"Okay, so add up your score and see your own evaluation of a most critical value of service component I call your Trust Quotient. If you got between 21 and 25 your Trust Quotient is pretty high. If you scored between 16 and 21, you could use some help in building trust faster or better with the people whose names you wrote on your relationship list from the last conference. I imagine you will be surprised as you build trust with those around you, how much better your relationships will be. If you scored at 15 or below then you definitely need to increase your Trust Quotient.

"The bottom line with trust is that when you have people's trust they will tell you what is really going on, so you can work together on resolution instead of massaging egos and emotions, which only leaves the problems causing mistrust unchanged and ready to surface again. The good news about trust is that it is built rather than depleted by use.

"The Trust Quotient is as much emotional as rational, involving comfort as well as confirmation. Too many times people with low trust PEPs are focused on creating a transaction instead of a transformation. A transaction is a short-term, one-time event. But transformation is centered on building trust and is more long-term relationship focused."

At this point Matt is writing as fast as he can. He realizes this is a key to helping him increase his division's effectiveness and to improving his relationship with Ann. As a group at work Matt thinks, "We are focused on quick and easy transactional events instead of transformational relationships that create lifetime clients. I am going to use this little assessment at this week's Department Coordinators' meeting."

Steve continues. "I have created a website for those of you who want more detail on the next section that we won't have time to cover today because of the limited time we have. The website is www.RiTraining.com/ALR. Generally speaking there are two areas that create mistrust: 1) The failure to get others to articulate what they would like their life to be like based on their dreams, not your dreams for them. And, 2) are situations that I call Trust Breakers.

"The first challenge comes from the imposition of your perception of their pain on your customers rather than getting them to acknowledge their own pain in their own words. For example: if you know someone who is addicted to drugs or alcohol, you will create mistrust in them if you call them a drug addict or an alcoholic before they acknowledge it. After they tell you about their pain, then you have permission to explore the possibilities of life without these challenges. But if you begin the conversation by talking about the effects of substance abuse, they will begin to defend the very thing that is causing them pain; simply because you imposed your perception on them, instead of allowing them to acknowledge their pain as their pain, and inviting you to discuss it with them.

"The second area that creates mistrust is called Trust Breakers. These seem to fit into two major categories: Disrespect and Lying. Any time you show disrespect towards others in any interaction, it feeds mistrust. Be careful that you don't make fun of or speak disparagingly about other cultures, religions, political ideologies, genders, or people's socio-economic status. It's very hard to regain trust if you offend someone in any of these areas.

"Secondly, there's lying. Of course lying will break down trust, but there is more to building trust than simply being honest. There are very subtle ways of lying, including things like exaggerating and setting unrealistic expectations with prospects, customers, and associates. When you contact, present, follow-up and enroll people in your business, you set several expectations for the new person. You are, in effect, setting certain expectations of the product, of the compensation plan, of their up-line's commitment to them. Not to mention expectations you set about how much time they will need to invest, how much effort and money it will take for a successful business, and what to expect with regards to personal improvement.

"A second major trust breaker is, being out of integrity. When people perceive that you are talking the talk, but not walking the walk. When your words are not the picture of your deeds, you are engaged in a major trust breaker. When you tell people that our company and team are of the utmost integrity, and then you don't do what you promise you will do, people will begin to think what you are doing is speaking so loudly, they can't hear a word you are saying.

"Okay enough of mistrust. I want to shift from trust breakers to trust makers." Steve talks about how trust is often grounded in people's evaluation of your ability, integrity, honesty, humility, gratitude, and courage. That is, the more people observe these characteristics in you; the higher their level of trust is likely to grow.

He continues with a dictionary definition and reads aloud, "Integrity is uncompromising adherence to moral and ethical principles." Expanding on the definition he adds, "Trust requires some sense that you are able to perform in a manner that meets your prospects', customers', and associates' expectations."

He proclaims passionately, "The world would function much smoother if honesty prevailed. Deceit creates distrust. Some people operate on a depraved level, adhering to unacceptable standards of personal conduct, dishonesty, and corruption. Rise above dishonesty. Money is abundant and can be obtained easily enough through fairness." On a bit of a roll now, he keeps right on going almost without taking a breath. "Humility," he says, "Is the opposite of pride and arrogance. People do not trust the arrogant, proud, or self-righteous. So get rid of any thoughts that you are better than others. Gratitude is a feeling of thankfulness. And evidence of gratitude is on the decline in our society.

"People appreciate graciousness and true appreciation for gifts, service, and friendship. When you cultivate a sense of gratitude for what you have instead of what you don't have, universal powers seem to work in your favor and trust is created. The last attribute of trust making is courage. Have the courage to live a higher standard. Face difficult situations bravely. Don't be afraid of the negative events that could happen, but think instead about the positive events that can happen as your opportunities unfold. Be wise, not afraid. Building trust takes time and effort.

"Mastering the critical skills related to trust is essential and you must take some risks getting to know people and letting them get to know and trust you. The value of your service will increase exponentially when people feel your intentions are to help them and know you are there to help take their life to a whole new level."

Steve is speaking almost as if he is in a trance. He continues by referring to his earlier comment about there being two parts to trust: a feeling part that indicates trust and a performance track record that confirms trust. "Trust," he says, "Is an active feeling of confidence based on your level of PEPs in relationship building and the value of your service.

"Trust is 'developed' or 'built' over time. It can't be created or fixed with one grand gesture. So your quest for being trusted begins with you taking many small steps towards a personal and then team culture of trust. You can do this by sending cards, letters, making calls, providing customer service, accepting returns of products, giving rides to events, or doing counseling sessions."

Continuing this focus on Trust Makers, he explains, "Put Trust Makers into the same two areas in your notes as you did Trust Breakers. What I mean is, there are things that contribute to feelings of trust and things that you can do that will create a history or track record of trust.

On the feeling's side he starts with empathy. He explains, "Take the time to put yourself in the shoes of others. Too often people act and react to circumstances with very little or no information. And what you think you know is often incorrect or misinterpreted. You need to get the other person talking and listen for clues that will give context to situations. Then ask yourself how would you react if you were that person? A good dose of empathy can be a tremendous tool in your quest for building trust. Empathy is a valued currency. It creates bonds of trust, and provides insights into what others are feeling and thinking; it can help you understand why people act and react to situations the way they do without creating prejudice against or malice towards them.

"Help them find a remedy or solution that they feel comfortable with. At all costs, avoid the phrase 'trust me.' If they have challenges you can't relate to, you can't build trust by simply telling them to believe you and do what you say to do. That's what the last guy said to them and look how that turned out. And then you wonder why this person doesn't trust anyone? Be curious and help them articulate their challenge, and then make them aware that you have a solution. Give them some options for engaging with you, and ask them which option works best for them. This builds huge trust with prospects and team members because you're not forcing a solution on them that solves a problem that you don't understand or care about."

Steve shifts to the next Trust Maker which he explains is, "To adopt the philosophy that others are just as important as you are. If you have to assert that you are the leader, boss, or parent, you aren't! Everyone in your sphere of influence is a volunteer and so you build trust by inspiring and encouraging, as opposed to ordering and dictating. Trust is earned not demanded. So don't demand trust, work to earn it. Treat people as individuals – one size does not fit all. Start by making it easy for your customers to do business with you. Make sure that you remove barriers to ordering, paying, and receiving products. Some customers would rather be on an autoship or autopay program and others would not. Some prefer to pay by credit card and others with a check. Some customers are comfortable with front door delivery and some would rather you deliver the products personally.

"In order to understand your customers, find out what results they would like to create by asking high-yielding questions and then, based on your skill in listening, product and company knowledge, and compensation plan information, recommend the appropriate products or income offering with the features that will produce the success they want. Make sure to teach and train your customers to properly use the products so that they will get the maximum benefit from them.

Steve continues the list of Trust Makers that create a feeling of trust with being authentic. "The notion of 'faking it till you make it' seldom works. And in the rare case when it does work, the time and level of success are shallow and short-lived. Being authentic means to be real, to be yourself. You don't have to put on airs, or pretend. All you have to do is learn and practice success principles and then apply them in their proper sequence as you master them.

"Being authentic means to risk not appearing perfect. An authentic person will always be the work in progress they really are. You don't have to know and do everything right to be trustworthy. In fact, people will trust you more when they know you are learning and growing at the feet of a master teacher or mentor. So admit when you don't know the answer, do the best you can, and work harder to make sure that what you say you will do can and will come to pass. Relationship sustainability is based on honesty and the truthfulness of your word.

"We communicate unseen messages to others about our core principles and our character through our desires, thoughts, and actions. Our words are influenced by our motives and intentions; and our consistency in word and action is very visible to those watching. This phenomenon is called authenticity. Trust is based on your ability to be authentic. So you need to seek alignment. Bring your thoughts, desires, and actions together under a higher standard of excellence; a legendary standard."

Steve takes a moment to tell us there are just two more concepts that we can use to create a feeling of trust for people.

This next one is, "Fix problems fast and fairly. An unhappy customer will become a loyal consumer if you handle their complaint fairly and do it fast. Every day you have the chance to transform mistakes and misunderstandings into returning customers – the kind who will tell three or four other people good things about you. Imagine that. Eighty percent of these people will come back to you if you've treated them fairly, and that percentage rises to the upper nineties if you respond immediately.

"The final idea of creating a feeling of trust is, accepting responsibility. When customers have a problem and you take responsibility to fix it, they're actually going to be even more satisfied than if they never had a problem in the first place. Your customers and team members don't discriminate between you, the product, or the company. To them, you are all one entity. These simple phrases will completely change people's emotions in a matter of seconds, and turn angry, disappointed or dissatisfied customers or team members into raving fans; the kind that recommend you and your business to three or four other people. You can say, 'It's my mistake' or 'I'm sorry; it's my fault' Or 'I'm sorry; I will take care of this right away. And it won't cost you anything.' Or you can say, 'That's terrible; please tell me what happened so I can make sure it never happens again.'

"It's completely natural to have trouble accepting responsibility, especially when it's not your fault," Steve continues. "But those words are going to make your angry customers and associates much happier and much more willing to stay customers and associates. So you're going to have to learn these phrases and use them if you want a strong and profitable business. And you're going to have to mean it."

Shifting his focus to items that help create a history or track record of trust for prospects, customers, and associates, Steve begins, "Concept number one is sharing information regularly. Let people in on what you are learning from your up-line mentors, the company, and the industry on a regular basis. Success is built on cooperation, not competition. So holding on to information will never serve your business interests.

"Concept number two is to hold yourself and others accountable. Everyone, including you should have goals for the week. First of all, make sure that you are doing what you are supposed to be doing. If you are not reading, listening, attending, contacting, presenting, edifying, asking people to take action, building relationships, creating duplication, and dream building then it's easy for your team to avoid doing those things as well. Make sure to evaluate how you are investing your time, as well as recording your conversion rates. Review how well you are keeping to your plan and schedule.

"Do what you say you will do, when you say you will do it. Steve introduces the principle by saying, "You can enhance how much others regard you as trustworthy when you behave in consistent and predictable ways. Ensure that your words are in harmony with your actions, and that you honor pledged commitments. Your integrity is reinforced, and the level of trust you gain is in direct proportion to how well you keep this commitment. It is not surprising that people crave trust from their leaders. There just aren't enough people walking the walk. In fact, there are many more people pretending to coach associates how to be successful, who themselves have never been successful in this industry.

"The next to the last concept of building a track record of trust with those you interact with is to communicate with intention. Clear, concise, and complete communication will help you avoid being misunderstood and will keep you from misunderstanding others. Successful trust-building communication hinges on intention, preparation, and application. It is also influenced by the way you view people, by your desire to help them succeed, and by your willingness to prepare to help others succeed on their own terms. All of these things are critical. Of course when we move beyond the intangibles of intention and preparation we come to the application of the skills you have acquired, and the level of PEPs you have worked to acquire in your communication skill."

Steve pauses for emphasis, "Building trust is vastly different from establishing who is right. The differences are obvious in how you communicate, depending on what your intentions are.

"Lastly, in this part of the training I want to discuss the idea of performing competently. You get paid for being personally competent in the critical skills of the business. Your prospects, customers and associates will evaluate how much to trust you by your qualifications and ability to perform.

"In summary, success in all areas of life is founded on trust embedded in good relationships. In order to build a strong and profitable business you must become effective at gaining trust. To do this you should focus on quickly increasing your Trust Quotient. You must eliminate trust breakers and purposely engage in trust makers that attract people to you and then with you.

"Of course you will want to build trust with everyone you meet. And most importantly you will want to ensure that you develop a high level of trust with those who are where you want to be. Your business will absolutely explode if you develop trust with people who have already succeeded. Having a trusting relationship with those who can give you advice, input, and counsel based on personal experience; who also have a vested interest in your success, is vital to the success of your own business. This kind of trusting relationship will propel your business forward faster and with less frustration."

Looking at the time Steve recognizes that his time for this session is gone. "There is so much more I have to share on this topic, but I know that your mind can only absorb what your rear end can endure. So after a short break, I want to complete this topic. Please take twenty minutes to take a short walk, stretch, check your messages and possibly begin improving your relationships by having a meaningful conversation with someone. We will begin on time in twenty minutes, so please be in your seats and ready to begin at that time."

Ann's team gathers around her to discuss what they learned. They ask her about her experience on the stage. She replies, "I think I will have a better idea of what this is all about after the next session. We only have a few minutes to visit the restroom and walk around. Let's discuss this at dinner, or after the evening session. I think we all need a moment to digest everything. This is Steve's strategy of taking a break. So let's take advantage of it."

Author's Note:
There is the mathematical equation in the appendix at the end of the book for this chapter.

5

Warning Labels

As usual, Steve starts right on time. Without any introduction he calls the business conference to order and without skipping a beat, jumps right into the training. He begins, as he always seems to, with a question: "What if *people* came with warning labels? We've talked about value of service, relationships, and trust. With those topics as context, let's look at warning labels. Most people go through their entire life without ever reading a single one; however, they are on every type of package from food to power tools. Becoming aware of labels has made me more aware of things hidden in plain sight, like the really small, unreadable print on medication bottles, and the people who talk really fast at the end of new, life-changing prescription medications.

"When I began to examine this 'oh-by-the-way language,' I was surprised at what I found. The side effects often seem to be worse than the pain they claim to relieve. So, as I was thinking lately about warning labels in general I began to wonder 'what if people came with warning labels?' What if you and the people around you came with a warning label? Can you imagine?

"Warning: this person may trigger irritation, inflammation, nausea, and vomiting. Side effects may include volatility and feelings of insanity. Continued use has been known to cause self-loathing, anxiety, and prolonged bouts of depression. If these symptoms persist, seek professional counseling immediately."

Matt notices that the energy in the room immediately changes. There is suddenly a lot of shifting around and squeaking of seats. A few chuckle out loud, but the uneasiness is undeniable. The implications of this question had a visible effect on many, and again hit me between the eyes like a two by four.

"Think about it," Steve continues. "Go back and look at the relationships list you made a few months ago and ask yourself, 'If they had come with a warning label: Would it have made a difference or been a deal-breaker?' Would you have even taken the time to read the label? Or, like me, would you perhaps have overlooked it until the results of that relationship made the warning label 'writing' move from 'the fine print' to graffiti on a public wall. Would you think then that maybe there is something about the warning label that is now a big red flag?' And even then, would it have made a difference?

"So what does any of this mean for you as a business owner? In keeping with the importance of relationships, and the critical nature of the value of your service to others, I ask you this; 'If you came with a warning label, what would it say? We are going to take a few moments now and go beyond theoretical consideration of this question. I invite you to take out a piece of paper and write your own warning label. Because none of you have probably ever done this before, I am going to give you a structure for the warning label and an example of what this might look like. Warning labels include four parts: 1) A main warning, 2) Side effects, 3) A 'continued use' statement and 4) follow up, or what to do if people experience any of the symptoms of your warning.

"There is only one rule for this exercise: you can't say something like 'Warning: working with me results in massive success.' This is not an advertisement or a features and benefits statement about how wonderful you are. This is intended to help you see yourself as others might. I want you to look at yourself through the eyes of others. One of the most positive things you can do from time to time is to assess areas where you can improve. The only way to do that is to take a close look at your personal relationship blemishes so you can make adjustments and improve the quality of your relationships and the value of your service.

"You may never have contemplated that people who engage with you might need to be warned about some kind of short or long term trauma that might occur by being around you, or that there could be any side-effects associated with your relationship at all. But if you search your memory, you will find experiences that indicate you have pushed people away from having a personal or professional relationship with you. Think about your high school days, church service, college experience, professional career. Examine your past and present relationships.

"Now, as you write you must focus on the causes of why your relationships either work or don't work. Don't look at the relationships themselves or judge whether they were or are good or bad. Just look at what those relationships are, without prejudice and without placing any kind of value judgment on them. I encourage you to really take this to a deep level so that you can identify anything that might be holding you back in your relationships. Each of us has something that is causing your relationships to be less than they could be. The good news about this assignment is that you all will be able to support each other and improve individually and collectively."

Steve gives us thirty minutes to complete the assignment, and he strongly encourages us to be back on time, in the room, and ready to resume within that timeframe. This comment gets a pretty good laugh from those who remember the previous incident. He takes a moment to see if there are any questions, then with a commanding voice announces, "The time starts now!"

The room immediately turns into a beehive of activity. I find that Steve is creative in the way he gets people to think about the foundational elements of powerful relationships. I don't think I have ever contemplated that people around me might need to be warned about possible short- or long-term trauma that could be associated with our relationship.

Ann and I climb the steps to the stage and sit on the chairs reserved for presenters and leaders. We move the chairs so that we are facing each other, and use our knees as a table for our notebooks. Ann seems lost in her own thoughts, and we sit quietly for a few minutes.

Almost in unison we look up at each other and suddenly Ann asks me, "Are there things you have discovered about me since our marriage that you wish you had known before we got married?"

At first I think that I really don't want to fall into this trap. If there is anything I have learned after years of marriage, it's to avoid questions that have no possible 'right' answers. After a brief moment of reflection I realize that I don't need to dodge this question. I shift my focus away from me and concentrate on what she is really asking me. I discover that this is her way of asking me to help her with her warning label. I reach out and grab her hand, and looking directly into her eyes I say, "You have to do this assignment without my input."

I stand and take a short walk around the room in an attempt to get my mind working. Then Ann and I decide to go for a walk outside together. It's too cold to sit outside, so we walk to the car in the parking lot. There it will be quiet and we won't be interrupted.

As I sit in the car, searching my memory for experiences where I have pushed away or offended people, I go back to my memories of high school, then my ranch and college experiences, and then my professional career. I examine my past and present relationship with Ann, and my relationships with my team at work, then turn to my relationships with my dad and Ann's family. I think deeply about those who became clients of mine at work, and those who didn't.

I search for reasons that people have chosen to move towards me and then with me, and jot a few of them down as if they are comfort food; they really are a buffer against the other memories that I have of being ineffective at building trusting relationships. Then I explore the relationships that haven't worked out as well as I had hoped. Using my relationship list, I start with the people with a number of six or less by their name. I stop to ask why these relationships aren't better.

I am saddened to realize that some portion of the blame for relationships gone bad rests squarely on my own shoulders. This feeling worsens when I understand that often I don't care about people as human beings as much as I care about what they can do for me. That thought is amazingly distasteful, but I begin to think that I actually do this. Then it occurs to me that the assignment isn't supposed to be depressing or a chastisement. It is just a starting point. I turn my thoughts to the cause of my relationships either working or not working and stop judging myself for where they are; believing that understanding the truth about them gives me an honest place to begin making adjustments.

I feel a little better as I begin to write my warning label. I remember that Steve said, "Knowing is always better than not knowing," and begin to write. I begin to feel that identifying these issues could help me change the things I am warning people about. When I reconcile myself to the fact that there are things about me I might need to warn people about, and then allow myself to identify what those things might be, a feeling of liberation washes over me. I think I just put myself in a position to become better than I have been.

Ann and I take turns reading our warning labels to each other. Mine reads,

"Warning: May cause intense emotional responses, repulsion, and offense. Side effects may include chaos and misunderstandings of critical details, inappropriate recommendations, and ineffective action steps. Continued use has been known to cause a feeling that results are more important than the people who create those results, side effects include: a prolonged disregard for feelings and differing opinions. If these symptoms persist, look for a mentor with whom you can foster a close relationship."

I look up at Ann as I finish, and the look on her face is astonishing. She can hardly believe what she heard. "Aren't you being a bit hard on yourself?" she says.

I reply, "I wanted to really take this to a deep level so that I could identify any blocks that might be holding me back in my relationships. I noticed that you rated your relationships better in general than I rated mine, so I figured there must be something causing that result. I wanted to dig really deep to see what it might be. So what does yours say?" I ask this question more to change the subject than to find out what it actually says.

Ann clears her throat as if this was going to be a theatrical performance,

"Warning: May cause profound feelings of abnormal safety, comfort, serenity, tranquility, and harmony. Side effects may include extreme desires to ignore facts and evidence that change is necessary. Continued use has been known to cause detrimental conflict aversion to the point of escalating discord due to inactivity. If these symptoms persist seek out my husband."

We both chuckle at the last line. We talk about being able to see our relationship barriers more clearly once we look specifically for them. Matt is really impressed. What a great exercise. The good news about this assignment is that now we can support each other and improve individually and with each other.

When we return, the doors to the auditorium are open. As soon as I walk in I get a sense that almost everyone invested a large amount of emotional energy on this. Not as many people are laughing and joking as there had been this morning. In fact, those that are talking are almost whispering to each other. Everyone is back early. Everyone is in their seats before Steve returns. Steve walks out on stage and smiles broadly. Somehow he seems energized by the sober nature of the participants. It feels like the energy in the room is exactly what he hoped to create with the exercise. Thinking back on the events of his training series, each section seems now to be a carefully laid plan.

Steve gets our attention by playing some music from the movie Lost in Space, which ends with the words from the robot, "Warning; Danger Will Robinson, Danger." The music is upbeat and the mood of the room improves. Steve asks us, "What did you learn from the exercise? What are your comments, observations, and insights? Would anyone like to read their warning label for us?"

It's silent for an uncomfortable amount of time, and so Steve interrupts the quiet and jokingly says, "The first question or comment is always the hardest so we will skip the first one and go on to the second." A man from a few rows behind us chuckles and says, "I am now more aware than ever that no one is really listening to me and that I am creating part of this inaction. I am so focused on short-term results that only benefit me that I never create long-term results that benefit everyone. I need to improve to increase the value of my service to my team by teaching them how to learn, practice, and apply correct principles in their proper sequence. My warning label says:

'Warning: May cause increased desire to ignore counsel, advice, or input. Side effects may include prolonged inactivity due to confusion and disorientation. Continued use may result in the denial of resolution, or relief of pain. If these symptoms persist seek out another source of inspiration or regular contact point.'"

Steve thanks him for his honesty and willingness to appear less than perfect. Then a woman in the front row shares, "I need to make sure to set realistic goals with customers and associates. I have been guilty of exaggerating product and income expectations, or allowing others who exaggerate those things to go unchallenged. I realize now that I am not helping anyone and that 'continued use', has been known to cause conflict and increased fallout rates." Here's what my warning label says:

'Warning, may cause the desire to set un-realistic goals and expectations. Side effects may include exaggerating actual results of product performance, income receipts and value of service. Continued use has been known to cause trying, testing and stressful relationships leading to accelerated dropout rates. If these symptoms persist ask for specific evidence that demonstrates the validity of claims, assertions and promises.'"

"Thank you for sharing," Steve continues. "These are amazing examples of what we can learn if we examine the results we create and the circumstances of our life in a non-judgmental way. These are incredible insights and clarity. The good news is that now you can take action to correct these challenges.

Having challenges doesn't make anyone bad or wrong. But doing nothing about what we know is holding us back denies us the chance of ever having the life we really want.

"Now please take three minutes to write down what was easy and what was hard about this activity."

Immediately Matt thinks that focusing solely on a bottom line breaks trust, hinders relationships, and lowers the value of his service. Ann writes, "It was easy to think of things that keep me from immediately connecting with people. It was really hard to reconcile that having a relationship with me may have side effects, and it was painful to think that there might be long-term or continued-use issues that could require professional treatment." Looking at Ann's notebook as she is writing Matt considers what she has learned. What a great observation. No wonder she has a higher quality of relationships than I do.

Steve breaks the silence by asking us to stop writing and close our note books for a moment. As soon as he has everyone's full attention he asks, "What have you learned from today's training, and how do you plan on putting it to work in your business with your prospects and team members?"

Christina, the woman Ann referred to earlier, and one of her Silver-level leaders, speaks right up saying, "We can fuel a revolution of success if we are willing to improve our skills in relationship building by uncovering people's pain and writing appropriate prescriptions that relieve that pain. We need to connect the dots in each circumstance for how XL-8 provides what they so desperately want."

Ann follows Christina with confidence, saying, "At a fundamental level, success is based on reaching down and lifting others up. In the past few months I have learned at least four ways where I can improve so that I can provide better and more valuable service to them. I am reminded of a quote from Mark Twain that says 'Only a life lived for others is worth living.' People who have skill and knowledge are needed to help the poor, the needy, the uneducated, and to recognize and assist those with great hope and aspirations of greatness but who have little opportunity to realize their own potential as human beings."

A woman sitting directly behind us declares, "Being able to calculate the quality of my relationships has been very valuable over the past months. Now that I have this information, I have even more work to do. However, I can begin to eliminate my warning label issues and improve the relationships that I don't feel are as strong as I would like."

A woman from the right side of the room stands and adds, "I learned that I have a warning label and that people pick up on it whether I am aware of it or whether I ignore it."

As she sits back down there is a moment of silence. Steve allows it to be quiet for a short time, letting the significance of the moment sink in. In the silence, I feel the need to share, "As an outsider, I originally felt like I should let everyone else share. Now I am beginning to think that an outside opinion might lend some additional credibility to the comments and training. It is so clear to me now that enrolling people in XL-8 or my business, or in any aspect of life is a result of trust rather than some sales technique.

"I see that trust is what motivates people to take action when they are asked to. People have to feel that we are there to help them, and we must also build a track record of performance that supports that feeling. When we do that, people will trust us, and they will freely tell us their concerns and challenges because they believe we can really help them resolve their issues and move them towards their goals. I also learned that we need to really focus on creating transformations instead of transactions."

Steve smiles, claps, and nods his head in agreement, then interjects, "That last comment comes from a man who is very successful in the financial services industry. So you see, these principles apply to more than your business. When I say they apply to all areas of life, I don't mean only your business life. They apply to everyone you meet and talk to in all aspects of their life. That means that how we approach our business may help people in all aspects of their lives, whether they participate with us or not. That means we bring to every relationship the goal to help people become the kind of person God meant them to be if they can grow into the kind of person others will listen to and follow. Thank you Matt for standing for something!"

Returning to address the whole audience Steve changes the subject a bit, "I also want you to know how much I appreciate your insights, observations, and comments on the training series. I use your feedback as a measurement of my own success, working toward a 'legendary' standard rather than a minimum standard. Tell me what you are remembering from this training."

A voice comes from the front of the auditorium, "I always judge my performance by what I think the Legends in our industry would do in any given circumstance."

Another voice from the back of the room says, "Showing up may be half of success, but showing up with a high value of service and showing up on time mark the difference between success and failure."

A woman from the front row stands up and faces all of us, waving her arms wildly as she exclaims, "We are enrolling people in their life by helping them take a proactive role in creating the results they want in their life."

A man from the right side of the room shouts, using his hands like a megaphone, "Success is simply getting people moving towards you, then with you, being interested instead of interesting."

One of Steve's leaders sitting in the front row shares his insight, "When people are done talking to me or engaging with me, can they do, think, say, or be anything positive that they couldn't do, think, say, or be before they interacted with me? Do people grow as human beings as a result of their relationship with me? Are they healthier, wealthier, wiser, and freer? Do they have an increased ability to serve in their circle of influence as they interact and associate with me?"

Before he calls on the next volunteer Steve interjects with great passion like an auctioneer, "These are excellent comments."

Then Sally Whitman, the woman Ann had partnered with a few months ago in one of Steve's workshops says, "There are only two kinds of relationships that reward and relationships that rob. Understanding the difference will propel me towards success. And I can manage and arrange my relationship portfolio."

Sally's husband and my partner from a few months ago follows right behind her saying, "I learned that trust is comprised of two parts. The feeling part is based on influencing people to move toward me because I am part of the solution to their pain, instead of pushing them away from me and becoming a further contribution to their pain. I also learned that trust and life long relationships are built on a track record of performance."

Steve thanks us all for sharing and applauds us for being authentic by acknowledging that we are not perfect and that there is much to learn. I am becoming increasingly aware of Steve's power as a speaker. He communicates with such clarity and depth of conviction it's undeniable that he believes the things we learn from him are critical elements to massive success.

I am focused, at this point, on internalizing what I believe is an incredibly powerful and liberating method of creating success. It makes me believe in a vision of success at any level. I am struck by how critical great relationships are to success. According to Steve, relationships are critical to success in everything in life. Caught in my own thoughts I become uncertain about the word "everything". Everything. Everything? I need more time to consider the scope of this statement.

My mental tangent is interrupted by Steve giving us an assignment to complete during the dinner break. He makes sure we know to pick up an assessment that will help prepare us for tonight and for the rest of our lives as professional relationship builders. He directs us to have it completed by the time the evening session starts, and not to wait to work on it during the recognition portion of the evening session. He enthusiastically excuses us for the break.

I take a deep breath, look at Ann as I wonder what this assessment is about. My experience with tests is limited to high school and college. I also remember the Personal Effectiveness Profile assessment reports that I have seen in Ann's folder. They seem to help her know which particular skills she needs to improve. My head is about to explode with new insights, ideas, and observations. I am not sure I can handle anything more. But my curiosity about the "test" helps me get up and take on this newest challenge. Ann's team members are so engrossed in making sure they can complete the assignment that they don't mob her in the aisle of the auditorium or in the lobby!

Ann and I pick up our assessment and head for the car. Neither of us really wants to start it. For my part, I know that the assessment is going to reveal something about me that needs to be improved, and I'm not sure I want any more scabs picked today. I already feel pretty bruised and bloodied. But when I was a kid I knew I had to eat the lima beans before I could leave the table; this is sort of like that. I start psyching myself up for the challenge once we get to the car.

Ann is a little quicker to investigate the assessment. As we drive down the road to dinner, she is already reading it. She isn't writing answers yet, but she is reading to get an idea of what it is and what it might mean. When we are seated in the restaurant, I wonder why I'm not getting that sinking feeling I used to get as a kid when I was avoiding homework I didn't want to do. Instead I actually feel excited to work on this assessment to see what it uncovers and how it might apply to my relationship with Ann, my team at work, and my climb up the corporate ladder.

The instructions say: "Read each question carefully and thoughtfully, then circle the most appropriate answer for your circumstances. Please be honest. This is NOT a test; it's a snapshot of how you currently feel about the topic of each question."

1. 1. When do you share your knowledge, skill, or wisdom with others?
   A) never   B) sometimes   C) frequently   D) on a scheduled basis   E) immediately
2. Are you the main source of information, advice, and counsel for your team?
   A) always   B) sometimes   C) frequently   D) as a last resort   E) never
3. Do you offer to help people, secretly wishing they will never call?
   A) yes   B) sometimes   C) regularly   D) depends on circumstances   E) never
4. When people call you on Saturday morning and ask for your help that might last the rest of the day, what do you do?
   A) make an excuse and not go   B) chastise them for calling on late notice   C) see if you can help them later in the day   D) reluctantly go and put on a happy face   E) willingly go and cheerfully work
5. What is your track record of consistently doing what you say you're going to do, when you say you're going to do it?
   A) I seldom do it   B) I sometimes do it   C) I frequently do it   D) I often do it   E) I always do it
6. How would your customers and associates rate you in regards to your having their best interests at heart?
   A) Cares more about him/her than me   B) Cares more about completing meeting than hearing what I want   C) ignores my circumstances   D) makes me aware of solutions to my challenges   E) Listens, proposes appropriate solutions, and asks me to take action

7. I hear people say they are telling me things they would never tell anyone else.
   A) never B) rarely C) sometimes D) regularly E) often

8. Do people perform at their highest level when they work with and for you?
   A) never B) rarely C) sometimes D) regularly E) often

9. Do you answer questions by asking questions to gain further understanding?
   A) never B) rarely C) sometimes D) regularly E) often

10. When talking with people, I ask them what they understand rather than assuming they understand.
    A) never B) rarely C) sometimes D) regularly E) often

11. During conversations I formulate my response or reply while the other person is still talking.
    A) never B) rarely C) sometimes D) regularly E) often -Backwards

12. If five of your associates, friends, or family members were asked to rate you on your effectiveness as a listener, which answer below best reflects what they would say?
    A) doesn't pay close attention to the speaker B) is easily distracted during conversations C) hears some of what is being said D) can repeat what was just said E) fully understands the words and meaning of what is being communicated

13. You adjust your language, questions, and presentation style to allow for different kinds of people?
    A) never B) rarely C) sometimes D) regularly E) often

14. When you ask people to make decisions and take action, do they do it?
    A) never B) rarely C) sometimes D) regularly E) often

15. How enduring are the relationships you build?
    A) conditional B) temporary based on value I receive C) stable for a few months or years D) strong and powerful E) life-long.

16. You call key team members to ensure everyone has information about upcoming events and business-building opportunities and other important information?
    A) never B) rarely C) sometimes D) regularly E) often

17. I focus on creating satisfactory solutions to others problems even if it doesn't help me in any way.
    A) never B) rarely C) sometimes D) regularly E) often

18. You follow up with your customers and team members to find out what their experience has been.
    A) never B) when there is a problem C) sometimes D) most of the time E) 100% of the time

19. I see people as a means to achieve my goals.
    A) I see everyone as a customer B) I see everyone as a business partner C) if it is to be it's up to me D) my goals can't be achieved without others contributing , E) I achieve my goals only when they achieve theirs

20. When I see people, I see them as
A) a way to accomplish my goals B) people with money to spend C) potential team members D) undervalued/unappreciated E) people with needs and wants that I have a solution for

21. When I talk to people, my focus is on helping them express what's missing in their life.
A) never B) rarely C) sometimes D) regularly E) often

22. Think of the last ten people you had a conversation with. While you were talking with them, what were you thinking about?
A) what you liked least about them B) whether you would introduce them to your family, friends, and neighbors C) what you liked best about them D) what amazed you about them E) what activities you would like to do with them

23. How often are people interesting to you?
A) never B) rarely C) sometimes D) regularly E) often

24. Do you allow your beliefs and values about people support others to achieve their goals, even if you disagree with their beliefs and values or the goal they are working for?
A) never B) rarely C) sometimes D) regularly E) often

25. What is your motivation for sharing XL-8 with others?
A) to make some money B) to get my products and service for free C) to save the world one person at a time D) to create job-dropping residual income E) because everyone should take advantage of the products or income offering of XL-8

Now that you have completed the assessment please add up the total number of responses that you made that were A's. Then repeat for B's, C's, D's and E's.

Total Responses	Points
A's___1___	___1___ (2)
B's___1___	___2___
C's___6___	___18___
D's___6___	___24___
E's___11___	___55___
Total___25___	___100___

Now calculate the value of your service. To do this:
1. Multiply the total number of A's by 1 and put the total points you received in the second column.
2. Multiply the total number of B's by 2 and put the total points you received in the second column.
3. Multiply the total number of C's by 3 and put the total points you received in the second column.
4. Multiply the total number of D's by 4 and put the total points you received in the second column.
5. Multiply the total number of E's by 5 and put the total points you received in the second column.
6. Finally, add the points you entered for each response type and put the total on the bottom line of the right-hand column. This is a numerical measurement of the value of your service.

After completing my assessment, I calculate my score and share with Ann, "I got a ninety five. What did you get?"

Ann smiles and replies like a kid, "Looks like I beat you again. I got a one hundred and two."

Not surprised that Ann is still better at this, I ask, "So what does that mean? There doesn't seem to be a way to find out what the points mean. Does this score mean I am good at something for a change? Or is this more bad news in terms of my ability to create long lasting, positive relationships?

Of course, there are no further instructions, and neither of us know what the numbers mean. I'm kind of mad. "This is not fair," I announce to everyone in the restaurant, "I don't want to wait to find out what this means and how to interpret it."

Ann just smiles and says reassuringly, "I am sure that Steve has something in store for us tonight to help us interpret the numbers."

"Aren't you even a little upset about being left in the dark about this?" I respond, still a little anxious.

Eagerly, Ann answers, "Nope. I am really pretty excited. The fact that Steve is making us wait means that this is going to be powerful. I know Steve well enough to know that if he wanted us to know right now what the results are, he would have given us a way to find out. I figure he wants to be able to work through what it all means together given a particular context. I am sure he will do it tonight. So you should probably just relax, and let Steve explain in his own way."

When the evening session starts and we get through the music, introductions, and announcements, Steve appears and begins the recognition portion of the meeting in typical fashion. I find this odd. He must know that the suspense of not knowing what the test results mean is affecting everyone.

Is he really going to wait until after the recognitions are complete before he lets us in on the secret? Just as Steve announces the winners of the first award, he is interrupted by a woman towards the back of the room who angrily shouts out, "What about the assignment? Aren't we going to discuss it at all? What does it mean? Why did we hurry to get it done before this meeting if we aren't going to discuss it right now?"

Steve cracks a little smile, just before he takes a drink of water while listening to this woman's concern. Somehow he knew someone would ask this question, so he doesn't seem annoyed or surprised.

"I was hoping to wait until the recognition part of our meeting was over," Steve offers. "But since you ask now, I will give you a glimpse. Please tell me your name."

"Alexandra," she responds.

"Alexandra, thank you for speaking up and asking this question. By the raise of hands, is there anyone else who wanted to ask or thought to ask, but didn't?"

My hand is one of the first in the air.

"For those of you who raised your hand, why didn't you ask? What kept you from getting clarity on this? It took someone with sufficient courage to stand against convention and speak out to resolve her confusion. So for that I give you full marks Alexandra.

Let me ask a simple question, Alexandra, do you and I have a relationship?"

She answers, "Yes, I suppose we do."

"How would you rate that relationship in this moment?" Steve asks.

"I think it's about a four or five," she says.

"I think I would agree," Steve responds. "My final question about our relationship is, do you think that your approach to this issue has drawn me closer to you or pushed me away from you?"

"Well now that we are discussing this it seems like we are farther apart than we were when we came in this morning," she replies.

Steve nods his head in agreement and tells her, "I applaud your desire to speak up. It is your method that has created the additional separation." Looking at Alexandra directly while motioning to the whole audience, Steve asks, "Why do you think I had you take the assessment?"

She responds defensively, "Based on my experiences with these conferences, it could be that you needed more ammunition to make us feel inadequate, or that you use this as a tool to drive home the point that we are not perfect and that we need to become more than we are now."

Acknowledging her emotional response, Steve asks a woman named Susan sitting on the front row what she thinks? Susan responds almost as if her answer is a question, "I think you want us to really connect with our beliefs and values about people?"

Steve turns to Tony, one of his leaders sitting on the stage and asks him, "What do you think? You've been coming here for many years. You've heard me speak many times all over the country. Why do you think I had you do this assignment?"

A little surprised by the conversation being turned on him, Tony responds, "In all the times I have heard you speak, I have never done this activity before. I don't yet know what your purpose might be, so I am left with two possibilities: Either the lesson is different for everyone of us, and we will be left to discover for ourselves what it is; or I should ask a clarifying question to find out more. On a roll now, Tony elaborates as we might expect a business leader to do. "From what I have learned in past conferences from you and others is that all will be known in due time. So I'm not too worried about understanding the importance of the activity. I have been in many training sessions with you, so I understand that you will tell us when the time is right; whether that's now or in the future."

Steve shakes Tony's hand turns back to the audience and says, "These are all interesting answers. I like Tony's the best and so let me continue the lesson by telling you a story. Whenever I speak around the world to audiences for XL-8, other direct selling companies, and even in companies outside of our industry, I always ask associates why people should buy, enroll, or engage with them. In fact, if I could have one wish it would be to teach every prospect to ask this simple question: 'Why should I get in with you?' The most common answer is something like 'because we have revolutionary products, a solid company, the best compensation plan and a really successful up-line.' These are very interesting answers, but they have nothing to do with the actual question: 'why should I engage with you? Remember that the customer does not differentiate between you, the product you share, and the company you represent. The single, biggest determinate of success is you. You are the magic. You are the reason most people engage. It's you that people are buying into.

"So what does this story have to do with anything, and why did I have you take that assessment and complete it before this meeting? Because whether you know it or not, whether you want to recognize it or not, prospects are asking themselves who are you and why should I care? They are asking 'what value do you bring to my life, dreams and passions?'

"Most associates, when pushed for an answer to the question, say something like 'because I can help you make your dreams come true.' Of course, the follow up question from the prospect to that response is, 'How do you know that?' 'What evidence do you have to support that position?' Some in XL-8 will even go so far as to say that they have access to the 3-step success pattern that creates predictability in the industry. That's a better response, but a system is still not you! As a prospect I would continue to ask, 'Why should

I follow you?' Most people hem and haw and never really give much of a compelling answer. Here's how I would answer this question:

"Why me? Because I have eighty-three PEPs, a relationship rating of 74, my Trust Quotient is 25, my value of service is 115, and my conversion ratios are better than 60%, 60%, 90%. And because of those factors, I can teach you how to take full advantage of the 3-step success pattern that creates predictability and to optimize our pay plan. I can actually help you play a proactive role in your life and create a life that you can be passionate about. That's why me!"

"Yeah, but I teach my team to have fun," Alexandra calls out defiantly. "They don't care about all those numbers. Figuring all that out takes too much time and distracts us from going out and sharing XL-8."

Steve smiles more broadly as he says, "As the husband of one of the most fun-loving women in the world let me tell you that she cares deeply about what I just said. In fact, lets invite her to tell you herself. Sara, please share some of your feelings about fun, details, and numbers."

"I would love to," she says standing up from the seats just behind Steve on the stage. "Let me ask all you women a question. When do you have the most fun? At work, grocery shopping, making dinner, doing the laundry, vacuuming floors? Those are not fun things to me. I would prefer to volunteer at my kid's school, be the room mother, volunteer at the homeless shelter, go to lunch with my friends, and pursue my greater causes and higher purposes. It's fun for me to be able to send my children to camps and attend their activities, no matter the time or location. I enjoy helping them pursue their likes and develop their talents. And if I want to write a $1,000 check to my favorite charity, I don't have to ask Steve. If I want to take the leaders in our group to Las Vegas for the weekend, we can go without worrying about cab fare or tipping the maître d'. If our kids want to have a pool party they can do it.

"The thing that makes all that fun possible is that when Steve shows up, no-one questions whether or not the business works. This happens because he has high PEPs, a high relationship rating, and the value of his service is off-the-chart high. In fact, his very presence does the teaching. When he takes action, the result is one hundred percent predictable. Nothing is left to chance. I often wonder why more people don't experience this kind of life. The answer always comes back to the same thing: because their answer to the question, "why me?' comes out as a plea to trust them.

"I wouldn't enroll with someone with low PEPs, a low relationship rating, and a low value of service, would you? The good news is that if you have a verifiable answer to this question, people won't ask *why* they should get in with you, they will ask how to get in with you! And that's when the fun begins."

Leaning back in his seat momentarily looking up at the ceiling Matt thinks, "Wow, I think that was the best two minute education I have ever had.

I have never considered that people might be asking themselves, 'why me?' That concept coupled with Steve's response to the question 'why me?' and Sara's bottom line observation about avoiding people with low scores are a critical lesson to learn for all my relationships."

Steve thanks Sara for sharing her perspective and asks all of us, "Does that answer your questions about this activity and what it means?"

No one offers either an affirmative or negative response. I think most everyone is caught off-guard by the simple, straightforward, truth of Sara's speech.

Steve continues, "This activity, like all the others I have shared with you are critical if you are building your business on purpose, with purpose. If you are okay with chance and luck, then you probably don't need to worry much about all this relationship stuff. These exercises and activities are only important in the context of taking meaningful action to create a predictable result. This is a relationship business, and you are the single, most important determinate of success. Now you know how to evaluate your ability to build relationships and be successful by measuring factors like PEPs, Relationship Ratings, the Value of Service, Trust Quotients, Conversion Ratios and other factors.

"The good news is that when you know your strengths and weaknesses you can take specific steps to improve, so more people will take the actions you recommend. You will touch more lives with our products and income offering, and you will make more money. That's what you want isn't it?" The silence in the room is deafening. The stillness signals for Steve to transition to the recognition portion of the evening.

Steve invites his leaders to come up and begin the recognition ceremonies. During the remainder of the evening, three of Ann's team members are promoted to the third level. Now she has four people in her organization who are at the same level she is. Sara lets Ann put the new Silver promotion level lapel pins on her new leaders. She also has seven team members reach the second level in her compensation plan. Another sixteen earn a promotion to the first level. Ann is, in fact, duplicating herself and teaching her team to do effective work. She has over sixty PEPs, a team of over one hundred Associates, and about forty-five customers. She has six team members who are consistently working and being promoted along with her. She is well on her way to joining the Thoms' at the Platinum or top level. I love that she's now earning about $4,000 per month. That's more than I made when I started as a financial planner right out of college. It's a good thing, too, that baby is getting closer and closer to making her entrance every day.

On the way home, Ann is very quiet. Lost in her own thoughts, she is feverishly writing in her planner. I have to ask a couple of times what she is writing before she realizes I am even talking. My question about how she is going to implement today's training for her team brings her back to reality.

Recommendations to help team grow faster!

"I'm going to have a weekly PEP call for everyone in the 'Improve Yourself' phase, and a separate call for everyone in the 'Build a Team' phase, and a third call for everyone in the 'Become a Leader' phase, so we can improve skill and knowledge in places that are critical to the phase that person is in. I think we can get several months' worth of training done in one month if we divide it up like this because the only information they are getting is specific to where they are.

"Then I plan to change the way I do my weekly trainings. I am going to begin each training meeting with some segment of relationship-building activity and then segregate the team into different groups, based on the success pattern phases and play the Residual Income® Game using the scenarios from the book RIGged For Success. Next, I am going to have personal coaching and counseling calls with the leader of each leg to help them take the most appropriate action, and work with the people who are committed to progress. Finally, I am going to focus more on creating transformations instead of transactions by increasing the teams' overall scores in PEPs, Relationship Ratings, and our Value of Service, all of which should improve our conversion ratios to at least 60%, 60%, 90%."

Pausing briefly she continues, "There must be a reason Steve invited you and me to the leadership retreat. My goal while we are there is to learn all I can about improving my skill level in developing relationships. I am hoping that this is what the leadership retreat is for: to learn how to fully implement how to have better relationships through increased value of service and higher Relationship Ratings. How are you going to implement this on your team Matt?" she asks me as we pull into the driveway.

Sitting there in the quiet of the car Matt eagerly replies, "I am going to start by sharing this training with my directors over the next few weeks in my weekly training meeting. I am going to continue to track their results each week as well. It's the only way I have of evaluating whether they are implementing these principles and teaching their team members as well. I have an especially challenging woman on my team named Shelly. She is a lot like Alexandra; independent and boisterous. My goal is to make her the biggest convert to the things Steve has been teaching us. My bet is that when she sees what I see, she will be the biggest advocate of relationship building as the cornerstone to financial planning in the whole company. I am also excited for the leadership retreat. I am hoping that I will learn the deeper lessons of how to start and develop meaningful relationships there."

Author's Note:
The instructions explaining the mathematical equation for this chapter is in the appendix at the end of the book.

6

PIKing the Lock

The time arrives for the leadership retreat. Ann finishes checking off the last item on her list just as Steve and Sara pull into the driveway to pick us up. Our bags are stowed safely in the trunk and now we are headed for the airport. Steve is in top form as we drive. He asks us what we are most looking forward to and what our conditions of victory are.

Needing clarification, I ask, "Conditions of Victory, what does that mean?"

Steve replies, "It means, 'how will you know if going to the retreat was worth your time and energy?' Most people call conditions of victory goals. But my experience is that people don't like 'goals' because they generally don't accomplish them so I made up a different way of saying the same thing so that people can respond to it and allow themselves to succeed."

Ann jumps in saying, "I think our overall goal is to learn all we can about improving our skill in developing life-long relationships through meaningful interactions. Do they talk about those kinds of things at these retreats?"

Steve, looking at us in the rear view mirror, explains, "What excites me most about leadership trainings is that no one holds back. The presenters assume that everyone is there to learn deeper lessons so that they can spread the gospel of success to their teams when we return. This particular retreat is focused on how to create relationships that influence people toward us instead of away from us. There are going to be fantastic leaders from XL-8 presenting and a special guest instructor: a world renowned expert on communication and human interaction."

After a long plane ride we arrive, retrieve our luggage, and check into the hotel. Steve and Sara leave to attend meetings intended only for leaders at their respective promotion level. Ann and I go for a swim and sit in the Jacuzzi for a while. It's nice to relax, but I am getting more and more anxious by the hour. What is this training going to be like? I wonder. And what did Steve mean when he specifically mentioned that the presenters don't hold back at all? It seems to me that he doesn't hold back in his trainings. Back in our room overlooking the mountains, I wonder how this educational journey can get more intense than Steve's meetings as I drift off to sleep.

The morning hasn't come fast enough for me, I think as I get out of bed. I spent the entire night tossing and turning in anticipation of the events of the day. I am reliving the training meetings, sitting next to Ann, listening to Steve, and praying that I will be able to apply his lessons and move up the corporate ladder. I remember my first promotion and the feeling of exhilaration of being appreciated for a job well done. I relive my most recent promotion and Bruce telling me that I was promoted essentially because I had mastered the skills Steve taught me.

I can't stop thinking about my clients and team members, and how they are counting on me to learn all I can so that I can truly help them. I agonize a bit over all the people who haven't let me into their lives yet, wanting to share my offering as a solution to pain I knew about or could feel when I talk to them. I have so many vivid memories of learning and growing while I have been climbing the leadership ladder. And the prize of that success is definitely worth the price. When the wake-up call comes, it is a welcome end to a sleepless night.

I hurry Ann as she gets ready to leave. She reminds me that no matter how early we leave, the meeting is still going to begin at the same time. When we get to the meeting area there are only a few people there. I wonder for a moment if we have the right time for the meeting. It seems weird that a leadership meeting for a multinational company with hundreds of millions of dollars in annual sales doesn't have more people than this. Jill, the woman at the registration desk asks us our names, I can tell that she is having a hard time spelling our last name so I spell out Ivey and then tell her, "Matt and Ann Ivey."

She remarks, "You must be new leaders in the company."

"Why would you say that?" I ask.

She responds, "Only the new people show up this early."

"Our instructions say that registration begins at 8:00 AM and the event starts at 9:00."

"Yes that's true," Jill agrees. "But it's only 7:45." She makes a check mark by our names and hands us name tags and a package. She gives us directions to where the first presentation is going to be held and sends us on our way.

The meeting room seems really big. Especially considering how many people were at the registration desk just now. The room looks like a stadium. There are several levels of seats arranged in a semi-circle rising above the speaker's podium so that everyone can see the presenter, projection screen, and white board. We find a seat towards the middle on the second row. We are the first to arrive, so we have a few minutes in the room by our selves.

Opening the package and taking out the agenda, I discover that today's first speaker is going to be the President of XL-8, Orson Flint, and later on someone named Olivia Vigotsky will be speaking. From her biography I read that she teaches people all over the world how to successfully build strong organizations through powerful relationships developed from meaningful interactions. The last section of the agenda includes the schedule of webinar presentations available, beginning with David McKay next month and then Glenna Hanks as the second webinar speaker. On the plane ride, Steve shared about XL-8's investment in a new video conferencing and teaching system. I wonder how well it works. If it's really good, I want to know how they did it so that I can implement something like it at my work.

I am so engrossed in reading the agenda, contemplating what Olivia Vigotsky will teach, and reading class descriptions that I have been completely oblivious to the fact that the room is filling up with people. I completely miss that Steve and Sara have come in.

Sara remarks, "It's so cool that Mr. Flint is here. This is a special treat. He doesn't usually do these events because of his travel schedule but he asked to be involved in this training for some reason."

Looking at Sara, I joke, "It's probably because he knew that we would be here."

Laughing, Sara shakes her head in disbelief and jokingly tells me, "You can think that if it makes you feel good."

A man comes to the podium and calls for everyone to take their seats so that we can get started. It's the Director of Marketing at XL-8, Mike Black. The meeting begins as all XL-8 meetings do, with a prayer and a call for all military veterans to stand and be recognized for their service. Mike then welcomes all of us to the leadership retreat and makes the usual announcements of bathroom locations and cell phone silencing. Mike continues by reminding us that when we began our careers in this business we enrolled in a lifetime personal improvement program. This retreat is an extension of that commitment. He details the agenda for the next few days and points out the locations of rooms for break-out sessions. He asks if any of us have any questions and lacking any response he introduces the President of XL-8, Mr. Flint and then turns the time over to him for his opening remarks and personal corporate welcome.

When is finishes his remarks everyone stands and applauds. As he climbs the steps to an empty seat towards the back of the room he announces, "I will be participating as a student along with you during the conference, and as such, for the next few days in the training please call me Orson and treat me like any other participant in the training." He then points to Mike Black as a signal to him to take it from here.

I can see the shock on Mike's face, who has probably never heard Mr. Flint allow anyone to call him by his first name. Mr. Flint seems very formal to me. Mike quickly regains his full composure and declares, "This kind of access is very rare. I encourage you all to take full advantage of this opportunity and get to know Mr. Flint. I, I, I mean Orson," he self corrects.

Mike moves forward saying, "Today we are going to focus on how to create meaningful, rewarding relationships that last a lifetime. We are going to get to learn from the foremost communication and interaction expert in the world. Her attendance here is the principal reason that we agreed to let guests come to this event. Orson wants all of you to learn from her, and I, personally, love to sit at the feet of a master and learn from her the skills and knowledge that make success possible. So without further delay, let's welcome Olivia Vigotsky."

She runs in from the side of the room directly onto center stage to the sound of a loud, appreciative and prolonged applause. Smiling widely she thanks us and invites everyone to be seated. "Let me start," she begins, "By saying the title of my presentation is not misspelled. The reason it's spelled in this non-traditional way will become clear as the day goes on. But before we get too deep into my lesson, let me set the stage with a story of a society of people desperate to connect with each other, but enduring massive cultural barriers to fulfilling a most basic need, human interaction.

"At first the community starts with the idea that feelings should not be shared, and that except for the very closest family and friends, people should be kept at 'arms' length. Then the culture moves emotionally even further away from each other with the advent of a global communication network. People begin to cocoon, and live within the walls of their homes. Actual human interaction with people outside their personal circle of influence becomes rare. This society then deteriorates further, building walls and layers of walls around the cocoon to insulate and protect them from the dangers of reaching out to others. What do you do with this culture, when one of the most basic needs we have is human interaction? So this society has a cultural dilemma: they have built a cultural interaction barrier to keep people away, but still have this human need for interaction. My friends, the community of my story is US! It is the world we live in today.

"This is why most people today are closed off. Real human interaction and real relationships are under attack. Think about this for a minute. Never in human history have we had more ways to communicate with each other, and at the same time we say less that's meaningful than ever before. Cell phones, instant messaging, email, texting, land lines, and video conferencing are everywhere, and everyone has access to most of these methods of communication. We live in a global village and yet as individuals we are withdrawing more and more into our own cocoons. Sadly, unlike caterpillars, we don't seem to be preparing for a grand metamorphosis and escape as new and changed characters. Instead we are building thicker and taller walls around our cocoons. We are fortifying ourselves against any possible entry by other human beings.

"The dilemma is that we are designed for human interaction. So our challenge is finding ways to penetrate the fortresses that we meet everyday in the form of family, friends, neighbors, colleagues, and people we don't know yet. The underlying question is, 'How do we gain entrance into people's lives so that we can actually help them achieve their divine purpose?' The truth is that we must learn to PIK the lock that bars entrance to the relationship gateway of those we know and those we are yet to meet. So today we are going to learn how to PIK locks.

"No I am not going to turn you into burglars. You are going to learn to PIK the lock that safeguards people's relationship gateway, enabling you to open the door to their life by gaining permission to start developing a relationship with them. PIKing locks in this case is spelled P.I.K. And it stands for Personal Interaction Key. Everyone has a preferred way of looking at the world and processing information, and everyone has a preferred method of interaction that they feel comfortable with. People protect themselves and safeguard their private life by locking the doors to their personal relationship gateway. The cynic that stands as a sentinel to the lock of their life is charged with keeping the world at bay. That cynical sentinel's job is to resist unwanted information and interactions; to sift the good from the bad. And because the overwhelming tenor of messages we receive is negative and laced with foul communication, the sentinel filters almost everything out. In fact, we have been carefully trained to ignore and disbelieve almost everything we read, hear, and see. A very small fragment of information is even considered by the gateway guard as safe and relevant.

"In order to get people to interact with you, you must get their sentinel to at least grant you access to the lock of the relationship gateway. Your job is to help them open up to you, to want to be responsive to you. You are a bit like a locksmith. Your goal is to find out how people want to be interacted with. Each person has a different lock that requires a unique key with distinctive teeth. To be successful you need to quickly decipher different clues so that you can PIK their lock, open the doors, and begin to develop, maintain, and strengthen the relationship. Without the correct key, the professionally trained sentinel will dismiss you with out argument.

"Identifying your prospects' Personal Interaction Key, and adapting your language and presentation approach to allow for the unique ways that people want to be interacted with, greatly increases the chances you will be heard. When you speak to people in the way they like to communicate and use terms they know and understand, it gives you credibility and builds trust quickly. This is NOT a method for determining a person's personality type. There are hundreds of books and training programs that discuss personality types. As interesting as they are, they only scratch the surface of understanding people, to say nothing of gaining access to their life and building a meaningful relationship through appropriate interactions. PIKing locks is a critical skill for anyone who wants to increase their Relationship Rating, Trust Quotient, Value of Service Score, PEPs, or eliminate their warning labels.

"I will start off by talking about the four general types of Personal

Interaction Keys and then will detail how to quickly identify each Key type via some simple observations you can make. We are also going to practice talking to, sharing with, and inviting a person of each Key form to take action in a way that will best serve their unique situations and circumstances.

"By the show of hands, how many of you are ready to begin working on this incredibly powerful skill?" Every hand in the audience shoots up. "That is awesome," she replies. "As we say often, that your brain can only absorb as much as your backside can endure. So let me give you a few instructions and an assignment before we take a fifteen minute break. First, one important part of relationships is looking out for each other. You can do this during the break by helping everyone return on time so that we can get right to work. And for the assignment, each of you must ask at least two people you didn't know before this retreat why becoming a professional lock PIKer is a requirement for success in their life. The break starts right now."

Ann heads directly for the restroom while I stop a man named Barry, who I assume is from Canada because I overheard him using the uniquely Canadian term 'Eh' during an earlier conversation with another associate. Barry also pronounces the word 'about' differently than most Americans.

Just to be sure, I ask him whether he is from Canada so as to eliminate any possibility of being wrong in my assumption.

Barry responds saying, "I live a few hours north of Toronto."

Then I ask the required exercise question, "What do you think of the concept of lock PIKing?"

"If it works as well as Olivia says this could be a huge differentiator between our teams and every other competitor we face. Being able to teach this concept to our team members should accelerate our growth by leaps and bounds."

In the interest of time we acknowledge that we still need to find another person to connect with, and shaking hands we split up to have our second conversation and time enough to visit the restroom before class starts again.

I learned from Steve awhile back that we certainly don't want to be late. Just then Ann comes back into the room looking as if she had already completed the assignment. I ask her if she is already done, fully expecting her to say yes.

She smiles, teasing me and then confesses, "I haven't talked to anyone yet. I wanted to make sure to be the first to the restroom so as not to be late coming back to class."

Laughing, because I had been thinking the same thing, I say, "Steve has certainly made an impression on us." I turn around just as a man named Lazaro is coming down the stairs, heading for the front of the room.

He asks if we can walk and talk while we make our way to the restroom.

I agree and ask him, "Where are you from?"

He answers with a very thick Spanish accent saying, "I am from Tegucigalpa."

"Tegucigalpa," I reply. "Isn't that in Honduras?"

He nods in agreement and then informs me, "I was one of the founding associates in XL-8 when they expanded into Honduras."

We shake hands, I welcome him to the US and then simultaneously we ask each other why we think PIKing locks might be a critical skill in our businesses. We both laugh. I answer first.

I tell him, "If I understand this correctly this should help us talk to more people, more effectively, and convert a higher percentage of prospects to customers and in your case associates."

He asks, "How did you get all that from what Ms. Vigotsky said?"

I reply matter-of-factly, "She said PIKing the lock would help us to get people to be more open to us, to share what they really want in life. She also said that we will then be able to adapt our language and presentation approach in a way that connects the dots between the life they have now and the life they could have if they engage with us."

Lazaro is impressed. "Wow," he says, "I think I must be missing something as she is talking. Let's talk more at lunch or later today about what else you are understanding."

When Olivia calls us to order, she asks, "What did you learn by talking to your classmates?"

Orson shares, "I learned that being able to identify how people want to be interacted with appears to be a great idea. But none of the people I talked to seem to have a clue as to how that would actually happen."

Tracy accentuates that point, saying, "I don't believe that we can really do this! It seems much simpler to just be curious and ask questions to get people to open up and talk. I talked to Sara Thoms and she has a very easy-going, natural way of talking that seems to effortlessly encourage everyone to talk to her. So how would it even be possible to teach that to anyone?"

Olivia smiles and explains, "Effective communication is the ability to transfer ideas from sender to the receiver. If you were to speak in German to a person who understood only Spanish, your message would not be received and your ability to help that person would be greatly diminished. Understanding what drives and motivates people helps you fulfill their needs, and consequently they will follow your advice, recommendations, and call to action like they would follow the pied piper! If you couldn't learn this, only a few people could be successful. The good news is that anyone can learn how to do this.

"Generally speaking, there are four different Personal Interaction Keys or Key for short. The next few minutes will be a basic overview of each. In order to keep this discussion simple, we will focus on identifying and communicating with the predominant Key of an individual under normal conditions.

"Identifying the correct Key is the most essential step of the whole relationship process. Without the right key, no communication technique, presentation style, or closing script will work to produce the result you want. To help you with the identification step, I have developed a picture set for you to see in your mind's eye. You won't need a formal test or assessment. Instead of using colors, animals, words, or letters as labels, I use the metaphor of automobiles so that you will be able to see not only what general Key category a person fits into but also what specifics are needed to crack the personalized lock of each individual. To do that you need to become a master locksmith. The car line up looks like this: There is the Sports Car, Minivan, Pickup Truck, and Hybrid.

"When I first started to describe these four types of cars and the specific differences between them I pictured how a person resembling each type would approach life in the context of participating in a house building project. Speedy Sports Car-type people see themselves as the boss or the person in charge of making decisions, and as such would be running about from one appointment to another, barking orders at each of the contractors and designers. The Minivan-type person would want to make sure that the color schemes are warm and inviting, that the landscaping is pleasing and beautiful, and that there will be space for everyone to feel comfortable. They would want to put a three-dimensional model of the finished project out in front so that everyone could experience what the finished project will be like. The Minivan would love to put those little scratch and sniff patches on the landscape parts of the model so that everyone could smell what the house would smell like in the neighborhood. The Pickup type would be about the work of actually building the house, bringing tools, supplies, and materials to the building site. The Hybrid person would be managing the details of the project. They would be tracking things like timelines, budgets, scheduling, inspections, and the like.

"A major concept you should all consider is that no-one is any one type. Everyone is some combination of the four instead of being all one type. But people often have a dominant or preferred way of being, and their life experience has helped them to adapt to include at least one or more other types that become dominant depending on the situation. In most situations they will operate from their dominate interaction perspective, and that's the Key that will get you through the relationship gateway. However, there are circumstances where people will exhibit their secondary way of being. For instance, a person who is predominantly Sports Car and secondarily Minivan will make sure that everyone has a vision of what the project is supposed to look like when it's completed, and that everyone has their proper assignments, and will make sure that everyone is having the mandatory fun in the process!

"As we examine each of the Personal Interaction Keys, remember that there is a three-step process to correctly identifying the kind of person or Key you are interacting with: 1) See, 2) Hear, and 3) Trust. First, and most important, you must stop judging people based on your own preferences and personal experiences. You are going to want to really tune into and trust what you see and hear. Observe facts and your personal observations instead of your preferences. Don't get hung up on 'she is really pretty,' or 'he's really handsome,' or 'I really like or dislike your house, outfit or accent'. Those are preferences, and they only serve to distract you from PIKing the lock. What you need is an acute awareness of the facts that are right before you. I liken this focus to tuning in to a specific station on the radio. If you find just the right frequency and get the best possible reception so there is not any variance at all, then every subsequent decision or action can be trusted, based on this initial attention.

"Let's begin with step one: 'what can you see?' As you begin your interactions, look at the general surroundings of the person you want to interact with. This is kind of an 'environmental awareness' check-up. If you are in their house, observe whether it's spotless, neat, or a bit disheveled. Are there pictures on the walls? Are they arranged in specific ways? Are they hanging straight? Are they dusty? If you are not in their environment, look more specifically at them, individually. Notice the way they are dressed. Are their clothes well-tailored? Does everything match? Or are they casual and comfortable? Watch their eye movements, gestures, and posture. Do they look up, down, or straight across when they talk about their passions or their past? This is like making fine adjustments to the frequency on your radio.

"Step two, 'what can you hear?' What words do they use? When you ask them a simple question like 'where are you from,' tune in and listen to how they respond. Do they paint a picture by saying, 'I'm from a pretty little town in southeastern Washington that sits against the Blue Mountains.' Or do they give you the precise details saying, 'I am from Blythe California, right on the California, Arizona border on the Colorado River, 223 miles east of Los Angeles and 152 miles west of Phoenix, Arizona.' Do they talk about how hot it is in Blythe and how people only go out at night and congregate at the community swimming pool? Do they give an approximate answer— something like 'I am from southeastern Washington?'

"If your radio is finely tuned you can immediately begin to determine what their unique Personal Interaction Key is. It is so much easier to get them to tell you more by being interested and curious, as you should have been learning in your training meetings for the past few months. This is why being curious and interested is critical to your success. Without the information you gather from seeing and hearing, you are left to guesses, chance, and luck, like trying to hit the bulls eye on a dartboard you can't see. Think of the city of Las

Vegas. Who do you think wins at the game of guesses, chance, and luck, the casino owners or the patrons? If your desire is to be successful in this business, and you determine that success is based on relationships and duplication, you should consider burying your old guess, chance, and luck strategy, and adopt a predictable pattern that enables you to build trust quickly, that helps people open up their life to you, and that invites them to move toward you and then with you.

"The last step in the process is trust. Once you have determined what their key is you must trust your observations and proceed with boldness to communicate your intention to give and share. Wavering will not serve you or them. They need to know three things about you to fully engage with you: can they trust you, are you good at what you do, and do you care about them. Once they know these three things they will engage with you and follow any recommendations you make because they feel you give them a vision of what they really want and are there to help them create that result. If you waiver in your approach, you signal to them that you are not trustworthy, that you are only mediocre at what you do, and that you are more concerned about your needs than theirs. If you have ever been in a non-English speaking country you know that even attempting to speak the local language allows people to respond much more readily to you because you are using an approach that most closely relates to their way of thinking, seeing, hearing, feeling, and being.

"Now that you know the three underlying principles to PIKing locks, let's examine each of the Personal Interaction Keys in more detail. In your notes you will need five sections for each Personal Interaction Key with these labels: General Description, Identification, Talking to, Asking to Take Action, and Encouragement, Recognition, and Rewards. These specifics are like the individual teeth of the personalized key that will allow you to unlock the relationship gateway for every person you meet. We will start with a general description of each, beginning with the Sports Car.

General Description of the Sports Car.

Olivia reminds us, "No one is all of any one type, and everyone has some characteristics of all four types. About thirty-two percent of people are Sports Cars. They think that everyone wants to be like them. They view themselves as the star of the show, the shiny example the one who gets things done quickly, where others can't. Getting the job started and finished is one of their primary concerns. To a Sports Car, their mission in life is making sure that everyone knows what the vision is for the completion of any project, and making sure that assignments are made to get the work done.

"Sports Cars are a positive force in our world because they feel tremendous gratification and value from getting things done. They assertively and swiftly deal with problems and tasks. Sports Cars tend to be fast-paced, task-driven people, who thrive on the challenge of problem solving. They are quick decision-makers and are impatient with shortcomings in themselves and others, and they have an opinion on just about everything. They don't wait to be given authority; they take it. Sports Cars make decisions quickly, frequently without sufficient information to make educated decisions. They arc interested in making or being the difference. Sports Cars view the world visually, in models or pictures. They trust that images are an effective basis for decision-making.

"The attributes that hinder Sports Cars from making positive contributions include speeding around, often without having a detailed plan of how to accomplish the work. Sports Cars often run roughshod over others. Getting the job done is more important to them than the needs of the people who are doing the job. Protecting relationships and peoples' feelings are not high priorities for them. They are outspoken, even when their opinion is not requested. Sometimes their self-confidence comes across as arrogance. They don't see how or why rules apply to them, especially if the rules are hindering the work. To a Sports Car, the rulcs apply to everyone else, and are there so that everyone else will stay out of their way. They are often competitivc, blunt, outspoken, restless, aggressive, and even defiant. They don't care about details. They have a short attention span."

General Description of the Minivan.

"About thirty-one percent of people are Minivans. They need to be with people. They are active, friendly, outgoing, relaxed, and optimistic. They want to include everyone in the group, and the more, the merrier. They wouldn't want to exclude anyone from participating with them. They are called 'people-people' because they love to talk, and they are always inviting others to stop by and visit.

"Minivans are a positive force in our world because they belong to the 'fun' group; they are the huggers and the party people. They are enthusiastic, entertaining, and they love to help others. They will take pain-staking steps to make sure that people do not get their feelings hurt or feel left out. A Minivan's primary goal is to make sure that everyone is enjoying the journey. Joy and relationships are always more important than getting work done. Being liked is important to them. They get their work done by making allies with others in amiable environments. They are fast-paced, and because they talk to everyone they are well-connected and highly influential. They usually have BIG goals, BIG dreams, and BIG ideas. They are eager to please and agreeable. They have lots of confidence and lots of friends.

"The attributes that hinder Minivans from making their most positive contributions are that details are completely lost to them. They often forget or ignore objectives and goals. They lose their cars in parking lots, and can't remember where their keys, phone, and other items are. Their desire to be liked and accepted can hinder their ability to ask people to take action for fear that the request will offend someone."

General Description of Pickup Trucks.

"About twenty-one percent of people are Pickup Trucks. Pickup Trucks are the 'worker bees' in every organization. The team doesn't function without them. They 'clean up' behind Sports Cars, and create clarity for Minivans. Their ultimate reward comes from actually getting projects completed. All they need is a plan and some resources and they will get the job done. They don't like change, especially change for the sake of change. They depend on listening or hearing to get the information they need to work. They love to have sound, music, or some kind of noise in their environment. Details about process are critical to their thinking, to their work, and to their decision processing. Knowing "how" is the critical question for them.

"Pickup Trucks are a positive force in our world because they know how to do the job; they know what systems will support their initiative and how to implement them. They create predictability through effective and precise process development. They move at a controlled, deliberate pace. They are great schedulers, and like to slow down and take time to ensure efficiency and effective use of resources. The contractor's saying 'measure twice and cut once' is their motto. They gather facts and create a plan of action before they make any decision. They are in control of their emotions, are patient, and they are good at listening to people and calming others when they get upset. They are best at getting along with many different personal interaction keys. They have high job security because their bosses know they can do their job well, get the job done and get it done with precision. They are comparison-oriented. They focus on cause and effect, meaning they understand if they do A, then B, then they get result C. When they read books or listen to audio programs, they plan out strategically how to implement the information they are learning. They take the hours of reading and listening that they do and put the highlights into bullet points for implementation into an existing process or procedure.

"The attribute that hinders Pickup Trucks from making the most positive contribution include a slowness of making decisions. They like to gather all the facts and figures before making a plan before they take action. This sometimes creates a situation where they have taken too long to get work done."

General Description of the Hybrid.

"About sixteen percent of people are Hybrids. They are concerned with precision, accuracy, and excel at complying with rules and regulations. They are cautious, calculating, well-disciplined, and extremely logical. Hybrids are cautious decision makers. Their mission is to be correct. They want to be right and set standards of 'rightness' that are almost impossible to achieve, and are not really necessary in established procedures. They depend on listening to get the information they need to work. They love to have tempered sound, soft music, or some kind of gentle noise in their environment. When they read books or listen to audio programs, they can tell you what page number each concept is on. They plan out strategically how to implement the information they are learning. They also take the information from their hours of reading and listening and put the highlights into bullet points for cross-referencing and indexing.

"Hybrids are a positive force in our world because they are good at focusing on the tiniest, most minute details. They take painstaking measures to make plans that comply with rules and established processes. They move at a controlled, deliberate pace. They are great planners, and like to slow down and take time to think. They gather facts, make lists, and do complete analysis before they make any decision. They are in control of their emotions and are patient. Details, quantifiable facts and figures are critical to their thinking, to their work and to their ability to make decisions. They want to know exactly what result they are planning to produce, so that they can determine what resources they will need in order to create that result, and how long it will take to accomplish it.

"The attributes that hinder hybrids from making the most positive contribution are that they focus on doing things in the right way, so change causes them great anguish. They analyze the situation and create the perfect solution. Because they pay inordinate amounts of attention making sure that every task is in its proper sequence, change unravels their plan and their certainty that the plan will be correct and complete. This is incredibly painful for a Hybrid. Furthermore, a Hybrid's primary concern and ultimate goal is having a correct, detailed plan. In fact, having the plan is more important than the completion of the project or accomplishment of the goals and objectives that their plans detail, so getting finished doesn't always happen."

Olivia pauses, "Okay, now that you know something about the different Personal Interaction Keys, how many of you think you know what your Key is?" Almost everyone raises their hand. Then she asks us, "Did you identify at least one person you know in each Key category as I described the four types?" Again almost every hand goes up. Then she instructs us to "Turn to the page in your notes where you wrote your relationship list from past conferences. The one where you rated your relationships with the people you know." The rustling of pages is pretty loud and almost immediately people begin talking to each other. She invites us to, "Take five minutes and put an abbreviation beside each name on the list, indicating what PIK Category we think they are in: SC for Sports Car, MV for Minivan, PT for Pickup Truck and HY for Hybrid." The room becomes silent as fast as it had become noisy a few minutes ago. It's weird how fast the sound level in the room can change. When the five minutes is up she asks, "How easy was it for you to put people into a general category based on nothing more than the general Key descriptions?"

A man from the back shares, "I think it's pretty easy to do, and now I can see that I have approached many of the people on my relationship list in ways that probably push them away instead of getting them to move towards me."

A woman exclaims, "I am sure in many cases, based solely on the general descriptions, that if I had a couple of clues to look for I might make better assessments of how to talk to people. I also agree with the first man that my relationships have probably suffered because of my inability to communicate properly with people."

The woman sitting next to Ann says, "I am pretty sure I have sabotaged many of my relationships because I talk with everyone as if they are like me, with the same interests and ways they want to be communicated with."

Olivia thanks those who shared and tells us, "The next few minutes might change our relationships for ever. We are going to discuss and practice identifying the clues, signs, and hints that would help us accurately classify people." To the second woman who responded, Olivia offers some consolation saying, "You didn't know what you didn't know, until now. And so from today on, you can tune your radio and make more precise adjustments to improve your relationships with people."

"Let's invest a couple of minutes talking about another part of the Key making process; the forging of distinctive teeth for each key. This begins with identifying people in each different Personal Interaction Key category. As I said before, there are three things to keep in mind as you identify the kind of person you are interacting with: 1) What do I see, 2) What to I hear, and 3) I must trust the information I gather." Gesturing at Tracy, Olivia continues, "This is how you begin to implement the idea of lock PIKing so that you can really tune into people and discover what they really want their life to be like. In your packet there is a picture of a car radio. During the next few exercises you might want to carry it with you as a reminder that you really need to tune in to who the other person is and what you need to do to quickly gain access to their inner-most feelings, creating a strong and powerful relationship."

Identification of Personal Interaction Keys.

"Identification should be the second section in your notes for Personal Interaction Keys. It should be directly after the General Description of each category. To make the notes easy to maintain, I will talk about them in the same order as I did earlier, starting with the Sports Cars.

"The ability to identify Sports Cars, or any other Key starts with 'What you can see in a general way'. Primarily, Sports Cars hate a mess. If you can see their desk, yard, house, car, or planner they are clean and well-organized. Everything has a place and everything is in its place."

Steve interjects with his personal experience saying, "When I visit people's homes I ask to use their restroom. The Sports Car's bathroom will be clean and organized. Towels will be hung in place and soap will be in a soap dish, and the mirror over the sink will be clean."

Shaking her head and slightly annoyed by the interruption (by a fellow-Sports Car) Olivia continues, "Once you have taken a general look at the environment, move on to what you can see more specifically. Sports Cars are well groomed, their clothes match, and they pay attention to looking good. Finally, when you are talking to them, watch their eye movements."

Steve can't resist this either. He says, "I ask prospects about the first car they ever owned, or what they would do if they could change anything about their life? Then I watch their eyes. The Sports Car will look up and to one side when remembering the car, and up and to the other side when describing the change they want to create in their life."

Olivia thanks Steve again for his help, and then asks him to get her a glass of water. He disappears into the foyer. She now can continue uninterrupted. "Sports Cars look directly at you while you're speaking. You can also easily identify a Sports Car by reaching out to shake his or her hand. They will face you straight on and hold their hand out as far from them as possible. They need some space between them and you. They aren't being rude, they just want to be able to see all of you.

"The last clue to pay attention to is 'what can you hear?' Sports Cars talk really fast and often they will finish your sentences for you. They are task-oriented and focus on getting things done. They are completely aware of the things they have to do, and the problems they face. They can always tell you what's wrong with things and people. They have an opinion about everything, and they are happy to share it with you whether you ask for the information or not. They rely more on vision than physical touch or hearing.

Identifying Minivans.
"Identifying a Minivan begins again with 'what can you see?' Environmentally, Minivans are a bit slobbish when compared to non-Minivans. They are completely oblivious to the fact that there is a mess everywhere around them. They leave stacks of clothes, mail, and papers all over the place. If you can see the top of their desk, it's probably a miracle. Their yard, house, and car are not well taken care of. If they have a planner it might be a set of post it notes left around their work space. There is no apparent order to anything. To use Steve's restroom trip from a few minutes ago, the Minivan's bathroom would be a mess. Everything that should be in a drawer or cabinet will be on the counter. Towels will likely be on the floor, and they use the same bar of soap for washing their hands as they do for bathing. It might be a bit difficult to see the mirror through the muck.

"Specifically, what can you see? Minivans are not too concerned with their dress and grooming standards. Their clothes won't necessarily match, but they will be loose, comfortable, and probably made of soft cottons. They are fond of big jewelry that they can feel. Minivans who are women like big earrings and pendants. They might take their shoes off right in front of you. Finally, ask them a question, and watch their eye movements.

"Ask them about their first car, or what they would change about their life. Pay close attention to the eye movements they make before they answer. The Minivan looks down and to one side when remembering the car, and down and to the other side when describing the change they want to create. The Minivan often looks down while you're speaking.

"You can also easily identify a Minivan by reaching out to shake his or her hand. They will be eager to shake your hand, but they won't extend their hand very far. They want you in their space. They will move close to you. In fact, sometimes they move in close enough to touch you. They might even give you a hug if they are at all acquainted with you. They have no sense of other's personal space. They aren't being rude, they just want to be able to touch you. They slouch when they sit, and are often hunched over when they are standing. They can't stay still. Some part of their body is always moving: tapping fingers, fidgeting feet, or bouncing knees. They rely more on physical touch than vision or hearing.

"And lastly, for identification purposes, 'what can you hear?' Minivans talk a bit slower than a person with a normal cadence. They use air that comes from the bottom of their belly, and it takes more time for that air to come to the top. Usually they talk with a softer voice that is lower and airy. They focus on people and their feelings more than on getting things done. They never speak negatively about others. They are always looking for the opportunity to turn every event into a party."

Identifying Pickup Trucks.

"Beginning with step one, general observations, you will find that Pickup Trucks create arranged chaos. Items in the bathroom and kitchen that are being used or will be used again soon, will be left out. But they will be arranged in a particular order so that they can be used according to the proper sequence. For example, if they are right-handed and brush their teeth first after showering, followed by drying and combing their hair, then putting on their makeup, then the toothbrush and toothpaste will be closest to the sink. To the right of those items will be the hair dryer and the hair brush, and still farther to the right will be their makeup. The makeup will be arranged in the order it is applied as well. They may have knick-knacks displayed on tables or counters, but they will be in a particular order, something like the chronological order that they were purchased or made. Pickup Trucks love to be recognized with letters of commendation and with awards. These will be displayed with pride; they will be clean and arranged in a particular order.

"More specifically, they are well groomed, clothes will be of high-utility, suitable for the work they are involved in. Finally, watch their eye movements when you ask them a question. If you ask about the first car they ever owned or what they would change about their lives, pay close attention to their eyes. The Pickup Truck looks straight across to one side when remembering the car, and straight across to the other side when describing the results they are working to create. The Pickup Truck might look above you when they are talking. A Pickup Truck reaches out to shake hands, but does not fully extend his or her arm. They like to stand farther away than the Minivan, but closer than the Sports Car. They stand or sit relaxed and slightly turned to the side, possibly with arms crossed or folded, and with their head tilted to the side. This lets them turn one ear closer to you so they can hear better. They stand close enough to hear, but certainly not close enough so as to be able to reach out to touch you. They often times touch their ears.

"What do you hear that might tip you off to a Pickup Truck? Well they can talk at a varied speed and volume. The fact that it's not always loud or soft gives you a clue that this person is not a Sports Car or a Minivan. There will almost always be music playing, or a radio on for background noise. Their voice usually has a melodious sound. They need to make some kind of noise by tapping their fingers or feet, whistling, or humming. They are warm but logical in their communication, and need to understand the facts about products and services. They want a clear understanding of how they will impact the whole organization and what processes will be impacted by a purchase. They are passive, reflective, and introspective. They rely more on hearing than touch or vision."

Identifying Hybrids.
"Generally speaking, Hybrids create efficient chaos. There will probably be items left out that are being used or that will be used again soon. In the bathroom, the items that are used daily are left out or put into a counter top box. Kitchen utensils will be left in the dish drainer or in a hanger of some kind on the counter top for easy access. They may have knick-knacks displayed on tables or counters, but they will be put into arrangements according to what they mean or ordered in relation to an event or project they are associated with.

"Individually their clothes probably don't match and will likely be out of fashion. But they will for sure be the best in cost and value. If you ask about the first car they ever owned or what they would change in their life, pay close attention to their eye movements. The Hybrid looks straight across to one side when remembering the car, and straight across to the other side when describing the results they are planning to create. A Hybrid's eyes are turned to the side when they are listening. When shaking your hand, a Hybrid reaches out but not with a fully extended arm. They like to stand close enough to easily hear you, but not close enough to invade your personal space. Like the Pickup Truck, they sit and stand slightly turned to the side, possibly with arms crossed or folded and with their head tilted to the side. This lets them turn one ear closer to you so they can hear better. They turn away when they need to think or find answers.

"So what audible hints do Hybrids give? They talk at a varied speed and volume, depending on the purpose of their communication and desired effect. When they are excited or upset they mimic the Sports Car, and when they want to make a dramatic point they can sound like a Minivan, speaking soft and slow and giving the details about all the details. They have a way of complicating everything they are involved with. There will almost always be music playing or a radio on for background noise. They will ask a lot of questions about the facts, figures, and other proof of any claim made about the products and services so that they can analyze the minutiae of every nuance to gain a clear understanding of how all of it works together as a system. They rely more on hearing than touch or vision."

When Olivia finishes talking about how to identify each of the Personal Interaction Keys, she takes a big drink of water and walks around the front of the room for a moment or two as she contemplates what will be the next most appropriate activity. Nodding her head as if she has finished talking to herself, she tells us, "There is a lot more information about each Personal Interaction Key, but I have decided to save that for after lunch. You have been sitting for a while, so I have decided to let you begin practicing.

"Okay, we are going to separate into groups and practice identifying Personal Interaction Keys. In your packet, you'll find a small stack of 3x5 cards. Your assignment will be to talk to five people in fifteen minutes and identify what you think their Key type is. As soon as you know or think you know what their Key is, stop the conversation, write their name down and what their Key is on a card that you will keep for reference at the end of the activity, and then write what you think their Key is on a second card and give that card to them. Then find someone else to talk to.

"Now before you make a mad dash to find people to talk to, let me give you a few instructions about where you will go for the next little while. If your last name starts with A-L please meet in the Pearl room. If your last name begins with M-Z please meet in the Oasis room. And if you are here with a spouse, significant other, or business partner, then make sure you are in different rooms. When the fifteen minutes is up, we will notify you. You will stay in the room you have been assigned to for the next assignment after that. Are there any questions?" She looks around while she takes another drink. With no one needing clarification, she announces, "The fifteen minutes starts now!"

It's like bedlam. Everyone is dashing to find the room they are supposed to be in and begin the assignment. I take a minute to consider the goal of this activity. What is Olivia really asking us to do? I am accustomed to having conversations with people to find out what they want their life to be like, but I don't think that's what the assignment is. We are only supposed to practice identifying the Personal Interaction Key of those we talk to, not actually communicating with them. I am ready to go now, thinking I have my conditions of victory.

As requested, Ann and I split up. I find myself in the Oasis room with Steve Thoms. Ann and Sara are together in the Pearl room. My strategy is to talk to a few people that I don't know first, and then talk to someone I think I might know; like Steve, Lazaro, or Barry the Canadian man I met earlier.

The room is really noisy, like a pep rally or a casino on a Saturday night. In fact, it's so loud that it's difficult to hear the person you are speaking to. I begin by reviewing the steps: 1) what can I see generally, 2) what can I see specifically, and 3) what can I hear. I locate my first subject; his name is Rick. He has a big smile, his shirt is untucked, and his hair isn't combed very neatly. I reach out to shake his hand from a comfortable distance for me, and he only sticks his hand out a little way. I have to move closer to him to grasp his hand. He stands uncomfortably close. I don't think he has any concept of personal space.

At this point I think I know that he is a Minivan but I want to make sure, so I ask him what he likes most about XL-8. He immediately looks down and to one side as he begins excitedly describing the people he has met and has been able to go on promotional trips with. He starts to describe the karaoke bar on last year's cruise when I interrupt him by saying "I got it!" I write his name and Minivan as his Personal Interaction Key on my card and give him a copy of the 3x5 card for him to use. It takes him about twenty seconds to ascertain my Key. It also takes him longer to write down my information and give me a card than it does for him to recognize my Key. I am a little shocked that I am that transparent, but he probably started sizing me up before we shook hands and during the time I was talking to him. I could see that he wrote Sports Car on my card. I feel a tap on my shoulder while Rick is folding the card with his assessment of my personal interaction key.

I turn around to find a well-groomed woman in a comfortable looking sweater and casual slacks that don't seem to match exactly. I start making my assessment of her before I even recognize that she stands a little farther away than Rick did, which is a bit more comfortable for me. Her desire to complete the assignment, whether or not Rick and I had finished starts me thinking she might be a Sports Car. But something is a bit off as I look at her. It takes me a second to recognize that she is slightly turned to the side while she introduces herself, pointing to her name tag as a kind of verification that her name is Alma.

She begins asking me what color my first car was and what the first repair I had to make on it was. I barely answer the color question, and am only about three words into the repair question when she stops me and starts writing. I don't even wait for her to finish writing and hand me my card before I ask her about her perfect vacation.

She doesn't answer immediately. Pausing a moment she looks straight across and to the side and then starts to describe how her last vacation was nearly perfect, and how if she had gone to Athens before Rome she would have had a better experience. So her perfect vacation would be like her last cruise, except she would like to be able to talk to a travel agent who had actually been on that cruise personally to get their input before she booked the trip. I am interested in her story of Athens and Rome, so I let her talk while I fill out the cards and give one to her with the words Pickup Truck on it. I am amazed at the feeling that I can actually discern a person's key in just a few seconds by paying attention to a few details.

I can see that this is a skill that is definitely going to pay major dividends. I think briefly of Dayna, Jaylin, Ray, Shelly, Mylisa, and Kayci, whom I want to help take the greatest advantage of this skill. I'm brought back to reality by a voice over the speakers, telling us that we have only eight minutes left to complete the exercise.

I quickly find my third person; his name is Chris. We get right down to business. His suit, tie, shoes, and pocket square all match. This is a sharp-looking guy who understands dressing for success. I start to ask him what his greatest challenge in his business is, and before I can finish he interrupts my question by finishing it for me while looking up and to one side. As if his answer is part of the question he tells me, "I need more people who will do what I ask them to do. No one seems to listen or take direction anymore."

I realize in the three or four seconds of this interaction that he is standing straight in front of me, that I am comfortable with the fact that he is a full arm's length away from me, and that his answer is fast, short, sweet, and to the point. Talking to Chris is like talking to myself, which is a little unnerving for a moment. I write on my cards and he completes his. Our interaction is completed in about thirty seconds, in classic Sports Car fashion.

I walk across the room and find a man named Ben. As I wait for him to finish his interaction I watch him talking to his prospect. He stands slightly turned to the side and crosses his arms. At first I thought he might be closed off or defensive with the whole crossed-arm bit. Then I remember that Olivia told us that Hybrids sometimes do this. He has on a tie that looks like it might have come out of the seventies and doesn't match his suit at all. This makes me think that I may be able to begin my PIK analysis even before I am directly engaged with people.

When he finishes I reach out to shake his hand and he only reaches out part-way, kind of like Alma did a few minutes ago. His posture with me is exactly like it was a minute earlier: slightly turned to the side with crossed arms. I ask him about his first car and he hesitates in his response. He looks straight across to the side while he contemplates how to answer. His voice is noticeably soft and kind of slow as he details the general specifications of the year, make, model, engine size, transmission, and rear differential gear ratios. As he moves to the specific manufacturer's color code for the paint job and the instruments, I begin to chuckle out loud. "I don't mean to be rude," I explain. He immediately knows what is so funny. We have a laugh together because he knows that he has just given himself away. It takes him about ten seconds to confirm his assessment of me as a Sports Car, and then we look for our last person.

I talk to a woman named Robin, and in less than a minute I discover that she is a Minivan. When she shakes my hand she doesn't let it go and she gives me an ear to ear smile. I quickly recognize that I have always been a little uncomfortable when I talk to Minivans. And now I know it's because I need some personal space. In this case, Robin doesn't seem to have any concept about it. As we talk, I identify her eyes as moving down and to the side when she remembers the past, and I notice that she can't seem to hold still.

It only takes her a few seconds to identify my Key. She asks me whether I care more about getting things done than the feelings of the people who were doing the work. And, of course, in classic Sports Car style, I don't even think before answering. I say, "What do feelings have to do with getting work done?" I can't believe that I have so easily given my true feelings away.

Just as Robin hands me my card with a huge multi-colored drawing of a red Sports Car, Olivia stops the meeting and gets everyone's attention. They open the folding wall between the two rooms, and she stands on a makeshift platform so that everyone in both rooms can see and hear her. She asks for some volunteers to come up and share their experience of the past few minutes. Five people come up, and she asks them to share how difficult it was to identify the Key of the person you were talking to.

They all agree that it wasn't that difficult to identify the Key of the other person.

One woman says, "It was a bit strange to have someone analyzing me, knowing what they were doing."

A man shares, "The hardest thing was to end the conversation so abruptly and start talking to another person in only a few seconds. I wanted to really interact on a more personal level once I knew what Key they were."

Another woman confesses, "I was at a loss for what to say that might be different from what I would normally say to people."

Olivia interjects, "The reason I gave you this specific assignment was to help you focus on identification without any other agenda. I want you to become an expert in identification before you worry about how to talk to a person from each Key category. So, what did you learn from this experience?"

A man says, "For the first time I really observed the person I was talking to. I think I was talking with them instead of talking at them."

One of the women adds, "I learned that not everyone is the same, and even though some might seem similar, they really do have different clues that tipped me off to what their preferred interaction style is."

Another man explains, "This was the first time I have ever talked to someone without any preconceived notion of what they might be about. I started with a clean slate, and then just took in what I could see generally and specifically, and then added what I heard, before I made any kind of judgment about how to interact with them."

Another woman concludes, "It was really refreshing to just look at and listen to another human being and be able to be totally present and totally engaged with everything that was going on in the interaction."

Olivia thanks the volunteers and then lets them return to the class. "Wow. What great insights and observations from just a fifteen-minute exercise. I want all of you to look at the cards you received from the people who interacted with you. By the raise of hands how many have cards that all say the same thing?"

Most of the hands go up.

"And by the raise of hands, how many have at least one different assessment of what your Personal Interaction Key might be?"

About twenty percent of the hands go up.

"Keep your hands up," Olivia insists. "Keep your hands up if you have two or more different answers."

About half of the hands went down.

"Keep your hands up if you have three or more, four? I would like three of those who got two or more different responses to come up here on the stage."

Once they are on the stage with Olivia she begins to ask them about their experience, "Do any of the assessments agree with what each of you think you are?"

Leslie, the woman in the middle, shakes her head no.

"How many different responses did you get?"

She holds up three fingers.

"So what do you think your Personal Interaction Key is that no-one else could figure out?"

Without hesitation Leslie responds saying, "I am a Pickup Truck."

There is an audible disagreeing buzz in the crowd. "Why do you think that," Olivia asks?

As she answers Olivia's question she rocks back and forth from one leg to the other. She says, looking down at her feet, "Because I have to be the one who organizes people into groups so that work will get done. I am always in charge of every organization that has difficult people who don't seem to be able to work in teams."

"Do you like working in these kinds of teams?" Olivia digs a little deeper.

She confesses, "I like to get the team to function as a cohesive unit, but I hate having to work under deadlines."

Olivia turns to the crowd and asks, "By the raise of hands, how many of you think she is a Pickup Truck?"

Not one hand goes up!

Leslie is shocked by the class response.

Then Olivia asks, "By a raise of hands how many of you think she is a Sports Car?"

Again no hands are raised.

"Is she a Hybrid?"

No hands go up.

Olivia then invites the people who talked to Leslie to come up to the stage. The five come up and Olivia quizzes them about what made them answer in the way they did while they were talking to her.

The first woman says, "She put Hybrid on Leslie's card because she told me about the details of a birthday party she once had. And so in the few seconds I had I made that judgment."

"Understandable mistake," Olivia concedes. Then she asks the second person, "What did you assess her Key as?"

"I thought she was a Sports Car because she was really in a hurry. She gave her answers really quickly so that she could complete the assignment. But, now that I see her here on the stage with no time constraint I have changed my assessment."

"So now what do you think she is," Olivia asks?

"She is a Minivan," he exclaims.

Olivia continues, "So you other three must have put that she was a Minivan as well and that assessment might have been accurate, it just disagreed with her judgment is that right?"

They all nod in agreement. Turning to the crowd she asks, "By the raise of hands who thinks Leslie is a Minivan?" Everyone raises their hand.

Olivia reiterates, "Remember that everyone has some characteristics of each of the identifiers. That is to say everyone has learned to behave in certain ways depending on specific circumstances. In this case, Leslie felt like she was under a deadline, so she had to get work done quickly in order to comply with the instructions. This made her give a few false signs to her natural way of being. So let's take a few volunteers from the class to share what it is about Leslie that tipped you off about her being a Minivan."

One man shouts, "Look where she is standing. She is in the middle where she can have people on both sides and everyone is very close to her."

A woman from the front says, "Instead of answering your questions verbally, she shook her head and held up her fingers, which seem to indicate that she is more physical than visual or verbal."

A man from the side of the room yells, "When you asked her about her own assessment she didn't pause at all to respond. And when she did she was looking down. Additionally, the whole time she has been up on the stage she has been rocking back and forth. She doesn't seem to be able to hold still."

Sara Thoms offers, "She also said she likes to get people to work together, and that she doesn't like the stress of a deadline. She seems to choose to be with people who are not getting the work done."

Olivia remarks, "These are great insights and observations. And they are all right on. I love it when we can see things that help others to get more in touch with who they really are. So now Leslie how do you feel?"

She moves right to Olivia and with a few tears, she gives her a hug saying, "For the first time I feel liberated and free from some negative feelings that I have had about my value to the organizations I have worked in and for."

Olivia continues to hold her hand while adding, "Leslie has simply missed the idea that it is okay to like people and to honor who they are because she was supposed to be a task master getting work done, regardless of the welfare of those she works with."

A cheer comes from the class and it's a bit overwhelming to anyone who tends to feel emotional. As a Sports Car myself I am proud that I uncovered the misdiagnosis and that this problem is solved.

Olivia then explains that we have two assignments to complete before we will be ready for this afternoon's sessions. I can't believe that it's close to lunch time already; where has the time gone? It's so interesting that when I am actively engaged with learning how fast the time goes by. Olivia interrupts Matt's wandering mind by saying, "I will give you the second assignment first. The lunch break will end at 1:30 PM. When you return we will all meet in the classroom that we were in this morning. So you need to make sure to eat something, complete the lunch assignment, and be back here before 1:30 PM. While you are at lunch you need to take another 3x5 card and have at least five conversations during the break. These can be people you know or people you don't know. But they must be five different people.

"Now for the first assignment, before you begin the lunch break, you need to repeat the activity you just did right here. You will meet with five people, exchange a card with them and keep one for yourself with their Personal Interaction Key. There is only one extra item you need to write down on the card you record your assessment on. You need to put down at least two things that tip you off about their Personal Interaction Key. For example, if you meet Sally and at the end of your interaction you put down that Sally's Key is Sports Car, then you also need to put what she did or said that make you think she is a Sports Car.

"So let me recap quickly. You are going to remain here in this room until you have interacted with at least five new people and have captured their name, Key, and reasons why you chose it. And then you will go on a lunch break that ends at 1:30 PM. During lunch you will have at least five more interactions, capturing their name, Key, and reasons for your assessment, and return to the main classroom." She pauses for a moment to see if there are any questions, and seeing no raised hands she declares that we should begin, Now!

Two quiet conference rooms instantly turn into a chaotic, swarming beehive of activity and noise. It seems everyone is hurrying so that they can get to lunch. I think we have plenty of time to complete the assignments, eat lunch and still get back where we need to be so I take a minute to go over in my mind the three steps again: What can I see generally; what can I see specifically; and what can I hear that will indicate what their Key is. I take out ten 3x5 cards and begin my search for willing subjects to practice with.

My first partner identifies himself as a Sports Car on two counts: He looks up and to the side when answering my question, and he describes his desk at work as perfectly organized with everything put away each night before he leaves his office. I identify my second person as a Sports Car the moment we shake hands. She extends her arm to full length, keeping me at a safe distance. She talks to me first, and while she is talking to me I confirm that she is a Sports Car because she faces straight at me and looks directly at me. My third partner takes a little more work to figure out. He shakes hands at an in-between distance, and he stands sideways to me, so I rule out the Sports Car and Minivan. The clue that helps me discern between Pickup Truck and Hybrid happens when he asks me for proof that having a financial planner increases a person's ability to retire more reliably. My fourth person is even more challenging. I think she may be purposely misleading me at first because she talks for a full two minutes about how she wants to end domestic violence and gives me complete details about the cause and effect of this kind of tragedy. However, I think I get that she is a Minivan when she reaches out and grabs my hand while describing the emotional trauma people go through during and after violent episodes. As soon as she touches me physically she really opens up and talks about the human side of her passion for this cause. The last person I talk to is a Hybrid named Greg. He gives himself away by detailing what motivated him to join XL-8. He talks about how he loves the compensation plan and especially the matching lateral bonus and unlimited depth of PVC when you have a Gold level member underneath another Gold level member. It is surprising to me that, given just a few minutes of simple conversation, it is becoming very easy to discover what everyone's Key is with complete accuracy. In fact, everyone I talk to easily identifies me as a Sports Car.

This is so cool and it is going to be incredibly useful when I learn what to do now that I can identify people's Personal Interaction Key. Picking the lock is going to be so much fun; I can't wait until this afternoon. I find Ann and we decide to go to the shopping mall to eat and find people to talk to. It's Saturday at noon so there should be lots of people there and a large selection of restaurants that will have food we can get quickly. On the way to the mall, Ann checks her watch and is amazed that it only took us about fifteen minutes to complete the first assignment.

We talk for a minute about what we learned the second time going through this activity. Ann explains that she is getting good at recognizing visual clues and that she knows what their natural way of being is before she hears them speak. She is a little anxious, however, to use this new found skill with people who aren't privy to what is going on.

I nod my head in agreement because I am thinking the same thing about using this on strangers in a public setting. I also share my excitement to actually PIK locks, get people to open up the relationship gateway, and help them take advantage of what we offer.

Arriving at the mall, we quickly find the food court. Ann and I almost never order the same kind of food so we head off to different restaurants. In true Sports Car fashion, I want to get the ball rolling as fast as I can, so I start talking to the man behind me in line while we wait to order. I introduce myself, and he is hesitant to shake my hand at first, backing up a half step as I talk to him. His reaction startles me at first because everyone we practiced on at the event was excited to engage with me.

Remembering the radio analogy from this morning, I get myself tuned into the process and quickly conclude that he might be a Sports Car because he wants some space to observe me. I confirm this when I ask him what he does professionally. He answers, very proudly, that he is the manager of a disaster clean-up company. I ask him how he likes it, and he actually takes a step towards me and excitedly says, "I love to restore order to people's lives after they have experienced a tragedy like a fire or flood or something like that."

The person behind him tells me it's my turn to order. I apologize, thank my new friend for sharing with me, and turn to order. The cashier has a huge smile on his face, welcomes me, and asks how he can serve me. I had been so engrossed in the conversation I was having in line that I have no idea what to order so I ask him what he would recommend.

He responds by saying, "The number five combo always puts me in a good mood for the rest of the day."

Without thinking, I ask him if he is a Minivan. He looks at me strangely as if I had just said something in Greek. I explain that the number five would be great. Then I pay for my food and return to our table to meet Ann. Sitting down with a big smile on my face as I think back on the two interactions I just had, I grin at Ann who gives me that look she gives the kids when she suspects they have just done something sneaky. I share my experiences about talking to the man in line and the cashier and we had a chuckle.

I proclaim proudly that I already have two of my five people.

She responds, "You are not the only one who can get things done quickly, buddy. I also talked to two people while ordering, and Sheila asked me to call her next week to share more about what I am doing."

Gloating inside a little Matt thinks, "What an awesome woman I had persuaded to marry me."

We finish eating and then split up, agreeing to meet back at the food court at 1:10. That will give us twenty minutes to get back to the event, which should only take about ten minutes.

My strategy is to talk to two people working in stores or kiosks and one person just walking around. It is becoming so easy and natural to identify the way people want to be interacted with, that the suspense of not knowing how to take advantage of this is beginning to kill me. Ann and I meet back at the food court and surprisingly we are both about ten minutes early. As we walk towards the doors we see Steve and Sara.

Sara asks us about our experience so far today and shares that they are ready to learn what to do with this skill. We all agree, and, as if it would make a difference in the start time of the afternoon session, we hurry to our cars and return to the event center. We arrive only to find that we are the first ones back in the training room.

Since we were all there together, I have to ask what everyone learned so far today.

Steve says, "I found out at the mall that I had to ask different kinds of questions to get those people to talk to me."

Ann shares, "I had to pay closer attention to them because they were unaware that I was conducting an assessment on their Personal Interaction Key."

Sara mentions, "I found that, not everyone is a willing participant. That is to say not everyone wanted to talk to me."

I found that store clerks seemed more interested in engaging than customers. Then, Lazaro my new friend from Honduras joins us and remarks, "People told me things I probably shouldn't know when I started talking to them."

Sara adds, "It was hard to end the conversation when I figured out what their Key was without being rude. So each conversation took a lot longer and was more in-depth than the assignment called for. I did meet some really interesting people who gave me their contact information and invited me to call them when I get home."

While we are immersed in our own conversation the room is filling up. Olivia has been eavesdropping on our conversation as she prepares for the afternoon session. She joins the conversation after Ann's comment, saying that people will begin to be very attracted to you, and in some cases they will actually move closer to you physically. To validate her comment, Ann relays my story of talking to the man in the lunch line who moved away at first as his Key would indicate, and then he actually moved a full step closer to me as we talked.

Olivia calls the group to order and she essentially repeats the instructions for the exercise that we just went through. She asks for volunteers to share what their experience was like and almost the exact same observations come out. Olivia uses my experience in the lunch line. By the end of this ninety-second interaction, the man was actually closer to Matt than he was in the beginning. She then asks me, "What is his Personal Interaction Key?"

"He is a Sports Car," I reply confidently.

Olivia reminds all of us, "The Sports Car is the category that wants the most physical space. Remember that success is getting people moving towards you, then with you. And being interested instead of interesting is the success magnet that draws people towards you." She congratulates Matt for PIKing this man's lock in broad daylight. She then asks us all, "By a raise of hands, how many of you had people give you, a perfect stranger their personal contact information by the end of the interaction." A fair number of hands go up, and Tracy shouts from the back of the room, "That wasn't the assignment. Weren't we only supposed to identify what category they were in?"

Olivia acknowledges that she correctly understood the specifics of the assignment; "I was only curious to see if anything happened beyond the obvious experiment. Tracy, it is going to be crucial for you to see beyond the explicit instructions and look farther than what you actually see and hear. You are going to have to make sense of the clues people give you, and discern what they indicate if you are going to have meaningful interactions with people that gets them to move towards you and then with you."

Matt momentarily thinks about his own circumstances, I find that the more Tracy talks, the more she reminds me of Shelly at my office. She resists anything and everything that might actually help her to grow and become the kind of person who others will actually listen to and follow. It seems that Tracy should really learn to absorb this information. After all she gets paid by results and performance. No attendance or managerial pay plan here.

Olivia continues, "If you are like most of my students, you are ready to move onto what you do after you identify people's Personal Interaction Key. If you are ready to move on, take the next three minutes to stand up, gather all of your belongings, and trade places with anyone in the room, so that everyone is sitting in a different place than they have been before."

When everyone is settled again she tells us to open our notebooks and get ready to learn how to talk to people in each category and also how to ask people of each type to take action.

Author's Note:
The instructions explaining the mathematical equation for this chapter is in the appendix at the end of the book.

## 7

The Relationship Gateway

Olivia begins the session right on time. "Now that you have PIKed the lock of your subject, you have earned the right to interact with them. I mean because they feel you understand how to communicate with them, they allow you to enter their relationship gateway and give you some attention. You have gained a certain level of trust with them and they are now willing to engage in some kind of relationship with you. Now, if you will recall, the last step in the process is trust. I don't mean you creating trust with others, but you trusting yourself enough to follow your observations and proceed with boldness to communicate your intentions to give and share. Wavering will not serve you or them.

"Here is how to talk to each Key category and also how to ask people to take action that will best serve both of you."

Talking to Sports Cars.

"Now that you have identified you are talking to a Sports Car, trust your analysis and feelings and talk to them with confidence and clarity. Be specific, brief, and to the point. Think in headlines or bullet points, not in details. You can solidify your initial analysis that they are a Sports Car when you notice they respond very quickly to your questions, sometimes without thinking about the answers they provide. Talk to them using logic to make your points. Make sure they can follow you by keeping your thought process in a logical sequence of ideas.

"They use image-making words and paint a picture when they talk. They readily relate to image making words when they listen. So when you talk to a Sports Car say things like: 'It appears to me;' 'It looks like;' 'As you can plainly see;' 'From my perspective;' 'Imagine what that would look like;' or 'Picture this.' If you ask them to clarify what they mean or ask them to tell you more about what they said, they might say something like 'let me show you what I mean.' They may even take your pencil or pen away from you to draw you a picture. When your interaction ends, they will say something like 'see you later.'"

Asking Sports Cars to Take Action.

Olivia stops for a drink of water, then continues. "Sports Cars love being on the cutting edge and thrive on providing or using new and innovative products and services. They will respond well to language that demonstrates quick, measurable results.

"Position your product as the best quality and value available. If you are prepared, well-organized and talk in basic terms, using models and pictures in a sequence, they will take action if it is relevant to some pain or challenge they can understand, even if that pain or challenge isn't theirs.

"Because they think, move, and talk quickly, they will be prepared to take action or make a buying decision right now. Be direct. Ask them how they see your offering working for them to solve their challenges. Ask them to take action and they will do what you ask them to, if you have helped them see how your recommendations will produce the result they want."

Talking to Minivans.

"Minivans talk slower; they are warm and emotional in their communication and respond quickly. People who are Minivans make eye contact, are usually friendly, and have a smile on their face. Use their name and ask questions so they can give their opinion. They will want to dominate the conversation, so make sure you ask questions that will guide them to the result or conclusion you want.

"Minivans avoid confrontation. They use big arm and hand gestures when they talk. When you talk to them, do not include a lot of details because they do not listen well and lose interest or become bored quickly.

"They are highly motivated to engage in learning programs because they love to talk to groups about how good the latest book, video, or conference call was, how they plan to implement it, and all the people they are going to share it with. They are always more concerned with people's feelings than getting things done.

"Minivans use feeling words and create a sense of emotion when they talk. They say things like 'it all boils down to,' 'that will give me a firm foundation,' 'that's a pain in the neck," I am so excited," I have a good grasp on that,' and 'I will be able to touch more lives.' If you ask them to clarify what they mean or ask them to tell you more about what they said, they might do something like scoot closer to you or lean towards you and say 'This is how it feels to me.' They may even grab your hand or reach out to touch your arm or shoulder to let you feel how they feel When your interaction ends, they will say something like 'We'll be in touch.'

Asking Minivans to Take Action.

"To get a Minivan to take action you need to explain that engaging with you will be fun and that it involves helping and interacting with people. Make sure to point out that using your products and services is easy and low maintenance.

Position your offering as providing incredible social value. Be sure to let them know that it will create occasions for their friends and neighbours to come over and ask them about it.

"Minivans don't want to be left out of the excitement or excluded from the group, so they will be prepared to take action today. Be direct and ask for their business by asking them how they feel about the products or services and helping others have a better life.

"However, I do have a couple of cautionary notes here: First if they are not interested they will be very reluctant to say so, because they don't ever want to offend anyone and saying no might seem offensive. Furthermore, they might say yes just to be part of the group. They might not want to do any of the work to build a business, but they will attend everything they can to participate as a team member. They might make excuses about things they are concerned about that aren't really concerns just so that they don't have to say no."

Talking to Pickup Trucks.

Olivia moves on to Pickup Trucks, saying, "When you talk to Pickup Trucks, make sure that you begin with a personal comment, including their name. They are really good at remembering names so make sure to use theirs often. Give them time to respond to your questions as they need time to think about their answers. Give a lot of encouragement and ask questions to build their trust. Do not be domineering or demanding.

"Pickups enjoy listening. They spend a lot of time gathering information so they can accurately process the ramifications of what the speaker is saying. How, is the most important word in their vocabulary. They want to know 'How do things work?' 'How are orders processed?' 'How do I talk to my friends and family?' and 'How does the compensation plan work? They talk through concepts to get clarity or more information so that they can work effectively and make educated decisions. Pickups think problems through by weighing the pros and cons before they make decisions. They have a long attention span, but are easily distracted by unusual noises or voices.

"They use words and phrases that represent hearing when they talk. They say things like 'That rings a bell,' 'I would like to voice my opinion,' 'In a manner of speaking,' 'To tell you the truth,' 'Could you explain what you mean?' or 'I wouldn't say that.' If you ask them to clarify what they mean or ask them to tell you more about what they said, they might say something like 'To tell you the truth,' 'Here is exactly how that works and how it compares to others.' When your interaction ends, they will say something like 'I look forward to hearing from you.'"

Asking Pickup Trucks to Take Action.

"When you ask a Pickup truck to take action, make sure you emphasize that your company is steady and reliable. State the facts about how many years your company has been in business and what the customer satisfaction rate is. Give them 'cause and effect' details that will help them weigh the efficacy of the products, services, and income offering. Make sure that you tell them that they will be more efficient and effective if they buy your product or service, and engage with you as a service provider or partner. They want to know that their productivity will increase as a result of using your product or service.

"Pickup trucks prefer to approach things cautiously; they like to gather all their facts and think about things before making decisions. They are not going to make the decision to enroll the first time you present to them. You should give them the option to enroll or to get more information so that they can make a more educated decision. In fact, you can anticipate that their first answer will be to get more information. They will need to understand how taking your recommendations will help them be more effective. They will want evidence that you offer proven, predictable processes and systems that create intentional results and bring things to completion.

"When you are working with a Pickup Truck, be patient, get a clear understanding of what information they need to make a decision and get it to them. The good news is that because it takes them multiple exposures to your products, services, and income offering before they will enroll, it will also take them a long time and much thinking to ever quit or become inactive."

Talking to a Hybrid.

Olivia pauses for a breath before she continues with the last Key type. "Hybrids are good at listening. This is their primary method of collecting the data and information they crave. They like to talk and ask questions so that they can hear the same information in multiple ways. This helps them gain enough facts and figures to take a stand on a position or belief, a stand which they base on evidence, rather than conjecture or trust. Hybrids think problems through from every angle. They love to weigh the pros and cons multiple times before they make decisions.

"When you talk to Hybrids, make sure that you prepare your information in advance. Give accurate, detailed information. Make sure your presentation is well-organized. Prepare a lot of facts, and stick to the subject at hand. Be professional and matter of fact when you speak. You also need to give a Hybrid time to respond to your questions, as they need time to think about what you have just said and to formulate their answers. Like a Pickup Truck, Hybrids respond better when they are given a lot of encouragement and are asked questions to build their trust. Do not be forceful or push them to make a decision or adopt a point of view. They will make a decision when they have enough reliable evidence.

"Hybrids have a long attention span and love to talk about problems so that they can hear their own words out loud to make sure that nothing is forgotten or missed. They use words and phrases like 'I question the validity of that,' 'Could you describe what you mean in detail,' 'Let me tell you what the website says word for word,' and 'A well-informed person would understand why this is the key to the whole system.' If you ask them to clarify what they mean, or ask them to tell you more about what they said, they might say something like, 'Let me tell you in detail how all these parts fit together into a perfect system.' When your interaction ends, they will say something like, 'I look forward to hearing more about this.'"

Asking Hybrids to Take Action.
"When you are ready to ask a Hybrid to take action, make sure to prepare factual information about your company. State the facts about your company's growth, the industry's growth, trend information, and always state your information with precise details. Do not generalize numbers or facts. Make sure they have enough information to make an educated decision. They need an unconditional money-back guarantee.

"Hybrids approach decisions very cautiously. Efficiency and cost are important. They will weigh the pros and cons of the decision based on its logical merit. They will want to read, hear, and see everything they can so that they can get as much information as they can in as many different ways as they can before making decisions.

"Also like Pickup Trucks, Hybrids are not going to make the decision to enroll the first time you present to them. Of course, you need to provide enrollment options and an invitation for them to choose one of the options so they can make an educated decision, but you can anticipate that their first response will be to get more information, and you should be prepared for them to take time to act. Be patient, get a clear understanding of what information they need to make a decision, and get it to them. Keep asking them if they have enough information to make a decision, and if they need more ask what information, specifically, do they need. They will decide when enough is enough. Because they take a long time to make decisions and they hate change, once they enroll, they're in for the long run."

Pausing for a brief moment to get a drink of water, catch her breath, and transition mentally to the next segment, Olivia continues, "Now with all that said, we are going to practice once again. I want you to master using the knowledge, not just have it rolling around in your head for a few minutes before you completely forget it all.

"Your assignment is to turn to a person sitting close to you that you don't know yet and invest ten minutes getting to know them. At the end of the time, each of you should know what type of key they require for you to unlock their relationship gateway, what they are passionate about, and what makes their feet hit the floor in the morning or what their greater causes and higher purposes are. You might begin by asking them 'What would they want to leave behind as a legacy for their great grandchildren?' Or, 'If they could wave a magic wand and get anything they wanted, how would they change the world to make a difference to those they care about?' Capture the information on a 3x5 card in as much detail as you can. You will be using this information later today for our final exercise."

Looking around to see if there are any questions about the exercise and noticing there are none, she declares, "The assignment begins now!"

Turning to his neighbour, Matt begins by asking her name and where she is from. She says her name is Patti, from Memphis, Tennessee, and after a few seconds Matt determines that she is a Hybrid, which in almost every way is exactly opposite of what he is. It doesn't take long for her to conclude that he is a Sports Car. Matt is unsure why but he feels nervous that there are going to be consequences coming from this conversation.

I am also nervous, Matt thinks, because Patti and I are dissimilar in almost every way, something that makes this exercise more challenging. She shares that she wants to set up homes where kids that complete their time in foster homes or other institutions, but aren't completely ready to fully function in the real world, could learn critical work, life, and relationship skills so that they can be fully contributing members of society. She believes that if she does this work on her own, her work would fall outside government oversight, and she would then be free to help them without the constraints of bureaucratic regulations.

It is really hard for me to resist offering to help her with advice and counsel about how to get this going; yet another clue as to my being a Sports Car. I ask her what is keeping her from making this happen, and she is pretty frank with the details of how much money she needs, what the money would be spent on, and the specific sequence of events that have to occur to get the first home in place. As I am scribbling the details of her passion Olivia calls time.

When she asks for some simple feedback about how we could apply what we just learned, the overwhelming response from all over the room is, "When I actually communicate in accordance with the way they want to be interacted with, they share so much more easily and seem not to hold anything back. The biggest difficulty I have is not just jumping in and saying 'I can help you make that happen,' and then telling them all about my solution for their challenge."

Olivia nods her head and explains, "That is the typical response I get when I do this exercise. People who want to build a big business and care about others are often eager to share what they offer as the key to improving people's lives. We want so much to just jump in and do what we can to help. The challenge is that you haven't yet earned the right to participate with others. This is mostly because those who can help have a hard time suspending their agenda long enough to offer help that is truly helpful and not a distraction from the overall goal of the person they want to help.

"Our next exercise will help bring this into the light." She begins instructing, "Everyone who was in the Oasis Room before lunch, you will return to that room and await instructions from Jill. Please leave all of your belongings here, including your notebooks. You may leave now. If you were in the Pearl room before lunch, please stay here until the Oasis team is completely gone.

As the Oasis Team enters their room. Jill, Mike Blacks assistant and the woman we met this morning at the registration desk, gives each person an envelope with $10,000 in monopoly money, and then gives them their instructions for this activity. She says, "Each member of the Pearl Team will be acting as travel agents. You are to pretend that you want to go on your perfect vacation. You have scrimped and saved for over five years to have the money to go, so this has to be absolutely perfect. Neither time nor money will be an issue, and she instructs them not to hold back on what their dream vacation looks like. Make sure to stay strong in your convictions of your dream vacation. The Pearl Team travel agents might want to sell you something besides what you are most interested in."

Meanwhile Olivia tells the Pearl Team, "Each of you is about to play a game, and the name of the game is, 'Make as Much as You Can.' Each of you will be playing the role of a travel agent. You need to proactively seek out two new prospects from the Oasis Team. Remember that your objective is to 'Make as Much as You Can.' You must talk to people you have not had conversations with before. Here is an added bonus for you. Your travel agency has been given an exclusive promotional trip that no other agency in the world has to offer.

"The spectacular trip is to visit the Bonneville Salt Flats on the Utah, Nevada border. The trip includes airfare, hotel, meals, rental car, a ride in a race car on the Salt Flats, and $500 in casino chips to use at any of the establishments in beautiful Wendover, Nevada. Your trip only costs $1,250 per person, and you will get a thousand dollars sales commission if you can sell this particular trip. If you do sell this promotional trip, have the person you are talking to give you $1,000 from their envelope as the final transaction. If you sell anything else, your prospect will give you a $500 sales commission no matter what the cost of that trip is. Make sure to collect the $500 as the final transaction. Again remember that the name of the game is to 'Make as Much as You Can.'

"Your assignment is to PIK their lock, talk to them in their appropriate language, and then ask them to take action based on your recommendation. You will have thirty minutes to complete the exercise. Make sure to write down the name of the person you talk to so that you may follow up with them later on." Looking around to see if there are any questions about the activity and seeing none, she shouts, "The training starts now!"

Matt decides to take Mike Black's initial offer and get to know Mr. Flint. Orson, as he invited us to call him, is a Hybrid. Wow, I think, another Hybrid;

that's two in a row. I begin by having him describe what his dream vacation is. As I listen initially, I am checking to see if anything about my Salt Flats / Wendover trip is going to work for him. He details a trip to Honduras to go scuba diving and parasailing behind his boat. He gives me the details about what fish you can see and the underwater caves he loves to explore. Almost nothing he shares has anything to do with my promotional destination. I ask, "Have you ever considered a new and different kind of vacation like driving on the Bonneville Salt Flats, the night life and entertainment of casinos, and the seclusion of an out of the way location?"

He politely declines and then explains, "I am much more interested in Honduras if I can do it with my business partners."

I quickly decide that selling something is better than selling nothing, and I'm more interested in creating a repeat customer and a transformation than making a single transactional sale. I quickly invent and share the details of a vacation package that meets his requirement and has a few extra things included that will add additional value for his group.

I include, "You can take ten of your partners with you on a ten-day excursion, which includes four days of scuba diving, a full day of parasailing for everyone in the group, two days of deep sea fishing, and three days spread out over the ten days for you and your partners to conduct some business while you are all there together. The hotel you will be staying at has all the scuba and fishing equipment, and the boats and crews would be waiting for you and your party when you arrive. Additionally, you won't have to decide which of your partners will be part of the trip until two weeks before the departure date, so if your people have to qualify for the trip, the promotion can last until two weeks before the trip begins. Of course, everyone will have to have their passport in place at least a month before the excursion."

I wait for a few seconds, giving him some time to process my recommendation and to think about the pros and cons of my proposal. The momentary silence doesn't bother me because I know that he is just weighing his options. He asks, "Please repeat the schedule of each day and the sequence of events so that I can begin planning the business part of the trip. Also, what is the cost per person and what alternate activities might be available for those who are not certified to scuba dive? I want to see how all this fits together into a seamless trip."

Without hesitation, I make up some more details and tell him, "It will cost $2,357 per person including airfare. Scuba gear will be an additional $214 for anyone who wants to participate in that activity. Parasailing and deep-sea fishing are included in the original price. Is there any other information that you need to make an educated decision about this trip?"

He responds, "If you can guarantee this price and the conditions as you have explained them in writing I will be willing to sign the agreement in the next week."

I make the follow-up appointment, we shake hands, he smiles at me and says, "I haven't heard that persuasive an argument to go to Honduras in all my life. He congratulates me and gives me my $500 out of his envelope. I write his name down and the details of his trip. Walking away I think, I didn't get the $1,000 but I did make a sale, and maybe the afternoon follow-up is about repeat business. This is so fun now that I can intentionally interact with people in meaningful ways. I know that Hybrids are detail-oriented, that he would need some kind of guarantee, and that he probably wouldn't transact in this first meeting. So I made it easy for him to get the information he needed and to transact once he heard what he wanted to hear: cha-ching.

I never would have guessed that Mr. Flint is a Hybrid before yesterday's presentation and our conversation today. I would have pegged him for a Sports Car like me. If I would have just rushed in and treated him as a Sports Car he would have rejected me, and no meaningful interaction would have happened.

Finishing making my notes about Orson I look up to see a woman named Yasmin standing there. She has a worried look on her face, so I ask, "Is everything okay?"

She replies, "No-one has approached me about taking my perfect vacation yet, and I am worried that I am doing something that pushes people away from me."

I ask, "Can I be your travel agent?"

She reaches out, grabs my hand, and with a huge smile says that it would make her feel a lot better.

My initial assessment, Minivan, comes from her telling me the reason for her worry, and the fact that she grabbed my hand when I offered to help. This is confirmed when I ask, "Tell me about your perfect vacation."

She describes, "I would love to go on a Caribbean fun cruise with a lot of different activities, like dancing, karaoke, night clubs, and time to socialize around the swimming pool. I want to see the Virgin Islands and go sailing on one of those ships where they provide a sunset dinner and return to the cruise ship late at night."

I ask, "If an out-of-the-way destination in the Utah and Nevada Desert with the night life and entertainment of casinos would interest her."

She responds asking, "How would that compare to the sailing ship sunset dinner?" and "Would the activities of a casino bring her friends together like a cruise ship?"

I am really tempted to invent a tale of fun and celebration that would surpass any cruise that she could ever go on. However, I reconsider when I think of my core value. If I am value-bound to do what's best for the other person no matter the consequences for me in the short term, I'm going to make her dream come true, not mine. For a brief moment I see the flushing of a $1,000 bill down the toilet. I look her in the eye and tell her (using her name, of course) that she will be much more comfortable on a cruise than in the desert. There goes my immediate $1,000. Oh well, it's the lifetime value of this relationship that I should be focused on, right?

I describe the cruise and the different activities on the ship using big arm and hand gestures. I focus on the fun she can have with all of the friends and family she can bring, and reassure her that they will talk about this vacation for years and the photos would be traded for generations to come. I include how easy a cruise is because the meals and other activities are all included. Then, because I know that Minivans will take immediate action, I ask her, "How do you feel about this vacation as a way to create a deeper connection between you and your family and friends? If this is something you feel good about, is there any reason why you wouldn't move ahead by booking the cruise right now?"

Before I completed my call to action, she is nodding her head and giving me my $500 commission from her envelope. I hurriedly write her information on my 3x5 card and put a period on the last sentence just as Olivia calls time.

Olivia gets everyone's attention and has each group return to their room. The folding wall is closed, dividing the rooms once again and Olivia gives us our instructions for the next part of the exercise. She gives all of us an envelope that contains $10,000 and explains, "The Oasis group is going to pretend to be contractors. Each of you is going to describe a remodeling or landscaping project for your home. You need to be wary of tricky sales techniques from those who might want to sell you something you don't want or need."

While Olivia is giving us our instructions, Jill is telling the Oasis group about the game called "Make as Much as You Can." She informs them that as contractors they get promotional items from time to time and that if the can effectively sell them they can get a $500 bonus added to their normal sales commission of $500. She tells them that if they sell anything else they will get only the normal commission of $500. The promotional item they are to sell to make the big bonus are decorative roofing shingles. This item will give their home or outside structure a distinctive look, and adds great value to any property by creating a distinguished and unique street appeal to a house, gazebo, patio, or porch. If you sell this item, you get the $1,000. Remember the name of the game is "Make as Much as You Can." Just as she finishes her instructions, the dividing wall suddenly opens and the sales frenzy is on.

It's really interesting to watch the pretend contractors thinking about what they see and hear, and then talking with purpose, based on what they think will be the most appropriate approach to their prospect's natural way of being.

I am approached first by Michael and then Beverly. Not knowing what their exact agenda is I describe my dream home project: an outdoor hot tub setup which flows into a swimming pool. Off to the side is a huge flat screen TV and barbeque grill with tables, counters, and sinks for food preparation and clean-up. In both cases they quickly identify my Personal Interaction Key and use appropriate language for a Sports Car.

Both Michael and Beverly weakly attempt to sell me the shingles using a pretty good argument. When I tell Beverly that the shingles aren't really going work into my plan, she quickly abandons the idea of promoting it any further. Michael, however, persists and continues to promote the value of a unique roof to my covered hot tub structure. I have to stop him in mid-sentence and exclaim, "If you are not willing to build what I want without this ridiculous roof you are trying to sell me, then I probably should look else where for a contractor that will do what I want."

He apologizes, realizing that he is about to loose the whole deal, and agrees to my request.

At the end of our discussion, both Michael and Beverly make similar comments about how much easier it is to carry on a conversation and ask for the business using lock PIKing, instead of having to guess or making stuff up to talk about before asking for the business, hoping to have said enough of the right things to make the sale.

When the thirty minutes is up, Olivia calls time and brings us all together, facing the front of the Pearl room. She asks us who made the most money saying, "By the raise of hands, who has at least $500?" Everyone raises a hand. "Keep your hands up if you have $1,000." No hands are lowered. "Keep them up if you have $1,500." Almost every hand goes down. "Who has $2,000?" No hands are left up. "So those of you who made $1,500 must have sold a promotional item, is that right?" Some nod in agreement, and others shout in excitement of making the most money. Olivia interrupts the celebration inviting, "If you bought a vacation to the Bonneville Salt Flats or the roofing shingles as part of your renovation project please come up on the stage."

A few people come up and Olivia asks, "Did you originally want that trip or the roofing shingles?"

They all respond, "No."

Wanting to clarify, Olivia asks, "Then why did you buy these things if you didn't want them?"

One woman says, "I felt sorry for the sales person, so I bought the Salt Flats trip and then went to the next agent and bought what I really wanted."

A man offers, "I bought the roofing shingles because I wanted to get rid of the sales person and they didn't cost much more money."

Another woman responds, "I didn't want or know how to say no."

Another adds, "I didn't want to hurt the sales person's feelings."

A man replies, "I didn't think the shingles would be a detriment to the project, and she was really persistent in talking about how great it would be."

The last volunteer says, "The sales person told me that they would get a bonus if I booked the Salt Flats trip and that she would split the bonus with me. She made the Utah and Nevada desert sound very picturesque, so I took the money and changed my plan."

The crowd responds to this with an immediate negative noise in the room. Olivia dismisses the purchasers with her thanks and gratitude for sharing with honesty.

"You see how easy it is to talk to people when you know how? How easy it is to get them to take action, and how easy it can be to take advantage of people who really don't want what we want, but are willing to comply? Will the $1,500 earners come up here on stage," Olivia invites.

Once on the stage, they all line up facing the crowd smiling and looking like the grand prize winners. Olivia gestures to them as if we should clap or cheer. Then she does something unexpected: In a congratulatory tone, high fiving them as she passes them in their line, she says, "It appears that you are the big winners!" When she gets to the other end of the stage, she turns to the crowd and declares, "Appearances however, can be deceiving. Let me demonstrate what I mean."

Olivia asks the Oasis Team, "By the raise of hands, how many of you would book your next vacation with the agent that talked to you? If you would buy from one or both of your travel agents quickly move to the left side of the room. Divide the money you have left in your envelope in half. In a minute your travel agents are going to come and visit you again to see if you would buy from them. If you would work again with both agents, give each agent an equal share of your remaining money; so that all of the money you started with is distributed. If, however, you would only buy again from one of the agents, make sure to compliment that agent and give him or her all of your remaining money, and let the other agent know why you would not buy from them again.

Travel agents, if the person you sold to has their hand up as a possible repeat buyer take the next five minutes to follow-up with them to see if it's you they would buy from again. When you collect your residual income and your feedback, please come back to the right side of the room."

The room is buzzing. Matt breathes a sigh of relief when he receives the feedback and cash from both of his clients. Then the process is duplicated for the Pearl team and their contractors. I am impressed with this exercise. Beverly comes up and I hand her an additional $9,000, all of what I have left in my envelope. Then Michael comes up. Somehow he knows he is only going to get some feedback from me. I share, "In the real world I may not have hired you at all, so it's a bit of a gift that I gave you the first $500. If you had listened to what I really wanted and served those needs without persisting with what you wanted to sell me, I may have returned to buy from you again. I just can't reward behavior that won't serve you once we leave this training."

Olivia has been walking around the room listening to the feedback and interactions and then rejoins the $1,500 earners on the stage. She calls us all to order and then asks, "Now, who has the most money?" There is a loud cheer. "By the raise of hands now who has at least $1,500?" Almost the entire group raises their hands. "Keep your hands up if you have at least $5,000." A few hands go down. "How about $6,000?" Over two- thirds of the room still has their hands up. "How about $9,000?" A few more hands retreat, "And $10,000?" she asks. Still, a majority of hands are up.

"What a remarkable sight," Matt shares with Ann as they observe the crowd dynamics.

Olivia concludes by asking, "So what creates the most lifetime income with the least amount of work?"

There is a resounding response, "Repeat buyers and lifetime customers."

Olivia points out for emphasis, "If you concentrate on single transactional sales, you will always have to replace the last customer with the next. Now, before we go on break does anyone have any questions, comments, observations, or insights?"

Tracy angrily asks, "Why did you give us directions to do one thing, and then reward us for doing something else?"

Unsure of the meaning of her question, Olivia responds, "I'm not sure I understand your question; could you clarify what you mean?"

Tracy discouragingly clarifies, "Well you told us to make as much money as you can, so I did exactly what you said. I sold the promotional trip, and in the end you told us that this was the wrong thing to do."

"This is an excellent question and one that needs a bit of explanation," Olivia begins. "Thank you for your desire to learn, Tracy. Earlier I said that each of you would have to begin looking beyond the obvious in order to take your business to the next level. The instructions were pretty clear, make as much as you can. You interpreted this to mean make as much as you could in the short term.

"Let me ask you a question Tracy. How much did you make from the promotional product sale you made?"

"$1,000," responds Tracy.

"Did you make a sale to the other prospect you had?" Olivia continues.

"Yes."

"And did that other person return to buy from you a second time?"

"Indeed they did," replies Tracy.

"Well then, how much did you make from the repeat customer relationship," Olivia asks?

"$5,000."

Quickly calculating Tracy's total sales, Olivia states, "So if my math is correct, you made $6,000, right? If your job was to make the most money you could, which relationship did you make the most money from?"

"Of course the return sales," replies Tracy.

And before Olivia can continue, Tracy adds an excuse for the misunderstanding, "You didn't tell us that we were going to be able to return to sell again, so I assumed that I only had one chance to make as much as I could."

Olivia responds, "That's an interesting challenge. It goes along with the concept that you will have to look beyond the explicit instructions to be able to most appropriately apply the principles I am teaching you here. You always have the opportunity to support those you serve multiple times, if you earn that right," Olivia continues as she turns to the whole group. "Your job was to make as much as you could, and there are many who made nine and ten thousand dollars. Some made even more; so you didn't make as much as you could in regards to your own sales opportunities: $1,000 versus $5,000. Furthermore, you didn't make as much as many of your classmates. I encourage you and everyone in the group to change your thinking if you are truly going to create massive success going forward.

"Okay it's time for a break. And during this twenty minute break you will need to meet two people whom you haven't been able to spend much time with yet. During your interactions you will want to PIK their lock, talk to them in ways that are meaningful for them, and then find out how they like to be encouraged, recognized, and rewarded for their contribution. Take a 3x5 card with you and make sure to write down what you learn about encouragement, recognition, and rewards and think about how they might relate to each Personal Interaction Key. When we meet again we will be in the main training room where we started this morning." Seeing that there aren't any questions about the assignment Olivia declares, "The training begins now!"

When Olivia comes into the training room everyone is back in their seats and the room is strangely quiet. Olivia breaks the silence by welcoming us back for our last segment of the day. "I hope you enjoyed your time on break. So tell me what did you learn?"

A man says, "The people I talked to seemed to like to be encouraged and rewarded in similar ways. That is to say, they both seemed to like to be rewarded with some kind of social gathering, and they said that the best encouragement comes from having long talks about how they will be able to better serve and support more people if they keep improving and working towards their goals. Interestingly, both of the people I talked to are Minivans."

A woman in the back stands and shares, "I talked to a Sports Car and a Hybrid and they seem completely different, so by the time I finished talking to each I was completely confused as to what I was really learning and figuring out." She finishes her comment by saying, "I am glad that this session is going to clarify this idea because I have been thinking for some time now about how to give recognition and rewards to my team members that will really mean something to them."

Olivia uses this as the perfect segue to talk about meaningful encouragement, recognition and rewards, based on Personal Interaction Keys. "So let's get started," Olivia announces as if it were a command to charge ahead. "I will discuss these in the same order that we have been talking about the other topics, beginning with Sports Cars."

Encouragement, Recognition and Rewards for Sports Cars.

"Because Sports Cars are very visual, they love to *see* that you appreciate them. They crave a big production put on in their behalf. They won't tell you this, but they want the spotlight and they want you to show others that you appreciate them and that they are being rewarded for achievement. When you give them recognition and rewards, do it very publicly and dramatically with a gift of some kind that befits the achievement. They love awards that make a visual statement, like a trophy or a fancy watch or other jewelry, something that can be shown off that gets them attention. Conversely, encouragement or correction should be done privately, as they will see this as a sign that all is not going as planned, and they would never want anyone to know they weren't achieving some spectacular victory. To a Sports Car failure or mediocre results are a sign of weakness and personal failure."

Encouragement, Recognition and Rewards for Minivans.

"Minivans love to *feel* how much you appreciate them. The greatest reward you can give them is your time. So a great reward would be something like a day with the leaders, or a dinner in their honor with their team. But they wouldn't like to sit at the head of the table, and they would want a round table so that they could reach out to everyone in the group. The second greatest reward is a well-timed hug, hand shake, dance, or just a simple holding of hands. They are always looking for a reason to have a party. Anything you can do to include people is an excellent way to reward them.

"Creating a reason to have social gatherings, any personal interaction, and talking in close groups are excellent ways to encourage and reward Minivan's. In fact, the more people present while they receive recognition, the better. They will embrace wholeheartedly the idea of a group hug. While they are receiving individual recognition, they will want to extend their recognition to include all of the people who have played any role in their success no matter the degree of their participation. Team awards and recognition mean more to them than individual accolades.

"They appreciate pictures that have people in them rather than certificates, trophies, or lapel pins. They will carry the picture around with them and from time to time they will take it out and touch the people in the picture as if they were with them in that moment. Encouragement should be done privately, so as not to notify others that they might be having difficulty. They want to shelter their team members from any idea that there might be pain and struggle involved in building their team."

Encouragement, Recognition and Rewards for Pickup Trucks.

"Pickup Trucks love to *hear* how much you appreciate them, what they are doing, and how much they contribute to the success of the whole team. Any act of service that you do for them tells them that you admire and value them. Kind, well-chosen words also affirm how much their efforts mean to the achievement of personal and team goals. Words of appreciation make all the difference, and inspire the Pickup Truck to do even more miraculous work. They are team players, and as such, are not too worried or desirous of the spotlight. All they need is for you to make sure to acknowledge how their contribution got things done and made a difference in the overall success of the team.

"They love certificates and plaques with inscriptions for accomplishments of efficiency and effective team work on a particular project. The more awards you can give them for this kind of work, the better. The awards don't have to be elaborate; they just need to be displayable. The words you use when you present the award or recognition will be more memorable to them than the award itself. A tangible award serves to remind them of the recognition ceremony and what they heard in the presentation. Encouragement should be done in a team atmosphere where everyone can hear what they as the leader of the "worker bee" club is being encouraged to achieve."

Encouragement, Recognition and Rewards for Hybrids.

"Hybrids also love to *hear* how much you appreciate them and what they are doing. More than anything else you could ever do, verbal compliments and kind words affirming your appreciation are powerful communicators of gratitude and encouragement to any Hybrid. Hybrids love to hear someone recite a bulleted list of the individual wins that led to the completion of a goal on time and as efficiently as possible. They don't want attention or the spotlight, so a certificate, plaque, or a letter detailing how their contribution has led to success is the best possible reward for their efforts. They will display the award and the letter together as a reminder of that success and to let everyone know that attention to detail is the way success is created. From time to time they will even take the time to read the letter out loud, so that they can replay the recognition ceremony. Make sure that the awards you give are of similar size and shape so that they can easily be shown off in a symmetrical display. Encouragement needs to be specific, and you must connect the encouragement to the achievement of particular goals.

"Now that you know all this, I want you to take out the 3x5 card on which you wrote information about the neighbor you talked to just after lunch. Your assignment is to take the next thirty minutes to create some kind of award or symbol of recognition to acknowledge the person you talked to as if they had achieved that greater cause, higher purpose, or fulfilled their passion today. What ever you create should be appropriate for their Personal Interaction Key, so that they will see, hear, or feel what it will be like to accomplish something they can leave as a legacy to future generations. We have all kinds of materials here in the front of the room for you to choose from in which to create your award for your new, team mate. Please spread out into all three rooms so that you can have some room to work, and remember this: We make a living by what we get. We make a life by what we give."

All of a sudden, Matt feels very small and inadequate as he contemplates the incredible and awesome responsibility to make sure to give proper recognition for achieving a life legacy goal. He thinks, this certainly isn't some gold star or sticker that I sometimes give out at department meetings, a relic from grade school. As I think about those stickers, it occurs to me that maybe I should re-evaluate what I am doing to reward achievement, including how to recognize different kinds of accomplishment. But I don't have time to think of that right now, and I return to the present. I need to focus on how to encourage, recognize, and reward my new friend Patti from Memphis.

I spend a few minutes contemplating what Patti needs. I make a plan, and then go to work. I only hope I can finish all that I want to accomplish for her in the next thirty minutes. My sole focus is on Patti. She is a Hybrid, so I create a plaque, a certificate, and a letter of congratulations that I will read detailing her achievement.

When the thirty minutes is up, Olivia calls time and then declares, "This is the moment of truth for many of you. It's time to recognize your colleague for accomplishing a major achievement. Please take the next twenty minutes and acknowledge each other as partners in the appropriate way. I will tell you when the first ten minutes are gone, so you can switch from giver to receiver."

Matt pauses to reflect a minute about the difference between being a giver and a receiver. I am so filled with gratitude for this opportunity to recognize Patti that I feel like I am receiving, even when I am giving. This is a great feeling to have. I am definitely committed to examine how I do recognition and rewards when I get home.

Olivia doesn't give any instructions on who should go first, and I feel like my manners should rule here: Patti, being a woman, should receive first. She agrees and I begin my presentation by handing her the plaque, which is a picture of a huge home that would serve as a home for the kids she is so passionate to help. The picture is mounted on cardboard that I took from a box on the table. The certificate is written on the blank side of a 3x5 card with an inscription that says, "More than an accomplishment or achievement, this certificate of conquest is awarded to Patti Doyle of XL-8 in honor of your meeting milestones including getting investors, and community and religious leaders to hear your call to action. For overcoming barriers of land developers, construction crews, and financiers. For enrolling teachers, volunteers, staff, parents, and transition teams to help young adults go from governmental programs to the private real world." As she reads the certificate she begins to cry.

Patti looks up and says, "Thank you," through the tears.

I told her, "I am not done yet," and read the letter of congratulations I wrote as a verbal reinforcement of all that she had accomplished. It reads, "As Governor of Tennessee, representing all the people in this state, and in conjunction with XL-8, I give you my congratulations and appreciation for hearing and answering a greater call to help an under-served group of our citizens. I congratulate you for meeting goals, including organizing the physical requirements of purchasing the land, building the home, enlisting the help and cooperation of community, religious, business, and medical leaders. You have done a masterful job of enrolling the necessary teachers, volunteers, staff, parents, and transition teams from the limited governmental organizations to assist in this phenomenal, privately run program. Your dedication, persistence, and commitment to excellence has brought this project to completion on time and as efficiently as possible. I celebrate the hundreds of hours of work, your call to action, and attention to detail which have made this tremendous service possible."

Reaching out to shake her hand and give her the letter, she uncharacteristically gives me a hug.

She whispers, "This is just the thing I needed to be persuaded to pursue this goal."

Now we are both crying. This is definitely one of those moments that I will never forget because of the human connection. I want to encourage her to pursue this passion because there are literally millions of kids who will benefit from the skills and knowledge that her program will provide, but it seems trivial to break up this moment by speaking.

Patti wipes the tears from her eyes and then gives me an origami trophy she made out of newspapers and paper clips in the shape of a Sports Car. I took a few minutes just looking at and admiring the ingenuity of this trophy. She wrote an inscription at the base and in true Hybrid style, feels compelled to read it to me.

She reads, "In honor of traveling through life at supersonic speed, inspiring others along your journey to achieve their greater causes and higher purposes."

What an inspired idea and a perfect reward for me to work for. I know just the place in my office to put this. We exchange a look of gratitude and love for a minute. It reminds me of the quote I learned from Ann, "Teach the gospel to everyone you meet, use words if necessary."

Just then Olivia calls time and invites everyone to return to the main training room. As I look around there isn't a dry eye anywhere. What a way to quickly bind hearts, minds, and lives together in just a few minutes. The appropriate use of encouragement, recognition, and rewards is certainly a powerful tool that I have obviously paid much too little attention to. I am certainly planning to use this new found skill and knowledge with Ann, as well as with my team members and clients at work.

Olivia can tell from the emotional outpouring that if she tried to do a debrief on this session it would just reopen emotional flood gates and that no one would be able to learn anything more important than they already had. She lets it be silent for a moment, and then she takes a few minutes to recap what we had been learning. She thanks us for being such a great group and shares her appreciation for our being willing to share and grow so that the world would be a better place for having us in it. She tells us, "There is one more assignment to complete and when you are done with it you need to see Mike Black to get the details on your next meeting, which will be conducted via the company's on-line video conference training system. After you have the details from Mr. Black you are free to go, or hang around and visit, make new friends, or just decompress. The final assignment," she explains, "You need to connect with yourself. Write in your notes, 'What value did you get from this event? How will you use it? What goals do you have now for the next month(s)?"

Matt takes a time out with his head in his hands for a full five minutes to gather his composure and reflect on what he has experienced today. I can't believe it has only been one day. It feels a lot longer, just because I feel I have learned so much. From PIKing locks to interacting with others through their natural way of being, and then appropriately recognizing people, I am swimming with new ideas and information. What does all this mean and how can I put it all together to make a bigger difference? I definitely need to confer with Ann about how I can support her to use all this to grow her team and get ideas about how I can use this to develop my team at work to provide better support for my company through increased value to clients.

I open my note book and start to write the first thoughts that come to my mind. It took me many months to get promoted to Department Coordinator and only a few months to be promoted to Division Manager. What changed, I wonder. Did my PEPs in building relationships really grow that much in a few months? Did the value of my service to clients transcend single transactions to transformations? Maybe it is the value of my service to both clients and team members that attracted attention. Whatever the case, it seems like what I am learning from Steve and now Olivia is transformative. It appears that I am leading my own transformation at work. So, back to the question Olivia asked us to ponder: what value did I get from this experience?

Primarily I see that I need to be 100% dedicated to the idea that to really serve those over whom I have stewardship I must focus on their interests, rather than my own. The only way to offer any value to their life is to initiate, develop, and maintain a relationship that rewards both of us for the effort. I have known for a long time now that people are different from each other. Now I can identify the differences before and during my interactions with people. I can talk to everyone in ways that attract them to me, and I can now invite people to take appropriate action that will serve their own interests, and by so doing I will be rewarded.

I guess the bottom line is that the only way for me to get what I want is by drawing people to me. I can do this by first PIKing the lock on their relationship gateway; second, interacting with them in appropriate ways that build trust, so third, they will articulate what they want and take the recommendations I prescribe because they consider me a valued partner in the relief of their pain.

I see now that I don't need to ride on the coattails of Bruce to the Executive Floor, I believe that by using what I learn here and mastering it over the next months, I will lead a changeover within my Division that will open doors to a Regional Manager level in the next six months! The executives will have to promote me to keep me in the company when we begin to create legendary rhino results.

While pondering this assignment, I look over to Ann who is deep in thought. Unbeknownst to me, she is asking herself whether it is possible that now she really understands how to build relationships that provide enough value to prospects, customers, and team members to reach the next level in her business? She thinks, I am at the Silver level, with four Silver level achievers on my team. I only need one more Silver team to qualify at the Gold Level. I am duplicating myself well. The two Silver teams I have each have two Silver groups within them, and many others who are climbing the promotion ladder. With this new information, I feel like I can help two more groups that are working towards and that are close to the Silver level achieve that milestone in the next month or two. Their success would result in my being promoted to the Gold level. Now that I think of it this way, this goal seems possible and possible soon.

Although I am already doing some of the things I have learned here today, I will need to make some changes to increase the value of my service. I also need to dedicate myself to the legendary measurement of work and results and increase the rating of my relationships. If Matt is willing to support me, I am committed to qualify for the next promotions and help anyone who wants to climb the promotion ladder with me to do so as well. I know for every prize there is a price, and for every price there is a prize. I am sure that this will be worth it from a price and prize perspective.

Ann stands up at this point, and Matt can see renewed determination on her face as she gathers her things together and stands up. She looks around the room for Matt, and sees that he stood up almost at the same time. They both take this as a sign that they seem to be in sync about moving forward.

Matt thinks as Ann walks over to him, even though we aren't invited to participate in all the meetings of the retreat we have time to plan our next moves and spend time with Steve and Sara. Sitting beside the hotel pool waiting for Ann to get done with her massage, I take some time to revisit the things I learned from Steve about Relationship Ratings and Value of Service Scores. Remembering my walk back to my office when I had been promoted, a couple of important numbers come to my mind: my own general Relationship Rating that increased from an 8 to a 32 in a few months, and each of his team members ratings, that increased by an average of twenty-five percent. As I contemplate this it occurs to me that I haven't really gone through this exercise with my Department Coordinators. I also haven't taken the time to evaluate my Trust Quotient or my Value of Service Score with them.

As I consider this, Steve's voice comes to my mind as vividly, as if he is standing right beside me. Steve emphatically responded to Alexandra's objection about the level of detail they required when discussing how relationships are critical to success, saying, "Why would anyone choose to engage with me? Why, because I have 83 PEPs, a Relationship Rating of 74, my Value of Service is 115, and my conversion ratios are better than 60%, 60%, 90%. And because of those factors, I can teach you how to take full advantage of the 3-step success pattern and how to optimize our pay plan. Why me? Because I can actually help you be proactive in your life and create a life that you can be passionate about. That's why me! Steve has also told me that this is a relationship business, and the things he is constantly teaching are all ingredients in the relationship recipe.

As I think about Steve's response to Alexandra, a similar question comes to my mind: why would my Department Coordinators engage with me? What value do I bring to them? How effective am I at teaching them how to be effective managers, leaders, and client service representatives? How effective am I at teaching them how to teach their teams to be effective? A moment of pain comes to my stomach, knowing that, based on what I learned about Personal Interaction Keys, I am not serving with as much effectiveness as I can. So what to do, I ask myself? I know exactly what to do: I need to start at the start by going through the exercises Steve taught me and that I have been sharing with my team.

Department Coordinators

	Relationship Rating Calculation:	
- Dayna, (7)		
- Jaylin, (8)		
- Ray, (8)	Total score	44.5
- Shelly, (6)	# of People	÷ 6
- Mylisa, (8.5)	Initial Score	7.4
- Kayci (7)	Multiplier	X 10
	Initial rating	74
	Discount (100-89)	- 26
	Adjusted Rating	48

I also re-read my notes on Trust Quotients and PEPs, and did the calculations, changing the questions so that they would apply solely to my Department Coordinators, and the score comes back as a 22 out of 25. Pretty good, according to what Steve had taught us. Lastly, I re-do the Value of Service assessment, again changing the questions to apply only to my team members. My Value of Service Score is 111 out of 125 with this group.

Although I feel bad about having a Relationship Rating of 48, I feel pretty good about a Trust Quotient of 22 and a Value of Service Score of 111. I start to plan how to create industry changing results with the team I have. The more I plan, the more uneasy I become. It occurs to me that I am falling into the "Make as Much Money as You Can" trap. I am jumping in and doing things that might solve short-term problems, but I am ignoring what I have just learned from Olivia about interacting with my team in the most appropriate ways for each of them. I need to take a moment to jot down some notes about each of them and determine what I think their Key category is before I go any further. I walk to the front desk to get a few more 3x5 cards so that I can write a note about each of my team members and review them regularly when I get home.

My first card reads, "Dayna is a Sports Car. She seems to thrive on the challenge of being the model Division in the company, and she is set on being the model department in our Division. She is the one who came to see me first. She doesn't worry too much about details, because she didn't even know why her department was not performing as well as mine. She is glad to have a mentor who can teach her how to succeed. Her office is always clean and well-organized. She is always well-dressed and she pays close attention to her hair and makeup. She talks really fast and has finished my sentences for me. And her reports always have little notes about the challenges she has to overcome to meet her objectives."

Jaylin's card reads, "Jaylin is a Minivan. In her introduction she pointed out that she is married with children, and that she met her husband at a social event. When she met me the first time she reached out to shake my hand and pulled me towards her a bit. Even though she is a new Department Coordinator, she knows everyone in the company, and oddly everyone seems to know her. She has come to our weekly meeting without a pen or notebook paper, and she lost last week's report on her very messy and unorganized desk. She wears comfortable clothes and everyday she has a different set of really big earrings."

Ray's card says, "Ray is a minivan. He enthusiastically jumps into conversations, often without thinking before he speaks. He seems more excited to be on the Olympic team than he is about winning or competing at a high level. I don't know how he gets anything done; there is always someone in his office chatting away. He has post-it notes all over his office and he looks like he gets dressed in the dark most days. A lot of the time he doesn't have his shoes on in the office and he makes me crazy when he taps his fingers on the table during our weekly meetings.

"Shelly is the group's Pickup Truck. She is the model worker-bee employee. She gets more done in a few hours than most everyone else gets done in a day. When I asked her to be the test department for tracking results she didn't or couldn't decide right then, and when she did agree she had a detailed plan of how she would do the test. Her department is the most predictable and consistent. She always takes time to think before she responds to questions or situations. She wants the details about process and expectations before she begins working. Her office is more like organized chaos than Jaylin's mess. There are items that get left out, but they seem to be arranged in some meaningful way. When I ask her to recall something or invent a creative solution she always seems to look straight across, not up or down. Her emotions are very measured. Her office door is always closed, so that she won't be disturbed, and so that no-one will hear the music she listens to.

"Mylisa is a Minivan. She loves sports cars, which indicates a free and fun loving spirit. She loves to be the center of attention. She is the captain of the company volleyball team, and sends all of us a report on their progress with an invitation to join the fun and camaraderie of playing. She loves working here, but dreams of having a non-profit organization to help domestic violence victims. Although I don't know how she will run a company when she can't keep track of her personal items. I find something that belongs to her almost everyday somewhere in our office.

"Kayci is the lone Hybrid in the group. She notices the details of everything. She gets her work done everyday with great precision, and according to the letter of the law written in the company policies and procedures manual. She is extremely logical and takes a long time to make decisions if I give her choices. She hates it when I change my mind about meetings or schedules. She loves her planner and keeps facts and figures about everything. When she goes home at night, there is a detailed list of things to do the next day typed and in order of how she needs to do them the next day. She also has a wide variety of knick-knacks well-ordered on her shelves in front of the books. When I talk to her, I feel like we are dancing. I want to stand directly in front of her and she always turns slightly to the side. She has a masterful way of complicating everything."

Looking at all this together I have a lot of ideas going through my head. I have a group with three Minivans, one Hybrid, one Pickup Truck, and only one who is like me: Dayna. That explains some of my challenges with Shelly. Of all my direct reports, I have the worst relationship with her. She worries about process and details, and I focus on bottom-line results. I'll bet she feels like a lone wolf in our group. Besides Kayci, she is the only one concerned about how things will get done. Jaylin, Ray, and Mylisa should be the easiest and most willing to learn about building relationships because that's right up their alley.

This is invaluable leadership insight. How does anyone effectively manage any team of people without knowing these things? I need to make sure all of my meetings have a consistent structure and sequence, including a process for how the results I expect will be achieved. I also want to begin each weekly meeting with some kind of recognition or award. Then I need to make sure to include a training segment each week to teach them how to teach their team members to thrive and prosper. Lastly I want to make sure to include a way for them to report on the Relationship Rating, Trust Quotient, Value of Service Score, and Key category for each of their team members. It seems that following Steve's advice about tracking results makes sense: if I measure it, I will be able to improve on it.

I have been home now for a while and have been implementing the ideas I had at the pool. My meetings are much more productive, and the morale of the group seems to be improving along with our relationships. I have used the past month since the leadership retreat to teach the concepts of identifying Key types, PIKing relationship gateway locks, talking to people according to their natural way of being, and using appropriate encouragement strategies.

The work is paying off. In just two months, our division moved from fourth to second in overall profitability. Our customer acquisition costs are down 22%, new accounts grew by over 14%. Customer up-sells increased by 17% and 53% of our business now comes from existing customers. Our retention rates increased by 9%. Our customer satisfaction surveys are now the highest in the entire company. Shelly and Dayna have the number one and two departments in the company. And in our own results tracking system, the average Relationship Rating increased by 120% for my direct reports, and 68% for the whole division. The average Trust Quotient improved by 47% for my leaders, and 52% for the division as a whole. And the Value of Service Score went up by 36% in the leaders and 39% for the division.

I lean back in my chair thinking about the enormity of this accomplishment, basking in the good news, and reflecting on this amazing success. I attribute our continued success to our understanding of the underlying three principles. 1) People do trust us, 2) We are good at what we do, and 3) We do care about our prospects and clients. As I look up, Shelly unexpectedly comes into my office.

She confidently tells me, "I want to report my findings for the conversion ratio project you asked me to test a few months ago. It has been a huge success. It has helped me as a Department Coordinator to be able to spot challenges that were hidden before. Because of that, I can take corrective action faster than ever before. I don't know how you learned this but it has been a great help to me."

Uncharacteristically pausing for a moment as I think about how to respond I say, "Congratulations Shelly. First of all you need to know that the division is now in second place in the company and your department is now in first place in the company in overall profitability. You have been a great inspiration to the whole division. I will talk to Kayci and she will arrange to have a special recognition lunch for your department next week so that we can congratulate your whole team."

Shelly's countenance changes immediately. She responds as she stands up to leave, looking to the side to hide the tear in her eye, "Thank you Matt. Thank you for all you do for us."

It takes a full five minutes for me to recover before calling Kayci. While I am sitting here, I recognize that without the principles I have learned and implemented, my relationship with Shelly and all the others would probably be adversarial at best. I take a moment to plan out the best way to recognize and reward Shelly and then I call Kayci, "Please order a plaque for Shelly and include her department's numbers for the month and a congratulatory remark about their number-one ranking in the company. I also need you to arrange a special lunch for her whole department next week. So please check with Shelly about the best day, and I will arrange my schedule to attend and make a presentation of the plaque to her in honor of her team."

Since returning from the leadership retreat, Ann is also making serious progress in her quest to achieve the Gold level in her business. On the plane ride home from the retreat she did the same activity I did by the pool. She recalculated her relationship numbers and got a Relationship Rating for her team members of 82, her Trust Quotient was 24, and her Value of Service Score is 114. She also wrote a brief note about each of her team member's Key with ideas on how she would interact with each of them differently to improve their relationship.

Almost every day we discuss how we are implementing Trust Quotients, Relationship Ratings, Value of Service, and PIKing locks; as we had learned. During one of our discussions Ann remarks, "We do have a major difference in the solutions we offer to people."

"Really? What is the difference," I ask.

"We both begin our conversations by finding out what people want, but you only have to concern yourself with choosing the right product or service to recommend based on the results they want to create. You have no income offering to consider. I have to focus on whether my prospects want the results of the features and benefits of my products and services, or whether they want the results my income offering provides by joining my team as an associate or both! It would be so much easier to just focus on the product side of my business, but I know that the majority of my XL-8 income comes from bonuses and overrides I receive by leveraging the revenues from my team members. It seems like there are two parts to my business: a product side generating quick income from relationships I build personally, and the team building side, which requires me to both build customer relationships and foster associate relationships from team building activity.

"So it seems that I must master these skills to a deeper level because I offer products and services that relieve people's pain, and I also offer a career opportunity to people who are not trained business people. Some days it makes me tired just thinking about it. The good news is that I am in control of my advancement and income, and you are at the mercy of a management hierarchy. So I guess there are trade offs."

Matt responds by saying, "That's why you make all the big money right?" We chuckle for a moment and then I share my victory with Shelly and the conversion ratio pilot test and ask Ann how the conversion ratio tracking process is working for her."

Ann responds with pride, "My results have been just as amazing as Shelly's. I have helped three of my groups achieve the next promotion level to Gold level since we've been back. This is far beyond what is required for my own promotion to Gold level."

During this week's team training, Ann continues a careful implementation of her success team program that she planned out a few months ago. She is focusing on growing leaders on her team and creating transformations instead of transactions. At her weekly training, after the introductions, announcements, and the brief Residual Income Business Building Simulation, Ann invests a few minutes to help her team realize the importance of building trust as a foundation for building a strong and profitable business.

"The bottom line with trust," Ann begins, "Is that when you have people's trust they will tell you what is really going on, so you can work together on resolution and on taking action that relieves pain. Trust is as much emotional as rational. People become suspicious when they feel disrespected and less valued. Mistrust is really an indication of broken or ineffective relationship development. The reason I often talk about PEPs is because people with low trust PEPs focus on transactions instead of transformations. They concentrate on trading long term, life-long relationships for short term, one time, transactional events.

"Enrolling people either as customers or associates is a result of trust rather than some sales technique. Trust is what motivates people to take action on the recommendations we prescribe for their specific pain. People must feel that we are there to help them in the short term, and life-long relationships are the result of building a track record of performance that supports their trust. When we do that, people will trust us, and they will freely tell us their concerns and challenges because they believe we really are there to help them resolve their issues and move them towards their goals."

Author's Note:
The instructions explaining the mathematical equation for this chapter is in the appendix at the end of the book.

8

Where's the Target?

Like we were at the retreat, I am sure that we will be the first ones to this training session too. But as we turn into the parking lot of the auditorium, there are already two cars parked in the spaces closest to the doors: two Jaguars, a sapphire blue convertible and a deep metallic red coupe. I recognize the blue jag as Steve Thoms'. I feel some jealousy because I assume the other Jaguar is Sara's. I think, but don't say to Ann, "Isn't that quaint: his and her Jaguars." Probably not my best moment. We park a little ways off from their cars so as not to attract attention to our less-than-Jaguar class sedan.

As we wait for the event to start, we talk about what we think this training will be about. I am secretly hoping that Steve will cover the details of high-yielding questions. But I don't want to get too overheated about what I think might be next. Steve has surprised me too many times now. I'm listening to Ann giving advice to one of her new Gold level associates when the music comes up and the auditorium lights dim. The host runs out, excitedly makes her announcements, and introduces Steve. Walking onto the stage to a huge ovation, which he graciously accepts, Steve invites everyone to sit down so that we can get started.

He begins, as he always does, by asking a question. Except this time the question is an invitation for two volunteers from the audience to join him on stage. I learned from working for my dad and watching hypnotist shows, not to volunteer for anything. By the time I talk myself out of volunteering; two willing participants have already leapt onto the stage. Steve asks them their names. Both are very energetic; one is Lori, the other Madeline.

Steve has a makeshift ten-foot wide, by ten-foot deep, by ten-foot high cubical brought out onto the stage. He hands Madeline a huge dartboard with a one-foot diameter bull's eye, and tells her, "If Lori misses the bull's eye you will get $100. You can put the dartboard anywhere you want inside the cubical." There is a camera mounted above the little room that shows everyone in the audience what's going on in the little room. As Madeline is hanging the dart board, Steve hands Lori one dart and explains, "If you can hit the bull's eye with one throw of the dart you will get $100."

Matt thinks, I don't remember either my dad or any of the hypnotists

I saw ever paying their volunteers. Maybe Steve isn't just entertaining us; maybe the greatest experience really is for the volunteers."

Steve then explains to everyone that Madeline will come out, blindfold Lori, lead her into the room, and slowly spin her around twice. His final instructions to Lori are that she can have Madeline in the room with her to answer any questions she has, or she can excuse Madeline and do this on her own. Just as he finishes, Madeline returns with a big, sneaky grin on her face from the small room where she put the dartboard near the floor in the corner of the west wall.

Steve hands Madeline the blindfold and tells her that if Lori asks her questions, she must answer honestly. The pair enters the room only visible to us via a camera projected on a couple of big screens in the front of the auditorium.

Not knowing what to do, Lori asks Madeline, "Where are we standing in the room?"

Madeline responds, "We are in the center of the room."

Lori asks, "What wall is the target on?"

Madeline tells her vaguely, "The wall to your left."

Not knowing exactly how far to the left to turn, Lori asks Madeline to turn her towards that wall.

As soon as she is facing the wall that had the target Lori throws her one and only dart. It makes a thud as it hits the wooden wall, missing the bull's eye by a full five feet. Lori removes the blindfold, and both women come out of the cube. Steve hands Madeline a crisp $100 bill.

Lori exclaims, "That's not fair! Madeline had a huge advantage, and she didn't have to do anything for her money. Throwing darts blindfolded is much more difficult than hanging a target and just standing there."

Steve smiles as he asks Lori, "What was your strategy in determining where and when you would throw the dart?"

Lori responds, "Once she told me which wall the target was on I imagined the target in the middle of that wall, and threw the dart where I thought the target would be."

"Why did you think the target was in the middle of the wall? Did Madeline tell you it was there?"

"No, she didn't help me at all. I guessed the middle of the wall because I have seen people playing darts on television, and that's where the target usually is."

Steve continues, "Did Madeline answer every question you asked her?"

"Well, yes," Lori answers, embarrassed at remembering that Madeline did exactly as much as she asked her to do.

"Then it was completely fair," Steve concludes as he invites them to take their seats, and asks for two new volunteers. There is almost a brawl as people run to get on the stage first. The next two participant's names are Dagen and Dean.

Steve repeats the instructions for hanging the dartboard to Dagen, and gives the dart-throwing instructions to Dean. They go inside the room and Dean immediately begins asking Dagen questions about their current location in the room, and information about where on the correct wall the dartboard is located. Dagen answers Dean's questions, and after a few minutes Dean throws his only dart, missing the target by only a few inches. When he hears the thud of his dart on the wall he takes off the blindfold and remarks, "That is a lot closer to hitting the mark."

Both Dagen and Dean come out of the cube. Steve gives Dagen her $100 prize, and asks Dean, "What made the difference in your attempt?"

"He answers, "I asked a lot of questions to get Dagen to tell me where the bull's eye was."

"Excellent observation and strategy," Steve says, as he excuses the pair. He turns to the audience and asks everyone, "What did you notice about both pairs?"

A man in front stands up and says, "They both threw their darts from the center of the room. They were both standing at least five feet away from the target when they threw their dart."

A woman from the right side of the room adds, "They asked some questions, but they didn't seem to get their partner to really tell them exactly where the target was."

Ann stands up and exclaims, "They only asked questions about the location of the dartboard. None of their questions were about how close they were standing to the bull's eye. And neither of them reached out to actually touch it before they made their attempt to put the dart in the target. It seems to me that they interpreted the word 'throw' to mean that they had to stand away from the target in order for it to count. I think it would have been better for them to ask their partner for specifics that would get them close enough to feel the board, and then simply insert the dart in the bull's eye."

"All of your observations are fantastic, and right on the money," Steve responds. "If Lori and Dean had asked more questions, and asked better or more focused questions, Madeline and Dagen would have told them exactly where the bull's eye was and how to reach it. So what does this have to do with building your business on purpose, with purpose you might be wondering? Let me ask you about what you just witnessed. You just saw two people throw darts in the dark. Think about this for a moment. What are the chances of anyone really hitting the bull's eye when they have no idea of where it is?

"Lori told us that she guessed because she saw a television show once. Throwing darts in the dark is the recipe for failure. The good news is that this kind of failure is predictable and duplicate-able. But none of us want to

THE BULL'S EYE

predictably create or duplicate failure. So what do you do about it? How do you turn the lights on, or how do you get your partner to tell you with absolute precision where the bull's eye is?

"Here's the secret: when you master asking high-yielding questions, your prospects will tell you exactly where their pain is. What they want their life to be like. How their present life is different from the one they want. Essentially they will tell you exactly where their bull's eye is and where you are in relation to it.

"Just like Madeline and Dagen, they won't just come right out and tell you; you will have to ask. You must learn to ask, listen, and then repeat the process because they may not trust you yet, or they may not know how to tell you where their bull's eye is at first. You may not have a close enough relationship that they believe what you offer will relieve their specific pain. Or perhaps the value of your service is not high enough yet, or you may be talking about relieving pain they don't have!

"Use the power of high-yielding questions to determine people's interest in learning more about what you offer as it relates to them. Resist the urge to 'answer' questions until after you know what your prospects want or need. Assure them that you will answer their questions when you understand them better, and that most of their questions are answered in your presentation and materials. Your goal should be to show them our entire offering and all of the benefits before they make a decision. So today we are going to talk about high-yielding questions, and then do a practice activity.

"When you are learning about your prospects, you need to ask questions that require more than a one word or one sentence answer. You are not looking for a specific answer like yes or no or today, or $2,000 per month. You are inviting them to articulate the cause and effect of their pain, or what the underlying desire for a specific result is. For example, if you ask someone how much money they want to make each month, you will probably get a specific answer like $2,000 per month. However, if you ask, 'What would you do if you were making extra income every month?' Once you have determined what they can't do now that they would like to do, you can always follow-up with 'how much would that cost?' or 'how much would you have to make in order to do that?'

"Here are some simple rules to follow that will inspire them to engage with you and enroll as an active participant in their own life."

1. "Learn to talk little; ask high-yielding questions and listen much. Substitute your opinion and advice with high-yielding questions. Use the time you normally spend talking in listening to the responses you elicit with high-yielding questions. Don't spew all over them with your dazzle and sparkle. People like people who show interest in them. Ask questions

and be interested in their responses. When the prospect is talking, listen carefully, because they will tell you exactly what to emphasize in your presentation, and in your invitation to take action. Invest more time learning to listen and less time talking, presenting, or overcoming objections. They will get that you care about their needs, and that you are sharing something that could affect their life.

"Without unlocking the relationship gateway to gain access to your prospect's mind, it is impossible to make an *appropriate* recommendation that will truly solve their need. High-yielding questions allow you to successfully uncover challenges and desires. Sometimes people haven't really thought about the cause of their pain; they just know they hurt. It may be that they simply haven't put two and two together, and high-yielding questions can help them make the connections.

"Most people don't understand that you never learn anything when you are talking. You can't learn what your prospects need, want, or care about if you can't be silent. You must learn to listen, and truly hear what they are saying, because you can't propose solutions to problems you haven't heard. First you must build rapport with them, so they sense that you are interested in what they want and need."

2. "Find out what is important to them. Find out what their pain is. It may be money, health, time, stress, debt, or something else. What do they love? What do they want more of in life? What do they want less of? If you don't know them very well, start with where they live and what they like best about it. Find out where they would live if they could live anywhere in the world. Ask about their work. How long have they been doing it? What do they like and dislike about it? Asking questions focuses you on the other person, and ensures that you fully understand their circumstances. This is critical in determining an actual solution for their challenges.

3. "Be enthusiastic about what you offer, and believe in the possibilities of a different future. Make sure you broadcast by your facial expressions and body language that you are listening, and are excited to help them solve the challenges they are sharing with you. Everyone wants excitement and the feeling of making progress towards their ideal life. You have a vehicle that can take them to their dreams! Make sure that they see you believe it."

4. "Don't worry too much about having exact memorized answers to all of the questions that people could ask. Most people are more interested in the fact that there *is* an answer than whether you have the actual answer right at that moment. But make sure you get back to them with the right answer, once you take time to find out what it is."

"After you have begun the questioning process, the next step is to adapt your questions to help your prospects in three important ways: 1) To help them become aware of their own issues. When they become aware of and can describe their problems, hopes, and passions, they will be more likely to *accept* and sign off on solutions that address those issues. 2) They will understand that you have an answer for the desires they have not yet realized. When you gain a greater understanding of what they want, you can provide value as a solution provider. 3) You will understand their priorities, difficulties, decision making processes, and their perception of risks, concerns, and pain. Knowing all this helps you position your products and services more effectively.

"In short, the more information you can gather, the better chance you have of proposing the right solution. Again, without complete data, you run the risk of throwing darts at a target you can't even see. And the result will be very much like what you saw here a few minutes ago.

"Before we go any further, I want to give you a surprise. I have been thinking and pondering how to best teach this lesson so that each of you would be able to fully understand it and begin using it by the end of this meeting. I felt inspired a few weeks ago to call one of my mentors in the business and ask for his advice on this subject. I called him specifically because he is the world's greatest authority on asking high-yielding questions, and during the conversation he volunteered to help me help you by coming here and teaching you himself. So with that, help me welcome to the stage Double Platinum, David McKay!"

As the tall professionally dressed man walks out onto the stage, everyone stands up and cheers for over two minutes. I remember meeting him at the retreat, but this group welcomes him as if he were one of the Beatles or something. He seems like a great guy, but, I find this reception kind of over the top. No one welcomes anyone at my office like this. Maybe I should invest a little more effort in recognizing my Department Coordinators and Floor Level Planners with this kind of recognition. As I remember the cars in the parking lot I conclude that this probably explains the second Jaguar in the parking lot. I am disappointed, a little, in myself. This is the second time that my judgment has been wrong today, and brought out my less worthy self. First I mocked the Thomses for having multiple luxury cars (and I was wrong about that), and then I laughed at the volunteers as if they were chumps for wanting to learn at the hands of a master trainer. Thinking back to the lesson about trust makers and trust breakers, I am certain now that jumping to conclusions with little or no information is probably a trust breaker for me. Maybe I should include it in my warning label. I write a note about this in my notebook and circle it with a couple of stars out to the side.

After this side note, I feel excited to get the inside scoop on high-yielding questions. I have had questions about this topic since the very first time I heard Steve mention it. And to learn this from the foremost authority on the subject is a bonus. I have my notepad out and make sure my pen is working while I wait for the crowd to settle down.

David begins by edifying Steve saying, "What a perfect demonstration about the importance of asking questions. Great job Steve, and thank you for the introduction and welcome." David starts his presentation telling us emphatically, "If you master what I am going to share with you today, every relationship you have or want to have will improve. Steve alluded earlier to a simple process that I learned from one of my best friends, Glenna Hanks, who discovered this formula while taking a shower one day before she gave a presentation as I will explain in a moment. The process I am going to share with you today came from that auspicious beginning and is called Ask, Listen, and Repeat.

"This process is the key to enhancing all relationships, and relationships are the foundation or bottom line to all successful activities and endeavors in this business and in your family, community, church, government and et cetera."

Matt shaking his head cynically says under his breath, "You've got to be kidding. I can't imagine that the relationship secret of the universe was discovered while someone read shampoo bottle directions one day in the twenty-first century. If it's that easy, how come more people don't know about it?" Ann's nudge brings me back to reality and brings to mind my previous thought that I need to stop judging when I have little or no information. I remember that many of the greatest discoveries have been made by accident, and attempt to regain my focus.

David continues the story, "While Glenna was taking a shower one day, contemplating how to communicate more effectively, she stumbled on the formula to successful human interaction. Yep, in the shower! You might be thinking I've lost my mind. But in all seriousness, when she read the three step instructions: wash, rinse and repeat on the shampoo bottle, it occurred to her that the process for successful communication is very similar to those three steps. In this case, a great communicator should ask, listen and repeat.

"The formula for failure in relationships is 'talk, and then talk more.' In fact, my experience is that some people have mastered talking to the point where they can talk people in and out of the business in the same conversation. If you want to engage more people as customers and associates, you might consider learning to ask, listen, and then repeat the cycle. For you to really understand what result your prospects, customers, and associates want, you get to ask, listen, and then repeat. Once you have invested the time and effort it takes to understand people, they will give you the opportunity and ability to make a powerful recommendation of our products, services, or income offering because you know exactly where their bull's eye is.

"Steve's demonstration this morning was fantastic. It clearly demonstrated your prospects' and team members' bull's eye is simply knowing what they want, why they want it and how committed they are to get it. I am certain you have heard the foundational principles, but to make sure no one missed the message, I want to reiterate it now. For people to really take you seriously, and ultimately take the action you ask them to take, they need to know three things: Can they trust you? Are you good at what you do? And do you care about them?

"When you ask high-yielding questions, listen to people, and then repeat the process to gain deeper understanding, people will trust you, they will be convinced that you are good at what you do, and they will know that you care about them. This happens because you are actively engaged in the conversation and are focused on them. It's a good idea to make mental or written notes about what is most important to this particular prospect, customer, or associate and tune into your prospects', customers', and team members' needs. If you don't get them to clearly express their wants and needs, you may be responding to a wrong or misinterpreted message. When you provide an ineffective response, your credibility will crash and so will your business.

"In order for you to provide solutions to your prospects problems you must first know what they are. Build rapport with them so that they get a sense that you are interested in understanding their challenges before you prescribe some form of pain relief. If you interact carefully with your prospects, they will tell you exactly where the bull's eye is. They will direct you as to what to say and do to get them to take action.

"Having a process like Asking, Listening and Repeating takes the emotion out of conversations. This is important because when you get emotional your adrenaline kicks in. Sadly, when your emotion or adrenaline goes up, your intelligence goes down. Bad communication creates damaged, non-functional relationships. When you communicate in a doped up, dumbed down state you perform badly. This is why, when you feel you have the most on the line you perform the worst. For example, if actors rehearse lines for their rolls when no one else is around they can freeze up when the spotlight is on and the audience shows up. Because in that situation, the adrenaline kicks in and mental function goes down.

"The same is true of business builders. If they spend time memorizing scripts and comebacks in a solitary place, they will lose all of their carefully studied scripts when the prospect, customer, or associate is standing in front of them. That's why I teach you to just be curious about people. There is no one, single, best question to ask in every situation. So don't worry about having to memorize what you hope is the correct question every time. Simply look and listen for something you can be curious about and pursue that for a moment or so, until your emotions settle down. It's much easier to calm yourself down when the other person is talking. You can be listening, trying to identify this person's bull's eye, by just looking for something that you can be curious about.

"You will invariably fail to persuade others to adopt new ideas, concepts, products, or services without understanding their needs and wants. And it's difficult to discover anything about others if you enter into their life in an emotional, incoherent, adrenaline-induced state."

As Matt relates what David is teaching to situations in his own life, he finds it explains a lot about why his relationship with his dad has always been difficult, and his relationships with Oscar Lambert and Bill Rena have always been easy and meaningful. I never bothered to ask my dad if he had plans for me and the ranch, and he never bothered to ask me what I wanted my life to be like; whereas Oscar and Bill were always curious about what I wanted to do.

By the time I come back to the presentation David is talking about liking and loving people. He says rather shockingly, "To be successful in this business you don't have to love people. In fact, you don't even have to like them. However, in order to create success, you must be curious about them. Curiosity is the foundation of your business. If you are curious about people, you will be looking for things they are passionate about. Whatever they are passionate about is your clue for helping them get an abundance of it, which will keep them coming back to you.

"For me, however, how to be curious has always been difficult to define: like someone telling me to relax. I have never been very clear on what I am supposed to do to relax. Similarly, at one time I lacked skill and knowledge about how to be curious about people. I was always afraid that others would think I was being overbearing or nosey. My goal today is to clarify, define, and describe how to be curious using a scientifically human approach. This is a method for getting your prospects and team members to tell you exactly where the bull's eye is.

"I had often heard that you couldn't really understand a person unless you had walked in their shoes a while. Curiosity helps you do that. It lets you see the world through their eyes. It gives you a glimpse of how they view the world. In order for you to be of value to others, you must learn what they think about, and how they think about those things. The idea here is to seek to understand before being understood. Curiosity allows you to ask questions and be interested instead of worrying about being interesting. Here are a couple of examples of what I mean:

"Close your eyes for a moment and picture yourself mining for gold. You use your pick to break up the ground in search of little nuggets beneath the surface. Each time you find one, no matter how big or small you pick it up and put it into your pocket. At the end of each day you go to the assay office, reach into your pocket, and pull out the handful of nuggets you collected. Picture in your mind each nugget in your hand as you give them to the assayer. As he weighs them, he gives you the total weight, and then pays you based on the value of gold that day. High-yielding questions are like a pick. They allow you to penetrate the surface and reveal the golden nuggets in people's lives that contain the greatest value. Every time you discover one, it is important that you pick it up and put it into your pocket.

"At the end of your conversations, pull the golden nuggets out of your pocket and show your customers that you know what they need. For instance you might say: 'I think I have something that can help you – pull the nuggets out of your pocket – 1) have more energy during the day, 2) sleep better at night and 3) lose weight.' Another example might go something like this: 'I think I have something that can help you – pull the nuggets out of your pocket – '1) Buy that new house, 2) pay off those credit cards, 3) fire your boss.'

"In the transition from step one to step two of your presentations you could say, pulling the nuggets out of your pocket, 'Here's what I found that will help you: 1) be more alert in the afternoon at work, 2) relieve your joint pain, 3) help you have better vitality.' Another example might be: 'Here's what I found that will help you: 1) increase your income, 2) save for your children's college, 3) retire without worrying about fixed benefits.'

"When you ask people to take action you might say something like— pulling the nuggets out of your pocket— 'Are you ready to: 1) experience being more rested when you wake up in the morning, 2) get rid of all those medications, 3) be able to play with the kids and grandkids again, 4) take action to increase your income, 5) take control of your lifestyle, 6) begin building a legacy and example for future generations?'

"All of the items you list off are the nuggets you discover when you talk to them asking, listening and repeating the process through high-yielding questions. The good news is that most everyone will gladly give you all the nuggets you need to help them see, feel, and hear how your offering helps them create the life they dream of.

"Here's another example: I watched a movie once about a family living in the American West in the mid-1800s. They were searching for life-giving water on their new farm. They didn't have the technology we have today, so they drilled wherever they thought they might find water. They drilled in one place with out success. They drilled another hole with the same result, and then another, and another. After five or six attempts, they finally pulled water out of an underground reservoir. The life-giving resource you are searching for are the circumstances, conditions, and situations in their life that they would like to change and are committed to create.

"Just like the early American settlers, sometimes our conversations lead to dead ends or discussions about topics that they are not passionate about. When this happens, don't hang your head and give up the search. Move to another spot and drill another well. If you don't hit water there, switch to another topic until you find yourself talking about something they are passionate about. Something that allows you to anticipate that they will take action to accomplish the changed situation they are talking about.

"For years, leaders in this industry have taught that excitement and enthusiasm are enough to attract the attention of your family, friends, and colleagues. That strategy may have worked in the 1960s, but today we need a different approach if we intend to make the promise of the industry come true for more people a greater percent of the time. A few years ago one of my leaders said: 'The tongue in your mouth must match the tongue in your shoes.' This means that running around frantically is interesting, but it's only effective if your goal is to create chaos. Everything you do you must do with purpose on purpose. Enthusiasm is good. It's better when combined with skill and knowledge about the company, products and income offering. Enthusiasm combined with skill and knowledge is best when engulfed with your ability to build a relationship and offer recommendations that actually benefit your prospects, customers and team members.

"In the past we concentrated on what we thought was exciting about the business and why we personally explored the promises that XL-8 made possible. We ran around saying things like 'I found the greatest thing ever, you need to check this out,' or 'Here's what I do and why I do it, you want to get in?' We told people what we found and why we thought it was the best thing since sliced bread, and then invited them to enroll with us. The challenge with the 'me, myself and I' approach is that it focuses on the wrong subject.

"The world has changed in the past few decades. People have been carefully taught to ask themselves, 'what's in it for me?' 'What do you offer that helps me?' In this day and age you need to focus on the prospects' circumstances, needs and wants first. And you can't learn what your prospects need, want, or care about if you are doing all the talking, especially if you're talking about you. The secret sauce to this approach is you must get them to express what they want more or less of. You may already see their challenges. You may be right in your opinion of their dilemma; but if you start telling them about it, they will begin to defend bad behavior and undesirable results. Suddenly they won't see their challenges as challenges at all. The issues that are keeping them from being completely happy will be nothing more than a judgment you make about them and are now foisting upon them. This approach pushes people away from you instead of drawing them closer.

"So learn to ask questions that will get your prospects to talk about what is working and what is not working in their life. I call this a curiosity dialogue. If you can find out what they want more or less of in their life, you can then give them a specific prescription to solve their pain. If you learn to do this, the world will be at your feet. Think about the last visit you made to your doctor's office. The doctor uses a very interesting process. First, the nurse asks a few general questions and then takes some vital signs. She writes her findings on the medical chart and then she takes you to the examination room. She puts the file in the pocket on the door for the doctor to review when he comes in to examine you. Based on the preliminary, golden nugget information he begins his examination by asking some very general questions about why you came to see him today before he does anything more specific. Once he has a general idea of where your pain is he pokes and prods a bit in some very specific places, then he asks very explicit questions before giving you his diagnosis and associated recommendation for relief. This is a perfect example of curiosity.

"Back to my original statement about loving, liking, and being curious. The doctor doesn't love you or his other patients. He may not even like you or them. But because he can be curious about his patients, investing a few minutes asking questions, he can get them to talk about their difficult circumstances. The doctor listens for specific, meaningful things that help guide him to the bull's eye: and appropriate diagnosis and treatment recommendation.

"What if he came in without reading the chart, but simply pulled out a bottle of pills and told you to take one of them in the morning, one more at night, and then instructed you to come back in two weeks to see him again? I will tell you that I wouldn't take any of those pills. I would never come back to that doctor; nor would I refer anyone else to him, would you? But isn't that what we do when we rush in and tell people about what we have and why we think it's so great?

"When we do this we are behaving like a snake oil salesman who has the miracle cure for everything, instead of a physician who takes the time to find out what is ailing people before he or she tells them what the cure is! You could easily make the case that being a business owner casts you in the roll of a doctor of sorts, and your recommendations to relieve their life-pain are like writing prescriptions for them to follow. With that being said, I give you a warning; writing prescriptions without a proper diagnosis is malpractice. When you contact, present, and follow-up, make sure you get a clear picture of their life as they dream of it. Listen attentively without prejudice, and respond with encouragement and support. Remember that your pain is not necessarily their pain. You may want more time and money. They may want better health, or some other benefit of your products and services.

"Here is a personal example: when my wife takes her car to the mechanic, she tells him that it's making a funny sound—something like ca-chingalug. The mechanic, of course, has no idea what this means, so he is forced to ask a lot of questions to get at the heart of the problem. But when I go to the mechanic, I tell him what I think is wrong with the car because I think I know something about it. He doesn't ask nearly as many questions, and invariably it takes longer and is more expensive to fix, because I think I know what's wrong and he thinks I know what I am talking about. We both waste a lot of time and I spend a lot more money because we both think we know what the other is talking about. This is what we do when we rush in, telling people what is so great about XL-8. It should be a surprise to no one when they reject us because neither of us really know what the other is talking about.

"Now that I think about it, aren't you glad that surgeons don't take our word for what's wrong and how to fix it? If we tell them it hurts on the right side, they don't say 'okay lets operate!' They take their time to evaluate the situation to ensure they have enough information before they recommend any procedure.

"And finally, when I go to a restaurant, I am glad that the server doesn't show me to my table and then bring food before I look at the menu and order what I want. How could they possibly know what I want if they don't ask?

"High-yielding questions are the key to communicating clearly and effectively. When we rush in with nothing more than enthusiasm and our products to show off, we are acting just like the snake oil salesman in my story, and me with the mechanic I told you about, the hasty surgeon, or the premature restaurant server. What makes XL-8 so great for you probably won't be what is so great for your prospects. For every person there is a need, a specific want, that they can't meet doing what they are doing now. And some part of what you offer is the solution. If you approach your prospects by telling them our products and services have given you more of what you want, but don't mention how the benefits will help them, they will not engage either as a customer or an associate on your team. Your prospects won't be interested, until they know how your products and services will alleviate their specific challenges. You have one mouth and two ears, use them in that proportion – solve their problems not yours.

"Here is a method of figuring out what they need: Have TINY conversations. T. I. N. Y. stands for Their Interests, Not Yours. Tiny conversations start with something as simple as: 'Do you live around here?' or 'What do you like most about living here?' or 'If you could live anywhere in the world, where would it be?' You can use the old acronym FORM to get the conversation started. F. O. R. M. stands for Family, Occupation, Recreation, or Money. Ask about their work. How long have they been doing it? What do they like and dislike about it? Here are a couple more conversation starters to get your TINY conversations going: 'Just out of curiosity, how do you increase your sales?' 'Just out of curiosity, how do you attract more customers?' 'Just out of curiosity, how do you get your family to eat right?' 'Who does your payroll?' 'How is the economy affecting your retirement plans?' Another approach could include: 'I need your help. I'm looking for a couple of people who are willing to learn how to make a six figure income in the next 2-3 years. Who do you know?'

"Let me demonstrate what a TINY conversation might be like." Before he finishes asking for a volunteer, a woman on Ann's team named Sue is on stage with him. He begins by asking her to pretend she isn't in XL-8 for a minute. He starts the conversation saying, "What is your name?"

"Sue," responds the volunteer.

"Do you work outside of your home, Sue?" David asks.

"I do. I work at the local University," Sue replies.

"What do you do there?" David continues.

"I work in the admissions office, checking to see if students have all their enrollment forms submitted."

"How long have you been working at the University?" he asks further.

"I have been there for seven years," she says with a sigh in her voice.

"What do you like best about working at the University?" he asks.

"The health benefits are the most attractive thing about my job now."

"What do you like least about your job?" David presses further.

"I hate the endless paper work, rules, and regulations I have to follow just to enroll one student in his dream to get a degree," she answers emphatically.

Noticing the passion in her response David asks, "Do you think they are paying you all that you are worth?"

"Not even close. If they doubled my salary, I still wouldn't be making enough to put up with the nonsense!" she says even more ardently.

"Have you ever thought about doing something else?" David asks, very curiously.

"I have thought about it, but I don't know what I would do," she offers, looking a little sad.

David reaches into his pocket, pulls out a gold nugget, and responds with a great question, "On a scale from 1 to 10, how serious are you about getting paid what you're worth doing something you love?"

Sue perks up a little and replies, "I am a 10! Why do you ask?"

"I think I may know of something that can help you get what you want. I need about a half hour to give you some details. Do you have thirty minutes on Thursday or Friday?" he asks.

"Friday after 5:00 PM would be best for me," Sue replies looking at her calendar.

"I have time at 6:30 PM or 8:00 PM. Which would be better for you?" David inquires.

"Eight is the best," Sue answers.

"Okay then," David explains, as he put the appointment in his calendar. "There is a coffee shop right down the street from here. Would that be a good place to meet?"

"That would be perfect," Sue agrees.

"I see you're putting this in your calendar, so I know you will be at the coffee shop at 8:00 on Friday night, right?" David confirms.

"I'll be there," Sue reconfirms.

David shakes her hand and says, "Sue it's been great to meet you today. I look forward to our meeting on Friday night at the coffee shop." David excuses Sue with applause for her willingness to risk being on stage as a volunteer.

"The key is to get the conversation started," David encourages. "Once you have begun the conversation with a question, you put them in the power role. They think, feel, and perceive that they are in control because they are doing all the talking. However, nothing could be farther from the truth. You are in control because you are guiding the conversation to find what's not working in their life through the questions you ask. I know a lot about Sue, but she knows almost nothing about me or whether what I offer that may relieve her pain. One thing she does know is that I am interested in her and what she wants, and because I focused on her instead of me she is going to meet with me so that I can present the explicit features and benefits of our offering that pertain specifically to her and her situation."

Recognizing that he is ahead of himself in his presentation sequence David says, "You'll have to excuse me; I get carried away sometimes and leap ahead. Let me get back on track here. High-yielding questions are also very important to use when you enroll new associates. These kinds of questions allow you to see what they want out of the business, and to establish their commitment level for achieving their goals. This is a business of relationships. And you will accelerate relationship building if you ask a few questions and let your prospects and associates talk about the things everyone loves to talk about most: themselves, their families, and the things they are dissatisfied with.

"Learn to talk little by limiting your end of the conversation to high-yielding questions and then listening carefully to their responses. Remember not to throw your darts too early. Everyone likes people who show interest in them, and being able to do this well is what our process is about.

"There are six types of high-yielding questions. There is no magical order to the sequence of question types, and you may use more than one type of question in any given conversation.

"The first type of high-yielding question is a Diagnostic question. Diagnostic questions uncover the cause of your prospect's pain. They enable you to get to the 'what' and 'why' of your prospects discomfort. They are great for beginning conversations and for transitioning to inviting people to take some kind of action that will best serve them as a next step. Here are some examples of diagnostic questions:"

Types of Questions

1. Diagnostic questions.

- If you could change anything in your (life, business, organization, community, relationships), what would it be?
- On a scale from 1 to 10, how serious are you about getting what you want?
- What do you do professionally, and what does that involve?
- If you could live anywhere in the world where would that place be?
- If you could create the ideal business, what would it be?
- What are you passionate about?
- What do you want more of in life?
- What do you want less of?
- What are your top priorities this year?
- What issues are of the most concern to your team?
- What goals have you set for your team?
- What are your biggest challenges?
- What obstacle is keeping you from reaching those goals?
- What type of budget have you set aside for your business this year?
- Who else is involved in making a decision?
- What do you need to make a decision?

"The second type of high-yielding question is Implication questions. Implication questions help you determine the effect of your prospect's pain. These questions can either focus on possible risk or possible benefit. Each serves a different purpose and can bring to light the danger of not acting on the problem, as well as the benefit of taking meaningful, purposeful action to resolve the problem."

2. Implication questions.

- What would your life be like if you had… (name the thing they just told you about).
- How would your life be different if (state what they want) occurred?
- Can you (imagine, see, picture, feel, hear) your life with… (whatever they just told you about).
- Do you think they are paying you all that you are worth?
- Would you keep going to work if they stopped paying you?
- What happens if you don't follow-up with your prospects in 24–48 hours?
- How would you benefit if you increased your income by 20% this year?
- What will your life be like if you do the same things others are doing?
- What would you do with the extra time you would have if you could quit that second job?
- How does having too much debt affect you?
- What will the result be if you do nothing?
- How do you propose to do that?

"The third type is Confirming questions. This type of question helps you create clarity. They help ensure that you understand the situation correctly and completely. Confirming questions are a way for you to use the golden nuggets you have been putting in your pocket. When people respond to confirming questions, they are opening themselves up to the possibility of working with you either as a customer or an associate. They are beginning to see that you are on their side. They believe that you are helping them create the life they want. They begin to move beyond the limiting beliefs and values that have created the circumstances they are unhappy with in the first place. Here are some confirming questions."

3. Confirming questions.
- So, if I understand you correctly (restate what you heard them say).
- Here's what I just heard you say (restate what you thought you heard them say).
- What will it take to eliminate that concern?
- If you didn't have (the concern they stated) is there any reason you wouldn't take action to create the result you want?
- If you had a way to get (insert the concern they stated) would you take action to turn your vision into a reality?
- How long have you been (state their situation)?
- What do you like best about (state their situation)?
- What do you like least about (state their situation)?
- How do you define success in (state their situation)?
- How can I help you meet those goals in (state their situation)?
- How important is (state any concern they have expressed. I.E. time, price, quality…) in your decision to move forward?
- How do you make your decisions about creating success in (state their situation)?
- What are you doing now to deal with (state their challenge)?

"The fourth high-yielding question type is called a "Have You Ever Considered…" question. Your goal in asking 'have you considered questions' is to get your prospect to say yes to something. This type of yes means that, at a minimum, they have at least thought about what you are asking them. It brings a positive answer to mind, even if they have only thought about it one time, for five seconds, ten years ago. Some 'have you ever considered…' questions are like these:"

4. Have you ever considered questions.
- Have you ever considered starting a home-based business?
- Have you ever considered bringing in extra income?
- Have you ever considered supplementing your income?
- Have you ever considered doing something else?

- Have you ever considered a different approach?
- Have you ever considered the XL-8 business opportunity?

"The fifth question type is a very powerful question form. They are called "What Keeps You From..." questions. These questions are very powerful because they lead you to the real reasons people aren't doing what they need to do to get what they want. When you understand what keeps them from doing what you want them to do, or when you see what causes them to do what you want them to do, you know how to recommend the appropriate solution. Here are a few examples of this type of question:"

5.   What kept or keeps you from questions.
- What kept you from doing it?
- What kept you from being successful?
- What keeps you from being interested in it?

"If you begin by asking them whether they have ever considered starting their own business, they might have said, 'Yes I thought about it, but I am really not interested.' I would respond with, 'When you thought about it, what kept you from doing it?' They will now respond by guiding you toward the bull's eye. You might then ask, 'What made it seem overwhelming?' and the conversation will continue because you have created trust from simple curiosity. Approaching people this way invites them to share their concerns. These concerns are very close to the center of the bull's eye. They will give you reasons why they didn't want to do it, or why they weren't successful at it, or why they weren't interested in it. When you are doing this, you must remember that the key to improving the Trust Quotient of this relationship using "What kept you from" questions is to focus on understanding them and their point of view; it is not to overcome them! People don't want to be overcome, they want to be understood.

"The final high-yielding question type is "What Caused You" questions. This type of question digs deeper into that person's underlying motivators. Usually people aren't going to change what they are doing unless some outside pain or circumstances forces movement. When you know what impels people to change, you know how to create a solution for their pain that they are likely to accept and take action on. Some "what caused you questions could be like these:"

6.   What caused you questions.
- What caused you to look into the XL-8 opportunity in the first place?
- What caused you to think about a different career?
- What caused you to consider moving to a new town?
- What factors are causing you concerns?

"The beauty of high-yielding questions is that you invite people to talk to you and open up to you. The best thing about this type of questioning is that they tell you how to help them persuade themselves, because when you can meet their specific needs with what you offer, their lives can begin to transform.

"Sometimes when you are having high-yielding question conversations, there can be some silence while your prospect is processing the question or formulating their response. Remember that Pickup Trucks and Hybrids do take some time before they respond to questions, problems, and situations. Some associates feel the need to insert their own word and opinions to shorten the silence. But I would recommend that you resist the temptation to rescue yourself from the silence with your own comment. Don't interrupt their thinking and response processes. Often your ideas and opinions are a distraction to their thinking rather than a help.

"With all that as a background for finding the bull's eye, it's still critical to hit the target with your dart. The critical question Steve asked Lori when she was in the little room with Madeline was, 'What was your strategy in determining where and when you would throw the dart?' What a great High Yielding Diagnostic Question. I learned so much about Lori when she responded to the simple question. However, I didn't learn what Lori is passionate about, or how her life would have been different if she had hit the bull's eye, or how serious she was about hitting it. To demonstrate I need a volunteer."

In less than a second a man jumps onto the stage from the front row without using the steps as an aid. Still facing the audience with the volunteer next to him David instructs, "I am going to play a game called 'Are We There Yet' with..." David stops, realizing he doesn't know the volunteer's name and indicates that he needs the man to fill in the last part of his question with his name.

The man responds, pointing to himself and says, "Me!" Everyone laughs at his response.

David smiles and asks, "What is your name, sir?"

Without realizing that he hasn't already told David his name, the man says, "My name is Katsumi!"

David reaches out to shake Katsumi's hand welcoming him to the stage and to a mini lock PIKing exercise. Katsumi's arm is at full stretch. Their hand-shaking demonstration creates a stark difference and Matt thinks but doesn't say, I can't help but notice the difference between Katsumi the Sports Car's and David the Pickup Truck or Hybrid's, hand-shaking preference. I actually think David is a Hybrid, rather than a Pickup Truck because he has given so much detail about high-yielding questions, and because his retelling of Glenna's discovery of this process included a lot of details. Who else does that but a Hybrid? If he were a Pickup Truck we would have been learning to apply the information way before now. Not that any of this matters at the moment, but classifying people by their Personal Interaction Key has started to become a part of my internal relationship awareness.

"Katsumi is an interesting name," David continues. "Does it have a special meaning?"

"It mean's self-controlled," answers Katsumi proudly.

"Excellent," replies David. "You are the perfect candidate for this exercise. 'Are We There Yet' is a game that resembles digging a well," David explains. "When you're digging a well your conditions of victory are to hit water. You know you have met your conditions when water comes out of the ground in the hole you are drilling. So when well drillers are digging they constantly see if they are there yet. Once they determine that they are there, they typically put a cap on the well with a pump so that it can be used any time the owner wants water.

"If you are building your business on purpose, with purpose then every conversation will have conditions of victory. I mean that you will know whether you had a meaningful interaction with someone or not. As you learn and practice high-yielding questions initially, your conditions of victory might be to get others to engage in conversation with you, period. Your conditions of victory might be to simply find out what people are passionate about, or you might want to invite your interaction partner to do something like meet with you personally, attend a meeting with you, visit a website, or something else. No matter what your conditions of victory are, you must constantly ask yourself 'are we to a point in this conversation where I can naturally ask them to take the action that will help them alleviate their pain?' In essence, you are assessing, 'Are We There Yet?'

"In the well-digging example it's obvious when you are there when water flows up from the ground. It's equally obvious for the high PEPper in high-yielding questions to see when he or she is there in the conversation as well. The easy way to explain it is this: you are there when the person you are talking to becomes passionate about what they are talking about. So what do you observe when you or someone else becomes passionate about something?"

A woman from the right side says, "They become really animated. They start waving their hands and arms. Some people even reach out to grab me while they are talking about the topic."

Another woman from right in front of us exclaims, "They seem to know a lot about the details of the topic. It is clear that they have given the topic a lot of thought before this conversation."

A man sitting next to her replies, "Their body language changes. They stand up straighter and become more focused, serious, and purposeful in the way they talk about the topic."

Another woman from behind us offers, "I agree with everything that has been said, and I also think they talk faster. I don't mean everyone talks super fast, but it seems that whatever their normal rate of talking is, they speed up from there."

"Excellent observations," David remarks, as if he is a bit surprised at the level of insight these answers show. "Now we know what the water of our conversations looks, feels, and sounds like; let's see an example of it. Incidentally, there is also a way for you to make sure we aren't fooled into thinking you are there, but aren't there yet. I will also teach you how to recover from that in a minute.

"Okay Katsumi, what do you do professionally?" David asks.

Katsumi responds, "I own my own business."

"What do you like best about owning your own business?"

"I love the freedom and flexibility I have as the owner."

"What kind of business do you own?" David asks curiously.

"I have partnered with a company called XL-8. Have you ever heard of them?" replies Katsumi.

"I have," answers David. "How long have you been an XL-8 associate?"

"I have been working with XL-8 for three years," responds Katsumi.

Pausing for a moment to ask the audience, "Are we there yet?" Everyone responds with a resounding No! "Do I know where the bull's eye is yet?" he asks referring to the dartboard game Steve had played. Again everyone answers in the negative.

Returning to the conversation with Katsumi, David asks, "What caused you to start your own business?"

"I wanted to increase my income so that I could retire while I am still able to do things," Katsumi says.

"You look pretty young to be thinking about retirement," David continues. "What would you like to do when you retire?"

"I would love to travel," replies Katsumi.

David naturally follows the conversation asking, "If you could go anywhere in the world, where would you go?"

Hesitating momentarily, Katsumi shares, "I would like to go to Japan and see the homeland of my grandparents."

"What excites you most about traveling to Japan?" David follows up.

"I would like to visit the city where my grandparents lived and tour the country to see where I came from," Katsumi answers as he contemplates his reasons.

David turns to the crowd and asks, "By the raise of hands, on a scale from 1 to 10, I want you to vote for how passionate you think Katsumi is about this idea—one being not excited at all and ten being 'he can't live another minute without achieving this.' Hold your hand up if you think he is a 10;" no hands are raised. "How many think he is a 9?" Still no hands, David continues down the scale: "7? 6? 5? 4? 3? 2?" Turning to Katsumi, David asks him, on a scale from 1 to 10 how serious are you about traveling to Japan?"

"Not very, I guess about a 1."

Turning to the crowd David says, "This is the point where most people fail in their conversations. If you keep talking about a dream that really isn't a dream, they are almost certainly not going to enroll either as a customer or an associate. And if he does enroll, what do you think the chances are that Katsumi is really going to do the work, learn, practice, and apply success principles in their proper sequence if the reason he enrolls is only at a 1 or 0 level? Not a chance!" David interjects with his own answer. "That's why we don't throw our dart too quickly. That's why we dig a little deeper before we think we are at water. In this case we are definitely not there yet.

"So what do we do now?" asks a woman in the front row, desperate to find the answer to her own personal communication challenges.

"Excellent question," David responds. "I usually don't get this kind of chance during the demonstration." Returning to Katsumi and pulling a golden nugget out of his pocket, David asks, "Is there anything you are more passionate about than visiting Japan?"

"I would love to build my own wood-working shop behind my house," replies Katsumi.

David turns to the audience and asks again, "Are we there yet?" There is a unanimously negative response. David continues, "What is it about wood-working that excites you?"

Katsumi says more emotionally, "I love to build beautiful things out of nothing but a block of wood. The feeling I get when I turn a piece of wood on a lathe, or the look on people's faces when they receive my finished work is so rewarding that I loose track of time when I am working."

Turning again to the crowd David motions as if to say, "Are We There Yet?" There begins to be a difference of opinion in the crowd. Some respond with a yes answer and some respond not yet.

One man says, "We know what wall the bull's eye is on and where it is on that wall, but we are still standing too far away to throw our dart."

David nods in agreement and proceeds, "What would your life be like if you had that shop?"

"I would spend all my spare time making furniture, mastering the art of wood carving and turning. I would love to design and build functional, beautiful, and expressive works that are meaningful to my clients," Katsumi answers without thinking.

David looks at us and asks again, "Are we there yet?" Most everyone responds in the affirmative. David, however, is not totally convinced yet and presses on, asking, "What's keeping you from getting that woodshop?"

"I don't have the money to build the shop, or the time to work in it if I had it," Katsumi complains.

"What do you think is holding you back in your XL-8 business?" David replies.

Katsumi says with more and more emotion, "I don't know. I feel like I am doing everything I am supposed to."

In a good rhythm now, David continues, "So if I understand you correctly, you are passionate about building a dream wood-working shop, and you enrolled in XL-8 because you thought it would provide the time and money to make this happen. But in three years the dream hasn't materialized. Is that right?"

"That sums it up perfectly," says Katsumi.

David turns to us and asks, "Are We There Yet?"

Everyone agrees that we are and David explains, "The reason this is critical is that we should be able to anticipate the answer to the question that will transition this conversation from simple curiosity to taking some kind of action. I knew when I asked Katsumi about travel that he was going to give me a very low score. And now I am predicting a very different answer about the woodshop. I am going to reach into my pocket and pull those little golden nuggets out and use them to deeply connect with Katsumi."

David turns to Katsumi and asks, "On a scale from 1 to 10 how serious are you about getting that wood-working shop and making the beautiful furniture and helping people get a feeling of joy from your creations?"

Katsumi quickly responds, "I think I am a 12!"

"Well Katsumi," David says confidently, "I think I have something that could help you get that shop."

"Really," replies Katsumi, "What is it?"

David stops the conversation and points out that if this were a contact he would tell Katsumi that he needed about thirty minutes to explain it to him. And if this were a presentation he would segue into the explanation of the features and benefits of XL-8 that pertain to income and how income translates into time, freedom, and the ability to pursue passions and dreams. Turning to the crowd David asks, "What did you observe?"

The answers come pretty quickly, "There doesn't seem to be a memorized sequence in the process you used. You asked him questions about that were based on his responses."

"You were focused on him."

"Katsumi did most of the talking. You asked a question and then he talked to you."

"You took whatever he gave you and asked about that."

"You didn't judge what he wanted."

"I thought we were there way before you did."

"I would have talked about how XL-8 makes traveling to Japan possible, when his real passion is something completely different."

"When he started talking about woodworking he started to become more energetic."

"He talked about specific tools and his feelings and the looks on people's faces. He also talked about loosing track of time because he became so immersed in his passion."

"These are excellent observations," David acknowledges. "And when I struck out on the first thing, being curious allowed me to discover something else that he is truly passionate about. There were literally hundreds of questions I could have asked that would have led to the same place. So there's really nothing magical about what I did with Katsumi, other than I was simply curious about what he cares deeply about. When I was more focused on understanding before being understood, he trusted me enough to openly share what he really wants. He knows almost nothing about what I have claimed can produce his workshop; but I know a lot about him and his passion. Now, before I have you practice this, there are a couple of things I want to make you aware of.

"In every aspect of our life, people buy results. If you have a boss, he or she wants results from your work. If you are the boss, you want results from your organization. If you are a business owner, you get to answer to share-holders, partners, bankers, or customers who all want results. In the personal side of life we want results which may be peace, security, fun, and inspiration. Mastering how to ask your prospects what they want their life to be like that it isn't like now, puts the focus of the conversation squarely where it needs to be: on the prospects desired result.

"In the story of Alice and Wonderland, Alice comes to a fork in the road. She meets a Cheshire cat there and she asks him which way she should go. He responds by asking her where she wants to end up. Essentially, the cat asks Alice 'what result do you want to create?' She answers by saying, I don't really care. The Cheshire cat tells her, 'Then it doesn't really matter what road you take, if you don't care where you end up.'

"When you ask what result people want, it's easy to get sidetracked or to stop before you know where the bull's eye is; before you are really at water; before you really are at the place they need to come to. For example, when Katsumi was talking about traveling, I could have easily stopped or taken imaginary trips to far off places with him. But we really weren't at water yet. Had I thrown my dart then, it would have landed with a thud as my dart hit the wall, missing the target by many feet.

"When Katsumi told me he wanted to have a workshop, it was clear that is the real result he wants. When I asked him how his life would be different if he had his workshop, he answered in great detail, with passion and emotion. It was at that point that I saw, heard, and felt that he was passionate about what we were talking about. I was standing directly in front of the target, ready to insert my dart with one last question to confirm my suspicion: 'On a scale from 1 to 10 how serious are you about creating that result?' I anticipated a ten and I got a twelve. If the answer is anything less than 8, you are not there yet. You can simply ask your prospect what they could be more passionate about, and they will probably tell you.

"If you are having a discussion about something and you are just not seeing, hearing, or feeling like your prospect is passionate about the topic, start digging your well in a different place. Don't deceive yourself with superficial quick-fix attack methods. These will distract you into thinking you are advancing towards some life-altering, deep-seeded, critical path end game result, when in fact your prospect has no passion for or commitment to whatever you are discussing. Superficial topics may be interesting and possibly even important, but if you have not discovered a result they can be passionate about and that is critical to them, they will not engage with you or enroll either as a customer or an associate and no one will be served by anything you have to offer."

Looking at his watch, David realizes he is twenty minutes over his allotted time. He jokingly says, "Why didn't anyone tell me the time is up?" The truth is, everyone is so engrossed in his training that no-one has been paying any attention to the time. "I hope this has been valuable to each of you," David continues. "I want you all to have an opportunity to have some skill mastery practice on this topic between now and the evening session. So here is what I want you to do in the next few hours. First, I want you to invest a few minutes writing down what value you got from this session and share it with someone else. Second, I want you to practice having a high-yielding question conversation with one person in the room. And third, you need to have at least one conversation with someone who is not in the room right now between this meeting and the evening session. Any questions?" he asks, hoping there are none. Seeing there aren't any questions he declares, "The break starts now!"

As Ann and Matt head out for the break, Matt tells her, "It's obvious that he is a Double Platinum. He must have 100 PEPs! I found his insights to be truly amazing. Then I ask her which part of the assignment she wants to do first and as she begins to answer, her team members gather around her like chicks to their mother hen. She smiles at me and says my team members need me right now, so I will do the writing assignment with you later. As she talks with her team and encourages them to make sure to get the assignment completed before the evening session, Matt writes down his impressions of the training and how he might use it at work in his notebook.

I think about how to have these kinds of conversations with my team members. I realize that I have had superficial relationships with my team leaders up to this point. In fact, I have had superficial relationships with the whole division. A feeling of gratitude comes over me for what I learned today. I have come to realize that I have been throwing darts blindfolded, and I have stopped drilling for water way too quickly with most people. As a consequence, I have been having conversations with people about fascinating things that were mostly inconsequential to them. My conditions of victory are not being met because the recommendations I make to clients aren't and don't create the result they are most passionate about. I now understand that high-yielding questions are a critical element to increasing my value of service and enhancing my relationships. And just maybe this can work with my relationship with my dad. He is about to become a grandfather again, and this will be a great time to reach out to him to repair our relationship now that I am something he can be proud of.

When I look up, Ann's team has disappeared to work on the assignment. In fact, we are some of the last remaining people in the auditorium. Ann is dialing her phone, calling one of her team members that hasn't been advancing in the business. "Hi Donna, this is Ann Ivey," I hear her say as she thumbs through her notes. "Do you have a minute to talk?" Ann asks as she turns away from me.

"I do have a few minutes," Donna replies.

"I am calling to see how you are doing," Ann continues. "How do you like your new house?"

"It's fine, but I wish I could spend more time working on the yard. It's a mess," Donna says.

"So if you could wave your magic wand, what would you like it to look like?" asks Ann.

"I would get rid of the shrubs and bushes around the yard. They are consuming the whole landscape. I want to plant two shade trees in the front yard, and a few fruit trees out back. I would plant flowers around the perimeter of the front and put in a new walkway from the street to the front door. You know, just make it look more pleasant," Donna answers passionately.

"Wow, sounds like you have some big plans for the yard," Ann replies. "What's your motivation behind all the changes to the yard?"

Donna goes on, "When I come home I don't feel cheery or excited to come in. I want my house to welcome me home and invite me to come inside."

"What I'm hearing you say is that you really want to remodel the yard so that your house will feel like your friend instead of a building, is that right?" Ann says confirmingly.

Donna responds with a sigh in her voice, "Yeah, I really want it to look like one of those houses you see on TV, with everything beautiful and charming."

"Well Donna, what is keeping you from making your yard the paradise you're dreaming about?" asks Ann.

"I just don't have the time or the money to make it happen," Donna responds gruffly.

"Donna, on a scale from 1 to 10 how serious are you about making your house into a home, beginning with the landscaping?"

Donna pausing for a moment says with a tear in her voice, "I think I am a ten!"

Knowing that Donna is passionate and serious Ann presses on, "What has changed in the past few months since you moved into that house?"

"I am sick and tired of being sick and tired," Donna answers longingly.

Ann lovingly reaches out and says, "You know Donna that I am here to support you in anyway I can. I would like to talk to you about the new things I am learning, and how they might help you build your XL-8 business to the point where you can have the time and money to do whatever you want to your new house. I would like to invite you to come to the evening session of conference tonight as a first step. I will save you a seat if you promise me you will come."

"New things? What new things?" asks Donna.

"You will be able to see better for yourself when you come, and we can talk afterwards. Will you come?" Ann repeats.

"I would like to come and meet with you all. I miss the group and the friendships," Donna admits.

"Okay, I'll save you a seat right next to me," Ann says reassuringly. "I look forward to seeing you, just before 7:00 PM, bye."

As she turns back to me, I give her a hug and tell her, "You are poetry in motion."

Ann replies, reflecting on her relationship with Donna, "I have known Donna for a long time. Even before you and I met in college. I thought when she enrolled in the business she wanted to travel and see exotic places. What she really wants is a place to come home to. I never would have known this if it wasn't for the things I learned today. She would have quit completely and those ugly bushes in her life would probably never go away."

Matt looks down at his notes and says just loud enough for Ann to hear, "It is exciting to hear how simple it is to have real-life, meaningful interactions with people. That's how we really help them have the life they want to create. Hearing you talk to Donna was inspiring. I love how you care for her. And because you were curious and interested, Donna opened up and told you exactly where the bull's eye was. What an amazing lesson."

Ann waits at the front door for Donna. When she arrives Ann gives her a big hug and brings her to our seats. She is so excited to see her, to have her here to listen to Sara Thoms, and to witness the progress of the team during the recognition part of the program. When the awards ceremony begins, Sara has Ann join her on the stage to help her present. This is an unusual request because Ann is at the Silver level, and awards are never given out by associates lower than the Gold level. As Ann walks to the stage, Steve and Sara start to announce the awards. Ann is on the stage to help welcome and congratulate twenty-three of her team members who have earned their first promotion level and receive their Copper lapel pins. Then she gets to personally welcome eleven more of her team members to the second level or Bronze title, and then two of her Bronze level team members advance to Silver, with each of them also having at least one Silver level member on their teams. One of these leaders is Sheila, the woman Ann met in the lunch line when we were at the leadership retreat with Steve and Sara. This means that Ann has earned a promotion to the fourth or Gold level. This is the second highest level in XL-8, and the first level of senior leadership. Duplication is a part of the Ann Ivey team and culture, as is learning to do effective work and teaching others to do the same. I am amazingly proud of her.

I sit, watching all of this unfold and I'm amazed at a few things: First, that Ann hasn't let on that she is going to be promoted tonight; second, that her team appears to be growing at a rapid rate; third, that her team members seem to be able to do what she is doing. Even Sheila, who lives in another State can do this. And four, I am loving how she is a whiz at learning and practicing the skill she needs to have the attributes she needs to advance before she is even at that level.

I keep an eye on Donna as she sits there watching. One of Ann's team members who enrolled the same night Donna did, crosses the stage as a new Silver, and Donna begins to cry a little. I don't think she is sad, but I think she is joyful that it can be done, and that she had an example of someone who has done it in the same time she has been enrolled. Ann is announced as a new Gold and her whole team stands up and cheers, including Donna. What an accomplishment. While they are announcing the awards, it becomes obvious that Ann is not only being promoted to Gold, but that she is perfectly positioned to reach Platinum, the highest level in a few months.

She has over seventy PEPs, a team of over two hundred Associates, and about seventy personal customers. She has twenty-one team members who are consistently working and being promoted along with her, and seventeen leaders. She is well on her way to joining the Thoms' at the Platinum or top level. I love that she's now earning enough money to feel confident talking to just about anyone, including doctors, attorneys and high-level business professionals.

I think about how grateful I am that Ann built this team the right way and is teaching them to start at the start and not in the middle by skipping steps in the success process. I also realize that between my job and Ann's business, our children will never want for anything. That is truly a humbling moment. The lights dim and Steve Thoms approaches the podium. Usually Sara introduces him and then relaxes while he speaks, but tonight they have a different agenda. Steve introduces Sara and turns the time over to her for the balance of the meeting.

While Sara is walking up to speak, everyone stands and gives her a very loud welcome. She begins by saying, "It's common for you to come to meetings like this and hear speakers say things like: 'If I can do it you can do it' and 'there's nothing really special about us. We just kept on building.' Well, that is almost true. Although you can do it if you hang in there, hanging in there doing the same ineffective things over and over again, hoping for a different result so that you can outlast failure, doesn't work. There is something special about the people who you just saw come across the stage here tonight. Yes, they stayed with it when it was difficult. But while they were staying with it they were becoming the kind of people others could count on and follow. They are paying the price not by simply staying in, but by learning and practicing critical skills so that their work is more effective than work that leads to disappointment or discouragement. The average associate can only produce average results. You must learn to become a superior performer. As we learned earlier today, the only way to do this is to focus on what you and others can be passionate about. With that being said, I want to talk about a topic that has been on my mind the past few months: dedication.

"Dedication to the life, circumstances, and situation you want is critical to achieving that life, those circumstances and situations. Dedication is a decision to succeed no matter what the circumstances, conditions, or obstacles. History is full of examples of people creating massive success despite incredible odds, hardships and challenges. Obstacles are what you see when you take your eye off the goal. I would like to encourage each of you to look at your life and identify a few things that keep you from building your business on a more consistent, predictable, meaningful basis. During your self-examination you will find there are things that distract you and keep you from getting up here on the stage as the leader you are capable of becoming. As you identify the distractions in your life, cast them aside. Get rid of the distractions and focus your full attention on that which will empower success. Arrange your life so that you can create balance. When you are with your family, be with them. When you are doing housework or yard work, then do that work. When you are building your business, build your business.

"Decide what you want your legacy to be, and then dedicate yourself to achieving it. Pursue it with relentless determination and chase it until you reach it. Don't worry about what others may think or say about what you are doing. Think of it this way. What if you saw a dog chasing a rabbit? The craziness of the dog running around, jumping over and through the bushes would make perfect sense right? Now think of the same scene, except that now you can't see the rabbit. What would you think if you could only see the dog? This is how you look to those who can't see what you are passionate about pursuing. They only see you running and jumping. They can't see the rabbit that is your dream, and so they think and sometimes comment on how foolish you look.

"The chasing dog knows not to give up what he wants most in the long run for what he wants in the moment. Turn off the TV for a while. Give up the softball league temporarily. Dedicate yourself to yourself and the life and legacy you want to create. No one fails. Everyone creates a result. If you examine your life and decide that the result you are creating right now is not the result you want, then change your approach. Now is the time to learn and practice skill and knowledge that will enable you to apply correct principles in their proper sequence. This also applies to the results you get when you communicate with others, and the quality of relationships you create.

"I've noticed something interesting about life: there is pain in everything we do. But the pain of success is always less painful than the pain of failure. The next time you watch a sporting event, look at the players after the game. The ones who have just lost always look defeated, battered, and bruised. The players on the winning side seem just as battered and bruised, but they are elated. So either the pain is less, or they don't feel it as intensely because they were victorious. Either way, success has a nullifying effect on pain. So remember that no matter whether you win or lose, there will be pain. You get to choose whether to endure pain and succeed, or endure pain and fail."

As Sara speaks, Donna is being touched in a very empowering way. It's as if Sara is reaching into her soul and tugging at her heart strings. Donna begins to get a vision of what can be if she turns herself into the dog on the chase. While Sara is speaking, Donna reaches out and grabs Ann's arm and hands her a note that says, "I dedicate myself to become your first Gold level team leader. Even though I am only a Copper now I am deciding that I want success more than I want failure. I am willing to endure the pain of success so that I won't have to endure the bitter pill of failure any longer." Ann grabs Donna's hand for a moment and squeezes it, with tears in her eyes.

Sara concludes saying, "Lastly tonight, I want to talk about being a sitter. The very first event Steve and I went to, we didn't receive any awards at all. It seemed that everyone went across the stage except us. We called ourselves 'sitters' because we just sat there while everyone else got up and received some kind of recognition. It hurt us to sit out in that audience. It hurt us to sit on the sideline. It hurt so much we made up our minds we would never come back again as a sitter. I want to encourage you to master the critical skills that are required by success. Dedicate your life to something, and then make a decision to achieve the highest level of success in that area. Feel the fear and pain and go do it anyway. Disregard the opinions of the uneducated, weak, dependent, security-seekers and pursue your passions with relentless determination. Chase it until you reach it." Finishing now with a slight bow to the crowd and a wave, everyone stands again and enthusiastically applauds. There isn't a dry eye in the house and both Ann and I double our dedication to achieving success in our own lives.

In the coming weeks I work hard to create an environment of success for my department coordinators. Shelly is making great progress in her work and leadership. She has become fantastically more productive, and is receiving recognition regularly from me, Bruce, and Mrs. Jensen. Last week was a landmark week in our relationship. We had a great conversation in my office about what is going on in her life. For some time Shelly has been enduring great emotional hardship in her personal relationships. Since she has begun to implement the lessons Steve has been teaching me, that I have been passing along to her and the others on the team, her personal relationships have turned around. She expresses profound gratitude for all she has been blessed with.

The results that the division created haven't gone unnoticed by executive management. Bruce calls me into his office, now on the top floor with his new regional manager colleagues. He asks about Ann and the kids and about my goals with the company. I must look a bit puzzled because he tells me, "There is a Regional Vice President position opening up later this year." He continues saying, "Mrs. Jensen and the other executives have been asking for names of Division Managers capable and deserving of moving up, and your name keeps coming up in the conversation. One question I have for you as your manager is, 'How serious are you about moving into senior management?'"

I respond, telling him, "It has been my goal since I joined the company; it's what I have been working and sacrificing time with my family for." Then I inquire about Josh and Jane and he shares, "They are stellar examples of traditional leaders. They are what the executives have always looked for in senior executives, but your work is opening their eyes to other possibilities. You seem to be some kind of 'Revolutionary.' Your approach is very different, with a focus on relationship building as the key element to your sales process. Josh is a great contributor as a Division Manager, but he lacks the human interaction skills to inspire and mentor other Division Managers down to the Floor Level Financial Planners to produce excellent results for our clients. Jane is still a Department Coordinator, but will be promoted to a Division Manager position this month. According to her, she owes this next promotion to your example and the things she is learning by watching you.

"To tell you the truth, we are all watching you. A few more months like the ones you have had lately, and I will be convinced that your approach is sound and stable. I would like to submit your name for the board to consider, but I need to make sure that your method can be taught, adopted, and duplicated through an entire region over a longer period of time. There are too many 'Flavors of the Month' styles that come and go, and when they go, they take our bottom line results with them. So you need to show me that your approach creates predictable, definitive, measureable results for a while longer, and I will be glad to recommend you to the board."

During the next few months Matt covertly works to conceal that the executives are watching his division and their results. But news has a way of leaking out, and before too many weeks pass Dayna and Jaylin begin to tease Matt about the promotion. Ray seems amused, but unaffected by their jokes. Shelly and Kayci seem genuinely excited; each saying during informal interviews that they both see an opportunity for them to move up with him. The good news is that everyone seems super motivated to work harder and smarter to create extraordinary results for each of their departments and for the division as a whole. Matt reflects on how interesting it is to think back to the first interactions he had with each of them and to see how those relationships have grown and blossomed into ones of trust, professionalism, and care.

Every week and month of the quarter I have had an interview with Bruce to discuss the results of each department, and he has given me an update on our division's standing within the company. Two of the top three departments in the company are in my division, and our division is number one in the region and the company. New accounts are growing; retention is increasing. Our up-sells are first in the region and our percentage of sales that come from existing customers is at a record high.

At the beginning of the next quarter, I am walking to Bruce's office for my quarterly review when Dayna reminds me to remember the little people when I come back as the new Regional Manager. Smiling and satisfied that our division is doing great, I take my normal chair in Bruce's office. He barely looks up from the report he is examining. Suddenly he closes the folder, smiles and in his normal passive demeanor exclaims, "The executives asked me to pass along their congratulations on another terrific quarter and they also want me to talk to you today because we are offering you a promotion to Regional Manager. If you decide to accept the position it will mean you will have three divisions under your direction. You will have the responsibility for the weakest performing region in the company, and so it will be a great challenge and a great opportunity to show what you're really made of. The position also requires you to travel more and to be headquartered 1,200 miles away in Minneapolis. This also means that there will be a vacancy in your position. Do you have any recommendations for your position? Someone who can lead the number one division in the company?"

Sitting there for a moment, not knowing what to think, feel, or say, I ask the only thing that enters my mind, "When does this new job begin?"

"As soon as you can get things arranged here and get going," Bruce responds emphatically.

"We have two small children at home, and so moving right now isn't the greatest time. I am worried about how this will affect my family."

"I went to bat for you big time on this promotion Matt. This is a chance of a lifetime," Bruce counters.

I am not happy with this answer, since I hate being manipulated and coerced. But I can't argue with him, no matter what my personal circumstances might be. I have been working as hard as anyone in the company and my results definitely reflect that I have been working smarter than most. The results Bruce alluded to certainly qualify me for this position. This is what I have been preparing myself for ever since my dad told me I was too dumb and irresponsible to ever be the boss. I have proven myself at last. Not only am I the boss, I am the number one boss in the entire company. Too bad my dad isn't here to see me now. I make a decision.

"I will accept the position, Bruce, and my recommendation for my replacement falls on only one person, Shelly. She is easily the most qualified and productive Department Coordinator in the company. She has increased the value of her service to the point that she is probably more qualified to be a Regional Manager than most Regional Managers are. I also have a second recommendation to make, but not about the Division Manager position.

"I want to make a recommendation for Kayci, my assistant. She was your assistant and has been my company confidante since I have been a Department Coordinator. The value of her service to this company has increased incredibly over the past year or so. Her value to the company is much greater than taking care of one Division Manager. I propose that the executive team, which I am now a part of, make her the training manager for all secretaries, executive assistants, receptionists, and support staff."

If in fact Bruce had "gone to bat" for me, and because he knew that I knew what I was talking about, it wasn't hard for him to accept both names on behalf of the executive team.

I leave his office on cloud nine. I'm not sure that my feet hit the floor once on the way to the elevator back to my office. In fact, I choose to take the stairs to work off some of the adrenaline and excitement before I get back to the second floor.

On the way home I proclaim to Stan, the evening bus driver, that this will be my last trip on the bus. Tomorrow, I am going shopping for a new car, one that befits the most valuable Senior Executive in the world. He smiles, shakes his head, and then my hand. I ask him for his recommendation about executive cars, and he explains that I should catch the bus in the morning and get off at the Rose Street stop. Go one block on Rose to Teague Motors. You will want to talk to Bob and tell him I sent you. He will talk to you like an adult. He will want to know what you want the car for, and then he will tell you whether he has something that will fit the bill or whether he needs to find the one you want. He only looks for customers that he can create a long-term relationship with so he's not just looking for ways to make a quick buck on a single sale. Tell him what you want, and he'll take care of you.

I thank Stan and get off at my usual stop. But no sooner do I start walking home, when Steve Thoms stops and offers me a ride in that very nice, sapphire-blue, convertible Jaguar. I have admired it for some time now, but this is the first time I've ever had a chance to ride in it. I tell Steve about my promotion, and ask about new cars, hoping to get Steve's recommendation.

Steve asks, "What are the most important features of this new car, Matt?"

I reply, somewhat superficially, "I want a car other executives will envy and that will serve to encourage and remind me everyday to keep pursuing my climb to the top."

Steve pats his jag on the dashboard and does a fantastic job promoting its features and benefits as an appropriate car to create that result.

Once again I am reminded that Steve doesn't just talk the talk. He walks the walk. Instead of just telling me to buy this or that kind of car because it is what he likes, he takes a moment, even in this casual, private conversation to find out what is important to me before he gives me advice. He recommends that I go to the same dealership Stan recommended. He also encourages me to make sure to talk to Bob and no one else. At this point, even if I wasn't going to buy a new car, I have to meet this guy Bob; whoever he is. Steve lets me out in front of the house, congratulates me on the promotion, and invites me to drop by and show him my new car when I get it. I wave and go into the house.

Once inside I play my own version of 'guess what I did today' with Ann. The problem is that my life is so predictable that Ann guesses right off. She answers saying, "I am so proud of you Matt. You deserve the recognition you are getting!" She is excited and worried at the same time. Sitting down at the dinner table she stares into empty space and says in a beleaguered tone, "This probably means more time away from me and the kids." I hadn't told her yet that I would be based in Minneapolis and that I would indeed be traveling more often.

I feebly explain, "The only reason any of this matters at all to me is so that you can have the life you deserve, and that I long to give you."

She looks up at me with a tear in her eye, and without saying a word says, "Things are nice but what I really want is you."

I assure her that once I put some systems in place at work I will be able to spend more time with her and the kids. But I can tell that my promise has fallen short, and I'm not sure she's wrong. It's a long, cold, sleepless night. I have successfully created the lifestyle her mother never had, and that my mother took for granted everyday. But something is missing here. Ann doesn't seem nearly as excited about this promotion as I do.

The next morning I make a side trip to the car dealership Stan and Steve recommended. I meet Bob, and at the end of an hour interview I drive away in a new Cashmere Metallic Jaguar XJ Supersport 510 hp 5.0-liter Supercharged V8, with jet seats and parchment leather headlining, a 1200 watt sound system, and gloss figured ebony with ribbon laser inlay, and a wood and leather heated steering wheel, with 20" Alloy wheels and performance tires. Try saying that in one breath!

Pulling into the parking lot at work, I park in the executive space painted with my name on it. I make my way to my office to tell Kayci that we have been promoted, and that she is going to have a new and much more demanding position. As I sit in my familiar chair, it occurs to me that there is nothing standing between me and a corner office and the seven figure salary that goes with it. Ann will come around when our kids and grandkids are financially set, I think in an attempt to justify my new position. As the day goes on I become more and more excited about the difference I am going to be able to make. The possibilities are almost limitless I think as I examine my Region's organization chart. This is the first real opportunity I have had to teach leaders of leaders. At this point I am training Division Managers to teach their Department Coordinators, who will teach their Floor Level Planners, who will teach their prospects and customers how to get the most out of their life. Nightfall comes without my noticing, so my first day as a Regional Manager comes to an end as I turn the office lights off. I catch myself whistling a catchy tune as I get off the elevator and head to my new car.

Ann is already in bed, but isn't sleeping as I walk in the door. She is staring at the ceiling. It's like she is in a far off land. She doesn't even seem to notice that I have come in at first. After a few minutes, she tells me, still looking at the ceiling, "Some nights I lay awake waiting for you to come home, dreaming of having a new home on a small piece of property with a few animals that our kids could learn to take care of. I would love a vacation to a nice resort where we can just relax, go swimming, and have fun with someone waiting on us for a bit of a break."

Breaking the mood, Matt knows it's time to discuss the pros and cons of moving or commuting to Minneapolis and other travel requirements. We agree that, for a while at least, it will be best for me to commute, especially while the kids are really young. Ann shares a serious innermost thought, "If you aren't going to be around much, maybe it would be good to use some of the money we are making to find a better situation for raising kids."

It takes Matt a minute to recover from the admission of her feelings of being alone as part of a plan to take some kind of action. Maybe this is a way to get me to really feel her pain, or maybe she's finally surrendered to the inevitability that I am just going to be gone a lot, or maybe it's a combination of both. Whatever it is, it cuts me to the core.

Author's Note:
The instructions explaining the mathematical equation for this chapter is in the appendix at the end of the book.

## 9

One Mouth and Two Ears

Ann shares her plans to go Platinum with Sara, "When I start making a six figure income it will be easy for Matt to see that he doesn't need to work eighty-hour weeks anymore, and that he can come home and enjoy our family." Now almost confessing Ann says, "I am a little frustrated. I have been telling Matt over and over again that he should spend more time with me, but he doesn't seem to be listening. I am not sure how to correct this because no matter how I tell him, he is not receiving the message that I need more time with him. Maybe I am just not talking in a way he can understand.

"Maybe he's just stressed about the kids and he wants to be in a good place professionally to ensure that we have everything we want. He is so focused on his next promotion. He is doing an awesome job, and he is on the fast track to be a senior executive. I guess I should be grateful, but I want to eat my cake and have it too. We have enough money, but we just don't seem to have any time to do any of the things we want. I don't know which is better, our situation of affluence, or our college friends' situation who became teachers. They seem to have time, but no money to enjoy it."

Sara reminds Ann, "You know I am here for you anytime you need to talk. And if Matt is traveling and you need anything, please let Steve and me help you take care of things."

"Thank you Sara," responds Ann. "You're a great friend and mentor."

"By the way," Sara says remembering one of the reasons she has called in the first place. "I want to give you a little advanced warning about this month's Conference topic. We are going to be talking about listening. You will want to get Matt there if you think he is having trouble getting your message."

"It would be great to have him there," replies Ann excitedly. "But he won't come unless Steve is presenting. I am afraid he doesn't have much confidence in anyone else. Steve has had a profound effect on him; Matt looks up to Steve as a great mentor."

"Maybe I should have Steve invite Matt this month," suggests Sara. "We are having a special guest speaker and I will tell you no one wants to miss this one. Our mentor, Glenna Hanks, is going to present, and she is fantastic. So the topic is perfect for you both and the speaker is going to be great. It's not often we get Glenna to come to these events anymore."

"If you could have Steve invite Matt that would help a lot," Ann responds, hoping Sara can deliver on her idea.

"Okay then, I will talk to Steve, and then I'll get back to you on our plan to get Matt to the meeting," Sara answers in a scheming voice.

"Thanks for everything Sara," Ann offers as she says goodbye and hangs up the phone.

Ann spends the next few minutes staring off into the distance, thinking about what it would be like to have Matt at home more. The phone ringing startles her back to reality. It's Matt!

"Hello dear, how are you?" I ask.

"Why are you calling me so early," Ann replies surprised to hear him.

"It's after 6:00 PM here," I answer. "So what have you been up to today?"

"Oh the usual stuff, washing clothes, decorating bedrooms and working in the yard. I just got off the phone with Sara, and she is super excited for this month's conference. I would love to have you come with me this month. Sara says that her mentor is presenting and she is going to talk about the next critical step in the relationship process. Can you fit it into your schedule?"

"I don't know," Matt answers, disappointed that I even have to wonder. "I have to go to Boston and then to Cleveland to train my Division Managers on Relationship Ratings before my first presentation to the Board of Directors early next month. Let me see what I can do to juggle my schedule."

"By the way," interjects Ann. "Guess what I did today?"

"Uh-oh, I know what that means," Matt says anticipating her announcement.

"I bought a horse! And I am going to keep him at Barker's place around the corner."

"A horse? Really? I wouldn't have guessed that in a million years," I respond. "I am happy that you found a horse suited to your taste. When will you find time to ride it?"

"Well I plan to take the kids with me and get them used to being around horses," Ann answers. "I want them to make friends with him and get used to being on him as I lead him around the corral. He will be there everyday waiting for us to bring him an apple or carrots," Ann shares hinting that the horse will fill the void she is feeling for Matt.

A few days later in our daily phone conversation and 'guess what I did today' ritual, Ann tells me, "Today I bought a horse trailer. I need a place to store my saddle and tack and a way to transport my new horse if I want to go riding away from Barkers."

"Where would you go if you went out riding?" Matt asks. "And what are you going to pull this horse trailer with anyway?"

"I can borrow Pam Barker's pickup if I need to," she answers quickly and forcefully. "A pickup truck maybe next on my list. It would be much cheaper for you to come home than for me to keep buying things to take your place."

It's silent for a few seconds. Matt doesn't quite know how to respond. I know we need to address this, and I know Ann is testing the waters to see what I will say. But just then my phone rings with a second call. It's Steve Thoms. I tell Ann, "It's Steve calling on the other line. I will consider what you said. I love you. I will call you tomorrow." I answer the other line. "Hello Steve," I answer the other line, not realizing at this point that I didn't hang up with Ann. "How can I help you?"

"I am calling to offer *you* some help," Steve says turning the tables on me. "We have been neighbors now for a while, and it occurred to me the other day after talking to Sara that you and I have never really done anything together. I know you're the big boss man now and so it seems fitting that we should invest a few days talking about how to really make a difference in the world. I would like to invite you on a four-wheeling trip with me in the mountains on a trail I have been scouting for a while now. We'll only be gone for a few days, and the trip might give us a chance to talk about how to really accelerate your success in your business.

"We can go four-wheeling in the days leading up to the business development conference. I know you don't usually attend the monthly business development conferences unless I present. But this one is going to rock your world."

Listening intently to the conversation Ann begins to take notes on how Steve is interacting with Matt.

"I would love to," Matt replies. "The trip would be fantastic, but any time I get away from work I want to spend with Ann. And what's this about the business development conference?"

Ann is touched by his genuine desire to spend time with her, and for the first time she starts to understand his point of view about providing a lifestyle befitting a queen.

"I know how you feel," Steve continues. "I felt the same way. I was just like that when I was teaching school and coaching. But Sara and Ann have plans for one of the days anyway. So from my perspective we might as well take advantage of the mountains instead of the mall, if you know what I mean. Imagine what it would look like, just you and me speeding around the lake and eating around the campfire, talking about how to create massive wealth and security for our families by setting new records for success. And the speaker at the conference is my mentor, Glenna Hanks. She will be talking about how to better understand what your prospects, customers, and team members want and need. She is going to be detailing the difference between hearing and listening, things you can do to improve your listening, roadblocks that keep you from being able to listen, and most importantly, the three-step cycle that allows your prospects to tell you how to sell to them."

As she listens, Ann realizes that Steve is talking to Matt using the language of a Sports Car. He is using succinct headlines or bullet points and image words to paint a picture.

Steve continues, "So what do you say? Are you ready to come with me to conquer the trails and then the business world?"

"That's it!" Ann thinks as she is listening. "I talk to Matt the Sports Car as if he were me, the Pickup Truck. I rarely ask him to take action directly. I hardly ever draw mental pictures, and I use way too many details about everything we talk about. How could I have been so blind? I know to do this when I am talking to prospects and team members. But in my own home and in the relationship that matters most I have failed to follow the rules of successful relationship building." Ann pauses to hear the last of the conversation.

"Thanks for thinking about me," Matt responds. "Looking at my schedule I do have a few days I can use before my Board of Directors meeting. Okay let's do it. I will call you when I get home on Wednesday night to get clear about the trip and logistics. Again, thanks for calling me Steve, I look forward to going with you, goodbye."

Ann is careful to hang up exactly when Steve does so as not to raise any suspicion about her having listened in. If Steve hadn't asked Matt directly he would never have gone, Ann realizes. I don't specifically ask him to take action, so he must think my requests are just suggestions, things that may or may not help him solve problems that are less critical than his vision of what success is for a husband. No wonder he dismisses my hints and clues.

After Matt hangs up with Steve, he calls Ann back to finish the conversation. I need to tell her about Steve's offer to go four-wheeling too.

"Hello there. Sorry for the interruption," I say apologetically. "So, guess what I did today?" Actually, I'm nervous enough about this conversation that I don't let Ann answer, "I agreed to take a four wheeling trip with Steve."

Making sure to sound surprised, Ann says, "Really? When are you going?"

"Two weeks from now, on Thursday and Friday," I answer eagerly, pleased that she didn't sound upset. "Then you and I can go to the business conference together on Saturday," I explain as if I have the inside scoop on a news story.

"That's wonderful," Ann replies not knowing whether she should elaborate on the fictitious plans with Sara. "I am excited you'll be home early that week." They exchange goodbyes again and hang up.

I lean back in my executive chair, staring out the window overlooking the city, thinking about the first few months of my new position. This job has been extremely taxing, and being gone 80% of the time from my family is wearing on me. I have been a Regional Manager for over two months now and as I pour over the numbers I'm getting from my Division Managers, I feel more and more inadequate.

Sitting alone in my office, and it is late right now, I say aloud that I have been teaching and preaching relationship skills since the day I got here. I have assigned my Division Managers to teach their teams about Value of Service, Relationship Ratings, Trust Quotients, and PIKing Relationship Gateway locks. I still have high-yielding questions, Listening, and Conversion Ratios to cover, along with whatever the next two principles are that Steve will cover. But the results I am expecting just aren't materializing.

The truth is, I am finding it really weird not reporting to Bruce anymore, and even more strange to be at the same level in the company organizational chart as he is. Now that I think about it, it seems odd that although Bruce recognizes some of the reasons I am being successful, he never has asked me to teach him what I am learning. Maybe he thinks it's too much of a risk for him to convert to what I am doing. And now that we are competing for bonuses, bragging rights, and possibly the next promotion, he is more likely than not to let me sink if my approach doesn't work. Maybe that is why I'm here, in the worst region in the company. I can't even imagine what my first quarterly review with my new manager Terri Hesslip is going to be like.

By the numbers, our region's customer acquisition costs are unchanged. Our new accounts have grown by a very small fraction, and customer up-sells increased by a measly .9%. Business coming from existing customers and client retention rates are all down slightly. Worst of all, our customer satisfaction surveys indicate that we are really struggling to grasp the idea of improving relationships while still asking people to take action. That's the bad news. But it's not all doom and gloom. None of my Divisions are in the bottom five any more, and our average Relationship Ratings are up by a point with Value of Service scores now over 65. No one yet seems to understand the importance of tracking conversion ratios. I am discouraged, but at that moment I remember what Bruce told me when I first joined the company and was struggling.

He congratulated me on changing how I was approaching prospects and clients, and encouraged me to keep getting better to become the kind of leader others would follow. He finished by reminding me that 'Rome wasn't built in a day,' and that personal improvement takes some time before it manifests itself in everyday life. Encouraged I remind myself that these principles do work. I have seen them at work with Steve and Sara, with Ann and her team, and with myself and team members at every level at Perpetual Wealth. Lying on the couch in my office I fall asleep thinking about Ann and what a miracle she is in my life.

During the next week I prepare for my presentation to the Board of Directors. It's challenging at best. I am working to put my Region in the best possible light, but there's really not much great news to share with them. During one of my evening calls with Ann I tell her that I am extremely discouraged and disappointed. I feel like I am letting Bruce down. He recommended me to the board, now the numbers are coming in and they are not what I anticipated.

Ann responds, "You took over a region that for a long time now has been the worst performing region in the whole company. It may take some time to turn this around. No matter what happens, I love you and believe in you and what you are doing. I feel like you need to stay the course. Sink or swim, you should stay with it and let the principles and skills do their work. It takes time for people to adopt a new philosophy, and then more time to get their skill levels up so that they will produce improved results. What I have learned during my time in XL-8 is that I need to have confidence that my team can and will master these skills, and that when they do, positive changes will occur. Don't abandon what got you to this point. I understand that the numbers are disappointing right now but have confidence that what Steve is teaching will work in the long run. I wish I were there with you to comfort you, but I believe in you and I know that you will figure out how to win. You will have a great trip with Steve this weekend, and we can talk more about this after the conference. I want to know what you learn from Steve, and we can discuss what we learn from Glenna Hanks." We talk for a few more minutes and then hang up.

I am on the ground and home again with Ann and the kids for a night, and then off four-wheeling with Steve. This little vacation is so liberating, I think, as Steve and I round a corner on the trail coming upon a long narrow meadow running parallel to the trail. We startle a cow elk with her calves; they had been foraging and take off running through the meadow along side the road. We follow them for a mile or so, when they turn into the trees just as we crest a hill overlooking the most beautiful lake. Stunned, I confess to Steve that I haven't ever seen such a breathtaking sight, as we stop to take a picture.

"I think this one is going to be suitable for framing," I comment. The evergreen trees along the trail and surrounding the lake with Aspens nestled in between, the beautiful colors of the bushes and underbrush, all of it is beautiful and still. Taking a deep breath, I feel the cool fresh air fill my lungs as it soothes my whole body. I can see for miles and miles: mountain after mountain. The birds are chirping and two squirrels are chasing each other, one having a nut in his mouth. The sound of a woodpecker pounding the side of a tree breaks the serenity of the moment like a jack hammer on the streets of a downtown construction project. "It is an awesome feeling." Steve remarks, "I always feel a special connection to God when I come out here in the wilderness, where nature is king and computers or phones don't distract me from what's really important."

Sitting around the warm campfire, sharing stories of our youth, Steve and I talk about his aspiration to be a major league baseball player, his experience as a coach and school teacher, how he met Sara, and the circumstances leading up to his involvement with XL-8. My admiration of him grows by the minute. "I was devastated," Steve shares. "When my father told me not to accept the baseball scholarship that would have put me at the top baseball program in the nation, and on the path to the dream I had worked all my life for."

It motivates Matt to share his own similar story saying, "Although I think my story has more drama, we are more alike than I had ever imagined." Steve then tells me that his motivation from that moment on, and what is still the driving force in his life is to become the kind of person who can succeed no matter what the conditions are. For Steve, learning how to win and then implementing success principles that create victory have become the driving force in his life. He's learned how to be a successful missionary in his church, and how to be a successful school teacher, coach, husband, father, and now leader in XL-8.

It occurs to me that I have never heard Steve talk like this before; here, he is talking and sharing instead of asking questions and elaborating on the teaching moment. It doesn't last too long, though. Steve finds his moment, and then asks, "So what motivates you? What drives you to work like you do, travel, and dedicate yourself to your job like you do? Why do your feet hit the floor in the morning?"

It takes Matt a minute to gather his thoughts and measure his response. When I am ready, I say, "I grew up idolizing my dad. He was larger than life to me. He was everything I ever wanted to be. He had everything I wanted to have someday. And I thought that working for and with him would be my ticket to success. When he ordered me off the property one day and told me that he had always been convinced that I would never amount to anything, something ignited within me. I think it was a passion to prove him wrong that summoned all the faculties, gifts, talents, and abilities God gave me to become someone of worth."

Steve interrupts asking, "Of worth according to whom?"

I respond, "I think that, secretly, I have been seeking his approval all my life."

"And so how is your relationship with your father today?" Steve presses.

"Sadly, I haven't spoken to him in years."

"Are you kidding?" Steve says curiously. "You have a college degree, a beautiful wife, great kids, a nice home, an executive position in a prestigious company, great skills, and a wonderful giving heart. What else do you think will gain his approval? And maybe the better question is, 'do you really need his approval anyway?' What if you get it? Will it make any real difference in the day-to-day living of your life?"

Odd how that line of questioning makes me feel defensive. I fire back, "His approval won't make much of a difference in my daily life, but I have been working for one more achievement since I was excused as a member of the family years ago, and that is to become an executive on the top floor of Perpetual Wealth Financial. That's when I think I will be ready to believe that I have become someone of value to the world and to the Ivey name."

"It seems to me," Steve picks up. "That you have lived your life at the mercy of others' endorsements: your father, college professors, and managers at work. What if you never make it to the top floor? Will that invalidate all you have accomplished? Will it make you less of a person? Let me ask you Matt, if you could wave your magic wand and have your life be anything you imagine what would it be like?"

"First of all," I respond more forcefully. "Not making it to the top is not an option. My dream is based on a hope for respect in my personal and professional life. Professionally I imagine a corner office with two windows, whatever car serves Ann's needs, a house on some acreage with a small river flowing on one side and a county maintained road on the other. Horses and a barn to keep them in so that Ann and the kids can enjoy them. The freedom to be able to attend my kid's activities and events. No debt, twenty thousand dollars in my wallet, no worries about money, a full college fund with one hundred thousand dollars for each child we have.

"Once that is all accomplished, I would love to travel to important religious and historic places, serve my church as a missionary, create a family bank for my kids and grandkids to use to build their dreams without the red tape, regulations, and impersonal decision-making, and my new addition to this list is four-wheelers to take on trips like this one."

Steve replies more softly now, "That's a great vision Matt. What keeps you from making that happen?"

I begin, "Well my personal experience and observation is that I don't seem to be able to be satisfied with the level of success I have at any moment in time. I am always chasing the next level of achievement, thinking it will be the magic potion to happiness. I often wonder why I continue to choose to follow in my father's footsteps, focusing on providing a high quality lifestyle for my family, even if it means I am absent most of the time."

Steve quickly responds saying, "Success is not limited to the things we acquire and the lifestyle we live. It also includes the reward we get for helping others become what they are intended to be. It also comes from being the kind of person that inspires and encourages people to pursue their dreams and passions with the same desire that motivates you to pursue your own goals. You have a great story of success, achievement, and overcoming obstacles, and it needs to be told to thousands of people all over the world. I would encourage you to consider how that might happen. Maybe through books, presentations, keynote speeches, and by telling your story one-on-one with your own family. How do Ann and your children fit into your grand scheme? They will need you more and more in the future. Your kids will need a mentor who can help teach and guide them on a personal and daily basis, and Ann will need a confidante and support partner while raising them."

Steve leans back and continues, "Here's what I mean about being a support partner. When Sara and I were first married I worked long hours away from home. She carried most of the burden of raising our children when they were small. I remember coming home one day and finding Sara on the front steps of our home. She had her face buried in her hands crying. The closer I got the more I began to wonder what had happened. Had something happened to our children and where *were* the children? As I approached her my heart sank in fear that she had snapped from the stress of being with small people all day and that I would find ours lying in a motionless pile somewhere in the house. But Sara simply said that she needed a time out. The kids were all upstairs playing. She had put the gate up at the top of the stairs so they wouldn't come tumbling down, and came outside for a few minutes to get a break from little people. We sat out on the stairs for a little while before I went in and took care of the kids. She needed me to be home to give her some relief and to support her in the endless duties of a mother." Matt is transfixed. He hadn't ever really considered how hard it is to be doing what Ann is doing without any help. He looks at Steve, who smiles for a moment, yawns, and says, "Well it's time to turn in. Tomorrow we will probably see many things like we did today. So get some rest." Happy to see that Matt understands better, and that he has met his condition of victory, Steve heads into his tent.

The sun comes up, and while taking down his tent Matt realizes that today is truly a new beginning. Riding in the mountains helps me clear my mind and relax my soul a bit. I am grateful to have such a great friend and mentor. On the way home I am lost in thoughts of Ann and the kids. Pulling in the driveway I see Ann working in the flower garden with the kids. My heart soars to see her, but sinks at the same time. This is the picture I envisioned growing up, and interestingly enough I am not present in the picture. What I haven't recognized until now is that my fantasy life growing up didn't actually include dad in any of the pictures either. My motivation to keep from turning into Oscar has driven me to become just like my father and to create an absentee lifestyle just like he had.

With renewed determination to have the lifestyle my dad achieved and somehow get myself in the picture with Ann and the kids, I find myself sitting in the front row so as not to miss anything in Glenna's presentation, feeling that being that close to her will somehow intensify the learning experience. Ann and I wait for her to enlighten us about the next relationship recipe ingredient, as Steve refers to what we are learning.

After the announcements and initial pageantry of the conference concludes, Steve introduces Glenna with the most compelling introduction I have ever heard. She begins with a bold statement, "The biggest communication challenge people have is listening too little and talking too much. You never learn anything when you are talking. You can't learn what your prospects need, want, and care about if you don't learn to listen. In order for you to provide appropriate solutions to people's problems, you must first know what they are. If you listen carefully to others, they will tell you exactly what to say and do to get them to take the action that will benefit them. For some it will be the value of your products and services they need initially. For others, it will be the opportunity of your business to create income and possibly give them more discretionary time. No matter what they are dissatisfied with, our business has the solution for it.

"During the first few minutes of your conversations and presentations, use the power of high-yielding questions and then follow with active listening to determine their interest in learning more about what you offer. Resist the urge to talk or answer their questions until after you know what your prospects want or need. Your goal should be to show them your entire solution and all of its benefits, so that they can make an informed, educated decision to take action.

"Remember that you are simply being curious, not interrogating them. You are interviewing them, not the other way around. As you listen to your prospect, there are three very important questions you should be asking yourself silently: 1) Is this person looking to find a solution to their pain or are they more interested in complaining or making excuses than taking action. Remember that people can make excuses or they can make money, but they can't make both. 2) Do you really want to invest your time and effort helping this person? And 3) Does this person really want to be helped?

"Today I am going to be talking about listening and how you can use it to build trust that allows your prospect to tell you what they need to know for them to agree to enroll with you as a customer or as an associate. You cannot establish trust if you cannot listen. A conversation is a microcosm relationship. Both speaker and listener play an active part, each attracting or repelling the other. Remember that listening is just as involved as speaking, and as a listener you will have as much to do with shaping the conversation as the person speaking.

"Listening is just as beneficial a skill as talking, particularly because you need to learn what your prospects need so you can promote the right features and benefits, or aspects of your offering. Don't misunderstand what I just said. I didn't say listening is more important than asking questions. Listening and asking high-yielding questions are equally important. Talking requires you to know something, and to have an opinion about what you think you know, even if that opinion is not based on facts, figures, or anything else concrete. So don't worry about talking; you will get your chance to talk and promote our products. But you will only get this opportunity if you have demonstrated you can listen, and only if you offer a product that actually serves their needs. Don't blow it by over-promoting a feature, benefit, or result that your prospect or customer has no interest in.

"So your first mandate is ask a high-yielding question, then listen carefully to their responses. When you know what they need, use your product, company, and relationship knowledge appropriately to help them resolve their challenges. Only when you can articulate the challenge that you can solve, and the product, service, or business offering that does the solving should you inform your prospects about the solution you have."

Matt is eager to hear all that she has to say after this rousing beginning. It's a subject that I thought I am already pretty good at, but now I'm not sure.

Glenna continues by asking us a question, "Have you ever been talking to someone whom you know wasn't listening to you, but seemed to be formulating his next question or statement before you finished talking? How did this make you feel?" Glenna is forceful when she tells us, "When you don't listen to others, it makes them feel like you really don't care about their point of view."

Matt thinks attentively, I am glued to her every word and movement. I find that I have unconsciously moved to the edge of my seat, and am clutching my pencil. I take a deep breath, relaxing enough to hear every word as if she is speaking directly to me.

She explains, "Your pain is not necessarily their pain. Your prospects are not particularly interested in what all your XL-8 stuff has done for you; and they won't be until they know how your products and services will alleviate their specific challenges. They may want more time and money. They may want better health and peace of mind. If you approach your prospects with a great story about how your products and services gave you more of what you wanted, but never show how these things will help them get what they want, they will not engage either as a customer or an associate on your team."

Glenna talks about the difference between hearing and listening, beginning by citing a public service announcement that aired on television. She describes the ad, saying, "They make a clear distinction between hearing and listening. Hearing is nothing more than a physical ability to process sound waves at specific frequencies. Hearing is a physical process that requires only your ears. Hearing happens as a matter of circumstance. For example, if you are in a room and people are talking, you hear noise whether you want to or not. Listening skills allow you to make sense of and understand the noise another person is making. In other words, listening skills allow you to understand what someone is 'talking about' and why it matters to them."

Matt ponders the many times he has "heard" Ann tell him she wants him to be home more with her. In the context of what Steve talked about around the campfire, and my own need to have a better relationship with Ann, it occurs to me that for most of my marriage, I have been hearing Ann, but not listening to her at all. Now I think I understand what Ann means when we are talking about her new horse and she says "He would be there everyday." I think I understand what she is really saying.

The truth is, it's been months, maybe years, since I have really listened to her plea. The little game of "Guess What I Did Today" is really her way of connecting. It is her Pickup Truck way of asking me to be part of her life, and she doesn't have any other way of asking me without coming right out and demanding it like a Sports Car would, something a Pickup Truck doesn't do naturally. It now occurs to me that I have no idea why she thinks it's so important for me to spend more time at home. I don't know what's really important to her and how it relates to our growing family.

She obviously has a vision of what a father and husband should be, and I have almost no clue what that looks like. She hasn't asked directly or demanded that I be home more. Maybe her mentioning it at all is a scream for her Personal Interaction Key type. Based on what Steve and I talked about around the campfire, I think I should find out what she's thinking and feeling.

When I rejoin the conversation Glenna is talking about being in business on purpose, and that purpose is to get and keep customers and associates. Glenna implores everyone here to, "Master this critical skill and begin to really understand what your customers want and need. Without that basic understanding very few will ever transact or transform with you, and soon your business will be a charity or social club."

She goes on to state, "In 1991 the United States Department of Labor identified five competencies and three foundational skills that are essential for those entering the workforce to have. Listening skills were among the foundational skills. According to the U.S. Department of Labor, good listening skills make workers more productive.

"So what are the benefits of high PEP listening? Here are a few things I want to share with you today: High PEP listening allows you to better understand your prospects, customers, and team members and know how to PIK their relationship gateway lock. In a few minutes, I will teach you a process that will help you build rapport, show interest, resolve problems, overcome objections, answer questions, understand the real needs and wants of your prospects, customers, and team members, and help your prospects, customers, and team members take the action you recommend. If you feel these are important or that they would help you build a strong and profitable business faster and with less frustration, then you should consider mastering this skill.

"The key to effective communication is to be interested instead of interesting! Listening is critical to this philosophy and will pay major dividends if you master it. Listening is a mental, emotional, and spiritual process. It is also a matter of choice. You choose to listen to or ignore what the other person is saying. If you choose you can emotionally, mentally, and spiritually process the words, feeling, and meaning of their communication.

"Good listening is a choice to interact with another person with curiosity. As you all already know, curiosity is the foundation of good listening, because if you are curious about what the other person is saying or curious about the other person in general, you will probably work to extend the conversation. Listening is about seeing the world through other people's eyes. It is like walking in their shoes for a while and understanding how they view the world.

If you are not curious you won't take the time to learn about others and the way they think. Learn to listen, and truly understand what they are saying.

"Okay enough background stuff, let's get down to the brass tacks of what keeps us from being high PEP listeners and talk about what you can do right now to increase your listening PEPs. I'll finish with a three-step cycle that will help you have powerful conversations with anyone about anything.

"Here are ten barriers people put up that discourage open, meaningful interaction:

1. "Bias or prejudice. All of us have negative thoughts or feelings about certain ideas. For example, I know a man who feels like people with tattoos who wear baggy pants and their hat pointed to the side are less likely to succeed than others. So when he interacts with anyone who fits this description, he starts the conversation with a prejudice that says this person is less educated or less intelligent or just plain less. Of course, this bias hinders his ability to communicate on a deep human level with this person. Hence he is restricted in his ability to provide value in any way to the individual.

2. "Language differences and accents. Because we live in a self-centered world, we assume that our way is the right way. I over heard a conversation between two women a while back. One was from England and the other from Alabama. As they listened to each other, each judged the other as less than cultured, educated, and capable because of the others accent.

    "Dialect and sentence structure also played a role in this conversation. The words the woman from England used to communicate had a different meaning for the same words as the Alabaman understood them. This caused a further divide between the women. Remember that the main thing in this business is to get people moving towards you and then with you. And these two women were definitely moving away from each other.

3. "Distractions. Noises in the room, text messages, phone calls, other people or activities in the room can be very distracting if you let them. Make the decision to stay focused on the person you are listening to.

4. "Worry, fear, or anger. Sometimes the things people say in conversations can be shocking, startling, or amazing when compared to our own philosophies. Often when we disagree we begin to shout louder and louder - if not with words, at least inwardly. We hang on fiercely to our own ideas, instead of listening and becoming quieter and comprehending more. When our emotions go up, our ability to think clearly goes down. Our ability to be curious and interested also decreases. When we let our emotions get the

best of us, our desire to be understood becomes the central goal of our interaction. We crush any hope of having meaningful interaction because our wish to be right overcomes our hope to help the other person.

5.   "Lack of attention span. Don't let your mind wander if the person you are talking to says something that reminds you of something else. It is really easy to start thinking of the other thing, but you can't let this happen. This doesn't build trust and it's definitely not professional, and it doesn't show that you care in the least about them.

6.   "Do not interrupt. Often people interrupt conversations in order to interject their own point of view or personal experiences. Interrupting devalues and de-edifies the other person. Interrupting others is just as effective at pushing someone away as you physically pushing them.

7.   "Finishing people's sentences. This is rude and like interrupting it devalues and de-edifies the other person and demonstrates that you think you know more about the person you are talking to than they do. This certainly pushes people away from you.

8.   "Quick draw responses. You know the kind of person who just waits for you to finish the story, or a paragraph, or sometimes even a sentence, so that they can have their turn. Sometimes this kind of person begins taking a breath in anticipation of your completion. This reminds me of a fantastic quote 'Some people have something to say, and others just have to say something.' Aristotle probably said it best, 'Wisdom is the reward you get for a lifetime spent listening when you would rather have been talking.'

      "Remember that your goal is to understand, not be understood. Pausing after the other person is finished talking also signifies that you are considering what they said.

9.   "Giving advice. It's common to want to give advice and fix problems immediately. Unless your prospect specifically asks for your help, don't. Even though you want to help, what might work for you might not work for them. Also, advice can feel condescending. Most people can find their own solutions if they just have the opportunity to talk and think their challenges through. Most want to find their own answers. Besides, when you fix other peoples' problems you make them dependant on you. So if you really want to help someone else, give them a listening ear.

10.   "Fidgeting. Shifting your body weight often, looking down, or checking your watch are conversation busters! All these things send a message that you are

bored, impatient, or not interested, and the chance that the person you are talking to will really let you in through their relationship gateway is zero.

"Listening is so critical to your success that I now want to share ten things you can put to use in your next conversation that will help you increase your ability to put aside your own agenda and focus your attention on others in order to build life-long relationships and add value to their life:

1. "Maintain eye contact with the person talking. Eye contact keeps you focused on the job at hand and keeps you involved in the conversation. It also helps you to look for visual clues about how the speaker is feeling. While you may be able to listen while looking down at the floor, doing so may indicate to the other person that you are not.

2. "Focus on content, not delivery. Have you ever counted the number of times a person clears his or her throat, uses the word 'um' or 'and' or 'so' when they are talking to you? If you have then you were focused on delivery instead of content.

3. "Stay in control of your emotions. Avoid emotional reactions to things people say and concepts that you may not agree with. When you are too emotionally involved while listening, you tend to hear what you want to hear—not what is actually being said. Remain objective and open-minded.

4. "Pay attention – Don't go on mental vacations. This means you need to stay present during the whole conversation. We've all had times when what someone says reminds us of something else, and our train of thought follows the other thing instead of the conversation. We've all been tempted to look around when noises are made in the room, or when someone walks in and out of our line of vision. Make the decision to stay focused on the person you are listening to. You may be able to pay attention while your mind wanders, but your prospect won't think you are listening at all.

5. "Treat listening as a challenging mental task. You can hear without listening. Listening is not a passive act—at least it shouldn't be. You need to concentrate on what is said so that you can process the information as you receive it.

6. "Stay active by asking mental questions. Active listening keeps you on your toes. Here are some questions you can ask yourself as you listen. What key point is the speaker making? How does this fit with what I know from previous conversations with this person and my own thoughts and beliefs?

7.   "Use the gap between the rate of speech and your rate of thought. You can think faster than the speaker can talk. That's one reason your mind may tend to wander. Your mind does have the capacity to listen, and ponder at the same time, but it does take practice to do this and stay present in the conversation.

8.   "Use nonverbal cues. A good listener knows that being attentive to what the speaker doesn't say is as important as being attentive to what he does say. Body language is a critical part of listening, and the old adage 'it takes two to tango' is in play here. Nonverbal cues include facial expressions and body language, both your own and the other speaker's. Sit still, nod your head, and lean toward the speaker.

9.   "Reframe what you hear. Summarize and repeat back what you understand the speaker is saying so they know you're understanding them, and you are focused on the emotions they might be feeling. You can say something like, 'This is really a problem for you. You have been feeling troubled for a long time now is that right?' Or, 'That's an interesting idea, could you tell me more about that?' Or, 'I'm not sure I completely understand. Could you tell me more about that?' are all good ways of reframing ideas.

"These confirming questions help you advance and deepen your conversations. They will help you to build trust by understanding what people are talking about and why they care about it. They also keep you in control of the conversation. A self-check on whether you are paying attention is to ask yourself if you could repeat at least one key point from the current conversation in the form of a question. For example, if your prospect just told you how excited she is about her new car, ask her what she likes best about it.

10. "Stay Present. Sometimes people pretend to listen, but they're really just waiting for the other person to stop talking so they can say whatever they've been mentally rehearsing while they've been acting the part of the interested listener. People can usually sense this, and it doesn't feel good. Also, they tend to miss what's being said because they're not focused. Live in the present moment. You may have to say to yourself: 'what is this person saying? I am taking in every word.' Then suddenly you begin to capture the exact words people are using and the message they want to convey. You will get a sense of what they want and need that they don't have now. Most people have a difficult time articulating their thoughts and feelings, especially when it comes to their dreams and passions.

"As you can tell, high PEP listening takes effort and practice. The good news is that mastering this skill will make you like honey to the bees. People will be attracted to you in ways you have never experienced before.

"Now that you know what barriers might be blocking your conversations and what you can do about removing them, I want to conclude with a reminder of the simple process that will help you PIK the relationship gateway and open the doors to the most amazing interactions you have ever had. Last month David McKay was here and he talked about high-yielding questions. He introduced you all to the success formula for relationship building. He taught you to 'Ask, Listen, and Repeat.' David and I have had so many wonderful conversations about this process. It's a little like the chicken or the egg debate: which came first, right? In this case, which is more important, asking or listening?

"I have concluded that neither is more important than the other. And often, the most important part of Ask, Listen and Repeat is actually repeating the process. Asking one question or listening to one response is never enough to provide you with enough context to really understand anyone's circumstances. Writing prescriptions without a proper diagnosis is dangerous and irresponsible.

"Listening is a creative force. Think how the friends that really listen to you are the ones you move toward in any particular conversation. When we are listened to we unfold and expand our vision of our own life experience. Ideas actually begin to grow within us and come to life. If a person laughs at your jokes you become funnier and funnier. If he does not, every joke in you withers and dies. That is the principle at work here. Listening makes people relaxed and free. If you are a high PEP listener, everybody around you becomes lively and interesting. When you listen to people there is an alternating current that recharges you so you never get tired of other people. You are constantly being recharged through listening with quiet, fascinated attention.

"David may have told you that I discovered the Ask, Listen, Repeat process while I was taking a shower one morning reading the instructions on the shampoo bottle. It occurred to me that the process for successful listening is very similar to washing your hair. Instead of wash, rinse, and repeat, a great listener should ask, listen, and repeat. The formula for failure in building relationships seems to be talk and then talk some more. Some people have mastered talking to the point where they can talk people into adopting their point of view, and out of adopting their point of view in the same conversation.

"This listening process will help you clearly understand what result your prospects, customers, and associates want. Once you have invested the time and effort in understanding, you will have the opportunity and information to make a powerfully accurate recommendation of the appropriate products and services because you know what result they want and why they want it.

"In order for people to really take you seriously, and ultimately for them to take the action you recommend, they need to know three things: can they trust you, are you good at what you do, and do you care about them? The ask, listen, and repeat cycle helps our prospects to get a clear, positive message about all three of these questions. In turn, they will take your recommendations. When you care about them, they will begin to trust you and have confidence in your recommendations and prescriptions to relieve their pain."

Glenna completes her presentation saying, "You have one mouth and two ears and you should use them in that proportion. Solve their problems, not yours," she implores us. "If you ask high-yielding questions to get them to talk, they will tell you what they need and how our products and services can help them to meet those needs. I hope you are all in business on purpose," she reminds. "The main purpose of business is to get and keep customers. Becoming a high PEP listener will help you more effectively communicate your intentions to be interested, instead of interesting, and to understand before being understood.

"At the end of the day, mastering listening is really not that hard. Why? Because you only have to control yourself. Everyone's favorite subject in the world is themselves. So you don't have to be a great conversationalist in order to show others that you are trustworthy and that you care for them. You only need to listen intently and ask a relevant question here and there.

"You may be feeling a little uncomfortable right now, learning that you might need some improvement in your listening skill PEPs. Or you may be thinking about someone else who needs some improvement in this area. But I think if you are feeling a little uncomfortable that might be good news. Because you might finally be realizing that you do need to improve. You might finally be able to see that your relationships will grow stronger much faster when you listen better."

"Some of you may have come today thinking you were a pretty good listener. If, after all this, you still think you are a really good listener, you should ask a few people who will tell you the truth. You can ask your boss, kids, friends, and spouse if you are a good listener, and you might get some pretty interesting feedback. From this day on," she challenges, "Listen to your wife, your husband, your father, your mother, your children, your friends. Listen to those who love you and those you don't, to those who bore you and even to your enemies. It will work a small miracle and perhaps a great one.

"When you decide to master this critical skill you will stand out in the crowd like the first star on a dark night. Listening enables you to connect with people in new and penetrating ways, and you will never have to be in the convincing business again. After all, you are in the people business. And people don't care how much you know or how cool our products are until they know how much you care about them. People will buy more of what you sell if you listen to what their needs and wants are because you will be different from everyone else. Thank you all for coming this afternoon, and I look forward to seeing you tonight." Just as fast as she arrived, Glenna vanishes from stage. The host gives us some instructions about when to be back in our seats for tonight and the auditorium lights come back up.

Matt turns to Donna, seated to his left and says, "I am blown away! I never knew that there is so much to know about listening. I am ashamed to admit that I am one of those she accused of coming into this meeting thinking I already knew all I needed to know about this. I guess it just goes to show you that it's what you learn after you think you know everything that matters."

Donna nods her head in agreement while closing her notebook. She tells me that she is more excited about tonight to find out how much everyone is progressing and to see the auditorium from the perspective of the stage looking out on the crowd.

The evening session starts out with the usual party-like atmosphere. I am actually beginning to enjoy the festivities of these events. Steve, Sara, Glenna, Ann, and the rest of the Gold level achievers are on stage to present the awards to the group. Ann has twenty-nine new people achieve the first or Copper level. The second level or Bronze achievers lined up to receive their recognition, and standing at the front of the line is Donna. In just a minute she will be looking out on the crowd from the stage for the first time instead of up at the stage from the crowd. Ann has seventeen new Bronze achievers and her three Silver teams have at least two new Silvers on their teams. Ann told me on the way to this session that next month's goal is to turn those Silvers into Golds and to get Donna and one other team to Silver.

Ann's team members seem to be able to do what she is doing. Her strategy seems a bit different from the other leaders. Instead of focusing on recruiting and hoping the cream will rise to the top, Ann focuses on teaching people to teach others how to build a strong and profitable business through powerful, meaningful life-long relationships. Her PEPs are now at eighty-two and she has a team of over 350 associates and about seventy-five personal customers. Twenty-nine of her team members are consistently working and being promoted along with her. She now has twenty-one leaders, and is making a great income.

As I sit there watching the procession of award earners I think, between my job and Ann's business I am now officially ready financially to feel comfortable living in our neighborhood. We still have the smallest house on the block, but we can afford to do most anything we want to do with a little planning. It seems interesting to think that I have had money and I have had none. And life always seems to go more smoothly when I have it.

On the ride home with Ann, as I contemplate what I learned at the event and how it might affect the teams in my Region, the thought finally penetrates my brain that I need to spend more time at home. I am worried that if I do that, then my career advancement and its associated income potential will diminish. My conversation with Steve while we were four-wheeling returns to inspire me: Steve said, "You have a great story that needs to be told in keynote addresses, books, and at home with your family." But my job as the husband is to provide temporally for my family, and so for now at least, I am going to commit to staying the course up the corporate ladder. As we come into the house I see a note on the dinning room table. It's a picture our kids drew while we were at the event. It's a picture of our family in front of our house. And right there in crayon I am included in the picture. In that moment I decide to reach out to my dad again and see if there is anyway to begin repairing that relationship.

Sitting in the front room, looking out the window at a spectacular morning, I picture what a conversation with my dad might look like after all this time. Impulsively I pick up the phone, feeling like there won't ever be a good time to call him, and so now is as good a time as any to dial the number. In a few seconds the phone rings once, twice, and then a third time. I begin to hope no one will answer, and just then the voice comes over the line, "Hello." I am relieved that it's my mother who answers. As I talk to her for a few minutes, I feel a little like I did in high school when I was talking to the friend of the girl I wanted to date, asking her if she thought the she would say yes.

I share my promotion news with her as a kind of test to see how she will react. She is very excited and suggests that I tell my dad personally. She tells me, "I think this wall between you both has been up far too long." As she's handing the phone to my dad I can hear her telling him to at least talk to me.

"Hello Matt," he says in his measured voice. "How are Ann and the kids doing?" He asks politely.

"They are doing fine," I respond. This conversation is a 1 on the relationship rating scale. I decide to take a risk and just come out with it. My dad is a Sports Car, and so I get right to the point. "I have some news to share with you. I have been promoted at work again. I am now a Regional Manager. I am working in our Minneapolis office and traveling quite a bit."

"That's great news," he replies with what I hope might be a smile on his face.

He always took great pride in my sisters when they did well. For the first time in years I don't feel like the bastard child who ran off to join the circus. Now that the conversation has begun, I ask how he is doing and ask a few questions about the horses and the ranch. I listen intently while he talks for about two or three minutes and then we cordially say goodbye with an admonishment to talk more often. In the strictest sense that could mean once in the next five years, but for this brief moment I communicated with my dad in ways I haven't in years, if ever. He shared things with me he never had shared before. Steve, David, Glenna, and Olivia are geniuses. The process of asking, listening, and then repeating the process even got my dad to open up.

I can't wait to tell Ann what I had just done. I find her in the bathroom and begin our daily game, "Guess what I did today?"

"I don't know," she replies. "But it must be good if you are this excited to tell me."

"I called my dad," I continue.

"And how did it go?" Ann asks apprehensively.

"It was awesome," I say excitedly. "He actually congratulated me on the promotion and we talked, well he talked openly and freely for a few minutes."

Curiously Ann asks, "What prompted you to call him?"

I reply without hesitation, "After listening to Glenna, I felt an urge to start working on some of my relationships and to really hear what their life is about and what makes them tick. I talked to my mom for a minute and then she just handed him the phone. Probably giving him that, 'you get to do this whether you want to or not' look. I am so surprised that he would even talk to me that I felt like it was a good idea to let him know firsthand about my promotion. When he congratulated me, I felt like maybe this was a good time to just let him talk for a few minutes without any pressure to do anything, or without any expectations. This might be the beginning of a new chapter in our relationship."

A few weeks have passed since I talked to my dad. But talking to him has given me the confidence to follow Ann's advice and stay the course. I am working hard to help my team members, and especially the Division Managers grasp the relationships-first approach. I am taking some consolation in the fact that Terri Hesslip hasn't called me yet. Either she is letting me get my feet under me before calling, or she is giving me enough rope to hang myself. Either way, I have a few months of data and can see general trends before I get to meet with her for my quarterly review. The region's numbers are only slightly better than they were when I got here. In fact, they are, in all reality, almost exactly the same. Customer acquisition costs, new accounts, and customer up-sells have increased slightly over the past three or four weeks. Business coming from existing customers and client retention rates both have improved some. Well, improved may be an overstatement, but they are no longer in decline. Relationship Ratings and Value of Service scores are up a bit. The best news of all is that two of my Division Managers are tracking conversion ratios and reporting them with insightful comments each week about what they might mean.

The morning sun is coming through the windows of my office. I love the morning; it makes me feel like everything has a chance to turn out differently, to be better today than yesterday. I am looking at the numbers that I have looked at a million times before, hoping that somehow today they would be different. Suddenly the phone rings, startling me and making my heart skip a beat. It's Terri Hesslip calling me unexpectedly. I look at my calendar to confirm that our quarterly review isn't scheduled until a few days from now.

I hesitantly answer the phone and Terri says, "Hello Matt. I wanted to call this morning and talk to you about your reports. I just couldn't wait any longer to comment on them. But before I give you my feedback, I want to know how you feel about your progress over the past few months?"

Cautiously Matt starts, "Generally speaking, I have done little except to stop the downward trend in almost all areas. We are not really improving though, so I am a little discouraged. I want to see improvement in more dramatic ways."

Terri asks, "I have a few questions about some of the numbers you are reporting like PEPs, Relationship Ratings, and Value of Service scores. I also want to know how tracking conversion ratios has helped you?"

I spend the next five or six minutes explaining how to measure, calculate, and track these items. "My focus has been to teach my Division Managers the importance of these items and to help them teach their team members so they can develop and maintain long term or life-long relationships with our clients."

Terri replies, "I have been eager to call you to congratulate you on the success you are having. I know it might seem like you are not making improvements. But you must recognize that your region has been the worst performing region in the company for over a decade. We have tried many different things and until now nothing has worked. That's why we put you there; for a fresh approach, knowing that if your methods work there we can take them to the rest of the company.

"I want to encourage you to keep your chin up. I am counting on you to weather the storm and bring your region to the top of the company. I also want you to relax; we put you in this position because we believe that you will turn this around and create long term success. If we wanted to implement the 'Flavor of the Month' we could have chosen almost anyone. We have tried that before, only to experience quick and short term increases, but no real long term results. Let me take a moment to teach you about the law of the harvest by telling you a brief story about a college classmate of mine."

Matt mutes his phone, takes a deep breath and sits back in his chair as he listens to Terri's story.

She proceeds, "My classmate was a very smart and capable man. His goal was to get a degree and get a good job. He took shortcuts for everything, and rather than paying the daily price of studying he learned to concentrate in his classes and to take thorough, exhaustive notes. He seldom studied, and crammed for tests the night before. He got good grades; in fact, he graduated with honors. But when he entered the workplace, something happened. His boss didn't care how much he knew or how much he could memorize. His employer cared only about what results he could create on a daily basis. Of course, my friend quickly became overwhelmed by the expectations of consistent, competent work. He called me one night and said, 'I have deceived myself. My old shortcuts don't work here. What can I do now? My boss demands more than I can deliver. Each day is like one of those college tests. But I can't cram each and every night!' For the first time in his life he faced real failure. I told him, 'The only way out of his situation was to learn some new habits.' He had to become diligent in his work each day, to persevere, and become self-reliant through long, late hours, mental sweat, and continuous struggle. And he has. He has paid a much higher price to overcome his past self-deception than he would have paid if he had just built the proper foundation to begin with.

"That brings me back to you Matt. We have been taking shortcuts in your region for years, trying to create a quick fix. The results have proven that we are paying a higher price for this philosophy than we would have if we had paid the price to build a proper foundation in the first place. You cannot force the growth process to happen overnight. We must follow the law of the harvest by planting, cultivating, and then the harvest will come. You have been planting, and now you get to cultivate. I believe you will have the opportunity to enjoy the harvest.

"I encourage you to listen to what your Division Managers are saying. Listen to the Department Coordinators and Floor Level Planners about their challenges with the process you are implementing, and see what they are saying and doing. Become aware of what is going on with your team, and adapt your implementation strategy to serve them so that they can better serve our clients. Keep up the good work. The first rule of emergency room triage is to stabilize the patient and then don't do anything that will make things worse. Then you can start to treat wounds and begin the healing process. You have done a fantastic job at planting and triage. Now you get to experience the fun of seeing the miracle of growth and healing begin." We talk for a few more minutes, schedule our next meeting, and hang up.

What a relief to know that she has enough confidence in me to take on the most challenging assignment in the company. Looking back on the past months I feel so blessed to have had this learning experience. It uniquely qualifies me for even greater challenges. I am grateful for having to really dig down deep into my personal conviction to the principles that have been so eloquently taught to me by Oscar, Bill, Steve, Mr. Jaynes and yes, even my father.

Author's Note:
The instructions explaining the mathematical equation for this chapter is in the appendix at the end of the book.

10

Collect and Connect the Dots

I can't believe how fast the time is going by, Matt thinks as he sits in his Minneapolis office. I have been a Regional Manager for almost six months now. Looking at the numbers, I think that Terri is right: over time things do get better if you apply correct principles in their proper sequence. We have moved out of last place as a region. Our region's customer acquisition costs are down 19%; while our new accounts have grown by over 11%; customer up-sells increased by 17%; business coming from existing customers is up by 8%; our client retention rate increased by 3%; and our customer satisfaction surveys indicate an improvement as well.

The two divisions that have been consistently tracking their conversion ratios have begun to move up the company rankings. None of my divisions are in the bottom five anymore. Just three months ago two were in the bottom five. The average PEP score for Floor Level Financial Planners has risen by 12 points. The Division Managers' Relationship Ratings are up 3 points, their Value of Service is over 85 and their conversion ratios are improving by about 4% per week. If things keep changing at this rate, we will be the number one region by my first year anniversary as Region Manager. That should give me a fighting chance at the rumored vacancy that will be left when my boss, Terri Hesslip, Vice President of Sales, retires soon. If the company follows its normal pattern they will replace her with one of the Regional Managers. And the only chance I have to be promoted to that position is to out-perform the other Regional Managers. Certainly I haven't been with the company long enough, or as a Regional Manager long enough to merit having my name under consideration for Terri's position. I need to sharpen my skills for transferring what I am learning so we can continue to create noticeable results for our clients and for our region. The good news is that I am conducting seminars in each region for the next few weeks, and that should give me some great practice teaching and training my leaders.

Preparing to board my flight on my way to visit my least effective division office I notice one of the gate attendants has on a different type of name badge than all the others I have seen before. The tag says "Manager in Training." That title seems really odd given the fact that this same person was working at the ticket desk a few minutes ago, and now she is taking tickets and helping people board the flight. I had seen many entry level employees in training learning to do these tasks, but not managers. When I ask her about their training regimen she says, "Every manager has to work a certain number of days in every position they are responsible for. It keeps all managers current on the latest systems and procedures, and also connects them to their employees, customers and front-line issues.

I love this idea so much that I spend the hour-long flight pondering this idea for my divisions. By the time I land I have a pilot program all laid out to begin immediately. And now that I think about it, I have noticed that most of the managers at Perpetual Wealth Financial don't really connect well with the Floor Level Financial Planners; or our customers for that matter. In fact, the higher they go up the corporate ladder, the more disconnected they become from the day-to-day issues. They also miss opportunities for growth when they can't see the problems our planners face on the front lines. I wonder what Ann might have to say about this within her experience in XL-8.

I call Ann during my taxi ride from the airport to the division office. My call takes her by surprise; we usually don't talk until evening. But today I am on a mission, and this new discovery might just land me back at the corporate building in Terri's corner office. "Ann," I begin as she answers the phone, "I have a question for you. In XL-8 organizations and in your up-line, what happens with new associates and customers as business builders rise up the promotion ladder?"

She responds, "The ones that learn directly from Steve, Glenna, and David McKay seem to be able to create success on a predictable basis—probably because they not only teach about creating relationships, they practice and live it. Remember that relationships are the foundation of the business, so the successful leaders build the deepest, long-lasting relationships with their customers and team members. Steve, Glenna, and David teach that the only way to create long term residual income and generational wealth is to teach others to teach others to teach others to build meaningful relationships.

"The only way you can be a teacher of teachers is to stay in touch with the new associates and customers. You have to be in living rooms with people who are struggling to create the life they dream of, to work in the trenches with new associates as they learn, practice, and apply success principles in there proper sequence. Why do you ask?"

Matt tells her, "On the way to the airport this morning I was thinking about how to get my Division Managers and Department Coordinators more involved in the day-to-day activities of the company. As I was boarding my flight this morning I saw a person training to be a manager of the airline doing things that entry level employees would normally do, and it got me to thinking that I might consider how this would or could work in my region."

Ann asks, "Remember Alexandra at the retreat? She is more indicative of popular philosophies of those who care more about individual, short term success. She and others like her seem to embrace the idea of just going out and talking to everyone, to be yourself, no need for any special skills, schools, or tools. She figures that we have been talking all our lives so we should be able to go and talk about XL-8 and get the results we want; we can throw mud at the wall because some will stick; It's the old 'fake it till you make it' philosophy. My experience and observation so far is that people who do those things don't last long in the business, and they make a lot of enemies along the way. The only ones who can just be themselves' are the ones who come to the business with really high PEPs. Those philosophies oddly are talked about and taught by some leaders like Alexandra. However, they seem to contradict what those leaders did themselves as they built their business empires.

"My experience is that people these days have a modern- day 'witching' stick. You know those Y shaped tools that pioneers used to find the location of water so they knew where to drill their wells. The modern day witching stick serves as a 'B.S. O-meter.' It seems that most people can very quickly sense someone who is selling one thing, but who is going to deliver another. The hype and hopium some use makes everyone suspicious and pushes people away. There were a lot of people there who don't have organizations capable of long term growth because of the foundational philosophies they were built on. Steve, Glenna, and David are already doing some of what Olivia was talking about, and so for them the retreat was really a green light for them to duplicate in more expansive ways the things they have been doing all along. I think Steve's method is going to be a greater focus going forward with Mr. Flint's leadership at the helm on the corporate side."

Matt says thankfully, "That is really powerful insight. Today I am going to institute a new program in my weakest division, and then if the results I expect to happen actually materialize, I am going to take this region wide."

"So what are you going to do?" Ann asks. "I am interested in the results of your experiment. If it works for you I might teach my team to do the same thing you do."

Matt shares his plan, saying, "I am going to have my Department Coordinators work on the floor one week per month, and my Division Managers will get to work on the floor one week per quarter and work along side the Department Coordinators one week per quarter as well. I am going to get this started this week. I anticipate a bit of push back and grumbling, but I expect that in a few months this is going to have a dramatic effect on our numbers for each office within the region. I can't see any downside, and the upside seems really positive. I love ideas that don't pose much risk but have huge upside potential. We'll see as I begin today.

"By the way, I also heard that Terri Hesslip, the Vice President of Sales, is retiring soon. If the company follows its normal pattern they will replace her with one of the Regional Managers. So I am highly motivated to test this new idea and focus on creating the most effective region in the company. If the rumor is true and I get the promotion, then I will be working back at corporate and my travel and work schedule will be much more manageable. The pay raise will be nice as well. Thanks dear, you have been a great help as always."

"Wait a minute Matt," Ann reacts suddenly enthused by the possibility of having Matt home more. "Your 'by the way' news is great! What can I do to help you on your quest to the top of the company?"

Not expecting a response Matt says, "The only thing I can think of right now is to teach me all you know and continue to believe in me and support me in becoming the kind of person others will listen to and follow. Of course you are already doing that so there really isn't anything new, different or extra that you need to do. I mean it with everything I have when I tell you how much I love and appreciate you. I need to get going to this meeting now. I will call you again tonight; I love you, bye!"

During my meeting with Rachel, the Division Manager for this area, I lay out my plan for her and the Department Coordinators. To my surprise, she is excited about it. As the newest Division Manager in the region she has plans to really make a difference. This division is the weakest in the company, and she knows it is a great opportunity to get noticed. She embraces the foundation of my philosophies and invents her own phrase for the idea: Relationships Create Real Results. Matt explains, "I want to work on the floor two days every week until I have visited every branch in every department in the region." She is quick to schedule my time in her Division before anyone else has the chance. I love her enthusiasm, commitment and the phrase, Relationships Create Real Results.

During my nightly conversation with Ann, I describe how my new idea was received and detail my grand plan of becoming uniquely qualified to implement and teach others how to implement the 'Relationships Create Real Results' philosophy at every level of the company. "I still need to learn the remaining skills in Steve's relationship training, though. Does he ever do any special or advanced training for those who want to go faster?"

"It's funny you should ask," Ann responds. "Guess what I did today?"

"Oh no, I think I know what that means," I reply.

"When you told me this morning that you were working to be considered for the VP position I called Steve and Sara and asked them if there was a way for you to get the training on a quicker schedule. Steve told me that he is going to be traveling to one of his out-of-town groups next week, and would be doing the next module in his training. I asked if you could accompany him on the trip and he agreed. I hope it doesn't cause a problem for your schedule, but you did ask, and learning the skills faster is what you want isn't it?"

"What a great leader you are Ann," I say very appreciative of her initiative. "I will probably need to meet him in the city he is traveling to, which will mean that I won't be home this weekend."

"I know," she says. "But if you get this promotion you will be home a lot more, so I am willing to postpone what I want right now to get what I want in the long run. You must promise me that you will share your notes when you come home, though, so that I can help my team take action faster as well."

Matt's secretary buys the last ticket on a flight landing almost at the same time Steve's does. As Matt comes down the escalator, Steve welcomes him and introduces him to his business partner Jerry. "Jerry," Steve explains, "Was the Vice Principle in the school where I used to teach and coach. He moved away to accept a promotion as a Superintendant in the school district here in town. Jerry is planning to retire soon, and he is making a huge push to become Platinum before he does. Jerry's team here is about three weeks ahead of Ann's in the training schedule."

On the way to the hotel, Jerry asks about Matt and his motivation for flying across the country to hear this training, and what his conditions of victory are for coming to the event. Matt thinks to himself, he sounds just like Steve, and further contemplates the power of duplication. No wonder Steve is so successful; he has high-yielding question clones all over the country. I tell Jerry that my wife Ann is in XL-8 and that I am a corporate executive in a financial services company. I explain that Steve has become a trusted mentor and friend, so anywhere Steve is teaching I want to be. I also share that there is going to be an opening soon for a Vice President position in my company and I want to learn the skills Steve is teaching at a more rapid pace so I can teach my people and continue to improve our results.

Steve, sitting by the door nods his head in agreement and says, "No matter what kind of business, job, or circumstance a person is in, "Results rule." Results are a consequence of effective action taken in its proper sequence. If you control the cause, the result will take care of itself. Tomorrow I am going to teach about being a professional dot-connector. That should answer a lot of questions you both have about who is in control of the pace of success in any area of life, including business."

Jerry changes the subject, asking Steve about logistics and recognition assignments. I spend the next few minutes thinking about what dot-connecting has to do with anything. The more I think about it, though, the more excited I become. I am always greatly surprised at Steve's training methods and the examples and unique practice opportunities he uses.

Steve and I stay in a hotel only two blocks from the auditorium where the event is being held. In the morning I choose to walk to the event instead of riding with Steve and Jerry. They have things to discuss, and I feel rather like a third-wheel. I arrive early enough to get a great seat in the front row;

and it's a good thing I came early. Only minutes after I sit down, people begin coming in at a pretty fast rate, filling in the auditorium, which is about as big as the one Ann and I usually go to. I am glad to have a bird's eye view of the proceedings. I can see and hear everything from my vantage point. The good news is that here, no-one knows who I am, and I won't be distracted by Ann's team. They are pretty enthusiastic, usually.

As I open my notebook and write a couple of thoughts about the idea of being a professional dot-connector, the lights dim and the session begins.

Jerry introduces Steve and the audience goes crazy, cheering, applauding, and whistling. This group is much more rowdy than the crowd at Ann's meetings. Maybe they are this excited because they don't get to see Steve that often, or maybe they are just more excited to be here. I don't really know, but they are seriously energetic for a Saturday morning. Steve begins in his usual way by asking a question which in this case is more of an invitation for whom ever is the most ready to become the next big leader to join him on the stage.

A man named Ken and a woman named Tina are fastest getting on the stage. Steve starts by asking Tina why she enrolled in XL-8.

Tina responds, "I initially enrolled so that I could get the products at a discount. But once I started to experience results for myself, I wanted to share them with others so they could enjoy the benefits I was getting."

Steve follows up, "And what has been the number one benefit you have experienced from using the products?"

"I have been able to get off all the medications I was taking for multiple conditions I no longer experience," Tina replies proudly.

"That is awesome," says Steve. "What can you do now that you couldn't before you enrolled in the business?"

"I can play with my grandkids and attend all of their activities including camping and hiking."

Steve continues, "What do you see as the greatest benefit that XL-8 offers to others?"

Tina replies, "The opportunity to have better health, and if you want it, a way to get paid for sharing with others."

Steve asks curiously, "Who introduced you to XL-8?"

"Jerry did," she answers as if she were the child of a movie star.

Steve presses on, "And now that you are actively building your business, what is your next goal?"

"I want to create enough income so that I can get my products for free, and then make enough money to quit my part-time job." she answers, seemingly without thought. But it was obvious that she had spent a great deal of time considering this before Steve asked today.

Steve continues, "How long have you been in the business, and what do you think is holding you back?"

Tina admits, "I have been in the business for about two months. I really don't know how to contact, and I am really nervous about asking people to take action."

Steve asks, "What would your life be like if you could overcome these two challenges?"

Tina answers excitedly, thinking about the possibility of getting help from Steve, "I would be able to help more people take advantage of the products I so dearly love, and I would make the kind of money that would allow me to focus on building my business by sharing with more people."

"Tina, on a scale from 1 to 10 how committed are you to learning how to contact more effectively and to overcoming the challenge of asking people to take action?"

Without hesitation she answers, "I am at least a ten."

"I intend to help you today to begin making that dream of yours come true," Steve concludes. "Thank you for sharing with us, Tina. Ken come over here and let's take a moment together."

Turning his attention from Tina to Ken, Steve begins by asking, "Ken how long have you been in XL-8?"

Ken responds, "This time about nine months. But I was enrolled a long time ago."

Steve is taken a bit by surprise and chuckling confirms what he thought he just heard, "You say you have been enrolled in XL-8 twice now?"

"That's right," Ken answers. "The first time no-one taught me how to do anything. They just said make a names list and go contact them all as fast as you can."

Steve uses an implication question asking, "And how did that work out for you?"

Laughing a little Ken says, "Not to well. I quickly became a member of the NFL club, which stands for No Friends Left."

Steve follows up using a diagnostic question, "So Ken, has there been a difference this time around?"

"This time I have really enjoyed learning more of what to do," Ken shares honestly. "The training program you have put into place has taught me skills that have given me the 'how to' for the 'what to' of the business."

Steve acknowledges the compliment and asks a confirming question, "It sounds like you enrolled both times with an emphasis on the business side of XL-8, is that right?"

Emphatically Ken exclaims, "I am in this to make money. There is no mistake about that. I have seen lots of people go across the stage who don't seem any more sharp than I am, and it frustrates me. So I am excited to learn how to take the next step that will help me recruit more people on my team and help them succeed once enrolled."

"I appreciate hearing that you are enjoying the business now. When you enrolled the first time and then again this time, what result did you envision your business would produce?" Steve asks using a diagnostic question.

Ken shares openly, but is a bit embarrassed when he says, "I have $73,000 in credit card debt, and I appear to be overqualified for any reasonable job in the corporate world. So I see this business as my only way of running my own business, and the only real way I am ever going to repay that debt."

Steve uses another diagnostic question, "What will your life be like when you get rid of all that debt and have money coming in every month?"

"I am sure both my blood pressure and stress level will go down," Ken continues. "Like Tina here, I will get rid of a few of the medications I am taking right now, and I will be able to volunteer more doing what I am passionate about, which is to help veterans to transition back into normal life when they return from their service assignments."

Steve follows up with yet another diagnostic question, "What are your greatest challenges in your business right now Ken?"

"I don't seem to be able to help people see how XL-8 benefits them and their particular circumstances," he concludes shaking his head.

Steve transitions the conversation using the golden nuggets Ken has given him, "Ken, on a scale from 1 to 10, how committed are you to learning how to connect with people better so that you can help them see the value of your service and the benefit of XL-8?"

Answering immediately Ken says, "I am a fifteen!"

Steve concludes saying, "What you are going to learn today should help you connect the dots for yourself and for your prospects. Thank you for sharing with us Ken. You can take your seat again."

Turning his full attention to the crowd, Steve explains, "These conversations were not random or without purpose. I had two reasons for having these conversations: First, I wanted to take another opportunity to demonstrate TINY, high-yielding question conversations; and second, I needed some information from a couple of volunteers to help me later on. Now that you all have mastered the Ask, Listen, and Repeat process, you should be able to inspire people to tell you many important and personal things that they are passionate about. When you get to the end of a simple High Yielding Conversation you probably have a lot of information to work with, so now you might want to know what you do with that information. For instance, after talking to Tina and Ken, what do I do with the information each gave me?

"Over the past few months I have been teaching you about relationships, the value of your service, trust, unlocking relationship gateways, high-yielding questions and the art of listening. I often get emails from many of you asking me, 'I have a bunch of pieces to a puzzle; now what do I do with them?' Well today I am going to teach you what to do with all the personal and pertinent information you gather from people. Let me illustrate this by telling you a couple of stories.

"One summer when I was a little boy I needed something to do to keep me busy. My mother thought it would be a good idea for me to paint a few pictures, so she bought me a few 'paint by numbers' sets. She taught me a few basic painting skills, and showed me how the numbers in each of the areas corresponded to a paint color, and then she let me paint to my heart's content. With each picture I completed, she found a place on the wall of her workroom to hang the newest masterpiece. All these years later, I think they might still be there. I painted enough deer, elk, and coyotes in meadows and on cliffs to keep all of them off any endangered species lists. So, what does this have to do with anything at all? Here is the connection: XL-8 is like the paints and your prospects' and team members' dreams are the canvas, but without the numbers that tell you which colors go in which area you will have the same challenge that Ken has. Without knowing what color goes where, you can't possibly make a painting look like your prospects or team members want it to. Without knowing the color key you are 'faking it till you make it,' and that is like throwing paint at a canvas and hoping by some miracle you will create a masterpiece. The chance that I would be successful painting a recognizable deer or elk was so low that my mother knew I needed the blueprint for matching colors to specific areas."

As Steve is talking Matt escapes on his own mental journey down memory lane. I recall building fences and mending corrals instead of painting by the numbers. The only numbers I remember are the priorities that were listed on my work chart everyday. The value of relationships wasn't very important in my family, so I am grateful to get this lesson now. Maybe I appreciate it more now because my parents were focused on different lessons. They didn't worry too much about having fun or making sure I felt good about myself, but I did learn how to work and stay focused on a job until it was done and done right. That is a lesson I will always be thankful for; it helped me get through school and become a good worker.

Steve, transitioning to a different example continues, "When I was a kid a friend and I bought paper cutouts of the space ship module that landed on the moon. We popped out pieces of cardboard that had instructions saying, 'fold tab A into slot B, and then fold tab B into slot C until we created what was supposed to look like a model of the actual space ship.

"At first we had a terrible time getting even one ship put together. The main problem was that we didn't pay too much attention to the tab and slot instructions in the beginning. After some frustrating minutes, it occurred to us that the instructions were there to help us put the model together predictably, and with a lot less frustration. Using the instructions, we figured it out, and soon we had a fleet of space ships, enough to populate the real moon surface.

And just like painting by numbers, the tab and slot instructions on the lunar module models helped us, because when we didn't use them we failed miserably, and at one point became so discouraged we wanted to quit.

"Finally, I want to share about another childhood experience I had. When I was a kid we used to go to a restaurant where the placemats had games on them. One of the games was a 'connect the dots' game. When we connected the dots, they made a picture of a clown or animal, Santa Claus, the Easter bunny, a house, fire station, or something interesting to kids. After a while, we used to guess what the picture was before we connected the dots. Of course we were never right because there were not enough dots and too much space between the dots to make much sense of the picture. The only way to complete the game and reveal the picture, was to follow the numbers: 1-2, 2-3, 3-4, 4-5 and so forth.

"Once we connected the dots, we had a picture. After a while we got good enough at this game to turn the placemat over and put our own dots on the blank side, making our own game of connect the dots. We put dots on the blank side and asked each other to guess what picture our dots made. Then we traded our dot-smattered pages and connected the dots to reveal the picture the other person created. Of course, we had to connect the dots in the correct order as marked by numbers next to the dots to create a picture that we could color as we waited for our meal to arrive.

"Connecting the dots in the context of building relationships is how we help others see that what we offer is a way to get what they want. Once again, you can't worry about what you want; you will get that as a result of helping others get what they want: health, energy, or financial security. The truth is, security in direct sales is achieved only when you help others get what they want. The more people you help, the more you will get. Too many people fail to learn how to focus on the picture that others want to paint. They get stuck going through the motions of contacting, presenting, being rejected, and starting the cycle over again.

"Those people will always be working to recruit new people to replace the ones who said no or who quit because they were never taught how to get their prospects to give them dots to connect. They weren't taught how to use high-yielding questions, effective listening, and dot-connecting skills. They weren't taught to help their prospects to create a beautiful tapestry representing their life as they dream of it. They focus on what will make them a sale, on what will get them recognized on stage, or what will get them to the next level. They ignore the needs, wants, and desires of others, and fail in the business because you can't create job-dropping residual income by yourself.

"Everyone you work with needs to see a picture of what their life could be like if they knew how to create it and had a vehicle and help to produce what they desire most in the world. When you focus on precisely what people want, on understanding them, their circumstances; when you understand their level of commitment and their goals, talents, and desire to create the picture they tell you about; then you can help them fold tab A into slot B and put the right colors in the correct spaces. Then you can show them how to connect the dots so that they can see how you are an integral part in accomplishing their greater causes and higher purposes.

"Connecting the dots requires dots; and it requires their dots, not yours! Most people you talk to will give you plenty of dots if you just ask them to. To take your business to the next level you must become professional dot collectors and then dot connectors. All of the things they say to you when they respond to your high-yielding questions are the dots that, when connected, paint a picture of the life they want. We've also heard these called 'golden nuggets.' For example, both Ken and Tina gave us dots. They threw a bunch of dots out there for us to collect and place on the paper. The dots they gave us make up a picture Ken and Tina want to hang on their wall. Their challenge and your opportunity is that they don't have a way to create that picture yet. XL-8 is the way to create or color in the picture. So first you need to help them give you dots so that you have something to connect when you discuss XL-8 and your recommendation that creates the outline of the picture they have imagined.

"Any time you converse with people, you aren't doing anything more than collecting and connecting the dots between what they want and what you offer that will enable them to draw, color, or build the picture they want their life to be. Once you have dots to connect, connecting them is simply a matter of saying, 'Here's how we create the 'more time' picture; here's how we create the 'more income' picture; here's how we create the 'better health' picture, or the 'better relationships' picture.' We tell them, we know how to build people, using our offering to overcome emotional or spiritual challenges, or whatever else the dots they have laid out for you.

"Your job is to collect the dots, put them on the paper or canvas, and then help people connect the dots: 1-2, 2-3, 3-4, 4-5 and et cetera. At the end of your interaction they will have a beautiful picture of their life drawn the way they want it, and a plan by which to get it with your help as a success partner. As you connect the dots, people will be able to see very tangibly how XL-8 is the solution to their pain, and how you are going to help them resolve that pain.

"So why does painting by numbers, folding tabs into slots, and connecting dots matter? Let me give you a brief list to help you connect the dots of dot-connecting:"

1. "This is the only way for you to determine how to really provide service or value to their life. You can't serve people effectively if you don't know them well.
2. "It's the only way to get people to take action that will help them begin to create the life or picture they want. Asking, Listening, and Repeating the

process is the way to invite them to give you dots. Your presentation or counseling sessions give you the time to connect them.

3.   "This is the way to get customers to see the value of everything you offer in a context that they can easily see, hear, and feel. It's the only way for you to empower people to really see how you are the answer to their prayers. When you ask them to take action they will say, 'Of course. Why wouldn't I do that?'

4.   "The conditions of victory for your interaction are to help their life be better through transformation, not just single transactional sales. "I know this is counter-intuitive, but if you Ask, Listen, and Repeat to get them to give you dots, and then provide a specific, solution that connects their dots into a representation of the life they want, more people will buy what you offer. This is the difference between being transaction focused and transformation centered.

5.   "You won't have to rummage around in the medicine cabinet looking for something that maybe, kind of, sort of, could possibly someday help relieve their pain.

6.   "You will never again have to guess what others want. No more guessing whether what you have will specifically help their individual challenges.

7.   "You can't enroll people in their own life if you don't know what they want their life to be. You can't be a support partner to people if you don't know what support they need or what action you can support them to take to create a result they want that you don't understand.

8.   "You can't enroll people to be an active participant in a life neither of you understand or can articulate.

9.   "If you don't connect the dots for people, they can't or won't do it by themselves. From your perspective you know everything about XL-8 and why it's so wonderful. They don't know anything about what you offer, and they don't or won't care about it if you can't show them how it resolves their specific, individual, and unique painful circumstances. People are simply not capable of connecting the dots themselves, or they are not motivated to do so.

"Let's talk about this for a minute. People can't connect their own dots for various reasons. First of all, no one teaches anyone to do this. Schools don't, churches don't, parents don't, most mentors don't, and politicians certainly don't. No one seems to be motivated to teach anyone how to evaluate the cause and effect of decisions and how to take purposeful action that will create an intentional result. People are taught to blindly follow the mandates of the leader, no matter the qualifications or experience of that person.

"People don't connect the dots because they are too busy, too lazy, don't know what you know, don't have a vehicle to take them to their destination, don't believe that you or XL-8 will be different, or a myriad of other reasons. All these reasons discourage people enough that they don't make an effort to figure it out without some help. If you collect and then connect the dots for them, they will take action with you because they will feel the three underlying principles of relationships exist between you: they can trust you, they know you are good at what you do, and that you care about them. Dot-connecting is an act of love not selling.

"So today I want to reverse the trend you may have experienced of your leaders failing to teach you to fold tab A along the dotted line and then slip it into slot B to create your lunar module; to help you learn to paint by the numbers and connect the dots of people's lives. I want to reverse the trend of you wondering why people aren't asking you how to engage. I know that you think and sometimes say, 'didn't I just show you a way to get what you want?' You wonder, 'why aren't you asking what credit cards I accept?' The answer is simple: because you don't connect their dots.

"When you go in with your 'guns blazin' and a picture of what you think their life should or could look like, you run right over the main point of the contact, presentation, follow-up, enrollment, team building, or leadership processes. You disregard, discount, and degrade what the other person wants, and they won't engage with you when you have created a picture they don't care much about. I would recommend that you stop 'Shoulding' on people. Anytime you find yourself saying 'you should have,' or 'you should do,' or 'you should say,' that is the time to find silence and start listening.

"You are giving counsel, advice, and a prescription that might solve the problem or make the situation worse. If you've connected the dots right, people will not only tell you what they would like their life to be like, but they will also tell you what they are willing to do about their situation. Make sure you are recommending something that will actually help them relieve their pain instead of prolonging it.

"There is a quote I love that goes like this, 'The man who stands in front of the stove and says, if you give me heat I will give you wood, will always be cold and hungry.' It also reminds me of a time I was eating lunch in the park down the street from my house. A little boy asked his mom to save some bread crumbs for him so that he could feed the pigeons. After he ate his lunch, he gathered the crumbs and enthusiastically ran screaming into the flock of pigeons with his handful of bread crumbs.

"In about two seconds all the pigeons scattered, flying away in fear for their lives. The boy was devastated because he had something he knew the pigeons wanted. But his attack approach only scared the pigeons, and they never got the treat he had for them because he wasn't focused on what would draw the pigeons to him. He pushed them away from him by running in, aimlessly yelling 'I have something you want and I want to give it to you now!' In the end neither the boy nor the pigeons got what would have been good for both; all because of the boy's thoughtless approach.

"The whole crux of your business is based on drawing people toward you, and then with you, collecting and then connecting dots for people. Find out what they want and then make them aware that there is a solution for their situation. Tailor your questions and delivery style to fit their preferred interaction style, and make recommendations specifically for their circumstances. This is the only way they will ever be able to understand the value proposition of your offering. It is the only way for you to ever fully understand how they see the world and what their commitment level is to making the most of their time, talents, and life-goals.

"Not long ago I was talking to an associate on my team. During our conversation she repeated the popular saying she heard from admired speakers, 'You can't say the wrong thing to the right person.' Then she asked me, 'Doesn't that make all this questioning and dot-connecting stuff irrelevant?' I told her, If you want to follow that philosophy then you will enroll about three to five percent of the people you meet. Not surprisingly that is the industry average. She continued, 'I have also heard that you can't say the right thing to the wrong person.' I agreed and said, No matter how effective you become at Asking, Listening, and Repeating, about three to five percent of the people you meet will not engage with you at all. I am not worried about the five percent who will engage despite your effectiveness, or the five percent who won't engage under any circumstance. I am concerned with helping you persuade the remaining ninety percent of the people you meet to pay attention to you.

"If you become a professional dot connector, ninety-five percent of those you meet can be positively influenced by you to see your point of view, adopt your ideas and apply your recommendations; three to five percent in spite of you, and ninety percent because you are interested instead of interesting. I prefer to tip the scale of predictability in my favor. I would rather draw people to me instead of being dismissed by them because I lack skill, and then blaming them for having a narrow mind and lack of vision. Those ninety percent will, at a minimum, open their relationship gateway and hear you if you PIK their lock, discover their pain by talking to them in their preferred communication style, and connect the dots between what they want and what you offer that will bring relief to them.

"After an event once, an associate came up to me, thanked me for coming, and then asked a few questions: 'I feel a lot of pressure when I approach people about the business. How do I take the pressure off me?' My response was, 'By letting them talk.' He continued, 'How do I get them to take action that will best serve them?' I answered, 'Connect the dots and give them options.' I explained further, 'People will tell you exactly what you need to say and do to get them interested, and they will tell you exactly what they are committed to do to remedy their pain if you will let them tell you. This is the difference between transactions and transformations; this is the difference between one-time sales and lifetime customers.

"Okay, you might be thinking, this all makes a lot of sense, but how do we do it? What do we do to help connect the dots for people?

"Begin by developing the mind set that you're helping your prospect solve some challenge they have identified during your conversation. With the right mind set, high personal effectiveness in product, company, and industry knowledge, combined with the ability to listen, build relationships, and use personal interaction key recognition skills, you will be able to convert more prospects to customers and associates. You will do this because you know what problem you are solving, and it is specific to your prospect. Connecting the dots is nothing more than your ability to present reasons that indicate that your solution will solve your prospect's problems. For many, their decision to engage with you as a customer or an associate lies in your ability to persuade them through social proof, research statistics, the arguments you put forth, and the questions you ask.

"When you contact, show your presentation, follow-up, answer questions, overcome objections, and ask them to take action, the most persuasive leaders use some statistics or facts and figures to make a point, in addition to their own personal testimony of the product, service, or income offering being presented. Instead of saying 'I know a guy who told my neighbor's brother that the products work,' or 'the company's founders have incredible integrity', connect the dots by sharing some raw facts, figures, or statistics to support your own knowledge and experience. Typically, some social proof or logical data can add a lot of credibility to your presentation.

"The most persuasive arguments for your product recommendation should be largely based on facts and figures. When you have indisputable evidence that your product, up-line mentor, or company will perform exactly as you have promised, your prospects will have more confidence than relying on your personal testimony alone. Believing that many others have experienced positive results is a powerful motivator for people to take action either as a customer or an associate. You could say something like, 'According to a study by the Direct Selling Association, 15 million people enrolled in a direct selling company in the U.S. last year. That is an increase of over 1 million from the year before. And U.S.-based sales went up by almost $2 billion two years ago, which was up by a billion the previous year, and three quarters of a billion the year before that. The study indicates that just over seventy-five percent of all sales were transacted face-to-face with sixty-seven percent occurring in a home.'

"There are generally speaking, four tools at your disposal:"

1.   "Reciprocation. People tend to return a favor. Thus, the pervasiveness of free samples in marketing and advertising. This philosophy says, 'If I give you a sample and you actually use it, you are more likely to buy something from me because you already got value from our relationship, and now you will give back by enrolling.'
2.   "Commitment and consistency. Once people commit to what they think is right, orally or in writing, they are more likely to honor that commitment, even if the original incentive or motivation is changed or taken away. For example, in car sales, suddenly raising the price at the last moment works because the buyer has already decided to buy.
3.   "Liking. People are more easily persuaded by people they like.
4.   "Reasoning. Reasoning is usually based on things like logical arguments or principles, scientific or social proof.

"Logic is systematically using probability, facts and figures, and cause and effect to deduce the truthfulness of a belief, statement, or argument. Here is what I mean: I could state; 'If you take the personal effectiveness profile, then you will know what specific skills you need to focus on and in what sequence, so that you can improve your ability to recruit, train, and retain people on your team. Those who have done this have increased their PEPs and have accelerated their business growth by 100% in 60 days, and that's what you want isn't it? If you would like to increase your business by 100% in the next two months, take the Personal Effectiveness Profile and begin the process today!'

"Scientific proof refers to research and experimentation that has been tested and produced empirical and measureable evidence to support a position or conclusion. Most of the facts and figures you present to your prospects will come from this kind of reasoning.

"Social proof is evidence from people doing things that they see other people doing. For example, in one experiment, one or more people would look up into the sky; people walking by or standing around would then look up into the sky to see what they were seeing. Social proof is the concept that even though you don't have scientific proof to back up your claim, your own experiences makes your assertion highly probable.

"Using these methods will help you gain dot-connecting skill. But remember that dot-connecting is not your attempt to make someone do something that he or she doesn't want to do. Dot-connecting is your ability to excite someone to take action or to pique their interest about something. In my experience, people only get emotional about things that they are interested in. This means that you can't get anyone to do anything that they don't want to do by connecting their dots. That is to say if you have high dot-connecting PEPs, and people make a decision to take action, they are only doing what they really wanted to do in the first place. You are simply giving them the reason or confidence to take the action that will create the result they are already motivated to create. In all reality you can't motivate or force anyone to do anything. So your ability to persuade only taps into people's internal desire for something. Some may really want more time or money. Or maybe they really want less of something like weight, or debt, or stress. It could be something that they want to get rid of, like a job or bad health. Or it may be something they want that they don't have at all right now, like peace, a new car, or a day off.

"Connecting the dots is not manipulation or coercion. Those two things are necessary ways to get people to do things they don't want to do. Persuasion happens when you discover people's challenges and then present a solution or a set of solutions that are in complete alignment with your prospect's desires. Dot-connecting provides clear choices and demonstrates the cause and effect of the outcomes of making those choices. It provides evidence that people can see, feel, or experience that creates trust and credibility between you. It appeals to their logic or emotions. In short, high PEPs in dot-connecting allows you to take some form of research, data, logic, or social proof and insert your prospects and their circumstances into the story so that they can see themselves having the same challenges as others and like others, overcoming them as a result of taking the specific action you recommend.

"Manipulation and coercion use trickery or force to get people to think, believe, say, and do things they normally wouldn't do. Manipulation, for instance, starts with the paradigm that you are going to get someone to do something whether they want to or not, whether it would be good for them or not. If necessary you are going to trick, overstate, or use hyperbole to control someone's emotions, decisions, or actions. High PEPs in manipulation can be seen when people over-state the performance or results of products, compensation, or company performance. I call this person a hopium salesman.

"The hopium salesman talks of great wealth and quick riches requiring little or no work and no need to learn, practice, or apply any special skill or knowledge. Manipulation tactics are also found in creating scarcity where there is none. Perceived scarcity generates false demand; perceived scarcity means there isn't enough to go around. For example, saying 'If you don't enroll tonight, you won't be able to join my team' encourages enrollments, but it usually creates buyer's remorse in a few days or weeks, especially when they hear you say this to others. Manipulation occurs when we intentionally deceive people by leaving out important, but inconvenient information, or embellishing facts and figures to make a point. Some people call this manipulation tactic propaganda.

"Propaganda in its most basic sense is often completely truthful, but selectively presents facts to encourage a particular synthesis, or gives loaded messages. For instance, I remember being at a meeting once when the presenter talked about a huge industry segment and all the money that was being spent on items in that market space. He got everyone there in an emotional frenzy, and of course many enrolled. What the presenter failed to share was that the company didn't have an affiliation with any of the partner companies he showed in his presentation. Nor did the marquee names in the presentation do or sell what his company was doing and selling. It was a little like telling everyone that people buy cars everyday, and then subtly shifting the focus to selling houses and implying that the same number of people who buy cars will also buy houses with garages because they need a place to park their cars.

"Another manipulation tactic is found in what is called exchange. This is the idea that because I have done something for you, it's time for you to do something for me. I had a lady in my business once who did favors for her neighbors and expected them to reciprocate by hearing her presentation or enrolling as customers or associates in her business. What a shame that she wasted all that good will with this tactic.

"Coercion is even more underhanded than manipulation because it is the practice of forcing, or controlling peoples' decisions and actions. Some people use their own authority to get people to obey their request for action. Coercion is a 'Do it or else' kind of attitude. You might think this doesn't happen in our industry, but it sometimes does. A parent or dominating member will 'tell' you to get in. Of course, they expect you to follow their admonition, and there are negative consequences, emotional or physical, if you don't. Coercion also takes the form of daring someone to do something. If a person who is highly regarded dares people with lesser PEPs to do something, those people feel like they have been challenged to take action. This creates a feeling of 'I don't dare not do it.' A dare can be phrased like, 'Only those who care about making their dreams come true will act boldly enough to start right now.'

"Manipulation and coercion always leave you with less credibility than when you started. Using manipulation and coercion tactics are how people end up in the NFL club, which, as Ken told us a few minutes ago stands for No Friends Left. This is a relationship business, not a 'do what I say because I say it' business. You get paid to help others get what they want, something that requires you to focus on them not you. Using manipulation and coercion are ways to trick or fool people into giving you what *you* want, not what your *team* and *prospects* want. If you have to resort to manipulation or coercion, then get ready to replace everyone who buys from you or joins your business in the next thirty to sixty days because they didn't want to buy or join! They were tricked or forced into it and when they come to their senses they will quit buying from you, working with you, and maybe even talking to you! That is not what you want. You want a strong, stable, powerful, profitable business. Successful business builders and leaders serve instead of manipulate or coerce their prospects.

"As you move away from coercion or manipulation, you move toward dot-connecting. Don't be afraid to try this. People will typically respond if you connect the dots and invite people to take action to resolve their pain. Dot-connecting takes the pressure off of you. It puts you in control of the presenting process by letting you make an understandable, compelling case for why your products will improve their life. You won't lose your relationship by dot-connecting. Your relationships aren't in jeopardy unless you put them there through manipulation or coercion.

"Here are a few techniques that can help you connect the dots for people more effectively:

1. "Connect each dot step-by-step. Your presentations can be organized in a variety of formats, from the traditional 1, 2, 3, approach, to a time line, to a series of causes and effects. It's important to regularly and blatantly let your prospect know where you are and where you are going.

2. "Make sure that you talk about your experience helping people create the result they are looking for. Take advantage of the competence of your up-line mentor, and include facts and figures. All of these things add credibility to your argument. Here are some specific words and phrases that people respond well to: Improved, Natural, Pure, Tested, and Recommended. Any word which expresses credibility ranks high with customers and associates.

3. "Quoting recognized authorities verifies that you have both done your homework, and that you know what you are talking about.

4. "Be concise, specific, and graphic in your argument. This gives you the aura of professionalism and authority. Listen to these statements and ask yourself which is more likely to persuade someone to donate to a children's charity: 'Please give to poor children overseas,' or 'Christina, a four year old, who must dig in the garbage just to stay alive everyday, needs your help.' Your prospects need concrete items, and mental pictures to relate to.

"After you have all the dots connected for people, the last part is to invite them to take some kind of action that will enable them to create the picture in their real life. There are many of you who have become very effective at asking high-yielding questions and listening, and some of you are already good at connecting the dots for people. However, many people get to the point of agreement with their prospect and then just quit, stop, change the subject, or excuse themselves and leave. Unless you are just honing your communication skills or enjoy making a point for the pure pleasure of making your point, you need to finish the picture by asking for some kind of feedback or response. For example you might say, 'Now that you know what the business is all about, and how it will help you bridge your income gap, are you ready to get started?'

"The basic rule is to keep your language concrete, descriptive and clear. People with high dot-connecting PEPs urge their prospects to do something with what they learn from the discussion. Avoid or Resist the temptation to just inform. Informing reveals and clarifies options, but leaves it up to the prospect to connect the dots as to how the information applies to their situation, and puts the responsibility of making purchasing decisions and taking purchasing actions on them.

"Here are a couple of illustrations of connecting the dots but failing to invite or encourage prospects to take action that will create the result they told you they want: 1) A man has a friend who has been complaining about the rising cost of gas. He tells his friend about a new fuel saving technology and makes a compelling argument about how much money he could save each day, week, and month on his commute alone. He cites research and provides authoritative endorsements and his own testimony of the fact that this really works. And then changes the subject by asking how his friend's children are doing. 2) A woman is at the grocery store and calls her friend to tell her that milk is on sale for 50% off the regular price. And then she talks about her busy schedule and quickly hangs up.

"Associates with low PEPs are usually informative and make people aware that there is a solution for their challenges, but then leave it up to the prospect to ask how they can get it. Associates with high PEPs get people talking, connect the dots, earn agreement, evoke emotions, and ask for committed action. The two examples I gave a minute ago might have been approached like this: The gas technology discussion could end with the man asking his friend if he wants more information about how to save $200 per month on his commute. Or he could ask if he would like a free sample of the product that creates this amazing result. The woman at the grocery store could ask if her friend would like her to pick up a few gallons of milk for her. In both cases the discussion was very informative, but all the talk in the world is wasted if you don't ask your prospect to take some action at the end of the conversation. If you learn this one lesson, your business will begin to explode.

"I have said many times before that people don't care how much you know until they know how much you care. And although it may sound kind of corny, it's really true. And when you center your attention on others, they will quickly learn how much you care. In turn they will become active participants in their journey to greater causes and higher purposes. As a natural result, you will find whatever you are looking for in this greatest industry of opportunity.

"I see that our time is well spent. Before we end this session, I want to give you your skill mastery practice activity to work on during the break. When you leave make sure to get a connect-the-dots paper from the assistants at each door. During the break, I want you to talk to at least four people and collect at least three golden nuggets that you might consider learning more about as you dig for their passions and dreams, searching for the dots that you will be able to connect. When you complete each conversation, connect ten dots on the picture page you are going to pick up at the door as you leave. When you finish talking to the first person connect dots one through ten. And when you complete your second conversation connect dots eleven through twenty, and so on.

"When you have completed connecting all the dots and the picture emerges, write what the picture could represent to each of the people you talked to, and what three things you offer that could help them create the picture they want their life to be like. For example, if the picture you discover is a fire hydrant, then put a one on your paper with the name of the person you talked to, and then write 'the fire hydrant represents putting out the fire of financial stress Bob is feeling.' Next, write down what your offering is: 'I offer my help, a predictable education system that can help Bob learn practice and apply critical skills, and knowledge in their proper sequence to accelerate his ability to make money from the compensation plan of XL-8.' Then do the same for each of the people you talk to. This should help you focus on gathering dots, making connections and helping people see you as the obvious answer to the life they dream of."

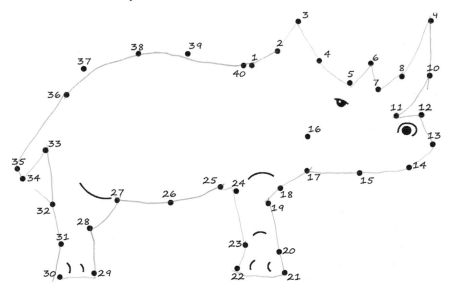

Steve concludes by thanking all of us for our energy and attention, reminds us to get a Connect-The-Dots paper as we leave and then he disappears backstage as the auditorium lights come back up.

Sitting alone, lost in his own thoughts, Matt begins thinking of what he would like his perfect life to be like, following Steve's connecting-the-dots process. I draw a line down the middle of the page and at the top of one side I write 'Professional Picture' and on the other side 'Personal Picture.'

Professional Picture	Personal Picture
• Corner office with two windows,	• Provide a comfortable lifestyle for Ann and the family.
• Have the highest rated departments in the company.	• Take four vacations per year. Two with Ann alone and two with the whole family.
• Have the number one, two and three highest rated Divisions in the company.	
• Customer acquisition costs to record low.	• A Car serves Ann's needs,
• New accounts growth record.	• Dream property I discussed with Steve in the mountains.
• Customer up-sells increased by 20%.	
• Business coming from existing customers 30%.	• Attend all my kids' activities and events.
• Client retention increased by 20%.	• No debt,
• Customer satisfaction ratings highest in company.	• Twenty thousand dollars in my wallet,
• Average PEP score of 40 for Floor level financial planners.	• College fund with one hundred thousand dollars for each child we have.
• The Division Managers relationship ratings 90	• Travel to important religious and historic places,
• Conversion ratios to 60, 60 and 90%.	• Serve my church as a missionary,
• Help team mates become what they were intended to be.	• Family bank for my kids and grandkids
• Inspire and encouragement team members to pursue their dreams and passions.	• Be mentor for kids and leader of family and partner with Ann
	• Reconcile my relationship with my dad.

    I begin to think of the most important things I can put down and finish my list with: Be mentor for kids, leader of my family, and partner with Ann, and reconcile relationship with dad. Speaking under my breath I say, "Those last two dots hit me in the heart. I would love to be able to spend personal time with all my kids, and that's what I am working for. I can be a mentor and encourager of hard work and dedication to a goal. Thinking about what it would be like to have a relationship rating of just fifty with my dad is hard to imagine. It would be fun to go fishing, play cards, or just have a discussion with him. My hope is waning on that front. He hasn't called or written me since our brief discussion a few months ago. Emerging from the emotional void I typically feel when I think of my dad, I turn my thoughts to what Steve would ask right now.

    I imagine him asking me, "How my life would be different if one or more of these things happened?" Using these two lists, it suddenly seems much easier to describe the picture I would like to paint. I can see how it would be easy to put the dots on paper. I can even see how the dots for my professional goals can be connected to create the outline of the corner office on the executive floor at the corporate headquarters. I can see how the dots for my personal goals could come together to create a utopia of family bliss. My challenge and growing stress is how to have these two pictures overlap and become the same picture. Steve did say that the same picture on our connect-the-dots sheet could represent the circumstances, conditions, and situations of different people. So maybe it's possible to draw the same picture and have it represent multiple success images.

I think I may count this conversation I am having with myself as two of the assigned conversations Steve gave us: one for the professional list and one for the personal list. Just before the evening session I call Ann, catch her up with what I learned, and ask for her professional and personal lists. I think I will put this to the test. This reminds me of an old TV show called the Newlywed Game where people who are newlyweds guess at how their mate will respond to particular questions. It makes me anxious to think that, without having an actual conversation with her, I really don't have much of a clue what dots she would give me or what picture she really wants. During our conversation I only correctly guess about fifty percent of what she says she wants. I wrote down her list of dots for me to connect.

Ann's Professional Picture

- Increase PEPs to at least 90.
- Green or yellow in all 50 skills in the success pattern.
- Increase team PEP average to at least 30.
- Have at least 500 team members.
- 15 or more leaders.
- 20+ serious business builders.
- 100 team members on autoship.
- 100 team members enrolled on education system.
- 100 team members regularly attending events.
- 50 team members recognized on stage at next event.
- Enroll two new personal associates each month
- Promote at least one leader each month. to pursue their dreams and passions.

Ann's Personal Picture

- Provide a comfortable home and supportive environment for the family.
- Attend kids' activities and events.
- No debt,
- Travel abroad with kids to introduce different cultures.
- Be mentor for kids
- Be support partner to Matt.
- Retire Matt from his corporate job.
- Landscape back yard.

At the end of my four conversations and have connected the dots for the practice sheet Steve gave us, and now I know that the picture the dots represents is a rhinoceros. What does a rhino mean for me, both my professional and my personal side? And likewise, what does this picture represent for Ann in these two areas? I write in the middle of my rhino picture:

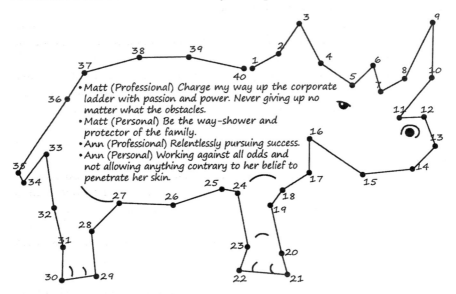

I meet Steve and Jerry at the hotel restaurant and we say goodbye. Steve has already told me about his plans to have Jerry and his wife speak at the evening session about how they became involved in XL-8, and why they were serious about building the business in the years leading up to their retirement. I decide that Jerry's story isn't particularly relevant to my goals for being here, and I also need to get back to the office and get caught up on having been absent for a few days already.

As I walk into my office in Minneapolis, I see that I have a message from Kayci from the home office on my phone. "This is Kayci," the message starts. "I just thought you might want to know that Josh has had a heart attack. He is in the hospital. They say he is going to be fine, but he will be out of commission for a while. I thought you would want to know. I miss you being here everyday. I hope all is well with you and Ann. Goodbye."

Of course I immediately call the hospital, and after a few transfers I am able to talk to Josh. He tells me, "I have ignored the signs of overwork and stress. I will confide in you, Matt, that being passed over for the promotion you got to Division Manager really got to me. Not that I didn't think that you were qualified, but I thought I was next in line for the job. It created real anxiety for me."

Matt assures him saying, "You are certainly qualified for a Division Manager position. Your chance will come. One thing I have learned over the past year or so is that patience really is a virtue, and that holding on to the principles that create success no matter what, create predictable results and achievement." We talk for almost an hour before the nurse comes in and orders him to hang up and get some rest.

Over the next few weeks I show up to Rachel's offices as scheduled, and am having so much fun working as a Floor Level Planner and Department Coordinator. I use my homemade name tag that says "Manager in Training," and wear it proudly as I work directly with clients for a day or so. My conversations are so much richer and more thorough than they were when I was actually doing these jobs. I am easily able to discover the passions and level of commitment to goals of my prospects and clients. I secretly wish that I had known then what I know now. I write a note to myself, we need to teach every employee that, "Relationships Create Real Results."

My experience with the Floor Level Planner and Department Coordinators is just as enlightening. Working with them gives me a whole new perspective and appreciation for the value of building strong and lasting relationships. Another note goes into my planner: We need to teach "Relationships Create Real Results" to all Department Coordinators, and we need to teach them to teach their Floor Level Planners on an annual basis." My meetings with Division Managers are also very interesting. Rachel reports that her experiment is going well, and that in just a month her results are closing the gap between her division and the others in the region. I am making my final preparations to leave for the airport to go home for the first time in a few weeks, just as Terri Hesslip calls to compliment me on my quarterly progress.

She says, "I usually call my Regional Managers more often, but I don't want you to feel like I am looking over your shoulder since your numbers are already showing great improvement." She gives me several verbal pats on the back, including calling me a 'Revolutionary' in my approach to business through relationship building. She wishes me luck, tells me to enjoy the weekend at home, and invites me to tell Ann hello on her behalf.

It seems she knows quite a bit more about me than she has been letting on. It's her job to keep very close track of my region's status, but she also knows that I am commuting, that I haven't been home for a while, and that my wife's name is Ann. It strikes me for an instant that I don't know this much about any of my Division Manager's personal lives. Maybe it's just her way of building relationships with her team, or maybe she is hinting that I should know this. Either way I need to make it a point to get to know more about them in a more personal way. Maybe the dot-connecting exercise Steve went through is a great way to do this. It also seems a little weird that both Bruce and Terri have now referred to me as a 'Revolutionary.'

Driving home from the airport I begin to really focus on Ann and how much I miss her. I stop quickly at the florist shop and pick up some flowers. As I open the door, Ann and the kids jump out from behind the furniture in the living room and yell, "Surprise!" Ann gives me a hug and says, "Guess what I did today? I have been showing our little daughter a big picture of you all week and saying 'daddy!' And today when I put the picture up she smiled. Isn't that cute?"

Matt doesn't respond well. "Yeah that's real cute." I say, deflated that my daughter thinks her father is a picture in a frame. Sighing as I sit down, I share, "I have had a real interesting few weeks. I thought things were going great at work, only to find out that I don't know anything I should know about my Division Managers. Josh nearly died last week, and now I find out that my daughter is getting to know me by proxy. Ann, you are the only thing in my life that is completely dependable. You are the rock of our relationship and marriage. Thank you for who you were, who you are, and for who you are becoming. The people in your XL-8 business should count themselves lucky to be on your team."

Ann embraces me and softly says, "It's really not me that they should be thankful for. My team and I are constantly exposed to a system and leadership that fosters success principles beginning with relationships and you and your team are not. I am lucky to have Steve and Sara as support partners in the business and I am in fact lucky to have you as a support partner in life. I am so proud of you for working to make our life comfortable and enjoyable. I am proud of you for hanging in there with your team leaders and believing in this approach. You are an amazing man, leader and example for me and our children to follow."

The next day Ann gets up early to prepare for the Saturday conference that Steve is giving about dot-connecting. I stay home during the afternoon session so that Ann can enjoy the presentation without any distractions. We attend the evening session together. I love to be at the recognition part. That is when I get to really see Ann's progress. Ann is on stage as the superstar student in this group of Steve's. She has thirty-four new people achieve the first or Copper level and twenty-two new Bronze achievers. Even better, Donna has achieved her goal of becoming a Silver this month; that gives Ann four Silver teams. As I am updating her organization chart it seems that each of her other Silver teams has at least three new Silvers on their teams as well. Steve keeps Ann on the stage for one last promotion level recognition: the new Gold level achievers. Ann's goal of turning her Silvers into Golds is happening. In true Rhino fashion, two of her Silvers achieved the Gold level, including Sheila from the leadership retreat lunch line. What a fascinating business model, being able to help people to help themselves. And this can be done even at a distance if necessary. It just goes to show you that relationships really are the key to success.

It is also very interesting to see that the principles that Steve is teaching work in every aspect of life. It works for me in the financial services industry. It works for Ann and Jerry and others on Steve's team in XL-8, and according to Shelly it seems to work on the personal side of life as well. Ann's PEPs are now at eighty-seven, and she has a team of over 600 associates. Over sixty-five of her team members are consistently working and being promoted along with her. She now has thirty-four leaders, and is making with bonuses and overrides more money than most Division Managers at my company. It seems that the pain of recognizing my shortcomings is helping me to grow and learn. I guess without any adversity I wouldn't become the kind of person others could look to for guidance and strength. I am so grateful for all that I am learning, and the trials associated with the journey to the top. Somewhere deep inside I wish that I could just get to the summit faster. In that moment it occurs to me that there might not be a summit. When you get to the highest peak you can see right now, maybe there are more mountains beyond the one you are on!

Author's Note:

The instructions explaining the mathematical equation for this chapter is in the appendix at the end of the book.

11

The Option Giver

I have invested months in my new program, I think as I stare out the window of my office. I have been traveling, teaching, and sharing everything I have learned from Steve. Department by department, division by division, and the results are coming in. Stunning, is all I can call them. Even so, I know there is one more lesson that will help our clients experience the full benefit of our offering, and put this region over the top. Steve alluded to it briefly in a dinner conversation we had while I was visiting Jerry's group. He told me, "All the skills we teach for initiating, building, and maintaining lasting relationships are critical ingredients to creating transformations. But there is one last critical element we need and that is what brings it all together. The last piece is what causes what he called a value exchange. This last step enables all participants to fully benefit from your offering, and it's what allows you to continue to share by staying in business. It is asking people to take action. Asking people to take action is evidence of your willingness to invite people to experience the full benefits of taking the actions that will bless their lives, based on the understanding you have of their circumstances, situations, and desires, so that they can create the result they want."

The question is, Matt wonders, how can I teach my people this final lesson and implement it before Terri retires? I wonder if I can convince Steve to teach my group this lesson all at once in one big training session. When I was a Division Manager, he declined because of the size of the group. But now I have a sizable team that he might find more appropriate for his time.

The day passes and the nagging question of how to get Steve to engage with my team keeps gnawing at me. At about 2:00 PM I remember something that Steve said in that very first conference about increasing your value of service; "You must become the kind of person others will follow before they actually follow you, and then you must become the kind of person other leaders will follow before you become the leader."

That's it, Matt thinks. I will invite the other Regional Managers to attend a workshop with my mentor Steve who has taught me how to create the results I have in my departments, divisions and region. Each division has five or six managers, and there are six regions, so that would be at least 30 people. The idea that an entire company would be affected by his workshop might tempt him to teach us. If Steve agrees, I will call Terri to see if I can get corporate approval to allow continuing education credits and a budget for the seminar. It will give me an additional reason to talk to her, and it might show some initiative to helping the whole company. It seems that this is a win, win, win plan.

I call Steve and while the phone rings a feeling of confidence and excitement come over me. This is different from the first time I asked for this favor; then I was scared and apprehensive. This is one of those moments when you realize that your PEPs really are high, and that this confidence comes from the hard work of increasing competence. Steve answers in his usual inviting and excited way. Just listening to him answer the phone is, in some respects, inspiring.

"Steve, this is Matt Ivey. Do you have a minute to talk? I have a question for you."

"I always have a minute to talk to you, Matt," he says.

"I remember you saying a few times that one of your passions is helping people both inside and outside of XL-8 to succeed by optimizing their relationships. Is that still true?" Matt asks.

Steve responds saying, "Inside XL-8 I love to teach my team, and as you can see the results are un-matched. I am becoming a highly sought-after speaker. Outside of XL-8, including my experience of working with you indirectly and seeing the difference I can make, excites my passion about that more than ever. Why do you ask?"

Matt confidently begins, "The reason I am calling is to offer a proposal and make a request."

"Okay, what's up," asks Steve in a puzzled voice.

"I want to have a seminar about the last step in the process that you have been teaching and include all the Regional Managers, Division Managers and Department Coordinators in my company; that is about thirty people. My request is to invite you to teach, inspire, and encourage every leader in my company to duplicate what you have been teaching me. I would like to have the workshop sometime in the next few weeks."

Steve, amazed at Matt's confident request, says, "Wow, you have learned the lessons well. That's a great example of what a contacting call should look like. No wonder you are rising as fast as you are. But, I don't have any free days in the next few weeks because I am speaking to one of my groups, and then I am having a business building boot camp in San Diego."

There is a moment of silence while Matt and Steve both contemplate the next step.

Steve breaks the silence saying, "On Friday of my boot camp I will be teaching the last step in the process, and encouraging each of my leaders to present this topic in their next monthly business development conferences like the one you attend with Ann. If you don't mind having your colleagues attend a network marketing training where I will be talking about how to build a strong and profitable XL-8 organization, then I would like to invite you all to attend."

Matt answers excitedly, "That shouldn't be a problem. I can set their expectations properly, and then my colleagues and I can meet Friday afternoon to discuss how your instruction fits into our business model. Frankly, there is really very little difference between what you teach for XL-8 associates and the application of the same principles for my business. That's why I am asking you to teach. You are a great teacher with a great track record of success."

Steve gives me the logistics for the conference and we hang up.

Okay, step one is a success I think, crossing off this item in my check list. Now on to step two: calling Mrs. Hesslip. As Terri's phone rings, my resolve to have this training for my team turns into a mission. She answers in her business tone. Not at all deterred by the difference between Steve the Sports Car and Terri the Pickup Truck, I spend a minute or two describing the learning process that I had been going through and introduce Steve Thoms to her. I detail how I have implemented what he taught me, and recount some of the results.

She stops me for a moment to say, "I have been watching you carefully for quite some time with admiration and appreciation for the time and effort you take to separate yourself from all the others."

Matt explains, "I have been considering having the Managers in my region attend a workshop with Steve in San Diego in a few weeks, and I am calling today to get approval to contact the other Regional Managers and have their managers attend with us. I am positive that having them attend would increase productivity and bottom-line results for every region as it has mine. What I love best about the training Steve does is that he focuses on how things work together in a system to produce reliable, predictable results."

"I like what I am hearing," Terri replies. "Increased productivity and bottom-line results are music to my ears. To tell you the truth Matt, I have been working on a plan to get you to teach the other Regional Managers what you have been doing, and this might be the way. I like that you have thought this through enough to include training the junior executives as well. Sounds like you have done your homework. I will need to look at the budget before I can make a decision."

Matt asks, "What information do you need that will help you to make a decision."

"I need your cost estimate and projections for sales and efficiency increases," she responds matter-of-factly. "If those numbers are compelling, I will go to Mrs. Jensen to get her approval. It will be important to get her buy in, and if your numbers are compelling enough to persuade me, and we realize them through this program, that should justify any expenditure."

"Thank you for your confidence," Matt says. "I ran the numbers before I called you and can send them to you right away."

"Excellent work Matt," she responds approvingly. "I look forward to hearing from you. I know you're pressed for time on this. I will get back to you with an answer in the next day or so."

I send the email with the numbers to her even before we hang up, and the anxious wait begins. By the time I hang up with Terri and complete my daily reporting, everyone in the office has already gone home for the day. Sometimes it's just nice to have a moment of silence, I think as I lean back in my chair. I wonder why Ann hasn't told me about this leadership meeting in San Diego. Certainly she would qualify as a leader by now.

Later that evening I ask about it. She is surprised that I know about the conference and says, "The meeting begins on a Friday morning which would mean that I would have to travel on Thursday and I wouldn't be back until Sunday. I can't just take off anymore, now that we have kids. Besides I didn't want you to feel bad because you wouldn't be here to tend the kids. I didn't figure it would be a positive conversation, so I didn't bring it up. Why do you ask anyway?"

"I talked to Steve today," Matt answers. "He offered to let my managers and the other managers at work attend the Friday morning session. I am pretty sure that I am going to get approval from Terri Hesslip for all of us to go. So I am wondering if I go, is there a way for you to go as well?"

It's silent for a moment while Ann considers the question. "I really haven't thought about it so I don't know. The meeting is in two weeks isn't it?"

"Yes it is," Matt responds encouragingly and continues, "Maybe your mother could take care of the kids and we could go together; what do you think?"

"It's pretty short notice," Ann answers anxiously. "I will have to call my mom and ask."

"Would you rather I call to ask?" Matt offers.

"You know, I think that would be the best idea." Ann says as she sighs in a bit of relief.

We talk for another ten minutes, and then I call Ann's mom. She is excited to take care of the kids and insists that she come and stay at our house while we are gone.

I immediately phone Ann back to share the news and she agrees to go. She starts listing all the things she needs to get done, and in a frenzied voice tells me she has to get started. Just as we hang up, I get an email notification from Terri. "Two thumbs up from Mrs. Jensen. And you have budgetary approval according to your numbers." The plan seems to be coming together; I feel energized by the news. The last hurdle will be talking to the Regional Managers and getting their buy-in. I have to remember that there is no pressure on me to enroll them; I have approval for the training, and if they don't agree to go, then they will miss out. My team and I will be going to San Diego and will be implementing what Steve teaches us. I will call them in the morning to lay out the plan and invitation. Excited about the opportunity, I head to my Minneapolis apartment for the evening.

With Terri's approval and encouragement I easily enroll the Regional Managers; all but one that is. The single dissenting voice is a lady named Alix, who tells me that there simply isn't time to get everything arranged. Her people have other plans, and some have vacations planned, and she has no reason to go to a training from a person she's never heard of. In some ways I am glad that someone decided not to go. This will provide a perfect case study to measure our results by. I don't wish any ill will on Alix, I just want to see the difference in results after the training.

The plans are set, people are excited, and most are in motion to receive this powerful training. Ann and I agree to sit with our respective teams so that we can keep our focus where it needs to be during the conference. I arrive early so that I can greet everyone as they begin to come in. I hand everyone a very small itinerary, including a place to gather tonight. I am surprised to see Darrell and Clarissa here since they are two of Alix's Division Managers. They explain that they already had planned to take vacations this week, so they simply changed their plans to include San Diego when they heard all of us were coming. They didn't want to miss out. Clarissa says, "Alix can keep me from coming on company time but she can't tell me what to do on my vacation days. So here I am!" Darrell nods in agreement and adds, "I have been watching you for a while now, and I have been amazed at what you have accomplished everywhere you have been in the company. So when I found out we were all invited, I wanted to come and see what you were promoting."

"Thank you for your confidence," Matt responds, reaching out to shake both their hands. "I thought it would be a good idea to brief you all on the context in which Steve will be presenting, and to assure you that in our meeting directly afterward we will be discussing how to implement what we learn in the context of our business. He is a tremendous teacher and a great mentor. Everything I have put into practice about relationship building I have learned from him."

Everyone seems excited, and most everyone has decided to make a weekend vacation out of the trip. I encourage everyone to get to the meeting room early, because these people actually start on time and the best seats fill up fast.

In the morning my team all meet together in the lobby and go together en masse to the meeting room. The whole team sits together and it's quite an impressive site if I do say so myself I think with a certain amount of pride. Jerry is the host, and comes out on stage a minute or two early to give the announcements and other logistics. He welcomes everyone gives a special recognition to the leadership team of Perpetual Wealth Financial.

He jokingly says, "Corporations are now coming to us for training." Bruce is not really amused at the recognition, observation, or comment. He defiantly sits there with his arms folded for a few minutes until Steve gets into his training.

Steve begins by saying, "All the skills required to build strong and lasting relationships are critical initial ingredients for creating transformations.

However, the final essential element in every recipe is whatever it takes to unify the ingredients into a coherent whole, be it simmering, baking, or chilling. For our recipe, it is asking people to take action. Up to this point you are preparing yourself and your prospect to synthesize and become something greater than each of you is by yourself. When you ask your customer to commit to action, you ignite the transformation process.

"Encouraging people to fully experience the benefits of your offering is vital in helping them take action. People often won't move forward, make a decision, or take action unless they are directly asked to do so. Once you know what result people want you can bless their life by finding out how committed they are to relieving their pain or frustration, solving their challenges, or creating the life they dream of.

"Some call this selling, closing, finishing, finalizing, winding up, concluding, or transacting. That is not how I look at it, because those words indicate the end of the relationship. My experience in this industry leads me to believe that to create lasting relationships, repeat buyers, converts, residual income, and generational wealth you need to begin thinking about this step as a mille borne as the French say it, meaning a waypoint or milestone. Thinking of the point where prospects make a decision to act as a beginning in our relationship journey helps me relax and see this step for what it is; a step in a process, not an end point or some eureka moment upon which everything hinges. Asking people to take action is a little like enrolling in college. No one gets a degree or certificate simply by enrolling. Once enrolled, the real work begins and the door opens for a lifetime of service and value exchange.

"Instead of bringing my relationships to a close, I prefer to offer options that let people decide what action they are willing and committed to take to create the circumstances and results they want. Remember that people buy results, and they always buy the results they want, not ones they necessarily need. If you build relationships based on trust and discover what results they want without bias, and then connect the dots, showing them how your offering is the means to produce the result they want, then a high percentage of the time people will engage with you either as a customer or an associate.

"It's like being a server in a restaurant. The server gives me a menu of options and asks which option I prefer. If I have questions about any of the options, the server doesn't get upset or nervous. He or she simply seeks to understand what I want by asking high-yielding questions to clarify which option will give me the result I want. If I ask for a recommendation but don't follow it, the server doesn't get angry. Even if he or she knows that my choice won't provide me with the exact result I say I want, there is no retribution. He or she simply takes the order and continues to serve me to the best of her ability, knowing that 'closing' or 'concluding' the relationship will result in short-term loss when I reduce my tip or don't tip at all. Or it might result in long-term loss if I walk out, never to return. In the latter case, the server might also lose her job.

"All the steps in the enrollment process up to this point focus on discovering the result people want, and their commitment level for creating that outcome plus an explanation of your offering that will produce the desired result. This final step is the invitation for them to take the action that will best serve the process of meeting their goals. Before I get into the nuts and bolts of giving options let me create some context for the whole process so that we are all on the same page.

"Everyone should be able to focus on resolving their prospect's pain, or on creating conditions that allow your prospect to do something they can't do now, doing what they are doing now. Here is a model that shows how the enrollment process works. In this model you have three responsibilities and your prospect has three responsibilities. Follow the boxes in their sequence from 1 to 6.

Your Responsibility	Prospect's Responsibility
1.	**2.**
Awareness–The first step and responsibility is to become fully Aware of your prospects circumstances, passions and commitment to do something to create a different result in some area of their life.	**Acknowledge**–Your prospects first responsibility to trust you enough to Acknowledge that they have some kind of discomfort and to explain some of the details about that pain and how their life would be different if their challenge went away.
3.	**4.**
Adapt–When you understand your prospects pain and their commitment to changing you must adapt your language, presentation style and explanation of your solution to meet their specific circumstances. Make sure to offer appropriate solutions and highlight specific features and benefits for their unique situation. If you offer crackers to people who want water or water to people who are hungry you won't be very successful.	**Adopt or Agree**–You must make sure that you are connecting the dots for your prospects so that they can easily understand how your solution really relieves their pain. This of course is the first part of step three of your presentations.
5.	**6.**
Ask–Your last responsibility begins once you gain agreement. When you pass step 4, you can stop "selling". They have adopted your solution as a plausible remedy to their pain. However, you must now invite them to take action to be able to realize the effects of your solution. Without this step they won't reap the benefits of what you offer. They will be aware that there is a solution to their pain but they will still experience the pain unless they take some kind of action.	**Apply**–Lastly, your prospect must apply the solution. I have met many people whose medicine cabinets and book shelves are filled with remedies that are still in their original packaging. I call this shelf help. For example, if a prospect says that they need more energy in the afternoon and you present a product that will give them what they want and they agree that your product will work for them and even if you ask them to take action by purchasing your product they still must take the product. So each step along the way is critical to their short and long term success in relieving their pain and also your long term business objectives of creating a lifetime customer.

"Today we are going to focus on step number five of this model, beginning with a couple of terms that often create problems for many people. We all know that sales are the bottom line for every business enterprise. Without sales, you don't have a business, because you can't stay in business without revenue from sales. For most people it's not that sales gets people on the path to pain relief that bothers them, it's how people are taught to sell that creates the anxiety. The truth is that I reject common sales methods because I prefer to build rather than test my relationships. When I see people I view them as people with challenges that I have solutions for; not as people with wallets to be lightened.

"Many have negative feelings about the words sales and selling. But even if you don't realize it, everyone is constantly in a selling mode. You sell yourself, your ideas, or your values all the time, everywhere you go. Your skill and comfort with sales will greatly impact your short-term income, residual income, and the achievement of your greater causes and higher purposes. Let me ask you a couple of questions: When you think of selling, what thoughts come to your mind?"

A man from the front says, as Steve begins writing answers on the whiteboard, "I have to do it."

The woman sitting next to him yells, "It's scary."

Bruce now with unfolded arms offers, "It's fun and exciting."

Without thinking Matt shouts, "It's a way to help people get what they need and want."

Clarissa is so excited she stands up and says, "It's a way for you to get what you want!"

After he captures the responses on the whiteboard, Steve smiles, looking directly at Jerry, "So who is teaching whom now?" He continues saying, "These are all great responses; thank you for sharing. The second question is: When the moment of truth comes and your prospects are at the point where they really need to make a decision about taking action, on a scale from 1 to 10, how comfortable are you at helping them make that decision?

"Take a moment and think about that. I know this is a workshop and the 'right' answer is 'ten.' But no one will know what you write down, so relax for a moment and answer truthfully to yourself."

The room is silent for at least two minutes when Steve interrupts the quiet saying, "Some people are so mentally, emotionally, or physically opposed to the traditional process of selling that they have a condition that I call 'sales paralysis.' In most cases sales paralysis is caused by fear, limiting beliefs, or attitudes about people.

"Let me take a minute to talk about these three things: First, fear is most often based on our pain at being rejected. We have mentally, emotionally, and spiritually tied our identity and feeling of self worth to being accepted.

When people don't take our recommendations, follow our advice or do what we want them to do, we feel rejected and our self-esteem drops a little or a lot depending on your level of PEPs. Many of the people who enroll on your team will struggle with sales. Some will be debilitated by sales paralysis, caused by a fear of rejection.

"Those caught in this trap think that if they don't ask for the business they won't be rejected, so they use all kinds of tricks and techniques hoping that people will magically ask them if they can buy or enroll. It is true, you won't get rejected, but your prospects won't enjoy the results they desperately desire, and you won't make any sales either! Another major reason people are fearful of selling is a lack of confidence. Many are afraid that they will look foolish or ignorant if they say something wrong or make a mistake. Now, there are thousands of stories that essentially tell you to, 'feel the fear and do it anyway,' but my experience tells me that the only thing that really helps people overcome fear is confidence—confidence in their ability to be effective at whatever they are doing.

"So here is my advice if fear of asking people to take action is holding you back: learn and practice each part of your sales process until you have mastered it in the mirror by yourself, one on one with your mentor, or by playing the Residual Income® Game. Then implement the skills you acquire into your real life. My experience tells me that confidence comes from competence! People who don't engage don't live the life they want, and so their opinion is irrelevant to your life and your success. Don't forget that you are responsible for handling your success, financial obligations, and opportunities for your family. So remember that you are in business, and creating residual income in this industry happens in direct proportion to your ability to help people take action. When they get what they want, you will have created the result you want as well.

"Second are limiting beliefs. Many people have been taught from a very early age that they are stupid, of little worth, or that no one cares about what they have to say. Almost all sales seminars and programs teach you to approach anyone and everyone you see. The paradox is this: if you believed no one cares about what you think or say, but that successful sales are based on talking to everyone, everywhere, you can see how contradictory this is. The hard truth is that not every one does care about what you have to say. And there are many who won't listen to you, or take action based on what you say and share.

"The good news is that there are some who will listen and act. As you increase your personal effectiveness you will be able to connect with and affect more and more people. There are also some who have the belief that selling to their family and friends will have a negative impact on their relationship. The truth is that most people who really care about you would be upset if you didn't share with them the way to achieve their goals and dreams; I would. Share the opportunity with everyone, but do it with the primary goal of building the relationship first. Finding out what they want that they don't have now first, instead of pouncing on them with what matters to you. Share is the key word here. Remember, you need to speak from your heart, rather than your head. This business is about relationships and helping people solve their pain by fostering great relationships. Keep in mind that the people you are talking to are buying into you, not only into the income opportunity, products, or services. Remember, the *way* you share is more important than what you share.

"Lastly there are attitudes about people." Pointing to the whiteboard with the answers to the first questions he presented, Steve asks, "If you said or agreed when someone answered the questions at the beginning of this lesson that sales: 'are a have to,' 'are scary,' 'uncomfortable', when inviting people to make decisions that will help them meet their goals or improve their lives, then your perspective needs some adjustment.

"For instance, successful associates always seem to like people, or at least they like to be curious about people and want to find out what makes them tick. They also have a passion for helping people get what they want, and they are outwardly excited about the possibilities of helping someone move in the direction of their goals. If you master the relationship skills I have been teaching for the past year or so, you will begin to have sufficient confidence. It will radiate to others and you will start to adopt a philosophy that selling is really sharing with an invitation to take advantage of something you found that will help them achieve their goals. In the end, they will be grateful that you helped them make a decision to take action.

"I believe that most people are born salespeople. Think back on your life. When you were in school, you sold your peers on accepting you and your teachers on giving you the best possible grades. You sold your parents on letting you stay out for activities at night or on buying a new toy or gadget. Unconsciously, you are already employing many of the aspects of selling, the power of persuasion, the art of negotiation, and the ultimate teenager's tactic: never take 'no' for an answer. By the time you reach adulthood you have learned how to position yourself to get what you want thousands of times. You have learned how to market your abilities and how to sell yourself in job interviews.

"Something mysterious happens however, when people enroll in a career in XL-8. Suddenly they forget how to sell. They question their own ability. Suddenly the techniques they've used all their lives become foreign and mysterious, as though they now had to go out and learn them for the first time. Yet the science of sharing is the conscious practice of a lot of things we already consciously or unconsciously know and have probably spent the better part of our lives learning, practicing, and applying.

"The challenge comes when personal effectiveness in language, product knowledge, persuasion, and other critical skills are being judged. Your reward and the reality of your creating a dream lifestyle is based on how you are judged by your prospects and team members. This can be intimidating, so many people respond by convincing themselves that they can't sell, they don't know how to sell, or they don't want to sell. Then they use these mental roadblocks to justify their lack of sales aptitude. But the real problems of selling have little to do with aptitude, and almost everything to do with how we perceive the process of selling itself.

"I believe that it's not only our lack of belief in ourselves and our competence in selling that keeps people from excelling in this area. I believe that our lack of belief in abundance also keeps us from relaxing and doing what we know how to do. The same thing happens in baseball games. We don't get to anxious or nervous in the first inning of the first game of the year. Why, because there will be many more games and many more chances to bat. But when there are two outs in the bottom of the ninth inning of the seventh game of the World Series, and the bases are loaded and your team is behind by one run; this is it! It's do-or-die for you and your team. This is how many associates feel in this business. I believe most don't feel like there will be an abundance of opportunities to share their presentation, or that there is a genuine lack of people to talk to who might actually be interested in the business. For those who either consciously or subconsciously believe this, they feel like they are thrust into bottom-of-the-ninth-inning pressure every time they engage in the selling process. Here is how I overcame this challenge in my own life even before XL-8, including when I enrolled in the business.

"Imagine with me for a moment the very first sale you have to make in this business. The greatest sale I ever made was the day I finally bought in to what I was doing–the day I finally saw the big picture, and the day I began believing in what I was doing and how it would help others along with me. The first sale you need to make is to yourself. Sell yourself and develop a strong belief in the products and services you offer. If you don't have a strong belief in our products and services, why would anyone purchase from you? The best way to become a believer in the products and services is to use them. Developing your own 'product story' is important, and will pay ongoing dividends down the road. If you have your own story your presentations will be more compelling. If you don't, then I would counsel you to get one as soon as possible. Pay close attention to how your products and services are changing your own life. When you have your own story of the benefits of your products, it will give you confidence, and it will be easier for you to share with your family and friends, inviting them to take action by asking for their business.

"Start building a network of people who will spread the word about you and your products to their circle of friends and neighbors. Share what we offer with everyone. Share is the key word here. Tell your family, friends and colleagues what you are doing, and invite them to check it out. You won't offend people if you expect them to check out what you have to offer. If you had a grocery store in town, wouldn't you expect your family and friends to shop there? I would. Well you have a business, and it is certainly reasonable that your family and friends would buy from you, if they knew what products and services they can buy from you.

"The second area of importance in sales is your beliefs. I talked earlier about how our beliefs tie into the fear of selling. Beliefs go much deeper than simply feeding our fears. I want to touch on two areas of beliefs here. First, if you think money is bad or that selling is taking advantage of your family and friends, then those beliefs will be reflected in your verbal and body language, and will send a very loud message to your prospects that you don't like what you are doing, or that somehow you feel like you are doing something wrong. The result is that you won't enroll new people in your business. You won't frequently transform or transact and your business will suffer. Second is your view of selling versus sharing. This is an industry that pays you to teach others about products and services they don't know about or think they can't afford. You are a messenger, not the message. Your job is to share and invite people to take advantage of the features and benefits of products and services that will improve their life.

"Of course the burden of integrity is upon you not to manipulate or coerce your prospects to buy items that only serve you through the transaction. If you act with integrity, people will choose to engage with you to purchase products and services that alleviate pain you both can articulate. The more effective you are at spreading the good news about your products and services, the more others can take advantage of them along with you. Sharing and encouraging others to share will give you the time and financial resources to achieve your own greater causes and higher purposes.

"Contrary to some peoples' beliefs, sharing with friends and neighbors what you have found is not taking advantage of the relationship. Your family and friends want to benefit from your experience. They want to know what you know, if it will improve their life. Think of it this way: if your friend had a way for you to become rich, or retire, or knew of a product that would improve your life, or if they had the antidote to poverty, or the antidote for driving to work in rush hour traffic each day, wouldn't you want them to tell you? I would! You have to understand that you are simply providing options, not limiting them to only your option.

"Before I get into the specifics of being an option giver, let me share some general tips: First, remember if you give your prospects options at the end of your presentation, they are more likely to follow one of your recommendations because they choose what they want to do. You are only the messenger offering great products and services to those who don't know about them. Ultimately they must decide what they want to do with the information you present and how they want to respond to your invitation to take action.

"Second, earn the right to ask for the business. Go through all the steps of making an effective presentation. If you do, then you won't ever be accused of being sly or tricking people. Furthermore, everything you do must be repeatable. Don't use tricks or fancy techniques because your prospects and team members will not be able to do the same. Following the Ask, Listen and Repeat process earns you the right to ask them for the business because they trust you. You will have confidence manifesting itself in your whole person that confirms you have suggested the right solution for the challenges they have shared with you.

"In each of the past business development conferences I have described many skills and attributes that you need to acquire in order to gain the trust of your clients. One of the most important things to remember is that sales is not a single event, but a series of events with commitment checks along the way. The way to create more sales is to know where you stand with people.

"It's common for people to be closed off or defensive at the beginning of your presentation. Their arms are folded, their legs and eyes are crossed; they have one hand on their wallet, so as not to let it get into your hands. This happens because people are simply unaware or uneducated about what you offer. Their skepticism originates from being "sold to" before. Your job is to know that most people start there, and to slowly and lovingly help them open up. They need to be open before they will be willing to listen and learn. Once they are open, they will share what their needs and wants are, and your desire to help them coupled with your PEPs in relationship building will inspire them to make commitments to take action.

"Most associates think that if they just talk enough, people will be sufficiently aware of their product or service and how it all fits together, and that when they understand the product, then people will ask how to buy or enroll. Many have the mistaken idea that if they can just keep talking their prospect will conclude that they need what the associate offers and will get an urgency to buy it. My friends, it's not the amount of talking you do that moves people to act. You need to find the Key that allows them to open up, then listen for the clues about their pain. Finally, when you connect the dots they have given you, you can offer options, and ask for them to take action.

"Relax, slow down, and take your time. Take some time to build that relationship. Even if they know you are initially only exchanging pleasantries, they will see you as a professional who at least appears to be interested and listening. The only way to get people to open up is to get them talking not you! And the best way to get them to talk to you is to make sure that you ask high-yielding questions. Once again, the key to dealing with your prospects is to understand them, not to overcome them. When you stop selling and start understanding your prospects needs and wants, they will tell you everything you need to know to help them engage. If you let them, they will tell you exactly what you need to say, show, and emphasize to clearly show that what you offer is exactly what they are looking for.

"Option Giving is really a two-fold process:

1. "It's an exciting way to inform people about products and services that they didn't know existed that will improve the quality of their life. For almost everyone in the industry that's the fun part.
2. "It is a responsibility to keep learning. You have a mandate to encourage people to do what you ask them to. That's why it's important to have high PEPs in all the critical relationship skills. The only way you will have consistent business growth is if people take the action you prescribe for them.

"As I said before, sales is not a single event, but a series of events with commitment checks along the way. For example, the purpose of contacting is to find out before the presentation that a person has some form of dissatisfaction and some level of interest and commitment to solving it. The purpose of presentations is to see if your prospect will commit to doing something about their dissatisfactory circumstances. The purpose of the follow-up is to answer any questions and make sure that your prospects know what their options are and how to take appropriate action to alleviate their pain.

"You may be wondering if there is some magical pixy dust to help you know if your prospects are committed to take action. The plain and simple truth is that there is! You must ask them! People will not take action they are not directly asked to take. At the end of each step in the overall sales process—contacting, presenting, following-up—and in the various steps of these activities, you are assessing your prospect's commitment to take the next step. Don't over complicate this! At the end of every step in the sharing process, your prospects have choices. It's your job to explain and offer options that will help them make educated decisions to create the results they are committed to. People seldom take action if they are not directly requested to do so. Asking for the business is a simple concept, and yet it is challenging for many people. Some do not want to seem pushy, which is why most people struggle and fail. Most people who join your team are not salespeople by trade, so many might regard asking for the business as something that could put their relationships with family and friends at risk.

"Asking people to take action is nothing more than establishing whether your prospect is ready to buy, needs additional information, or simply is not interested in your product or income offering right now. If properly done, your relationship with family and friends should never be at risk, no matter what their response to your invitation. When you know what they are committed to do, you can support their decision and take the most appropriate action by enrolling them as a customer or as an associate on your team, or asking for a referral and making an appointment for a few months from now to share your progress.

"Here is a basic overview of the four-step process for effectively asking people to take action. Transition from presenting or telling the features and benefits of the products, services and income offering by asking, 'What did you like best about what you saw or heard?' This is a high-yielding question which serves as a test to see if they can see the picture of their dots being connected by you. When they respond, ask them to tell you more about that. It is their response to this high-yielding question that helps you know exactly how well they are receiving your message. Before you invite them to take any action at all, ask them about their desire and commitment to do anything about their circumstances by asking, 'How serious are you about' and list off the golden nuggets you have in your pocket that reflect the pain they shared with you to this point. The last step is called 'Next Steps.' It is the point where you simply give them some options that will predictably produce the result they are committed to create.

"Here are the details of each of these four steps. After you know what their challenges are and you have presented specific solutions to their challenges, start the enrollment process by asking, 'What did you like best about what you saw or heard?' You could say something like,' So Bob, what do you like best about the business idea I just showed you?' No matter what he says, move on to step two by asking him to tell you more about his answer.

"Step two is to invite him to tell you more about what he liked best about your solution to his pain. Keep drilling for water by saying something like, 'Tell me more about that,' or 'Why does that excite you?' Here's an example: if he says in step one; 'I love the way I can order products online and I don't have to go to the store to get them.' You could respond by saying, 'Why does that excite you so much?' Whatever he says will give you the exact language you need in the fourth step.

"Before you begin step three, you should have a pretty good idea about what Bob likes about what you offer that relates directly to his circumstances. Don't continue to sell him. If he gets to this step he is already convinced that the products, services, or income opportunity you offer meet his needs and wants. You should be able to anticipate how he is going to answer your next question. If you are convinced that on a scale from 1 to 10 that Bob's commitment is at least an eight, then go ahead and ask him how serious he is about getting what he wants. Be direct and simply ask, 'Bob, on a scale from 1 to 10 how serious are you about not having to go to the store to get the products you use everyday, having them sent directly to your front door, saving both time and money in the process?' This allows you to evaluate whether you want to work with Bob and most of all, it's a mille borne or milestone point to check where they are in the process.

"If you do both steps one and two, they will be selling themselves by now. You won't be the one doing the selling. Here are a few more examples of 'How serious are you about that' questions: 'How serious are you about making the money you talked about,' or 'Getting your life back from your boss,' or 'Feeling better,' or what ever they tell you their pain was. If they don't tell you that they are at least an eight, nine or ten then you chose the wrong features, benefits, or offering to relieve the pain they shared. Or the pain they shared isn't very severe. People simply will not take action to solve pain that is not severe enough to cause them to move. The story of the dog howling on the porch comes to mind. Let me tell you this story.

"There was a man sitting on his front porch when a neighbor came up to talk. After a minute or two the dog let out a howl and then went back to sleep. The neighbor went on talking and again the dog howled and went back to sleep. This went on a few more times until the neighbor asked what was wrong with the dog. The man said, 'oh he's lying on a nail sticking up in the porch.' The neighbor asked why doesn't the dog just move? The man answered that, he would rather howl than get up and move.

"You need to know that there are some people who would rather complain than take action to resolve their pain. That's what you are finding out in this step. If they answer your initial how serious are you about that question with something less than an eight, you need to drill your well in a different spot. You do this by asking 'What could you be passionate enough about to take action to change?' They will either tell you what that is or continue to avoid being serious. In either case you know if they are lying on a nail and would rather howl than move; if they are committed to howl, then it's time for you to move on.

"Finally, step four—next steps. This is the decision step in this process. The only thing left to do here is to start working towards whatever they told you they wanted. If they told you they wanted to enroll as a customer, then go through the process of ordering. If they told you they are interested in making more money or they indicated they wanted to join your team, then lead them through the sign-up process. Don't ever be afraid to help people know what they need to do to be successful. Make sure that you get them to take the Personal Effectiveness Profile and enroll them in the training program including seminars, weekly trainings, the Residual Income® game, and training books like Six Figures in Six Months. Take the time to set their expectations correctly. Talk to them about their level of time and financial commitment and help them see the best, worst, and probable results based in their level of commitment.

"I want to go back, for a moment and talk about option giving. There are a couple of 'Option Giving' approaches that lead people toward making a decision about what they want to do. After all, you want them to make a decision, even if that decision is not to engage with you right now. Remember that knowing is always better than not knowing. After you have transitioned from gathering information to making them aware that there is a solution to their pain, then it's time to ask them as sincerely as you possibly can, one of these very simple questions. Then let them answer! This is like the server in the restaurant asking what you have decided to order.

"Let them know what the next steps are and then ask them a final question. For example you can say, 'Suzie, now that you know about our company, products, and different ways of making money, there are a few choices you can make, and I will support you in whatever you decide.' If your prospect is a Sports Car or a Minivan, there are only three options in this approach, because they will be able to make a decision immediately.

"Say something like, 'Suzie, you can:

1. Do nothing and your life will go on pretty much as it is now.
2. You can enroll as a customer and take advantage of the benefits of the products we talked about.
3. You can enroll as an associate and take advantage not only of the personal benefits of the products and services, but begin earning income and take control of your future.

Which of these interests you most?'

"Then LET THEM ANSWER!"

"If your prospect is a Pickup Truck or a Hybrid, and this is the first time they have seen your presentation, you will need to add an option to your approach, because they will not make a purchasing decision right now.

"Say something like, 'Suzie, you can:

1. Do nothing and your life will go on pretty much as it is now.
2. You can take a day or so and review more information if you need it to make a decision. *(an educated)*
3. You can enroll as a customer and take advantage of the benefits of the products we talked about.
4. You can enroll as an associate and take advantage not only of the personal benefits of the products and services, but begin earning income and take control of your future.

Which of these interests you most?

"Then LET THEM ANSWER!

"You want to handle your prospect's decisions objectively. It's natural to feel excited, happy, disappointed, or angry when prospects tell you what action they are committed to take, especially if you've already formed your own expectations for them. Be careful here because when your emotions go up, your intelligence goes down, so expect the best and recognize the possibility of anything less. Here's how to respond to their choice of options you presented:

"**Option one**. If they choose to do nothing, ask for a referral by saying, 'Bob, now that you know what I am doing at a basic level do you know anyone that might be a good candidate and a match for what I am looking for?' A referral is a much better lead than someone you have no connection with, so take the time to ask for them. Get the name and make sure the contact information is accurate. Wish your prospect well, and ask if you can reconnect with them in the coming months to update them on your progress. Make sure to contact the referral as soon as possible. Follow-up with the prospect to let him or her know how the referral went. If the referral decides to do something with the business, either as a customer or an associate, then ask the prospect if they want to enroll above or below their referral.

"**Option two.** If they want some time to gather facts, data, or just process all of the information—and most Hybrids or Pickup Trucks will want more time—say something like, 'If it looks good tonight, it'll look good tomorrow.' Or ask them, 'What are you going to think about?' Give them some guidance about making an educated decision. Ask them, 'What information do you need to make an informed decision?' Tell them, 'My commitment to you is to help you accomplish (whatever they told you during the presentation) if you will work with me. My goal is to help people achieve their goals, greater causes, and higher purposes. I'd like to help you achieve yours.' If your prospect chooses this option, and you know they are a Hybrid or a Pickup Truck, then you know they aren't just putting off telling you their not interested.

"**Option three.** If they choose to become a customer, take advantage of this opportunity to serve their needs. This will create income for you and will give you the opportunity to connect on a consistent basis with them. Many people who begin as customers will convert to associates after they become converted to your products and the value of your customer service. The idea here is for you to make the first order on the spot. Go through the ordering process with them to get them familiar with the process and products. Once they have made an initial order, it will be easier for them to make the next order as well. Of course, you will want to follow-up with them in a few days and again in the coming weeks to make sure that everything is going well. Make sure that they received their product and answer any questions they have about products, the company, and the ordering process.

"**Option four**. If they choose to become an associate make sure that they become their own best customer by buying the products you offer. Tell them about the autoship program and have them sign up for it. As a business owner they need to set the example for those who will join their team. What they do will be duplicated by those they enroll. Autoship is definitely something they want to duplicate. Using the products will build their testimony of the value and quality of the products and services, our company, and the up-line. Being on autoship will also give them confidence by belonging to the team, and will help them feel like they can go out and talk with confidence to their family and friends because they have committed to receive the world's greatest products on a scheduled basis. Make sure that you get them engaged in a regular training program. This should include business development conferences, weekly trainings, playing the Residual Income® Game regularly, and reading books from highly successful people in this industry. Make sure to promote the next event. Ask your new associate if you could come to their job tomorrow and do it as well as they do? Tell them that in order to become a professional in this business they need to learn from professionals. Don't ever be afraid to help people know what they can do to be successful.

"Please make sure to set their expectations correctly. Make sure that they know that there are different levels of commitment in time, finances, personal improvement, commitment to team, and customer service. Talk to them about their level of commitment and what they can reasonably expect with regards to income and goal achievement based on their level of commitment. Tell them the date, time, and cost of the next event. If tickets are required, make sure they buy them from you. This shows their commitment that they are serious about building the business.

"No matter what they say, you will know what their commitment level for taking action is. Even if they decide not to join you or buy from you, knowing is always better than not knowing. If they object to enrolling, but they seem like they want to do something, then make sure they become customers for a while. Reassure them that there is a money-back-guarantee on the products. Ask them to take some action. The worst case scenario is for them to keep you in suspense.

"I remember a couple who kept telling me that they wanted to enroll, but that the time wasn't quite right, or they didn't have the money right now, and a million other excuses. They kept leading me on. And for months I let them do this. I wanted someone in my business so badly I actually put up with this nonsense. Then one day it occurred to me that they were never going to opt in, and if they did, they would do the same thing in regards to building their business that they were doing with me. I suddenly saw myself returning over and over again to help them build an organization, only to hear that the parrot broke his beak, or that the gold fish drowned, or that they sprained their eyelash, and they just couldn't see themselves going out to talk to anyone.

"My desire to enroll this couple waned once I could see what was going to happen if I actually got them to enroll as associates. I was losing a lot of time and money by making repeated visits too. I think for the longest time they thought I was in the socializing business. We were great friends, but that was not my only goal, and it didn't fully serve them to continue not using my products or engaging with me as a business builder. It also occurred to me that I was showing them that if I let them do this, then they would continue. So I finally had to get them to make a decision. No matter what the decision was, this had to stop. I took them through the, 'You Have a Few Choices' scenario. And they became great customers. They ordered regularly and were extremely loyal to my products. But this would never have happened if I hadn't given them some options and invited them to make a decision about one of them.

"Here's another way of looking at being an 'Option Giver.' There used to be a television show called Let's Make a Deal hosted by a man whose name was Monte Hall. The idea of the show was for a contestant to choose a door, and whatever was behind the door was what they got. After they saw what was behind the door they chose initially, they could choose to trade it for another door. The challenge was that they didn't know what was behind the second door. This was all very exciting, and Mr. Hall was a master at giving options and enticing people to make choices that created great TV drama. I want you to think about this for a moment.

"In our business and in life we want people to make a choice, and the best way to persuade them to do that is to let them choose out of options that they can see and understand. That way no one feels tricked. We're not playing Let's Make a Deal. We are offering real solutions with all the doors opened, and are simply asking people what they would like to do, based on choices they can clearly see. Door number one is purchase and use products that will relieve specific pain a prospect has. Door number two is help prospects get their products for free by offering pain relief to their family and friends by sharing our products with them. And door number three is help prospects build a strong and profitable business by teaching them to teach others how to offer pain relief by sharing our products and business offering.

"You might not fully understand this story, so let me boil it down to numbers. Let's say that for every person you know who chooses door number one you make ten dollars. That is to say, every time you find someone new to buy the products we offer you make a crisp ten dollar bill. Not a bad deal right? Now let's look at door number two. You make three dollars every time your team members get someone to choose door number one. The downside is that you make less per person choosing doors. But you can ask more people to choose with a team of people helping you find people who might choose door number two. Door number two is more appealing if you want to just supplement your income or get your products for free. And what about door number three? You make one dollar for every person you and your team can encourage to choose any one of the doors.

"The major benefit of choosing door number three is that in our business it has a compounding effect not found in most other business models. This is the most lucrative choice a person can make. But it does have a cost. You must learn, practice, and apply critical skills in relationship building, and specifically in how to invite people to play with you. Then you must learn to teach them how to invite others to play with them and continue duplicating yourself. My experience is that some are willing to learn how to do it themselves. But few learn how to teach others to teach others. Like the ancient story of option giving: giving a man a fish and feeding him for a day or teaching a man to fish and feeding him for a lifetime or teaching a man to teach others to fish exalting him. So if you had access to the three magic doors, which would you choose; door number one, door number two or door number three and why?"

A man in the back shouts, "Door number three!"

Steve asks, "Why number three?"

The man responds, "Because it allows me to take a day off once in a while because others can do what I can do without me having to be there."

A woman in our row says, "Door number three. It's the only way to leverage time."

Another woman from in front adds, "Door number three! It's the only way to reward people for reaching their maximum potential."

Her neighbor says, "Door number three is the only way to reach the greatest number of people with what we offer."

A few more people stand or shout their reasoning, but everyone agrees that door number three is the best answer.

"The greatest rewards," Steve continues, "Are always in teaching others to teach others. That's the very nature of leadership, and is the essential element that we have.

"Look at your own life and the options you choose every day. Each day you are presented with hundreds of options. Do you routinely choose door number one, two, or three? When you analyze your opportunity in this business, which door are you most often choosing? When you interact with people and you ask them to take action, do you tell them what to do, manipulate them into doing what you want them to do, or do you give them options to choose from?

"It takes time to create success. Until the new person has at least thirty to thirty-five Personal Effectiveness Points or PEPs, they don't have the skills, knowledge, belief, or attitude to be very effective at relationship building, recruiting, training, retaining, selling, or creating duplication. The more effective you are at transferring effective skill and appropriate knowledge, the faster your team will be able to progress through the success pattern, learn how to build relationships, write prescriptions that will alleviate pain, and ask people to take action to build a strong and profitable business for themselves and residual income and financial security for you. Why? Because the bottom line with most people is the person doing the presentation! Not the product or service. People need what we have. Without effective associates, however, the whole system breaks down and the journey to financial freedom, greater causes, and higher purposes will be long and frustrating for you and each member of your team."

As Matt sits there he thinks about the current customer relationship philosophy at Perpetual Wealth Financial. It seems that we don't offer options to prospects or clients. Steve's explanation of the doors makes so much sense that it starts me thinking about what the options are in my business. As I contemplate the options we give our prospects and clients, I am reminded of a saying I have heard: those who have eyes to see and ears to hear will. And those who don't, won't. Maybe now I am beginning to see and hear. This has been an unbelievable revelation to me. The door number one, two, and three option giving metaphor is phenomenal. Just becoming aware that there are options if we are looking for them has been worth the price of attendance here.

Steve concludes this session with the announcement that there will be a thirty-minute break. During the break we have a skill mastery assignment, and after we leave the event we have another assignment. Steve instructs, "During the break each of you need to talk to two people and use what we just learned by choosing one of the methods or approaches for asking people to take action. After each of your conversations, write the feedback you get from the person you practice with. Finally, during the break, when you have completed the two conversations, sit down and write your invitation for people to take action at the end of your presentations. To speed up your conversations, simply ask your conversation partner; 'If they could change anything in their life what would it be?' Pretend that you have just given the perfect solution to the thing they would like to change, and then move through the steps of asking people to take action.

"The assignment for the week after the event is practice the approach you wrote down at least ten times. Your first two practices should be with people who already know about your business: a spouse, friend, or mentor. Then write the feedback you get from your ten practice turns, and keep polishing your skill in this area at least five more times this week in your real presentations". Not seeing any hands raised for questions, he excuses us reminding us to be back in the room in thirty minutes.

Matt's group meets in the lobby just outside the training room. We decide that we should complete the two conversation assignment before we meet together to discuss what we learned. I suggest, and we agree to meet together with Steve and the XL-8 group briefly to participate in Steve's debrief, and then do our own debrief. We can all leave as he transitions to his next topic without a lot of commotion. I will let him know what we are doing so that he won't be surprised when we all exit. We split up and begin the assignment.

Matt first meets a woman named Joan from Kansas City. She is an XL-8 associate and wants to increase her conversion ratios of contacts to presentations. I start the process Steve talked about by asking her, "What she liked best about what I just showed her that could increase her conversion ratios?"

She pretends that I showed her the secret to contacting, and then responds by saying that it seems really simple and might help her overcome her fear of contacting."

I continue, "Tell me about being afraid of contacting."

Joan tells me, "I feel like people who don't want to meet with me are rejecting me personally."

I follow-up by asking, "Joan, how serious are you about overcoming your fear of contacting and increasing your conversion rates?"

With conviction in her voice Joan answers, "I am a ten!"

I say, "I am glad you have so much passion to achieve your goals." I slightly change the options for Joan saying, "Joan, now that you know most of what is required for you to overcome your contacting challenges, you are left with some choices to make:

1. "You can do exactly what you have been doing to this point, and you will receive the same or similar results.
2. "You can begin to change your situation by enrolling in a training system that includes real life practice so that you can increase your competence in contacting, or
3. "You can begin by taking control over your fear by partnering with your high PEP mentor who can show you how to contact effectively, critique you on your approach, and then provide feedback on how to make contacting a natural part of your everyday life.

"Which of these options interests you most?"

Before I can complete asking her the question, she responds saying, "You make this sound so easy. Are you a Platinum in XL-8?"

I explain, "I am not in XL-8. I work for a financial services company. I am a visitor here for today's meeting."

"You would be great in our business," she responds. "If you were giving me these options, I would choose number three. It seems like you have enough PEPs to really help me if I were in your group."

Matt smiles and offers, "Thank you for your compliment. Now it's your turn."

Joan asks me about what I would change. I reply, "I would want to spend more time with my family. I work out of town a lot, and my wife is left to take care of the kids and everything else during the week."

Joan starts the process by asking me, "What I liked best about what she just showed me that could help me spend more time at home without decreasing my income?"

I pretend that she has shown me the secret to being at home more often and then I respond by saying, "It would be great if this really works like you say it will."

Joan continues, "Tell me about your family."

I tell her about our kids and our youngest smiling at a picture of me, and her growing up without the real me in her life.

Joan follows-up by asking, "Matt, how serious are you about spending time with your family, and playing a more significant role in your children's life?"

Her question cuts me to the core. The practice is all too real in this moment. I answer with a tear in my eye, "I think I am a twenty!"

Joan completes the process telling me, "Now that you know about our company, products, and different ways of taking control of your time, there are a few choices you can make, and I will support you in whatever you decide. You can:

1. Do nothing and your life will go on pretty much as it is now.
2. You can take a day or so and review more information if you need it to make a decision.
3. You can enroll as a customer and take advantage of the benefits of the products we talked about.
4. You can enroll as a business partner with me and begin taking control of your future so that you can spend more time with your family.

Which of these options interests you most?"

In my natural Sports Car way I want so badly to say, "Number four of course." But in my more tempered high PEP way, I answer, "I want a day or two to get more information and to think about it."

She responds beautifully by asking, "What information do you need in order to make an educated decision?"

I tell her, "I need to meet with Steve and Ann to further discuss the possibilities."

She pushes on, forgetting that this is a practice, saying, "I can arrange that for you."

She is actually asking to make an appointment to talk to Steve. I explain, "An appointment won't be necessary. Steve is a close friend and is the one who invited me and my colleagues here to the training." I thank her and compliment her on her skill. I also encourage her to keep talking to people. She is very good at connecting the dots, asking high-yielding questions, listening, and asking people to take action. And I look forward to seeing her on stage someday as a Platinum level achiever.

It takes me a minute to capture my thoughts about what I would ask differently or more effectively when I ask people to take action. Although this scenario is similar to ours, it occurs to me that option giving is critical to every part of my life. I don't really have much to add or critique to my performance, and when I look up ready to repeat the process again, I see Clarissa waiting for me to finish.

I duplicate the process with her, and when it comes time for me to choose an option she says, "Matt, now that you know the different ways I can help you, I can offer you a few options to choose from: First, you can do nothing and your life will go on pretty much as it is now. Second, you can take a day or so and review more information if you need it to make a decision, and third, you can begin working to create the results you talked about by taking advantage of the benefits of the products and services we discussed. Which of these options interests you most?"

I compliment her on a job well done and say, "That was a great adaptation of what Steve is talking about. If you do that at work you will soon be a superstar in the company."

She thanks me for my compliment and everyone goes inside to get seats together toward the back so that we won't be a distraction when we leave after Steve's debriefing.

Steve calls the group back to order and asks a great high-yielding question; "What did you learn and how can you use what you learned in your daily life?" The answers come as fast as people can stand up or speak out. I can barely keep up with writing their responses.

One man says, "It was so much easier than what I have been doing. They gave me everything they wanted to achieve; all I had to do was fill in the blanks for the options to get what they wanted."

A woman exclaims, "They essentially gave me permission to invite them to act in a way that will help them without it being personal to me. They weren't saying yes or no to me, they were choosing to opt in to or out of having what they wanted."

Another offers, "As a prospect, I felt like choosing to do nothing was a stupid choice. I can't imagine anyone making that choice if we follow this sequence."

Yet another speaks right up, "Asking people to take action this way makes it so much easier. I didn't feel like I was coercing them into doing something they didn't want to do."

From somewhere in front of me, "Asking people to take action in this way helps them to tell me what they really want to do without the pressure of trying to make up their own answer."

From across the room, "It seems that this will keep people from leading me on when they don't want to do something, but don't want to tell me they don't want to do anything."

Clarissa says confidently, "It lets me know exactly how to serve people. No matter what option they pick, I know exactly what to do next to serve them and myself better."

A man way up in front explains, "It helps prospects know what their real choices are. Yes and no answers really don't mean anything because we don't know what they are saying yes or no to."

Steve puts his hands up and says, "Okay I think we have a great set of responses. If I were to ask each of you individually, 'If you could change anything in your XL-8 Business or Perpetual Wealth Financial career, what would it be?' many of you would say, more customers and associates. How do I know this? Because I ask this everywhere I travel. I follow that question by asking you to tell me more about that, and you would tell me something like 'I just can't get people to listen to me or to enroll at the end of my presentations.' So I would continue by asking 'On a scale from 1 to 10, how serious are you about getting more customers and associates?' To which you would respond with 'Ten.'

"So with that scenario, here is another example of option giving:

"First, I ask each of you to choose one of the following options:

1. Keep doing what you are doing now, and be okay with getting the same result.
2. Learn what is holding you back and practice those skills to increase your PEPs.
3. Change your approach, and begin implementing this new found skill right now. If you have at least thirty PEPs, begin enrolling a higher percentage of prospects as customers or associates.

"Choosing the first option will ensure that you keep getting the same results, and those results will motivate you to quit. Choosing the second option will help you overcome any shortcomings you may have in building relationships of trust based on the value of your service. Choosing option three will propel your business forward faster and with less frustration.

"I want to thank you all for fully participating in this exercise. For some of you it was more than just a practice exercise. I also want to remind you of your assignment to talk to ten people who know you, followed by five people you want to enroll in some kind of action that will benefit them. Before I switch topics I want to thank the Perpetual Wealth Financial Group for being here with us, and for so freely sharing their gifts and talents here today."

Matt and his team recognize that this is their cue to excuse themselves. They walk upstairs to discuss their feelings, observations, and insights on the meeting and to understand how it will impact their day-to-day work.

Matt repeats the exercise Steve just finished. There are some who just say 'ditto' to what the big group had said. There are a few who add to the list of things they learned saying. "This should increase our conversion ratios."

Another adds, "This approach makes it so much easier for my prospects to know what they are choosing."

Shelly declares, "It should put them at ease because I am at ease when the moment of decision comes."

Rachel responds, "This approach helped me understand what I was asking them to do, and it seemed to create clarity for them. Overall, it should help me to know how to better serve our clients."

"By the raise of hands," Matt asks. "How many of you plan to implement this into your daily work as managers and also plan to teach this skill to your team members?" Everyone raises their hands. It is unanimous then.

"Raise your hands again if this training was at least a nine on a ten point scale for you?" Again everyone raises their hand.

"I encourage each of you to compose a brief statement about what you learned and how you can implement it into your work, and teach at least one other person in the company what you learned. I invite everyone to send me a copy, and if they choose to they can send a copy to Mrs. Hesslip." At this point I remind them about the ten and five-person practice assignment Steve gave and after we all eat the pizza I had delivered, the meeting breaks up.

Some leave immediately to begin their weekend vacation, others mill around the room discussing what they learned and get caught up with old friends and colleagues. On a personal note, Shelly, Kayci, Josh, Rachel, and Clarissa all approach me and ask me about different topics that were referred to that they were unfamiliar with. All of them ask how they can have more training like this. I explain, "We are going to have more and more of this kind of training, and it's up to you to make sure that you receive more training like this."

The meeting breaks up and in the quiet of the afternoon I take a few moments to organize my personal message to Terri. I spend the weekend at the boot camp event with Ann. I attend a few of the sessions with her and prepare my report for Terri explaining the training, including feedback on our experience. I know she will want a full description as soon as possible, so I send it to her on Saturday evening just as the event is concluding.

On Monday I am back in my office pacing around. I am eager to find out what Terri has heard through the grapevine, but I am anxious at the same time. I decide to end the agony of waiting and pick up the phone to call her. As the phone rings, the feeling washes over me that somehow my reputation is on the line, and that if this wasn't well-received by the others, I would be in some kind of trouble. Most of the time when I call Terri, I only reach her voice mail, so I formulate the message I plan to leave her in my mind. However, this morning there is a live voice on the other end saying, "Hello Matt. I am so glad you called. I have been thinking about you this weekend and am excited to hear your report."

Not having expected her to answer, my reply feels clumsy, "I only called to schedule time with you to discuss just that."

"I have some time right now if that is okay with you," she responds.

Okay. I pause momentarily, take a drink from the water bottle on my desk and begin, "You have my report with some details, and so I will give you a few of the highlights from my perspective. We learned that relationships are what create long-term results, and that the catalyst for creating long-term relationships is asking people to take action that will improve their life. We also learned that traditional methods of selling and closing can lead to transactional sales, but they don't create life-long customers or repeat buyers. And we had an opportunity to learn and practice specific methods to easily ask people to take action that will excite them to choose into what we offer as a realistic solution for creating the results our prospects and clients want. That's the high level overview of what we learned. The details are in my report. I am curious what you may have heard from the others who attended."

Eagerly she responds, "I received a few updates and messages from the Regional Managers, and a few of the Division Managers. They were all positive, and filled with gratitude for the depth and breadth of training they received. They used terms you and I have briefly discussed, but that I still don't completely understand like high-yielding questions, PEPs, Conversion Ratios, and Relationship Ratings, and they asked how we could receive the training you have been privy to for the past year or so. I told them that I want to see if they were actually implementing the training they already received, or if this was going to be the 'Flavor of the Month.' I am excited to see how this pans out and what effect it has on our Floor Level Planners and managers at all levels. Thank you for taking the chance to promote this. I know it's not always easy to take a risk like this. Mrs. Jensen also passes along her admiration for your initiative to make the company more prosperous."

Wow, Matt thinks, putting the needs and wants of others first does make a difference even at the highest corporate level. "Thank you Terri for your confidence in my judgment on this. I know the company invested heavily to make it happen. I am certain that we will experience a recognizable effect as a result of participating in this training." We talk for a few minutes about particular situations in the region and then hang up.

Over the next several weeks, every region in the company improves, even Alixes. Darrell and Clarissa's divisions start to outperform the other divisions in Alix's region. Terri notices the improvement and easily tracks the cause of Alix's improvement. Terri is looking for it, based on the information in my report on the participants list, along with the reimbursement forms for the event.

In the next few months my region pulls even with Bruce's. We are tied for first place in overall profitability. Since the event, my region's customer acquisition costs decline 6%; new accounts grow by over 5%; customer up-sells increase by 7%; 55% of our business now comes from existing customers;

our retention rates increase by 4%; and our customer satisfaction surveys are the highest in the entire company. In our own results-tracking system, the average Relationship Rating improves by 63% for my direct reports and 48% for the whole region. The average Trust Quotient goes up by 31% for my leaders and 58% for the region as a whole. Our Value of Service score raises by 23% in the leaders and 44% for the region.

I am looking out the window over the Minneapolis skyline, watching the sunset and basking in the feeling of having overcome immense obstacles when the phone rings. It is Terri. She wants to take a moment to give me a corporate update since the event in San Diego. "In every respect," she shares, "Our numbers are all moving in a positive direction. I thought you might want to know, and this also gives me a reason to call and congratulate you personally. You know it seems that the difference in our results in the past quarters can be attributed to a few of the things I read in our customer satisfaction surveys. People seem to trust us more now than they ever have, they compliment us more on how professional we are, and they do business with us because, unlike our competitors, they feel like we really care about them." We talk for a minute or two more and then hang up.

Rachel is right I reflect fondly: "Relationships Create Real Results." Those relationships are founded on the three underlying principles that Terri just finished discovering for herself. I am grateful beyond my ability to express. And even though these past years have been difficult, I have been blessed with great mentors and support partners: My dad for teaching me to work hard without much encouragement; Oscar with his relationship advice; Bill with his emotional support and clarifying discussions on important matters; Josh and Jane for their correction in the beginning of my career here; Bruce for his belief in me; Steve for allowing me to participate in his trainings and his example of walking the walk; and of course there is Ann, who begins teaching how to lead just by showing up. The lessons I have learned from each of these people are invaluable to me.

Ann's team is experiencing similar, if not even better results than mine. She is qualifying more new people at new promotion levels than ever before. She has over thirty new people at the Copper level, almost thirty at Bronze level, promoted two new personally sponsored Silver teams, and qualifies two more Gold teams. Donna steals the show at the latest event by achieving her goal of becoming a Gold. Ann needs only one more team to achieve the Gold Level and her goal of becoming a Platinum will be a reality. Her leadership down-line teams are duplicating her. They are promoting new Silvers, and their teams are promoting new Coppers, Bronzes and Silvers as well. Her team is lucky to have her as their mentor.

On the plane back to Minneapolis it occurs to me that I am lucky to have Ann as my partner and example of success. The time I have to spend away from her is really wearing on me. During the week I become almost desperate, hoping that my results and increasing reputation will make enough of an impression on the executive team for them to decide to promote me when Terri retires.

I have started taking a walk each evening after dinner to relieve the stress of waiting for my future to unfold. Tonight is different however. Not only because the weather is beginning to turn cool, but because I have life changing news to share with Ann. As I walk tonight the cool air makes my hands shake a little as I make my nightly call to Ann. She answers, and before she can say anything I ask, "Guess what I did today?"

Puzzled at my boyish excitement she responds, "I have no idea, tell me!"

Matt replies a bit short of breath, "I cancelled my future plane reservations bound for Minneapolis."

"Cancelled? I don't understand, what happened?" Ann asks.

"This afternoon I got a call from Terri Hesslip. I did it Ann. Rather we did it! I have been approved for promotion to take her place as the Vice President of Sales!"

Ann screams and excitedly says, "That's awesome Matt! That means you will be working from the home office, and that's why you cancelled your Minneapolis trips. I am so excited to have you home every night. What a blessing. But what happened to Bruce? Why were you selected over him to take Terri's position? How is he taking all this?"

"He called to congratulate me and said I earned it," Matt answers. "He said the extra work, initiative, and personal improvement put me over the top for sure. He is glad it's me who advanced ahead of him. He didn't think he could take it if it had been anyone else. I asked Terri the same question. She said, 'I was her choice and her recommendation to the board. Mrs. Jensen and the board members' only hesitation and concern was the short amount of time I have worked here. But at the end of the meeting both Mrs. Jensen and Terri agreed that results rule. And even though I had a shorter track record, it was filled with nothing but success at every level in the company, especially my most recent achievement of taking the worst performing region with possible closures and layoffs pending and turning it into the number one producer. They really didn't have much of a choice but to try to duplicate this throughout the company.'

"And my initiative to do the training workshop in San Diego was a great help as well. Terri apparently stood up and told the board, 'Matt took a risk revealing his secrets by teaching everyone else what he knows. It shows that he is concerned about the whole company and not just his personal stewardship.' I'll be home tomorrow to start our new life together again; once and for all."

Author's Note:

The instructions explaining the mathematical equation for this chapter is in the appendix at the end of the book.

12

Guess What I Did Today?

Driving to work on my first day as the new Vice President of Sales, it hits me, my dad has been wrong all along. I have become something. I do make a difference. I have a big smile on my face as I pull up in my new parking place with its specially marked sign signifying the owner of this coveted, priceless, nine-by-fifteen foot, parking lot real estate. It is a bright, sunny morning, but the air is getting too cold to really enjoy having the top down on my Jaguar. It doesn't matter. Today is a special day and I am going to relish the scene no matter how cold it is. When I get to my new office it's empty of any of Terri's personal belongings. Terri left it in spotless condition with a note propped up on the desk.

I sit down to open and read the note, which says, "Congratulations on making the climb to the top floor and a corner office. Take care of this stewardship and the people entrusted to you. You have a great responsibility to help the company grow and become like you: vibrant, innovative, and most of all client-service-oriented. The only advice I will give you is that aside from the things you have learned that got you here, don't assume there is anything wrong with your people, our processes, or the products and services we offer. One day you will leave a note for the person who follows you. Leave the position better than you found it and you will be able to look back with fond memories and no regrets. Good luck and good work. Terri Hesslip."

I turn to look out the corner windows to get my first real look over the city from this panoramic view. I'm surprised that it's raining on that sunny morning. It's not really raining, but the note Terri left me reminds me that people, not things, processes, or products were her focus; and even in this quiet moment alone she teaches me again that people are the most important thing to me as well. In fact, that's what she wrote about that got me into this office in the first place.

Terri is a great example of what a leader should be. She is so good at influencing people that her day-to-day example by itself is the teacher. This reminds me of the time Sara Thoms stood up in a conference one day and explained, "When Steve shows up, no one questions whether or not the business works, because he has high PEPs, a high Relationship Rating and the value of his service is off-the-chart high, his very presence does the teaching. When he takes action, the result is one hundred percent predictable. Nothing is left to chance." Steve and Terri are very much the kind of leaders that make the world a better place for everyone to live in. I think I will have this letter framed and put on my top shelf to remind me of Terri, the legacy she left here, and what she stands for.

There is a knock at the door. It's Darla, my new assistant. Actually, Darla has been the Vice President's assistant for many years. I think Kayci learned from Darla. Between the two of them, there is very little they don't know about what goes on here. Darla is eager to meet me and lets me know that she is excited to work with me. She asks if there is anything I need her to do, and then fills me in on my schedule for the day and week. She gives me the details on regular meetings that I am supposed to attend, and helps me get acquainted with the schedule that Terri set up. Remembering Terri's advice not to assume anything is wrong with the processes she established, I encourage Darla to help keep me on track with schedules, appointments and everything else for a while. The fact is, she knows more about what goes on in this venue than I do. She smiles agreeably and tells me that Kayci is here to see me.

Kayci comes in and gives me a big hug. "Congratulations, Matt. You have made a pretty big impact on things around here, and you deserve the promotion. I want to tell you how much I appreciate all you have done for me. I found out that you were the one who created the position I have now and recommended me for the job. I have always been grateful that you have cared for me professionally and personally."

Darla comes back in and announces that there are others who want to see me as well, and asks if she should show Shelly, Josh, and Jane in? Thinking that this is turning into a real party, I ask Darla if she could get some orange juice and doughnuts from the cafeteria. This kind of celebration needs a toast. By the time Darla brings the refreshments in, Rachel and Clarissa are on the conference speaker line. Shelly starts what becomes a round of congratulatory speeches.

She starts by saying, "Congratulations, boss-man! This seems like a perfect time to tell you how much I admire you for sticking with me when I was so difficult to get along with in the beginning. I found out that you were the one who recommended me to take your place as a Division Manager. There is really no way for me to thank you enough for taking a chance on me with the conversion ratio experiment, for teaching me to really care about others, and showing me how to increase my Relationship Rating. It has had a profound effect on my marriage and my relationships with my children. So what are you going to do now that you made it all the way up here?"

Matt answers eagerly, "The advice Terri gave me is to help the company grow and be vibrant, innovative, and most of all client-service-oriented, and to leave the position better than I found it. So I am going to begin improving upon what she has in place by teaching, expounding, and exhorting the Regional Managers and others to steadily and consistently improve their Value of Service Score, Relationship Rating, Trust Quotient, PEPs, high-yielding questions, listening skills, dot-connecting skills, asking people to take action capabilities, and, as you mentioned, Shelly, their conversion ratios. The challenge, of course, is that I need to help them personally improve. I need to teach them how to teach their Division Managers, I need to teach Division Managers to teach Department Coordinators, all the way to the Floor Level Planners."

Josh jumps in, "Nice job on the promotion. I think you should share some of that big fat salary with me, though. I had to nearly die so that you could get promoted ahead of me. Again. In all seriousness, you have risen far beyond what I could have with the opportunity you were given. I look forward to working with you."

Jane adds to Josh's request about sharing some of that bonus money, "Just remember that I gave you the advice to erase that white board, and got you going on the path that got you here."

Rachel on the phone says, "Congratulations from the field office here in Minneapolis. How's the view from the top floor? I am excited to learn more about leadership from you. I also want to thank you for recommending me for the Regional Manager position. It will be a great challenge and I look forward to learning, growing, and following in your footsteps."

Clarissa takes her turn saying, "Way to go Matt. I look forward to working with you and learning what you know so that I can have a greater effect on those I work with each day."

Raising his orange juice glass Matt offers a toast, "To the best team of winners in the company. I love working with each of you, and look forward to years and years of prosperity for all of us! Now let's prove why we deserve the positions of influence we have. If any of you need anything at all, please call me. Thanks for all you do and are. You are all amazing."

We all talk for a few more minutes, taking a moment to enjoy the success we created and deepening our relationships with each other. Then slowly, everyone disappears. After they leave, I sit in my chair, admiring the view from my top story, corner office for a moment. The heating fan comes on and it reminds me of driving to work with the wind in my face this morning, while I thought of my dad and how wrong he has been. That thought quickly turns to my fireside conversation with Steve, while we were four-wheeling. I reflect on what I told Steve that night: "I idolized my dad and thought that he was everything I ever wanted to be. He had everything I wanted to have someday, and as a result of our toxic relationship a passion to prove him wrong ignited within me."

Sitting here I finally feel like I have become the kind of person he can be proud of. This is the scene I have dreamed of for years, since I was sleeping in horse trailer bunk beds, and crashing into telephone poles. In that moment I decide to call him. I am feeling pretty confident about my ability to build strong relationships at this point. I think I will invite him to come see Ann and the kids. Okay, maybe I am not really as interested in him seeing Ann and the kids as I am having him visit my office and seeing that I am not the loser he proclaimed I was.

Funny that even now, in my executive office I am nervous as I dial the phone. Once again, a feeling of relief comes over me when my mom answers. As I talk to her for a few minutes I am feeling a little nervous, but not like I had before. That first conversation went well enough to give me sufficient confidence that I can repeat it. I share my promotion news with her and she calls for my dad to pick up the phone telling him, "It's Matt."

"Hello Matt," he says, careful not to over extend his friendliness. "How are Ann and the kids doing?" he asks politely.

"They are doing fine," I respond and then think, well, no one is dead or on the defensive yet. "I have some news to share with you. I have been promoted at work again. I am now the Vice President of Sales. I am working out of the corporate offices again."

"That's great news," he replies.

The conversation is going pretty well so far, so I decide to take a risk, telling him, "I have been thinking for a while now about putting our differences aside and spending some time together."

He quickly responds, "What did you have in mind?"

I follow-up saying, "I want to invite you to come and visit us before it gets too cold and snowy to travel." I want him to say yes, but I know there is a good chance that he won't want to mend our relationship, so he might just make an excuse and say no. The phone is silent for an uncomfortable amount of time. I can feel the tension building as I wait for him to respond.

He breaks the silence by agreeing that this would be a good time to mend fences. He says, "I have been thinking about how to put our relationship on the right track ever since we last talked; but I just haven't known how to bridge the gap that has been growing between us. We would love to come and visit."

My heart almost leaps out of my chest. I can hear the relief in my mother's voice on the extension line as we discuss a date for their visit and then hang up.

Beaming with pride and excitement, I can't wait to call Ann and tell her. Dialing with great anticipation, I hear her answer, and before she can even finish saying hello, I ask, "Guess what I did today?"

"I don't know, but it must be good if you are calling me this early in the day," she replies.

"I called my dad!"

"And how did it go?" Ann asks apprehensively.

Excitedly I share, "It was awesome. He actually congratulated me on the promotion. I invited him and my mom to come and visit. I hope you don't mind."

Ann curiously asks, "What motivated you to call him, and what made you think he would accept an invitation to come visit us?"

Without hesitation I say, "I felt it was a good idea to let him know first-hand about my promotion and to finally put our family together. When he congratulated me, I felt like maybe this was a good time to make an assertive declaration that he should come. And he said yes. I am so excited. This is the beginning of a whole new chapter in our relationship."

Ann is cautious, "You need to get control of yourself, Matt. So far you have successfully gotten him to take the next step in your relationship. The reality check is going to hit when he gets here to visit us, and the last time you were together, it didn't go well for either of you. I am not trying to rain on your parade; I just want to set your expectations correctly about what you might expect from their visit."

She's right, of course. I try to readjust my expectations as Ann and I talk for another minute or so and then hang up.

I walk around in my new office for another five minutes, thinking about Terri's note and her invitation to keep doing what got me into this office and Shelly's question about what I am going to do now. When I start to make some notes on my whiteboard about teaching people to teach others to teach others, Bruce's name comes to mind. I wonder where he is this morning. He was nowhere in sight when we were celebrating a while ago.

Sitting down, I think, even though he congratulated me on the promotion, he's probably pretty upset about the fact that I am now his manager, and that he recommended me for the Regional Manager job which led to this position as his boss. If he hadn't promoted me as his replacement up the ladder as he rose in the company and recommended me for the Minneapolis job, I certainly wouldn't be here now. I want his buy in and belief that we are all on the same team and working for the same goals. As I ponder what to do about this, two conversations come to mind: the one with Terri after my promotion to Regional Manager, and the one with Bruce when he extended the Regional Manager position to me.

Terri made it a point to call her Region Managers and build a great relationship with them by giving them verbal pats on the back and encouragement, including an invitation to call and discuss anything, anytime. Bruce told me when he extended the offer to become a Regional Manager that I was promoted because of my human interaction skills that help me inspire and mentor others and my ability to teach others to produce excellent results for our clients in industry changing style. In that moment my gratitude for Terri's example grows to a whole new level. I call Darla and ask her to schedule a meeting with Bruce at his earliest convenience. And then I return to planning how to create duplication in our company.

The questions on my mind, as I stand in front of my whiteboard are 'what does Steve do to create duplication that we don't?' and 'How, when, and where does he teach?' I write on the board: He holds a monthly business development conference, which is a fancy name for our Sales Seminars. Following his pattern of success, I will organize division conferences. In the first session I will demonstrate to the Division Managers how to teach their people to build strong and lasting relationships like Steve does. Again, following the same pattern, we will break for lunch and then resume with a recognition segment, followed by a presentation from a Regional Manager or some other corporate executive. This means I am going to have to first teach Regional Managers the same lessons I will be teaching Division Managers so they can give these presentations. As I am looking at my calendar to begin scheduling Regional and Division Manager training events, Bruce knocks on my door.

"Darla said you wanted to meet with me?" he says sheepishly.

"Come in Bruce," I say, reaching out to shake my hand. Bruce shakes my hand with a slightly bent elbow and sits down in the chair farthest away from me, folding his arms, crossing his legs, leaning back in the chair, turned slightly to one side with his head tilted, just as he had at the training event in San Diego. He sits there as if to dare me to penetrate his defenses, and in perfect Pickup Truck position, tapping one foot.

I begin, "Bruce, I want to meet with you for a couple of reasons. First, I want to thank you for promoting me as your replacement each time you rose up in the company, and for recommending me for the Minneapolis job as a Regional Manager. Without all of that, I certainly wouldn't be here now. You are a great example of integrity, and a credit to the company."

Bruce sits up a little straighter and unfolds his arms. Not knowing yet if his relationship gateway is fully unlocked I continue, "I also want to thank you for calling to congratulate me on the promotion. It means a lot to me to have a mentor call when I succeed."

He uncrosses his legs and shares, "Matt you have always been a great team player, and I want to also tell you that you have made me look awfully good since you joined the company. I don't think I would have been promoted to Regional Manager without your Department's success. So thank you for your diligence, sacrifice, and hard work. What can we do from here to make it look like the board made the right decision by promoting you?"

Bruce's answer takes me by surprise. I pause for a moment to think before I respond, saying, "I want to ask you how you would rate our relationship on a scale from 1 to 10?"

Taking a second to consider the question, not wanting to over - or underestimate what he thought I might say if he had asked me the same question. Bruce answers, "I guess it's always been pretty good."

"So on a scale from 1 to 10 where does pretty good fit?" I press for a more exact estimate.

"I would say it's about an," pausing for a second before venturing a number, "8."

"Excellent," Matt says. "I agree that we do have a positive relationship. The question really isn't a test; there isn't a right or wrong answer. I just want to help that 8 become a 9 or 10. I want to teach you something that Steve from the XL-8 training taught me a while back about relationships, and what our estimations and assumptions of them really mean. Steve taught me that if we have an eight relationship with someone that might seem really positive; and I agree that you and I do have a positive relationship."

Walking to the whiteboard to do the Relationship Rating calculation I continue, "The challenge is that you think that our relationship is better than it really is. Here's what I mean, if we have an 8 relationship, then that means at least twenty percent of the time we are not on the same page, or that things are not in harmony between us. The reality however, is that the twenty percent takes away from the eight relationship we feel so good about.

"Effectively the twenty percent is discounted from the estimate of eight. So that really leaves us with a relationship rating of six instead of eight. Picture this for a minute. If you asked Shelly to rate your relationship with her, and she responded with a six instead of an eight, would it alarm you and would it make a difference in your approach to her in your working relationship?"

"Of course," Bruce responds emphatically. "I need her to be part of the team, and anything that is keeping us from pulling in the same direction creates a drag on all of us."

"That's exactly right," Matt agrees. "The problem is that we are often fooled by our estimate of the quality of our relationships. In fact, the difference between a 6 relationship, as opposed to an 8 relationship is pretty significant. But when we only view our relationships at the higher number, it keeps us from doing those extra things that develop it into a powerful, productive, meaningful relationship. It's that slight difference in thinking that prevents us from taking the day-to-day action that draws people towards us and then with us. This is true of all of our relationships. Now that you know what your estimate of our relationship means, we can become more aware of how we can increase the value of our service to one another in a joint effort to put our company over the top."

Scratching his head, Bruce says, "I never thought of it quite that way before. I guess the Board really did know what they were doing when they put you in that chair instead of me. Thank you for the lesson. I need to run to another meeting, thanks for the time Matt. I really do mean it when I say congratulations on the promotion. I look forward to working with you in the future. Rumor has it that our meetings will be very different than the typical meetings we have around here."

We shake hands as he leaves with a big smile on his face and a bounce in his step that he didn't have when he came in. Darla looks at me standing in the doorway, analyzing my posture in an attempt to get a sense of how the meeting went. I smile and nod to her as if I had just made it through the last hidden door to the treasure room. She taps her watch, reminding me that I need to finish preparing for my presentation to the board.

Sitting in the boardroom for the first time, I choose a seat as far away from the front as possible. I have no idea what to expect so I intend to keep a low profile this first day. However, the first order of business for Mrs. Jensen is to call on me to introduce myself to the board members and to present the sales numbers for the past month.

I start, "Over the past few weeks the company's customer acquisition costs are down 2%, while our new accounts have grown by over 1%. Customer up-sells increased by 3%. Business coming from existing customers is up by .5%. Our client retention rate increased by .75%. And our customer satisfaction surveys indicate an improvement as well. The average PEP score for Floor Level Financial Planners has risen by 3 points. The Regional Managers relationship ratings are up by a full point, their value of service is over 60 and their conversion ratios are improving by about 1% per week. By way of comparison, from the average for the past six months our numbers are all increasing and we have reversed the downward trend in both business coming from existing customers and client retention."

Henry, one of the board members asks, "What surprises you most about these numbers given you have never had access to the entire company's reports before?"

Turning to face him directly I reply, "The effects I want to see on the whole company are slow. This is like driving an ocean liner. It takes a while to really see the cause and effect in measureable ways."

Henry smiles, knowing that I don't understand the bottom line effect of these numbers, and how good this report really is. He offers, "I don't think you realize the difference that a .5% increase in business coming from existing customers, and a .75% increase in client retention rate make. These two numbers alone equate to about a 7% annual growth rate. Coupled with the rest of the numbers you reported, our annualized growth rate would be about 14%, which is a 21% increase over last year. Impressive, to say the very least. Don't worry. You'll get the sense of it all soon. Well done!"

As he is speaking, it strikes me that he is clearly a Hybrid, and that if I need to address him in the future I will know how to adjust my language and approach.

Mrs. Jensen asks, "What are PEPs and Relationship Ratings? What are you measuring in regards to conversion ratios, and how do you calculate someone's value of service?"

I spend the next five or six minutes explaining how to measure, calculate, and track these items that no one else has paid attention to in the past and explain, "My major initiative over the next year is going to be to teach everyone in the company what these terms are and how to increase each of them to collectively improve our ability to create and maintain long-term or life-long relationships with our clients. It is these numbers, along with the traditional numbers we have always been reporting that have enabled me to see exactly what is happening in our sales, and to quickly improve performance in specific areas that they indicate are holding us back."

"Bravo," remarks another of the board members. "Someone is thinking outside the box for a change. You have my support and admiration for putting these procedures in place."

Seeing that there are no more questions or comments, I take my seat in the back of the room, relieved that I didn't wilt in the face of the questions, and thankful that my news was apparently good news. As I sit there listening to the rest of the meeting, I start keeping notes on the Personal Interaction Keys of each person in the room. The woman who praised me for being innovative is a Pickup Truck for sure. I am going to make sure to keep a little Personal Interaction Key note for every member of the board. The meeting adjourns, and surprisingly most everyone stays and talks for a while. I didn't expect this group to want to stick around and just talk. Another message from the universe: people at high levels of business develop and maintain relationships. Go figure.

A few days pass and as I reach for a report book on my top shelf, I see the framed note from Terri. It prompts me to call Rachel. As we are talking I slightly adapt the language from Terri's note and read it as a congratulatory note to her. She is appreciative of the thought and thanks me for our last lesson at the Regional Managers' meeting on value of service. She shares, "I noticed that Alix wasn't too engaged, and seemed to refuse to accept most of what you had to say." Coincidentally, while we are talking I receive an email from Alix, notifying me that she is resigning and wants to talk to me about a severance and logistics of her quitting. I resist the temptation to hurry my conversation with Rachel in order to get on the phone with Alix.

I figure my relationship with Rachel is more critical to the long term success of the company than my relationship with a manager who announces she is quitting via email. Rachel and I talk for a few more minutes and then say goodbye. Before I call Alix, I want to talk to my old friend Craig in Human Resources to get his advice on what I should and can say and do.

While the phone rings, I look back at Terri's note, then my mind shifts as I see the origami trophy Patti gave me at the leadership retreat. Together these two mementos remind me to tune in my Sports Car radio and pay close attention to what Alix's Personal Interaction Key is. When Alix answers the phone she seems annoyed that it took me so long to get back to her. I am instantly reminded that all my interactions with her in the past indicate that she is also a Sports Car.

I tell her, "I got your email. I am sorry for the delay in getting back to you. I was on a critical phone call." Taking a deep breath to regain my composure I continue, "I am very sorry you feel like you have to resign. What is it that is making you unhappy enough to bring you to this decision?"

She responds defiantly, "Don't use any of that high questioning stuff with me. You aren't going to trick me into staying. There are a lot of reasons, but mainly I just can't support you. I just can't get over the fact that you were promoted ahead of me. And even if I could get passed that, I think the whole idea of Relationship Ratings, PEPs, Value of Service scores, and the rest is an incredible waste of time and company resources."

Matt responds empathetically, "I don't want you to quit because of personal issues between you and me. Is there anything that can be done to make you happy and on board here?"

In true Sports Car fashion, Alix replies, "No. I just want to work out my settlement and get on with my life without the nonsense the company is putting on me."

"It sounds like you are firm in your decision to quit then?" I state, sounding as if it were a question.

Alix answers, "I must not be speaking English. I am resigning, and now I just want to work out my severance."

We talk for over an hour about sensitive client issues, the penalties of disclosing company information and discuss replacement candidates.

She tells me, "I would certainly not recommend either Darrell or Clarissa. They are the worst choices in the whole region to take my place."

I ask, "Why do you say that?"

She shares, "They are deceptive, dishonest, and deceitful."

I request justification for that claim, given that neither of them had ever shown up on any report as being trouble makers.

Alix responds, "Among other things they went behind my back to attend the training in San Diego with you!"

"Weren't they on vacation those days?" I ask for confirmation.

"Yes they were," Alix admits. "But neither of them was going to San Diego when we talked about their vacation plans. I didn't want them to go to the training if everyone couldn't go, and they snuck off and went anyway against my wishes."

"Did either of them know you didn't want them to go?" I ask, trying to find out what the truth is. "I believe you opted out of the San Diego training because there wasn't time to get everyone organized to attend and because a few of your managers were going on vacation. I don't want to ruin your story with the facts Alix, but it seems like the ones who really wanted to go were willing to use vacation time to better themselves and rearrange their life to allow for this training. We should be applauding and rewarding them for their proactivity, not chastising and reprimanding them."

"You see Matt," She says angrily. "It is this very difference in thinking, and your refusal to see common sense that makes it impossible for me to continue to work here."

Putting an end to this kind of discussion, I rebuff her saying, "The challenge you must learn sometime in your life Alix, is that relationships are all that matter. They are the single most important thing you can develop because they are the foundation of all success. I am truly sorry that you refuse to learn this lesson here with us in your current job.

"What exactly are your expectations for severance, future benefits, and stock options," I ask interested in finding out how unreasonable her request might be, and needing to move away from the more volatile subject?

"I would like six-months pay and full benefits for a year," she replies as if I can just give her anything I want or she demands. "It's a hard economy to find a job in, you know," she concludes in a demanding tone.

The first thought that comes to my mind as she talks is, she is such a Sports Car. This kind of demanding, guns blazin' approach might work with others, but as a Sports Car myself I understand too much of what is going on with her. It is amusing to watch an angry Sports Car in action. I repeat the advice Craig gave me about company policy in these matters.

She listens for a moment and before I can finish with my counter offer she interrupts me saying, "Your offer is completely unacceptable. I will call Mrs. Jensen and take care of this." And she hangs up.

I immediately call Mrs. Jensen to brief her on the situation. I explain to her that I had talked to Craig, and that he would be glad to provide her with any details of the circumstances. Mrs. Jensen tells me not to worry about this any further, that she will handle this herself, and concludes by asking with a sigh in her voice, "Do you have a recommendation to take her place? I would prefer to replace her with someone who is already working in that region. Is there anyone who is qualified to replace her?"

I quickly respond, "I have been pouring over the numbers each week since our last board meeting to make sure I understand all of the nuances of what we track. Based on those results and your desire to promote from within that region, I think Clarissa Gentry is the best choice."

"Okay Matt," she replies. "How sure are you about this choice?"

"I don't think I could be more certain," I answer.

"Then I don't think we need to wait to make a decision if you're sure," she declares. "Go ahead and call her and make the offer." Clarissa accepts the position and begins her tenure as the newest Regional Manager. The good news is that she is already pretty well-versed in building relationships as the foundation of building a strong and profitable organization.

A few weeks pass, and while sitting at the airport I find myself very anxious as I wait for my parent's plane to land. I put their luggage in the car and as we drive home we have a real conversation for the first time in years. It seems like my dad doesn't see me as a good-for-nothing child anymore. He compliments me on my promotion and when he comments on my car, a big grin comes to my face! We pull in the driveway and my mom comments on how beautiful the yard and landscaping look. My dad says, "I see you found the smallest house in the neighborhood."

Ann and the kids run out to greet us. My parents swoon over the kids for a few hours until it's time for the little ones to take a nap. We move out on the back deck and mom and dad talk to Ann for a long time. They have never really gotten to know her since we haven't really talked most of our married life. As we are talking I notice mannerisms about my parents that I haven't before, and now I am beginning to connect the dots as to why they behave the way they do.

My mom, for instance, has a big smile on her face and is very relaxed. Now that I think of it, this has always been true. While she is talking to Ann she uses her hands and arms, making huge motions to make overly dramatic points. I think if her hands were tied together she wouldn't be able to talk at all. She dominates the conversation and creates emotion when she talks. She has been saying things like 'that's a pain in the neck,' 'I am so excited,' 'do you have a handle on that' and 'your business gives you the ability to touch more lives'. Her clothes don't match at all and they are loose and comfortable. Thinking back now I remember times when I have been embarrassed by her "unkempt" appearance. Today for instance, she took off her shoes as soon as she got out of the car. In fact, they are probably still in the front entry way, and she won't likely remember where they are. She is definitely a Minivan. No wonder she has never challenged my dad. She has probably always been too terrified to jeopardize their relationship. So when he decided to exclude and ignore me she went along with him, not wanting to put their relationship at risk.

Moving to my dad, I notice that he looks up and to one side when he recalls details about his past, and I become really self-conscious with his penetrating and direct eye contact. A moment ago the conversation shifted from talking about general things like the yard, jobs, and kids to Ann more specifically. When she began talking, he turned directly toward her. I notice now, but I have never been conscious of it before that he touches his chin while he talks. After a while my dad and I decide to take a walk over to see Ann's horse.

The time alone gives us a chance to talk for at least a few minutes. Knowing that he is a Sports Car is very helpful. Even if I hadn't known him before today, I could have identified him as a Sports Car from his unsolicited opinion about the size of our house and by observing him while talking in the back yard. I begin the conversation asking him, "What surprises you most about seeing the kids?"

He answers, "They are so big, and are more active than I thought they would be."

I follow-up with, "They seem to grow up right before my eyes."

He says, "I remember when you and the girls were that age. You were all a handful. Your mother and I never got a moment's rest."

I continue, "How much do you remember about grandpa? I mean your dad."

Dad replies, "I remember that we didn't have much of anything. We went to the movie in town on Saturday sometimes if all our work was done. We all had chores, and certainly earned our keep. Grandpa worked really hard to make sure we had a roof over our heads and something to eat."

Then I ask, "If you could have changed anything about your relationship with him what would it have been?"

Dad stops walking and uncharacteristically pauses for a moment while he replays some of his childhood memories. He starts walking again as he says, "I think I would have liked to have him spend time with me, teaching me how he thought and made decisions."

Matt presses on, "What kept you from being closer to him?"

He answers abruptly, "He was way too busy to spend time with a kid."

The way he answers surprises me, but it says a lot about why he views the world the way he does. We walk for a few minutes in silence. My dad seems to be caught up in this trip down memory lane. Walking quietly, I think about his experience growing up and his Personal Interaction Key. Together they don't lend themselves to cultivating powerful caring relationships. Certainly the general description Olivia gave us fits perfectly here: "Getting the job done is more important than the people doing the job." I suddenly find myself with empathy for this man whom I have spent years accusing of ruining my life. Funny how his life was similar to mine.

We arrive at the pasture where Ann's horse is and he leans on the fence with one foot up on the bottom rail and drapes his left arm over the top. I have a picture of him standing this way etched in my mind since I could barely walk. He often stood this way, and usually it meant that he was relaxed and enjoying himself. I listen to him talk about the attributes of Ann's horse and how she has done a good job of caring for him.

He can't resist taking a shot at me by saying, "She probably takes care of the horse without any help."

I resist the temptation to fire a shot back across his bow, and simply offer, "I have been pretty busy at work to mess around with the horse. And actually Ann is teaching the kids to take care of him."

On the way back to the house my hands begin to sweat when I consider making this conversation really personal. I am conscious of every step, knowing that my time alone with him is growing shorter with every passing stride. I decide I have nothing to lose and so I take the risk asking him, "So if you could change anything about our relationship what would it be?"

Without any hesitation at all he answers, "I wish that we could have talked like this more often. I was always busy working or running to a fair or race somewhere. As you were growing up we were growing apart. It made me angry that I didn't have a better relationship with you, and that anger came out at you through harsh words and feelings that somehow our broken relationship was your fault. I have regretted the day I told you to go away ever since the moment the door closed behind me."

"I know how you feel," Matt says with a pained voice. "I have felt the same way. And that's why I called you those months ago, and why I invited you and mom here now for this visit because what I have found out is that relationships are the key to success and happiness."

"You sound like Oscar," Dad replies, with a smile on his face. "By the way he sends his good wishes to you."

Ann and my mom meet us in the front yard. They have been sharing their common passion for flower gardens and seem to have struck up a pretty strong friendship.

The next day my dad and I take a tour of my office complex. I introduce him to a few of the Floor Level Financial Planners and a couple of Department Coordinators. Each of them expresses a thought of gratitude to my dad for raising such a great leader and mentor. As we walk from the first floor to Kayci's office, I explain to him what we do and how we help people meet their short- and long term financial goals. I introduce him to Kayci and while they talk, I remember my conversation with Steve about accomplishing one final goal that I think should finally convince my dad that I am of worth and I do contribute in a positive way. From Kayci's office we take the elevator to my little corner of the world.

Darla greets us and welcomes my dad to the office. I sit in my chair and my dad circles the office. Passing the floor to ceiling windows, he stops briefly to take a look. I am relishing the moment expecting my dad to tell me how impressed he is that I have indeed become something. Years of planning and working have led to this moment.

He sits down and says, "You know, if I hadn't taught you how to work hard and if I had allowed you to come back that day in the driveway, you would never have learned the lessons necessary to become the person you are now."

I sit in disbelief for a few very tense seconds. In those seconds, everything I believed about proving myself to my dad collapsed. I fire right back as only a Sports Car can; appearing to agree but in a sarcastic tone say, "That's probably right, and one of the most important lessons I have learned on my way up the corporate ladder is that the one thing truly responsible for my success is the value of meaningful, life-long relationships. Cars, houses, money and all success is a result of creating, fostering, and maintaining strong and powerful relationships. I sit here now as a product of learning a lesson that I could never have learned from you."

My response stuns him. I don't think he expected me to say anything at all, let alone proactively assert that I have become successful in spite of him. He stands up and walks over to the corner windows, turns and looks at me and replies, "You are wrong about not being able to learn to have relationships from me. I am truly sorry for what I said to you all those years ago. I felt betrayed and belittled by you. I wanted to teach you a lesson that day about relationships; that treating people the way you treated me and your mother wasn't okay. My temper got away from me, but you must know now that I never meant to drive you completely out of our lives."

Matt's mind is racing, and in the few seconds it takes him to walk over and close the door he considers how to respond to a Sports Car who is acting like a Sports Car. I also consider that I am acting like a Sports Car too. I realize that my empathy is waning and my emotion level is climbing, which means my intelligence is declining. I have to get a grip on myself, or this will turn into another unforgettably bad moment.

On the way back to my chair I think about what my goals have been, and recognize that they have been to get what I want: to convince my dad that I am a big shot and that he should care about that somehow. I have completely ignored what my dad cares deeply about: an efficiently running, profitable ranch. This change in perspective helps me concentrate on how to create a transformation instead of a one-time transactional victory. I might win the argument that is about to begin, but I will certainly lose the war. If I don't change my approach, this could be the last conversation we will ever have. I need to relax and use my skill and knowledge to be interested instead of interesting.

I pour two glasses of water, one for myself and one for my father. Taking a drink to buy myself a few more seconds to strategize, I consider the dots I have and how I can connect them, knowing he is a Sports Car. I don't know how much time has passed while I am in mental deposition. It seems like a long time, even though I am sure only a second or two have passed.

Walking over to the window, standing a few feet away from my dad, I face him straight on, look directly into his eyes and declare calmly but firmly, "Dad, when I asked you yesterday about what you wished you could change about your relationship with grandpa, you told me you wanted to learn more about him and his way of thinking. What caused you to want to learn more about his thinking processes?"

My response takes him by surprise. He is expecting a childlike fit, and my questioning approach instantly relaxes him. He responds saying, "I would like to have learned more about how he thought so that I can make better decisions about how to make the ranch the envy of everyone in the horse world."

I dig a little deeper, "Why do you want to have the model ranch?"

Dad looks up and declares, "I want everyone to know just how proud I am of the legacy grandpa left for me. I want them to know how hard work and persistence can pay off, and probably most of all I want your mother and you kids to be proud of me and to take pride in our family name."

I can tell that dad is very serious about this goal and continue, "How will you know when you have achieved your goal?"

Dad looks away and starts pacing back and forth in front of the whiteboard on the wall across from my desk and says, "I don't think I will ever be done achieving it. I don't think you realize, Matt, how much it hurt me when you disappeared with Larry. It was like you abandoned the family, and the ranch, and everything I held near and dear to my heart."

Ignoring the obvious accusation of blame, I clarify what dad said saying, "So what I hear you saying dad, is that you want people to look to you as an icon of success, and that you want the family to appreciate you for all that you do to make our lives better. Is that right?"

Dad responds casually, "Yeah, I think that sums it up. I know that some in the family do appreciate what I do, but not everyone does. Maybe including you!"

Feeling in control of myself at this point, I declare, "I know how you feel. I felt the same way. Let me tell you what I found out about this. I have had to decide what success looks, feels, and sounds like to me regardless of what others say success is. Secondly, I have had to learn how to recognize the different ways people show their appreciation. So how would your life be different if you became a success icon and you did feel appreciated for all you have done?"

Dad sits down in the chair by my desk that visitors usually use and admits, "I have never considered that question before." After a few seconds he stands up and walks to the whiteboard. He begins to draw a picture representing each of my siblings' families working together on the ranch. "From my perspective," he continues, "Success looks like all of us sharing in the family ranch business, making every other family business around covet not only the overall success of the ranch, but the way in which it is successful."

Walking to the door and leaning against it Matt asks, "So dad, on a scale from 1 to 10, how serious are you about making that picture a reality?"

"You make it sound like you have become the kind of person who can somehow make that happen. What are you going to do, wave your magic wand and 'presto,' there it is?" dad replies sarcastically.

Now in full control of my emotions I press on without hesitation, saying, "I don't have a magic wand, but I do know that for every prize there is a price. If you are not serious about creating the result you drew on my whiteboard, you will never pay the price to achieve the prize. So how serious are you really about achieving your goal?"

For the first time in my life I saw my dad looking perplexed. He pauses for a moment considering how to respond and answers, "In all seriousness I think I am a 10. So what does that mean Mr. Corporate Executive?"

I sit down in the chair next to my dad and say, "It seems to me that you have a few options. First, you can keep working your guts out and feeling unappreciated and unfulfilled. Second, you can create massive financial success and hope for the best in the appreciation category. Or third, you can create massive financial success and leave a legacy of strong and powerful relationships with your family, friends, and employees, and get a sense of fulfillment being surrounded by people who love to be around you. So which of these choices will work better for you?"

For the first time in my life I see my dad unable to respond. He's just standing there in silence, stunned for a full two minutes, staring at his glass of water as if it has the answer. During the stillness, I anticipate him responding in a cynical or defensive manner to my invitation to make a decision. In those few moments he seems to surrender to his reluctance to recognize me as a person of value. Finally he looks up with a tear in his eye, and for the first time in my life he motions for me to come to him. This mountain of a man, the rock of emotional stability begins to shake as he reaches out and gives me a great big bear hug.

Crying now he tells me through the tears, "I am so sorry for the hurt I caused you. Please forgive me."

We stand there for a few minutes, just enjoying what might have been the first affectionate moment we had ever shared. He backs away and congratulates me on the life I have created, including a great job, fantastic family, and great future in front of me. He asks, "I would like to be involved in you and Ann's life in a more meaningful way if you are okay with that?"

Given that this is really what I have always wanted, I respond with a big smile on my face, "There is nothing that would give me more pleasure. I have wanted this for years now."

The remainder of the visit is awesome. It seems like we are able to talk about anything from that moment on. Dad even seems more relaxed around Ann, as if somehow he stopped judging her for being stupid enough to marry someone he had previously considered to be a no-account like me.

Sitting in my office a few weeks after my parents' visit, I am developing a training event based on the weekly accountability reports I receive from my Regional Managers when Darla notifies me that I have a phone call, someone named Steve Thoms? I tell her to put him through.

"Hello Matt," Steve says. "I hope I haven't interrupted you. I know calling in the middle of the day is always a little risky."

"I always have time for you," I reply, turning his welcoming message around on him. He laughs and says, "I am taking a day trip in the next few days to look at some land that David McKay and Glenna Hanks are developing in the foothills by the mountains where we went four-wheeling. I want to get your opinion on its financial value as an investment property, or as a place for Sara and me to build our dream home."

I answer, "The day after tomorrow would be best for me."

"Great, I look forward to it then," Steve replies. "I'll pick you up about 8:00 AM at the house."

Right on time, Steve pulls into the driveway to pick me up. What a perfect day to take a drive through the country and up into the foothills. We talk about how much we each enjoy our cars, and on a day like this the word enjoy is an understatement.

Steve says, "I want to take this opportunity to congratulate you for the success you have had by learning, practicing, and applying the Ask, Listen, and Repeat strategy, foundational principles, and skills. I also want to thank you for believing in me, for placing your professional life in my hands, and also for supporting Ann in her business activities. I am grateful to know that the principles I teach my team work in all areas of our life, even outside of XL-8."

Matt smiles in response and gives him an acknowledging pat on the shoulders. Just then, we drive over a small hill and can see the land Steve is interested in.

"So what do you think," Steve asks as we get out and start walking around the twenty acre lot he is most interested in, surrounded by a few other lots like it.

Lost in my own vision and dream I respond saying, "It's perfect: a mountain view on twenty acres of land with a river flowing through one side, and a county-maintained road on the other. Over there I could put the house I have been dreaming of since my childhood."

Steve clears his throat interrupting my verbal daydream. "I was actually asking if you thought it would be a good investment property for me, or if it would make better sense for us to buy it and build our dream home here. But now that we are here, I guess it's a great question to ask. Would you buy a parcel? And if you would, would you buy it as an investment or as a place to live?"

What a professional option-giver Steve is, I think. Even now he is giving me options to choose from. I am so enthralled in my own daydreams that I don't answer immediately. Walking down to the narrow, shallow stream I am captivated by the view of the valley and the idea of waking up to a new day, the smell of fresh morning air, the feel of dew on the wild grass, the sound of birds chirping, and the taste of the pure mountain water in the stream.

Finally I get around to answering Steve's question, "I don't have the kind of money or patience to buy this only as an investment asset. I have been looking for a place like this to build my dream home all my life. How would you feel about buying adjacent parcels, and becoming neighbors up here instead of on the block where we live now?"

Steve responds, "I haven't thought about that, but it seems like a great idea. I know you and Ann are in a financial position to do so. Your corporate compensation alone should allow you to buy this."

"And by the way," Matt says, "I am super-excited to help Ann achieve the Platinum level."

Steve smiles as he says, "You're a bit too late to help her go Platinum. Her fifth team just qualified for Gold, and so next week at the conference she is going to be promoted. You know, looking out over this property and watching you and Ann inspires me to go for Triple Platinum." We shake hands and make the commitment to buy the adjoining plots and begin planning our personal utopia.

As Ann and I drive to the conference I can't keep from smiling, and she keeps asking me what I am enjoying so much. Of course, I can't tell her, but it's a fantastic feeling to know that she is about to achieve a great goal, one that she has worked hard and sacrificed for. Of course, Ann knows that she has qualified as a new Platinum; she helped Mikki to qualify as her fifth Gold team. But she doesn't know that I know. Ann gets to speak for about a half hour about what it means to achieve this monumental goal. During her presentation she shares about the lives that she has seen change, including her own. While she is speaking Matt experiences the event from a whole new perspective. He looks at the crowd and imagines his managers speaking at leadership and training events like this one.

After the event we go to the best restaurant in town to celebrate. As we walk to our table in a quiet corner of the restaurant, Ann thanks me for recognizing her achievement by taking her to this restaurant.

I tell her, "It is a testament to your willingness to win no matter what the circumstances and your dedication to help others get what they want." Sitting down I begin our favorite game saying, "Guess what I did today?"

She looks at me, amused by the game and, taking a drink of her water, she shrugs her shoulders as if to say, "I have no idea, surprise me."

Slyly Matt shares, "I bought some land bordering the parcel of property Steve and Sara recently purchased in the foothills on the west side of town. You, me, and the kids can design and build a dream home and horse ranch there. When Steve and I went to look at the property before the conference, he told me that you qualified as a Platinum, and I figured this would serve as a reward for you, for my promotion, and for my reconciliation with my dad."

She reaches out and takes my hand in hers. She looks deeply into my eyes and says, "Except for our wedding day and the birth of our children, this is the greatest day of my life. The relationship we have now is all I had hoped for when we were dating. I am so happy, now that you seem content with your place in the world. It seems so long ago that we were in that basement apartment looking up at the world as if it were a mountain in front of us. I am always amazed that our rise out of that hole in the ground is a result of something so simple and yet illusive: long lasting, meaningful relationships."

I love taking Ann out to fancy places. For me, being with this woman in this place is definitely validation that I have achieved something important. The rest of the evening is great, and arriving home we check on the kids who are sleeping. Standing in the door way of our bedroom, we look at each other, smile, and share a warm embrace.

Back at the office the next week I remember Steve's congratulatory words while we were driving, which makes me reflect on what has happened over the past years. I tell myself: I have a great wife, awesome children, I am on the executive floor in a corner office with full double wall windows. I am my first mentors' boss, and I make a six figure income. By the numbers our customer acquisition costs are down. New accounts have grown. Customer up-sells have increased. Business coming from existing customers is up. Our client retention rate has also increased, and our customer satisfaction surveys indicate an improvement as well. The average PEP score at every level has risen, as well as Relationship Ratings, Trust Quotients, Value of Service scores, and our conversion ratios are improving. These numbers are great and I love the results we are creating. I recognize that moments like these are rare and fleeting. I am so excited to come to work, and satisfied that I have made it to the top by making a difference in peoples' lives.

I also remember the feeling I had when Oscar shared his dream of owning his own ranch. That thought melds into my experience floating down the river with Larry years ago. The warmth of that sunny day comes to mind with the conversation Larry and I had about abundance and life-giving water that the river offers. Then Bill Rena's voice enters my head. He remarked that he was wondering when I would realize that I was more than a ranch hand, and that all I really needed was a mentor to teach me how to be successful.

Oscar's fortune cookie from years ago again comes across my mind like the repeating message on my computer's screen saver; "If you don't change your direction, you are likely to end up where you are headed." The realization that I ended up here because I focused on and followed a single direction forced me to sit down so that I wouldn't fall down. How could a fortune cookie from years ago mean so much?

I have a sudden urge to call Mrs. Jensen and express my gratitude for her and the opportunity she and the Board of Directors have given me. I decide to skip making an appointment and walk directly to her office. I justify my impulse, thinking this feeling might not come again soon, and that I should act now. I am very anxious as I walk to her office, contemplating what I am going to say that will communicate my appreciation for her and the opportunities she has provided for me to learn, grow, and develop into the kind of person others listen to and follow. I pass Mrs. Jensen's assistant and, like Craig and I had before, I just walk into her office.

Mrs. Jensen is a very petite woman, and I hadn't noticed this when Craig and I visited her before but she looks a little strange sitting in what looks like one of those captain's chairs in a Star Trek movie, perched behind her huge black desk. Her chair and desk make her look even smaller. She looks up at me from a stack of papers, extends her arm fully to shake my hand and asks, "What can I do to help you Matt?" Craig was right when he told me, "She does get right to the point," I remember. No wasted time with pleasantries or any personal touch á la Terri; just a clear focus on the next problem and quickly finding its solution. It is great to be able to so easily identify people's natural way of being. In her case she is a Sports Car.

"Mrs. Jensen," I begin. "You have done everything possible to help me get to this place in my career. I want to take a minute to tell you how grateful I am for the support you have given me and the freedom to reach more people than I ever have before. The reason I wanted to see you is to let you know personally how much I appreciate all that you do to make this company a place where people can grow and become what they were intended to become."

Not expecting this kind of meeting, she is caught off guard. She takes off her glasses, leans back in her chair, looks deep into my eyes and says, "I am proud to have you as a member of the elite leaders here. You have worked so hard to get where you are. You have sacrificed, learned, and have made a great contribution here. You have had a tremendous impact on our people, processes, and the bottom line. You have helped us get back to our roots of serving people by focusing specifically on their goals and dreams."

She stands up, sighs, smiles briefly, and shakes my hand again. Then she sits right back down and picks up her glasses and then the phone, as if I should understand that our business is over and that I should excuse myself because she is now on to the next order of business in her busy schedule from which I have interrupted with my unannounced visit.

I happily, but unceremoniously return to my office. On my way past Darla's desk, she lets me know that I have a call waiting from that guy named Steve Thoms. I hurry into my office to pick up the phone. "Hello Steve," I say short of breath from my office sprint. "What can I do for you today?"

He begins, "I wonder if you remember the conversation we had by the campfire when we were four-wheeling."

"Of course I do," I reply.

Steve continues, "I am talking specifically about the part where I told you that you have a great story of success, achievement, and overcoming obstacles, and it needs to be told to thousands of people, and that you should consider sharing it through keynote speeches?"

"I remember," I answer suspiciously.

"The reason I am calling today Matt," Steve goes on, "Is to invite you to be the keynote speaker at our Super Convention next month. I would love to have you talk about Asking, Listening, and Repeating, and how it has impacted your life professionally and personally." It's silent for a moment while I think about what Steve is asking me to do.

"I have never given that kind of speech before," I start. "Why would you choose me to speak to a big group of network marketers?"

Without any pause Steve responds, "Because you and Ann have mastered the principles and skills necessary to build life-long relationships and are living proof that the process works in all aspects of life. I am going to invite Ann to speak as well. Can you check your schedule and let me know as soon as possible. I need to get this booked and on the schedule for the event."

I answer before Steve can put the period on his sentence. "I can tell you right now that I am honored that you would invite me. It would be a privilege to speak with Ann at the convention."

"That's great," Steve says. "Please don't tell Ann yet. I would like to invite her personally. You will be hearing from someone from the XL-8 corporate offices in the next week or so about logistics, travel arrangements, and schedules. Thanks for all you do and are Matt. You are a great example of a winner walking."

I don't even hang up the receiver on my phone. Immediately I call Ann and ask her to get a baby sitter and make a reservation at our favorite restaurant. I tell her, "We need a quiet place to talk about something very important to both you and me."

"What's going on?" Ann asks. "Is there anything I can do?"

"No it's not an emergency," Matt replies. "I just need to talk to you about something I learned today." Ann is perplexed and confused about the ominous tone of Matt's language as she makes the reservation. "Did he get promoted?" she wonders. "Did he get fired? Did he get hired by another company? Does he have a health problem like Josh's that is just now coming to light? I hate surprises, but I know there is no way he is going to tell me until tonight. This is the perfect time to tell him my little surprise as well. After all turn about is fair play. I will make our reservations as early as possible, Ann thinks. Waiting to hear his surprise and tell him mine is killing me.

When we get to the restaurant, Michelle the hostess meets us at the door and personally shows us to our table. Ann is giddy with excitement. She has a smile from ear to ear. She looks radiant in the soft candle light and sits next to me instead of across the table.

To her credit she waits for our server to take our order before she starts prodding me to tell her my news, Matt thinks. I haven't felt like this since I asked her to marry me. Only then I had plenty of time to practice what I was going to say. This seems all too sudden and unrehearsed. The only words that come to my mind are; "Guess what I did today?" This little game we've been playing for a long time now is going to come to my rescue. I take a drink of water and out it comes; "Guess what I did today?" There is a slight moment of silence as I wait for Ann to respond.

In that moment Ann's excitement overcomes her and instead of saying, "What or I don't know tell me," she blurts out her news in perfect timing with his announcement. I share, "I am the keynote speaker at the Super Convention" at exactly the same time Ann says, "I'm pregnant!" And as if we had written this script for a scene in a movie we both respond simultaneously to the others news saying, "What!"

Ann starts the explanations saying, "I found out today that we are going to have our third child. I am a few weeks along, but we are adding to our family. Isn't that exciting?" She asks rhetorically. "I thought you knew somehow, and that's why you called and asked to talk about something you learned today."

Shocked and surprised I lean over to give her a hug and reply in a verbal frenzy, "What great news! I am so excited. When are you due? Is there anything you need? What can I do to help?"

Ann interrupts my rapid-fire questioning saying, "You don't need to do anything except be here with us. So what is this keynote speaker stuff all about?"

My turn now, I begin, "When I got to the office this morning I had an overwhelming feeling of gratitude for what my life has become and I shared with Mrs. Jensen. When I got back to the office Steve called and invited me to be the main speaker at the upcoming Super Convention. I wanted you to know so that you could help me create a great presentation. I want to make sure to help you in every way I can to build the Ann Ivey XL-8 empire. This speaking assignment is a way for me to partner with you in the crusade to further the work you have already begun."

Ann responds, "I am so glad to have you home more and that you have risen to the top. I always knew you could do it, and now being invited to speak at the convention makes that appreciation even greater. You shouldn't have any trouble with the presentation. You have been learning and practicing the skills we talk about all the time. Plus you have been to many of our events, so you should not be surprised by the environment. Just tell your story and talk about what helped you overcome the challenges of climbing to the top of your company. I will be glad to help you, but I have the sneaky feeling that they are going to ask me to speak as well, now that I am a new Platinum."

Matt smiles slyly and tells Ann, "You are right. Steve or someone else is going to call you and ask you to speak. It's very interesting that both of us will be in front of 20,000 people speaking about how to be successful. Who would have thought this day would be possible when we bumped into each other in our Biology class or when we lived in that basement apartment!" As we prepare for this up coming assignment we spend time reviewing the journey that led us to the spotlight of the stage, including the importance of learning the difficult lessons of building and maintaining lasting relationships.

During those weeks, Ann, the kids, and I visit our land in the foothills often. Our favorite time to get there is just as the sun comes up. We imagine the house, barn, pastures, fences, garden, and everything else, and how they will look using all of our senses. We walk through our imaginary home countless times and make many changes. We smell the flowers and imagine tasting the fruits and vegetables from the garden. We hear the birds chirping in the trees and feel the cool water running over our feet as we stand in the small river flowing through the back side of the property. A few days before the annual Super Convention we stand there in that river and I turn to Ann and say, "Guess what I did today?"

Relaxed by the warm sun on her face and cool water rushing over her feet she is completely caught off guard by my question. She lazily asks, "What did you do today, Matt?"

Matt pauses in silence until she opens her eyes to look at him. "Today I asked my dad to come and help us design the ranch part of our property!"

"That is a great idea," Ann agrees. "I am so glad that you invited him to come and help us. Maybe he can come with us and see us on the stage at convention. My mom and dad have already agreed to come hear you speak about your journey and me about mine."

The next weeks pass very quickly and I remind Ann one evening as we stand in our river, "There are only a few days remaining before we are going to be standing on the stage speaking to all those people."

"Don't remind me. I am very nervous to speak." Ann replies, moving closer to me while I offer some comfort, "Just remember that everyone in that crowd will be rooting for you. They want you to do your very best. So there's really nothing to be worried or anxious about."

She smiles and says to me, "Your obedience and diligence to stay the course, to never give up, to follow correct principles, and your willingness to learn, practice, and apply skills and knowledge to create lasting, rewarding, and meaningful relationships is what got you to the top of Perpetual Wealth Financial, and here in this river with me. I am so proud of you Matt. We've come a long way, baby. And speaking in front of that crowd will be very exciting. Feel my stomach, our new baby is jumping for joy as well."

The day arrives for our presentations. As I watch the first speakers it occurs to me that if the janitor walked out on the stage the crowd would cheer. Ann is right, I think, there really isn't anything to fear. When it comes our turn, we retreat to a quiet room back stage and wait for Steve to announce us. He tells the story of how we met and some of his experiences teaching Ann and me. He shares with almost fatherly pride that he witnessed us becoming the kind of people on whom success could rest. And then he turns and introduces me. As I walk out on the stage the entire audience stands, claps, and cheers.

Remembering how Steve handles these kinds of situations I acknowledge the crowd by waving and slightly bowing. I begin my remarks by thanking Steve and the other leaders in XL-8 for inviting and trusting me to talk about what it takes to get to the top. I congratulate everyone in the audience for showing up. Then I begin much like Steve had a few years ago by telling them, "Showing up is of course important but it's only about 40% of success. The rest of success is determined by your personal effectiveness in initiating, developing, and maintaining strong and powerful relationships. I had a mentor once who told me that the foundation of success in anything we do in life is based on the quality of the relationships we have. Another mentor taught me only to listen to people who were where I wanted to be. He told me to listen to those who had paid the price and walked the walk, creating the results I wanted. When I met Steve Thoms I knew I had met a man who could and would tell me how to get what I wanted without worrying about whether the truth would make me wither.

"Over the past years I have listened to and learned from the master teachers in building life-long relationships. Oscar Lambert my fairgrounds mentor, Bill Rena family friend and confidant, My father-in-law Phil Wentz, my first professional manager Mr. Jaynes, Steve Thoms, Olivia Vigotsky, David McKay, Glenna Hanks and of course my wife, Ann. They have all been fantastic support partners, instructors, and participants in my quest to become someone who adds value to the lives of others. I have been able to learn, practice, and apply the lessons each has so willingly shared with me. The key to my success and the success of anyone in any endeavor is the resolution to become better and the commitment to apply success principles no matter what; even when things don't appear to be working."

I talk for another thirty minutes about Asking, Listening, and Repeating, and why the three underlying principles make that process work. I share my insights and observations about value of service, relationship ratings, transactions versus transformations, lock PIKing, high-yielding questions, listening, dot-connecting, and asking people to take action by giving options. I share personal stories of how each principle acts as an ingredient in the whole success recipe and say, "Without each element, the recipe is sure to create confusion and failure. We must qualify for success. Not by punching a time clock, or working a long time, but by using our time and efforts to learn, grow, develop, become something ourselves, and to help others to do the same.

"Success is earned and achieved, not won or inherited. No one is born with a 'success gene'. Those who are born into advantageous circumstances quickly lose their advantages if they fail to learn how to build relationships with others. Relationships are an enabling power that helps you as the leader to show the way, and allows you to demonstrate how to achieve success. Being interested instead of interesting allows others to see that you care about them more than you care about you. Successful people begin just as we all do; with the first step, and then the next, and the next, and the next, until they wake up one day, and they have become a success over years of learning and hard work."

I conclude saying, "As a Sports Car I am not prone to heartfelt emotions but here in front of you all they are taking over." With tears in my eyes and a crack in my voice I look down at my dad sitting on the front row and thank him for teaching me how to work hard and be accountable. I motion for Steve to come stand next to me. Putting my arm around him I share, "Last but certainly not least, thank you Steve for mentoring me and showing me how to create meaningful, positive, life-long relationships that are the foundation of the path to success in everything I do everyday." I give Steve a big hug and together we wave to the crowd indicating that I am finished with my presentation. While everyone stands, claps, and cheers it begins to rain in that convention center. It isn't really raining of course; the truth is that I am crying so hard it looks like rain.

Steve lets the applause go for a full minute before he begins to restore order. It takes him a minute or two, and still most people are still standing when he introduces new Platinum level achiever Ann Ivey! The crowd goes crazy again. It's many minutes before it is quiet enough for Ann to begin.

Ann starts saying, "I don't really know what to say that can add to what has already been said. So I will share the feelings I have in my heart. When I started in this business I had a goal to make some money to decorate my little house and make sure our children had the little things that make a big difference in their lives, like piano lessons, and summer camps. When I achieved that goal, Sara invited me to set a new goal: a big, hairy, audacious goal. My goal was to help my husband get to a position in his company so that he could be home more, because more than things, camps, and lessons, my children needed a dad. They needed someone to take them on hikes, have late night talks, go fishing and four-wheeling with them. To share what it means to be a man, father, and partner with me in leading our family.

"I am happy to let you all know that because of what Steve and Sara have taught us, my kids will not only have an example of hard work, accountability, and success to look up to, they have their father to drive them to school, go to activities with them, and have him right there beside them to love, encourage, and support them. Even greater than that, I have my partner home with me every night so that we can keep the covenants we made when we got married to love, honor, and cherish each other. All this has happened because we have learned to develop and improve relationships as the backbone of a life spent building something. So I want to thank all of you for everything you do each day because it matters to those who are watching, listening, waiting and praying for you to come into their lives and help them achieve their greater causes and higher purposes." When she hands the microphone to Sara Thoms there isn't a dry eye in the crowd.

Sara motions for Glenna to come out, and while she is walking onto the stage David McKay comes out with her holding a huge statue of a hand sculpted Rhinoceros. Steve escorts me from the other side of the stage. Just before they present Ann and me with this beautiful gift as a token of their appreciation for our being there to share, Mr. Flint brings my parents and Ann's parents out on the stage to share this moment with us. Glenna talks for a moment about Steve being a great example of what it means to pursue his passions relentlessly, no matter what the weather or circumstances. She commends him for his desire to help everyone succeed, even those outside XL-8, and as she gives me the statue she says that this is their way of showing Ann and I what we really mean to them as leaders and showers of the way, not talkers of the way.

I am on such an emotional high for the remainder of the convention that I don't really concentrate much on anything else that is being said in other presentations. I spend the next few hours in deep thought and gratitude for all I had learned and that had happened. Reflecting back on it now, it's kind of like when you drive home from work or the store and you pull in the driveway, but can't remember anything about the trip home.

For most of the next week, I am able to spend time with my dad, walking around the property and planning the placement of buildings, barns, pastures, fences, electric, and water lines. As I am talking to him it occurs to me that I should have been consulting with him all along, especially about this. He is an expert rancher, and can give me some excellent insight if I stop talking long enough for him to give it to me. I ask his opinion about our plan, and he shares a couple of thoughts that are critical to making the layout really work well and that will be better for the animals. I must admit that I was convinced we had this all figured out, but once again I am reminded that it's what you learn after you think you know everything that really matters. I am glad that I have been able to put this into practice in my personal life.

Indeed, Ask, Listen, and Repeat is a critical element of success in everything we do. And this is just one more sign that proves it. I'm glad my dad has been able to be here to see Ann and me in our shining moment on stage. But more than that, or the property design time, I'm glad he is here to experience his grandchildren. He beams like a beacon on a dark cloudy night. He cuts some of our outings short so that he can hold and play with the kids before he has to return home.

The following year is spent implementing our property plan and building a house befitting a queen. Ann is settled into the house and establishes a new schedule for our entire household with me as an integral part of the daily routine. Steve and I make it a point to meet regularly to make sure I am still teaching and helping others to teach others to teach others, as he had done with me.

One Saturday morning Clarissa calls me at home and after a brief apology for calling me on the weekend and at home she excitedly tells me she has some very interesting news to share saying, "I was just in a training meeting with my team. We were talking about conversion ratios, and during the conversation one of my team members who has been in the industry for a long time, but until now has not been particularly successful, talked about her experience in other companies."

Clarissa's team member said, "Other companies teach that this business is just a numbers game."

"The problem seems to be," Clarissa interjects her own observation, "That most people don't know or understand how to develop relationships or measure their effectiveness in this area using numbers that really matter, or know how to track them. Matt, no one I know knows more about cause and effect, relationships, and the numbers of this business better than you do.

So the reason for my weekend interruption is to ask you to come and do a two or three day leadership retreat and teach the whole Ask, Listen, and Repeat process and the underlying principles. The sooner the better, please, because I run into people everyday who think that prospects are expendable, relationships don't really matter, and that low conversion ratios are acceptable.

"On a related note, Alix called me yesterday and told me about her job search. I listened for a few minutes while she explained that everyone in the industry has heard about what you are doing here at Perpetual Wealth Financial and that just as soon as they find out she worked for you they ask her to teach them what you do here with us. Of course she doesn't have any idea what we do or why we do it and in a moment of desperation she asked me if there was any way she could quickly learn the lessons you teach."

Matt pauses for a moment and then responds, "I am grateful for what I have learned and am happy to share it. It is interesting that others have seen the results relationships create. But Clarissa, you have been doing this for months now. Are you sure you don't want to do the seminar yourself?"

She answers, "I would love to see you teach the whole process all in one event. That would help me and everyone else to connect the dots better."

"I see your point and I would love to do it. And what might be even better is to get the master himself to facilitate the training. Maybe now after all this time and asking, I can get Steve to do it with me. It is my grandest wish to help you teach others to teach others to build stronger and more meaningful relationships. Thanks for all you do and are Clarissa. You are truly amazing. And make sure to invite Alix to the workshop. She's paid a heavy price for not knowing what you and I do. I will get back to you on a schedule for the event. For now, send them and your team members to: **www.RiTraining.com/ALR** for their free download of the **Personal Interaction Key Mini-Guide**.

"Take care of yourself and those you meet every day. They are counting on you to help them achieve greatness. See you later."

A

Appendix

Formulas, Equations, and Calculations

Relationship Rating from Chapter 3

Basic Relationship Rating.

Step 1. Write down the different kinds of relationships you have: parents, a spouse, customers, or neighbors. You might write your relationships in terms of categories like romantic, familial, professional, friendship, or collegiate.

Step 2. Write some specific names of people with whom you have relationships within each category.

Step 3. Rate each relationship from 1 to 10. One is a relationship that robs you and might be one you are considering ending or learning how to strengthen. A 10 is a relationship that is so powerful that nothing could ever pull you apart.

Step 4. Add all the scores you put beside each relationship.

- If you put some kind of range beside a kind of relationship like a volunteer group you work with, then you need to take the lowest number of that group.
- If you failed to put a number beside a relationship then you don't get any points for that relationship.

Step 5. Divide the total score of all the relationships you wrote down by the number of relationships you wrote down and that's your Basic Relationship Rating.

Step 6. Take your Basic Relationship Rating number and multiply it by 10. For example if you have an initial number of 6.2, then multiplying that by 10 would give you a 62.

- Generally speaking if the number from step two is below 50 then you are doing things either consciously or unconsciously to push people away from you more than half the time.

Equation – If you add all the numbers of the relationships you have together and they equal one hundred. And then you count the number of all the different relationships you have and they equal twenty then you take one hundred and divide it by twenty. In this case it is twenty out of one hundred or five; $(100 \div 20 = 5)$ and multiply this number by ten $(5 \times 10 = 50)$.

- You can also do this activity for each category of relationships you have and analyze your relationships that way.
- You can also take individual relationships and work through this exact same process.

Final Relationship Rating.
Tells you the bottom line or discounted results of what's truly going on in your relationship with people.
Step 1. Take your Basic Relationship.
Step 2. Subtract your Basic Relationship Rating from 100.
Step 3. Subtract that number from your Basic Relationship Rating and your Relationship Rating is the number that remains.

Equation – If your Basic Relationship Rating is 70; you would subtract 70 from 100 equaling 30. Then subtract 30 from the Basic Relationship Rating (70) and the remaining number is your Final Relationship Rating. In this case it is forty out of one hundred; (100 - 70 = 30) then (70 - 30 = 40).

Relationship Rating Calculation	
Total score	44.5
# of People	÷ 6
Base score	**7.4**
Multiplier	x10
Basic Relationship Rating	**74**
Discount (100-74)	- 26
Final Relationship Rating	**48**

Trust Quotient from Chapter 4

Step 1. Rate yourself on your paper from 1 to 5 on the following questions. One is absolutely not or no and five is completely or absolutely yes.

1. Think for a moment about whether your team members, customers, neighbors, and co-workers really trust you? Do they absolutely know that you will do what you say you're going to do when you say you're going to do it? Remember the question is, 'do they believe in you?' Not, 'do you believe in you?'
2. Do your customers and associates believe that you have their best interests at heart?

3. If one of your team members came across information that was potentially damaging, would they share it with you or hide it from you?
4. Do people tell you things they would never tell anyone else?
5. Do people perform at their highest level when they work with and for you?

Step 2. Add up your score from each question. This is your current Trust Quotient.
*   If you got between 21 and 25 your Trust Quotient is pretty high.
*   If you scored between 16 and 21, you could use some help in building trust faster or better.
*   If you scored at 15 or below then you definitely need to increase your Trust Quotient.

Equation – If you answered a 3 on the first two questions and 2 on questions three and four and a 5 on question five then your equation would look like this: $(3 + 3 + 2 + 2 + 5 = 15)$

Trust Quotient Calculation	
Score from question 1	3
Score from question 2	3
Score from question 3	2
Score from question 4	2
Score from question 5	5
Total score from questions	**15**
Trust Quotient	**15**

Warning Label from Chapter 5

Anatomy of a Warning Labels:
1. A main warning,
2. Side effects,
3. A continued use statement and
4. What to do if they experience any of the symptoms of your warning.

```
         Warning Label Anatomy (Example)

   Part 1—Main Warning—Warning: this person may trigger irritation,
   inflammation, nausea and vomiting.

   Part 2—Side Effects—Side effects may include: volatility and
   feelings of insanity.

   Part 3—Continued Use—Continued use has been known to cause
   self-loathing, anxiety and prolonged bouts of depression.

   Part 4—What to do—If these symptoms persist seek professional
   counseling immediately.
```

Value of Service Score from Chapter 5

Step 1. Answer the questions for the Value of Service assessment in Chapter 5.
Step 2. Total number of times you responded to the assessment questions with either an A, B, C, D or E and put that number in the column Total Responses.
Step 3. Multiply and add in the following sequence:
- Multiply the total number of As by 1.
- Put the total points for As in the column titled Points.
- Multiply the total number of Bs by 2.
- Put the total points for Bs in the column titled Points.
- Multiply the total number of Cs by 3.
- Put the total points for Cs in the column titled Points.
- Multiply the total number of Ds by 4.
- Put the total points for Ds in the column titled Points.
- Multiply the total number of Es by 5.
- Put the total points for Es in the column titled Points.

Step 4. Add the points you entered for each response type and put the total on the bottom line of the column titled Points. This is a numerical measurement of the value of your service. The greatest value of service score is 125.

Value of Service Score Equation		
	Total Responses	Points
As	4	4
Bs	6	12
Cs	5	15
Ds	3	12
Es	7	28
Total	25	71

Value of Service Score 71 out of 125

Conversion Ratios from Chapters 2, 3, 4, 5, 8, 10, 11, 12, 13

Conversion Ratio Calculation	
# of Contacts	100
Conversion Ratio (60 ÷ 100)	60%
# of Presentations	60
Conversion Ratio (60 x .60)	60%
# of Follow-ups	36
Conversion Ratio (36 x 90)	90%
# of Enrollments	27
Conversion Ratio (27 ÷ 100)	90%
Total number or contacts converted to enrollments = 27%	

PEPs from Chapters 2, 3, 4, 5, 7, 8, 9, 10, 11, 12, 13
Visit **www.RiTraining.com** to take the skill and knowledge assessment.

About the Author

Clay Stevens' career path has included service in the military and as a public school teacher, corporate training executive, Fortune 500 trainer and successful direct seller.

For the past 30 years Mr. Stevens has been working with pioneers and visionaries in the training and education field and has taught at the public, private, college and university levels. Working with Avon, Amway, World Financial Group, Juice Plus+, Legal Shield, U.S. Department of Education, NASA, Stanford University, Nielson Media Research, Washington and New York State Departments of Education, Mercy Health Care, Hewlett-Packard, Intel, John Deere, Kansas City Royals Baseball Club Clay delivered hundreds of workshops, seminars and webinars to diversified groups of business owners, entrepreneurs, community leaders and students.

Mr. Stevens holds three degrees from major universities in Instructional Design Technologies and is the creator of innovative and effective learning methodologies; Relevant Emotional Practice (REP Learning), and Results Oriented Instruction (ROI).

Clay has written seven books and owns four patents. He is an award winning training program developer and speaker and author. He founded Ri Training to help distributors and leaders learn how to improve their abilities to build strong and productive relationships that result in multidimensional goal achievement. He is a sought after Key-Note speaker and national/international T.V. and radio guest.

FREE DOWN LOADS!

www.RiTraining.com/ALR

- Personal Interaction Key Mini-Guide
- The deleted scenes from *Ask, Listen & Repeat*

Another great novel by Clay Stevens, *Six Figures in Six Months* covers the inside track of building a business from the beginning to a six-figure income in six months. Feel the emotions, experience the frustrations and fears, and learn the key to success in building your own direct selling business.